WORLD POLITICS AND YOU

WORLD POLITICS AND YOU

DAN CALDWELL
Pepperdine University

PRENTICE HALL, Upper Saddle River, New Jersey 07458

Library of Congress Cataloging-in-Publication Data

CALDWELL, DAN
    World politics and you/Dan Caldwell.
        p.   cm.
    Includes bibliographical references and index.
    ISBN 0-13-954728-2 (alk. paper)
    1. World politics.   I. Title.
  D31.C35   2000
  909.82—dc21   99-27555
                                              CIP

Editorial director: Charlyce Jones Owen
Editor-in-chief: Nancy Roberts
Senior acquisitions editor: Beth Gillett Mejia
Associate editor: Nicole Conforti
AVP, director of production and manufacturing: Barbara Kittle
Editorial/production supervision: Rob DeGeorge
Copyeditor: Barbara Christenberry
Buyer: Ben Smith
Manufacturing manager: Nick Sklitsis
Electronic art creation: Hadel Studio
Line art coordinator: Guy Ruggiero
Creative design director: Leslie Osher
Interior and cover design: Kenny Beck
Marketing manager: Christopher DeJohn
Photo researcher: Melinda Alexander
Image specialist: Beth Boyd
Manager, Rights and Permissions: Kay Dellosa
Director, image resource center: Melinda Reo

This book was set in 10.5/13 Palatino by Preparé Inc.,
and was printed and bound by RR Donnelley & Sons Company.
The cover was printed by Phoenix Color Corp.

Printed in the United States of America

10   9   8   7   6   5   4   3   2   1

ISBN 0-13-954728-2

Contents

Chapter 3
The State System and the Balance of Power   36

Chapter 4
Actors, Power, and Interdependence in World Politics   52

PART   II
WHAT IS THE HISTORY OF WORLD POLITICS?

PART III
WHAT ARE THE SIGNIFICANT ISSUES OF WORLD POLITICS?

Chapter 8
War, Peace, and International Security   142

PART   IV
WHAT IS THE FUTURE OF WORLD POLITICS?

Critical Thinking Exercises (Critex)

Preface

THE DISTINGUISHING FEATURES OF THIS BOOK

A nineteenth century intellectual, A. Bronson Alcott, wrote: "That is a good book which is opened with expectation, and closed with profit."[1] It is my hope that you have opened this book with expectation, but that even if you have not, you will read it with profit. I have that hope for several reasons.

First, I have written this book with students' interest in mind, first and foremost. Many textbooks are written by professors with their colleagues, rather than their students, in mind. Very few students in an introductory course are interested in specialized academic disputes over what they view as esoteric, at best. This book adopts an *atheoretical* perspective; those professors or students who are interested in a more theoretically based approach should consult other textbooks.[2]

Second, keeping students' interests in mind, I have developed an approach to introduce and engage students in the substantive issues of each of the chapters. I call the introductory critical thinking exercises in each of the chapters "critexes." These focus on a number of different issues and require students to complete various types of exercises. Hopefully, the critexes will increase both students' interest and their knowledge about significant issues in world politics.

Third, a distinguishing aspect of this book is that it contains practical information for students about how they can obtain information about internships, graduate school, and careers related to international relations; few other textbooks do this, yet many students are interested in "what they can do" with the information that they learn in courses. Eleven of the fifteen chapters have sections about practical information for students.

Fourth, this book emphasizes history and does so for several reasons. Many students entering college do not have a very good grasp of history, but understanding history is necessary for comprehending contemporary world politics. For example, it is impossible to understand the depth of hostility and hatred in Bosnia and Kosovo without knowledge of the history of that volatile region.

Fifth, for better or worse, many people today get much, if not most, of the information that they have about the world through multimedia sources and the internet; yet many international relations textbooks do not address these sources extensively. That is probably because their authors are more comfortable with print sources. This book makes extensive use of internet sources and lists a number of multimedia sources.

THE ORGANIZATION OF THIS BOOK

This book is divided into four major sections that focus on the questions:

- Who or what are the actors in world politics?
- What is the history of international relations?
- What are the significant issues of contemporary world politics?
- What is the future of world politics?

Several chapters are devoted to each of these questions. Throughout the book, key concepts, historical events, and personalities are indicated in boldface type. A glossary that defines a number of the terms is included in an appendix.

ACKNOWLEDGMENTS

No author writes a book alone; the author has a number of friends, colleagues, and critics who become *de facto* collaborators along the way. I would like to acknowledge and thank those who have assisted me in the writing of this book.

My friends and colleagues who have commented on the book are: Stephen Garrett, Louis Sell, John R. Todd, and Robert Williams. I would also like to thank the following reviewers who provided a number of helpful suggestions for the book: Patricia Davis, University of Notre Dame; Michael J. Lenaghan, Miami-Dade Community College; Stanley Melnick, Valencia Community College; Elisabeth Prügl, Florida International University.

Many of the sections on "You in World Politics" were based on a paper by Roy Licklider, and I appreciate his permission to use this material.

At Prentice Hall, I would like to thank Beth Gillett Mejia, Nicole Conforti, Rob DeGeorge, Barbara Christenberry, Elizabeth Kaster, and Michael Bickerstaff.

DEDICATION

One of (if not the best) aspects of writing a book is thinking about the dedication. Because of their encouragement and support, I have dedicated my previous books to members of my family, Edward J. Laurance (my best friend), and to my intellectual mentor, Alexander L. George. I continue to be indebted to these friends and members of my family.

I thought long and hard about the dedication of this book and decided to dedicate it to the memory of my friends who died for the cause of peace in the world. Elgin Juri was a Marine who died in Vietnam in 1969. Don Barrington and Eric Washam died from illnesses that resulted from contact with Agent Orange while serving in Vietnam. Joe Kruzel was one of three American diplomats who died tragically in 1995 while trying to broker an end to the fighting in Bosnia. Rest in peace, my friends.

---

[1] A. BRONSON ALCOTT, *Table Talk*, I, 1877, quoted in H.L. Mencken, ed., *A New Dictionary of Quotations on Historical Principles from Ancient and Modern Sources* (New York: Alfred A. Knopf, 1978), p. 118.

[2] There are approximately thirty introductory textbooks on international relations in print in English. Of these, several of the best more theoretically oriented books are: K. J. Holsti, *International Politics: A Framework for Analysis*, 7th ed. (Upper Saddle River, NJ: Prentice Hall, 1995), Charles W. Kegley, Jr. and Eugene R. Wittkopf, *World Politics: Trend and Transformation*, 7th ed. (New York: St. Martin's, 1999), and Bruce Russett and Harvey Starr, *World Politics: The Menu for Choice*, 5th ed. (New York: W. H. Freeman, 1996).

WORLD
POLITICS
AND YOU

World Politics and You: An Introduction

INTRODUCTION

MAYBE you've registered for this course, maybe not. Perhaps you are "just shopping around," taking a look at the class and the required text in order to decide whether you will sign up for the class, buy and read this book, take the exams and complete the other requirements for the course. There may be another class that meets at a more convenient time, or another one might be easier.

Why would someone take this class, other than the obvious reasons—it is offered at a convenient time; it's easy (maybe or maybe not—better check with other students!); or it's required? A distinguishing feature of this book is that it contains "critical thinking exercises" (abbreviated throughout the book as "Critex") at the beginning of each chapter, to introduce you to the topic under consideration. Before you decide whether or not you are going to register for this class

3

and/or buy this book, work through this first critex. This will give you an idea of both the approach taken in this book and the substantive area it covers.

The Man in the Net

The photograph below is, sadly, a photograph of an actual person; this is not a publicity photo for a movie, and the man in the net is not an actor playing a role. It is a photograph of a human being who has just been captured and whose life is about to be changed forever. How do you think that you would feel if you were this person? Your professor may want you to discuss your feelings or may have you write a brief letter expressing your feelings from the perspective of this person. Once you have written this letter, exchange letters with other members of the class. Were there different perspectives in the class? The following are excerpts from other college students' letters written as if they were the man in the net:

"The Man in the Net"

- Where are they taking me in this huge ship? How will my family survive without me? How can I, as a noble leader, be treated so unjustly? They appear to be as human as I, but they must be servants for an evil god. They are so cruel. Do they not know how to interact with other humans? I could almost pity them if they were not so cruel.

- Here I sit in my native land. Bowed by shackles that I do not understand. The likes of these cords I have never seen. They are strong and binding. I cannot escape. My captors are men with features I have never encountered before.

- Why is this happening to me?
  Have I done something wrong that justifies this action against me?
  Will I ever see my—
  > friends,
  > my family,
  > my homeland?

- What kind of people are doing this to me?
  How can they justify doing this to me?
  They must consider me no better than an animal that they would capture and send to a zoo.
  What will the rest of my life be like?
  What will happen to—
  > my hopes,
  > my dreams,
  > my aspirations?

- What will slavery do to me as a person?
  Will I become as uncaring and inhuman as my captors?
  How can I retain some dignity as a person and not be overcome and dominated by hatred?

It is possible that the great grandchildren of this person are fellow classmates of yours. How would you feel if one of your friends were the great grandchild of this person? Here are some reactions to this question:

- You have a right to be so angry. I can only empathize faintly with how you must feel. I wish that I could take it back—undo history—fix it somehow. Slavery should never have happened, and today's racism is directly related to slavery.

- Your ancestors were victimized by a racism that manipulated the economic, social, and political worlds. How can hope exist? The only hope that exists is based on the general acceptance of equality based on race, religion, gender, and ethnicity.

LEVELS OF ANALYSIS AND THE CAUSES OF SLAVERY

Everyone knows that slavery no longer exists, but the effects of it linger. What role did world politics play in perpetuating slavery?

Slavery existed from ancient times until the mid-twentieth century. Beginning in 1500 and continuing for the next 350 years, Africans were captured and taken to the "new world" of the Americas. During this period of time, it is estimated that between 10 and 15 million Africans were brought to the Americas and that 4 to 6 million more died en route from Africa. Thus, a total of 14 to 21 million people were taken from their homes in Africa.[1]

The explanations concerning the reasons for slavery's existence can be thought of in three ways. Political scientists are similar to other scientists in that they focus on different aspects of a phenomenon in order to explain it. For example, biologists may focus on individual cells; they may study one particular species; or they may focus on the interaction of various species in a particular ecosystem. Similarly, political scientists may focus on individuals, specific countries and/or the interaction of the actors in international relations. These different foci are called **levels of analysis.**

Racial Prejudice from Ancient Times to the Present

First, the causes of slavery were in the minds of individuals, and prejudiced people implemented the slavery system. The preamble of the United Nations Educational, Scientific, and Cultural Organization's (UNESCO) Charter states: "Since war begins in the minds of men, it is in the minds of these men who are most influenced in decisions for or against war that the defenses of peace must be constructed."[2] Similarly, racial prejudice also began in the minds of human beings. Even the great Greek philosopher, Aristotle, was racially prejudiced. To Aristotle, those who lived in northern Europe were lacking "in spirit, and this is why they continue to be peoples of subjects and slaves.... It is clear that just as some are by nature free, so others are by nature slaves, and for these latter the condition of slavery is both beneficial and just."[3] Sadly, Aristotle's prejudice was not an isolated example; Herodotus—often called "the father of history"— and the Roman historian Tacitus were also racially prejudiced. Over time, as historian Paul Gordon Lauren points out, "Black came to represent evil, depravity, filth, ugliness, baseness, wickedness, danger, death, and sin."[4] As prejudice grew, international relations gradually, but increasingly and inextricably, came to be interracial relations.[5]

Economics of the Slave Trade

Second, a number of companies and countries made vast profits from the slave trade and therefore supported it. One historian has claimed that western civilization itself "rested on the backs of African slaves, and the products of colonial plantations were enjoyed by complacent Europeans who gave little thought to the millions of blacks whose labor made these products possible. The capture, transportation, and sale of `black ivory' became one of the most lucrative branches of transatlantic commerce. The Portuguese, Dutch, French, and English competed for the privilege of supplying plantation owners, from Brazil through Virginia, with blacks who had been carried away by force from their African homelands to toil in the white man's service."[6] Owing their success and profits to the slave trade were many of the largest and most successful companies of the seventeenth century, including the Dutch West India Company, the East India Company, the British East India Company and the Royal African Company. **Marxist analysis** contends that capitalism invariably takes advantage of poorer people. Marxists, then, would argue that slavery was caused by capitalists trying to reap profits from the slave trade.

Lack of Will or Authority to Prevent Slavery

Third, some would argue that the slave trade was allowed to develop because there was no overarching authority to prevent it from occurring. As reformers in various countries criticized the evils of human bondage, slavery was outlawed country by country. Citizens of democratic countries were able to organize and pressure their governments to prohibit slavery. There was no central government of the world. Therefore, there was no central authority to prohibit slavery; in fact, slavery was not formally outlawed in all countries until 1962. There are recent, disturbing reports that slavery still exists in several countries, including Sudan.[7] From the international-system perspective, slavery resulted from the anarchic nature of the international system and the nonexistence of any hierarchical power.

Any one of level of analysis is usually necessary but not sufficient to explain the complex phenomena that make up world politics. Students, therefore, should be wary of any explanations that focus on only one of these levels. Such **"monocausal" explanations** are simpler and easier to understand than **multicausal explanations,** but they are usually too simple. Throughout this book, we will return to these three levels of analysis to explain various phenomena.

Before turning to an introduction to *The World and You*, there is one other point related to "the man in the net" for you to think about: Are there issues in today's world that future generations will view as evil and obscene as we view slavery today? What about war? Past generations have viewed this as an unfortunate, but integral, part of world politics. What about the degradation of the environment? As you read this book, think about other issues that may be viewed as unacceptable in the future and think about what you can do to address those issues.

WHY STUDY WORLD POLITICS?

There are four principal reasons to study world politics. First, almost two thousand years ago, Aristotle wrote: "The good of man must be the end of the science of politics."[8] If you want to make your community, or even the world, a better place, then an understanding of politics is a good starting place.

Second, the principal focus of international relations is on countries (which are most commonly called "states" in the field of world politics), and states differ from any other form of social organization in that they claim a legal monopoly on the use of coercive force. No other form of social organization may legally put its members to death and go to war. States can and do, and that makes them important.

Third, membership in the state is involuntary and cannot be escaped. Anyone reading this book can leave college, a marriage, a church or synagogue, a job or a profession. But no one can escape the power of states. Even if you are not a citizen of a country, you are still subject to the laws of that country when you are within its territory. For example, if you were to drink an alcoholic beverage in Saudi Arabia, you could be arrested and imprisoned because the Saudi government follows a strict Islamic policy which prohibits alcohol. Or, if you live and work in a country, you are subject to paying taxes on your earnings in that state, even if you are not a citizen.

Fourth, and perhaps most important, an understanding of politics can be relevant and significant for your entire life. Every citizen of every country has the opportunity to influence his or her government. This influence may be minimal in a country, such as Iraq, ruled by a dictator. In democratic countries, however, the opportunities for influencing public policy are much greater. This course, therefore, has the potential of being relevant to your life as a citizen; it can help you to make more informed, intelligent decisions. That is not to say that this book will attempt to influence the way in which you vote; however, it will teach you how to analyze and think about some of the most important issues and problems that individuals, organizations, states, and the international community confront.

When we look at the problems facing the world, we can easily be overwhelmed by the number and/or magnitude of these problems. Pessimists will look at the world and proclaim, as a now obscure Greek did thousands of years ago, that "the world is going to the dogs." Our world has problems that our parents and grandparents did not have to confront or even imagine, and the task for each of us is to determine how we, as individuals, can effectively deal with such problems. This book is designed to help you deal with that central question.

It also provides an overview of how you can become directly involved in addressing the issues and problems of contemporary world politics. You could, for example, work as an intern in a governmental or non-governmental organization dealing with hunger relief or human rights. You might be interested in going on to graduate school or even pursuing a career related to world politics. Suggestions and resources mentioned throughout will give you an idea of where to start, should you want to go on in this field.

YOU IN WORLD POLITICS

So you're interested in a career in political science or international relations? Many college students are attracted to the idea of a job in political science or international studies. A very useful introduction to career possibilities is *Careers and the Study of Political Science: A Guide for Undergraduates,* which is published and distributed by the American Political Science Association (1527 New Hampshire Avenue, N.W., Washington, D.C. 20036).

A useful website that addresses the oft-asked question (particularly by parents): "What can I do with a major in political science?" The University of North Carolina at Wilmington addresses this question for a variety of majors and provides links to discipline-specific websites, to the U.S. federal government's Occupational Outlook Handbook, to internship sites, and to job search sites that provide advice on resumé writing, interviewing skills, and a variety of other valuable topics. Check out:
http://www.uncwil.edu/stuaff/career/majors.htm

HOW WORLD POLITICS DIFFERS FROM DOMESTIC POLITICS

Fortunately for their citizens, most of the world's 194 states operate relatively effectively. There are, of course, some notable and tragic exceptions to this generalization, but most countries "work"; if they don't, there is pressure to change the government. Why, then, can't international relations work the way that domestic governments operate?

There are several requirements for a **domestic political system** to operate effectively. First, the members of the state must feel a sense of loyalty to the central government; if they do not, the ties that bind citizens are fragile and can be easily undone as the disintegration of the Soviet Union and Yugoslavia demonstrated during the 1990s. Second, there must be a legal system that is recognized and respected by all members of the state. Third, an effective economic system is required. Fourth, the government must possess a monopoly of organized violence. Where this is not the case, the central government is merely a façade, and real power is exercised by powerful groups operating in the background. The difficulties that the government of Colombia has had in controlling the powerful Cali drug cartel in that country illustrate the importance of this point. Some observers would go as far as to suggest that the government of Colombia has ceased to exist, in a formal sense, because it cannot subject the Cali cartel to its control.

Now, let us consider these requirements and the contemporary **international political system.** There is no central international government. The United Nations comes the closest to such a political entity, but independence—what is called **sovereignty** in international relations—remains with the 185 member states of the UN. There are a number of competing legal systems in the world. For example, many Islamic countries base their legal systems on the holy book of Islam, the Koran; the British and American legal systems are based on common law; and the French legal system is founded on laws originally developed by Napoleon. An international economic system exists, but it is not centrally controlled and regulated. And last, there is no international monopoly on organized violence; each state retains the right to support and maintain military forces for their own national security (and some nonstate actors, such as the Cali drug cartel, act independently of states).

The differences between domestic and international political systems listed in Table 1.1 result in a number of significant implications. Danger and uncertainty characterize international politics more than domestic politics. The international system is a decentralized political system in which power is held and exercised by the 194 states in different ways and

---

TABLE 1.1

Domestic and International Political Systems

Domestic Systems	International Systems
1. Sense of loyalty to a central government.	1. There is no central government; instead, there are 194 sovereign states.
2. Legal system with mandatory jurisdiction.	2. Each of the 194 states has its own legal system.
3. Centralized, regulated economic system.	3. Decentralized economic system, with limited regulation.
4. The central government claims a legal monopoly on means of violence.	4. No monopoly on means of violence; all 194 states control the means of violence.

in varying degrees. Democratic processes that characterize the procedures of many of the world's states do not characterize international politics. Even where democracy seems to reign, there are problems. For example, in the United Nations General Assembly, each member state has one vote. Because of this seemingly laudatory democratic principle, the People's Republic of China, with a population of 1,200,000,000, and "micro-states" such as the European principality of San Marino with a population of 24,000, each have one vote.

In the chapters that follow, we will consider in greater detail the differences between domestic and international politics and the implications of these differences for people, groups, corporations, states, and the contemporary international community.

SOURCES OF INFORMATION: PRIMARY AND SECONDARY

When you have a conversation with a friend and that person says something that strikes you as curious or even outrageous, the first question that comes into your mind is "How do you know that?" You will read a number of things that strike you as curious—if not outrageous—in this book, and the question "How do you know that?" will enter your mind. Let me tell you how I know what I have written in this book and, incidentally, how you can become a more informed and therefore more powerful person.

Scholars typically divide their sources of information into two broad categories. **Primary sources** are the basic building blocks of history and political science and include such things as newspaper articles, politicians' speeches and memoirs, governmental documents and basic statistics. **Secondary sources** consist of materials that are based on primary sources and include articles and books by journalists and scholars. Secondary sources by definition involve interpreting data and are, therefore, subjective. But, of course, subjectivity is a relative term and an article or book can be more or less subjective (or objective) in its presentation and interpretation of the facts. A difficult task that will confront you as a student, as a citizen, and as an intelligent, thoughtful person is to evaluate your sources of information in order to determine how subjective (and in what ways) they are. The primary sources used in the writing of this book include a number of newspapers, magazines, and journals.

I could not have written this book without relying on, paraphrasing, and citing many secondary analyses of world politics. These sources are cited in the endnotes and in the selected readings that I have listed at the end of each chapter. I strongly recommend that students peruse at least some of these recommended readings, for they will give you a much more complete idea of what world politics is about than is possible in this relatively brief, introductory textbook.

What we "know" about a subject does not come only from newspapers, magazine and journal articles and books. We learn, for better or worse, a great deal from television and movies. In fact, in American households, the television is on for an average of 7 hours per day, and American teenagers watch an average of 24 hours of television per week. Movies are much more popular than books; to confirm this claim simply stand outside your local video rental outlet and local bookstore on a Friday or Saturday night and count the customers. (In 1988, for the first time Americans checked out more videotapes from rental stores than books from libraries.) Because of the popularity of videos and movies and because we do learn from these "sources of information," I have included a listing of relevant videos and films at the end of each chapter.

Enter the Internet

Twenty years ago, this is where the "sources of information" section would have ended, and unfortunately, this is where this section ends for many textbooks. This is because textbook authors, like many generations before them, obtained their information primarily from printed sources. Many students and scholars today, however, obtain their information from not only printed sources, they rely on computer sources of information. The **internet** is a vast, worldwide network of computers linked together so that information held in this network can be made available to anyone. Access to the internet requires a computer (the "hardware"), the proper program (the "software"), and a modem to link your computer with the internet network.

Throughout this book, I have indicated relevant internet sites of information for those students who have access to the internet. Such access does not require you to own an expensive computer system; check with your local public library or the library or computer center on your campus to see how you can access the internet. A word of warning, however, is necessary. Unlike newspapers, magazines, journals, or books (including this one) over which editors exercise quality control, many internet sites have no such quality control. Therefore, be alert to the level of quality of information obtained on the internet and, if you use information obtained from the internet in papers or other school work, be sure to indicate its complete source, as I have done for the internet sources I have listed at the end of each chapter.

> **BOX 1.1   The Internet**
>
> The internet was originally developed by computer scientists funded by the Advanced Research Projects Agency (ARPA), an arm of the U.S. Department of Defense. It was developed in order to provide the capability to communicate in the event of a nuclear war. Computers all over the world were interlinked with one another so that if a military base or city were attacked and destroyed, communications could be routed through computers in other cities or military bases. Strange that a system originally designed to cope with nuclear war should provide what many consider to be the greatest step forward in communications since the invention of the printing press by Gutenberg!

USING LIBRARY SOURCES

Many years ago, British philosopher Francis Bacon wrote, "Information is power." He was correct, and even more so today than when he originally wrote those words. If you want to become a more powerful person, become more informed.

There are many types of information, and this textbook will introduce you to some of the major types. Just as monocausal explanations are suspect, so too are analyses based on one source or even one type of information. It is far better to rely on multiple streams of evidence.

In finding out more about a topic in which you are interested, start with the information source—newspaper, internet, books—that you prefer. Let's assume that you are on-line on the internet and that you want to find out more about a particular topic. Use one of the standard search engines, such as Yahoo, Alta Vista, Excite, Hotbot or Lycos, and enter the name of the event, person, country or concept you are interested in examining. For this example, let's say that you are interested in finding out more about an important concept in world politics, the balance of power. For broad subjects such as this, you may not find very much about the particular concept you are interested in. You may get "hits" on the *balance* beam, *power* ratings of baseball hitters—information about balance and power that is irrelevant to your interest.

Even if you are successful in finding some (or even a lot of) information on your topic of interest, you should also check the library for additional sources. Despite the wealth of sources available on the internet, certain types of information, including importantly, books, cannot generally be accessed on-line. In the case of the balance of power, you would only be able to access and read most of the books on this subject in the library.

After you check the subject catalog in the card file or computer (depending upon the degree of computerization of your library), also check several guides to newspaper, journal, and magazine articles. Among the most useful guides for students studying politics, social science, and international relations are *The Readers' Guide to Periodical Literature*, *Social Science Abstracts* and *The New York Times Index*.

DISCUSSION QUESTIONS

1. Why should someone study world politics, even if he or she is not a political science or international relations major?
2. In what ways are domestic politics and world politics similar? How do they differ?
3. What sort of information will increase the probability that a particular explanation is accurate?

KEY TERMS

domestic political system
international political system
internet
levels of analysis
Marxist analysis

monocausal explanation
multicausal explanation
primary source
secondary source
sovereignty

RECOMMENDED PRINT, MULTIMEDIA, AND INTERNET SOURCES

Print

BROWN, SEYOM. *New Forces, Old Forces and the Future of World Politics: Post Cold War Edition*. New York: HarperCollins, 1995.

DRESCHER, SEYMOUR and STANLEY L. ENGERMAN, eds. *A Historical Guide to World Slavery*. New York: Oxford University Press, 1998.

LAUREN, PAUL GORDON. *Power and Prejudice: The Politics and Diplomacy of Racial Discrimination*, 2nd ed. Boulder, CO: Westview Press, 1996.

THOMAS, HUGH. *The Slave Trade.* New York: Simon & Schuster, 1997.
WALTZ, KENNETH N. *Man, the State and War.* New York: Columbia University Press, 1959.

Video

Amistad: A movie depicting an uprising by slaves on a ship.
Roots: The epic movie based on the book by Alex Haley.

CD-ROM

U.S. Central Intelligence Agency, *The World Factbook,* published annually in both hard-copy and CD-ROM versions. The latter is published by Wayzata Technology, Grand Rapids, Minnesota (also available on the internet; see below).

Internet

Amistad website: Provides historical information on the Amistad case: http://amistad.mysticseaport.org/

CNN on-line: Provides hourly up-dated text, photos, and video of late-breaking news: http://www.cnn.com

Central Intelligence Agency home page: Information about the CIA and its publications; particularly valuable is *The World Factbook* which contains data on all 194 states in the world: http://www.odci.gov/cia

Department of State home page: Contains press statements and information about issues related to U.S. foreign policy: http://www.state.gov

Foreign Policy Association: A public interest organization based in the U.S. with information on contemporary issues of world politics: www.fpa.org

International Affairs Network: Contains links to many sources related to international relations: www.pitt.edu/~ian/ianres.html

Simon Wiesenthal Center, Museum of Tolerance web site: includes 1,200 items concerning the Holocaust and World War II: http://motic.wiesenthal.com

White House home page: Information on the president and vice president; also includes a database on press releases back to 1993: http://www.whitehouse.gov

Many countries have their own internet sites to provide information to anyone who requests it; see, for example:

Canada: http://www.statcan.ca/welcome.html
Czech Republic:
http://www.czech.cz/washington/general/pol-plsy.html
Israel: http://pmo.gov.il/english/websites/index.html
Japan (Ministry of Foreign Affairs): http://www.mofa.go.jp/
Norway: http://odin.dep.no/
Sweden: http://www.sb.gov.se/
South Africa: http://www.southafrica.net/

ENDNOTES

[1] HOWARD W. FRENCH, "On Both Sides, Reason for Remorse," *The New York Times*, April 5, 1998, sec. 4, p. 1.

[2] Quoted by KENNETH N. WALTZ, *Man, the State and War: A Theoretical Analysis* (New York: Columbia University Press, 1959), p. 63.

[3] Quoted by PAUL GORDON LAUREN, *Power and Prejudice: The Politics and Diplomacy of Racial Discrimination*, 2nd ed. (Boulder, CO: Westview, 1996), p. 6.

[4] Lauren, p. 9.

[5] This is the theme of Professor Lauren's excellent, provocative book.

[6] ROBERT HERZSTEIN, *Western Civilization* (Boston: Houghton Mifflin, 1975), p. 428; quoted in Lauren, p. 17.

[7] CBS Nightly News, February 1, 1999.

[8] ARISTOTLE, *The Nicomachean Ethics*, I. It should be noted that Aristotle wrote at a time in which gender specific language was used because men were the only participants in the political system. Throughout this book, gender neutral language is used except when the original source, such as Aristotle, used gender specific language.

Who Are the Actors in World Politics?

PART 1

2

The Evolution of the State

CRITEX:
The Melian Dialogue

*t*HE drive to be useful is encoded in our genes. But when we gather in very large numbers, as in the modern nation-state, we seem capable of levels of folly and self-destruction to be found nowhere else in all of nature.

Dr. Lewis Thomas[1]

In this quotation, Dr. Lewis Thomas, a much-respected physician, expresses a very critical view of the modern nation-state. Do "folly and self-destruction" accurately characterize modern states? And if so, were previous gatherings of large groups of human beings similarly characterized? In order to consider Dr. Thomas' claim, let's look back in history.

Archaeological evidence indicates that hunter-gatherers were the first form of social organization. These people used stone tools and had to forage for their food. Since the end of the last ice age, approximately 13,000 years ago, two other types of societies developed. As people began to farm, they did not have to be constantly on the move and were able to produce, store and even trade food with others. Some of these nonliterate, farming societies developed metal tools and weapons. Over time, these implements were used to conquer and exterminate other societies, such as the one "the man in the net" came from.[2]

Over many centuries, groups of people came together and formed villages, towns, and cities. Two-and-a-half millennia ago, the cities in what we now know as Greece developed into independent political entities. Cities such as Athens, Corinth, Sparta, Philippi, and Thessalonica were the basic unit of political life in ancient Greece. The people at this time identified themselves with the city from which they came, rather than with Greece. If we were somehow able to transport ourselves back through time to one of these cities and were to stop someone on the street and ask, "What are you?" no one would say that he or she was Greek; rather, people would say that they were Athenians, Spartans, Philippians, and so on.

The cities of Greece competed with one another in a number of different ways. Of course, everyone knows that the Olympics began in Greece as an athletic competition among the major cities. More serious was the political, economic, and military competition among the cities. In 460 B.C., the first war between Athens and Sparta began. Because both of these cities were situated on the Peloponnesian Peninsula (see Map 2.1), the war was called the **Peloponnesian War.** Throughout the ensuing half century, Athens and Sparta continued their conflict. A former general named **Thucydides,** who had fought in the war, wrote a history of the conflict, which was the first systematic description and analysis of international relations.[3] For this reason, many consider Thucydides to be the "father of international relations."

In his much acclaimed book, Thucydides recounted a terrible choice that the citizens of the island of Melos had to make. Melos was an island colony of Sparta, and its people refused the offer of Athens to become its ally. Melos was neutral until Athens attacked it and then demanded that it join forces with it. In the resulting discussion—the **Melian Dialogue**—representatives of Athens went to Melos and spoke bluntly:

> … we on our side will use no fine phrases saying, for example, that we have a right to our empire because we defeated the Persians, or that we have done against you now because of the injuries that you have done to us—a great mass of words that nobody would believe. And we ask you on your side not to imagine that you will influence us by saying that you, though a colony of Sparta, have not joined Sparta in the war, or that you have never done us any harm.

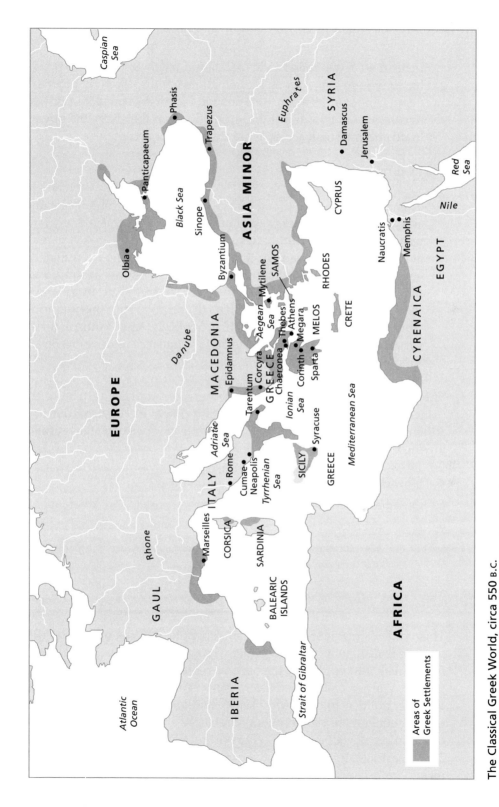

The Classical Greek World, circa 550 B.C.
Source: Joseph S. Nye, Jr. *Understanding International Conflicts: An Introduction to Theory and History,* 2nd ed. New York: Longman, 1997, p. 10. Reprinted by permission of Addison-Wesley Educational Publishers, Inc.

Instead we recommend that you should try to get what it is possible for you to get.... when these matters are discussed by practical people, the standard of justice depends upon the equality of power to compel and that in fact the strong do what they have the power to do and the weak accept what they have to accept.

For their part, the Melians argued:

Then in our view (since you force us to leave justice out of account and to confine ourselves to self-interest)—in our view it is at any rate useful that you should not destroy a principle that is to the general good of all men—namely, that in the case of all who fall into danger there should be such a thing as fair play and just dealing, and that such people should be allowed to use and to profit by arguments that fall short of a mathematical accuracy. And this is a principle which affects you as much as anybody, since your own fall would be visited by the most terrible vengeance and would be an example to the world.[4]

The citizens of Melos had to choose between remaining true to their principles and fighting to almost certain defeat or to surrender to the Athenians. Think about this exchange of views, and then answer the following questions:

- How did the Athenians define their interests?
- On what basis did the Melians make their case to the Athenians?
- If you were faced with this choice, what would you do?

THE PELOPONNESIAN WARS AND THUCYDIDES

Thucydides' great work has captivated people for two-and-a-half millennia. The British political philosopher, Thomas Hobbes, translated the book from Greek into English in the early seventeenth century. A later translator, Rex Warner, called *The History of the Peloponnesian War* "the greatest work on politics, in the widest sense, that has ever been written."[5] Succeeding generations of international-relations students have pondered this observation as well as many others originally presented by Thucydides 2,500 years ago. In fact, if you were to continue your studies of world politics in graduate school, in all probability you would read all or part of

Thucydides' great work. This means that were the book you are now reading to achieve the acclaim of Thucydides, it would be in print and read in the year 4,500—a truly remarkable feat!

Thucydides was born around 460 B.C. The war between Athens and Sparta began in 431 B.C., and it seems that Thucydides participated in some of the early conflicts of the war. Somewhere around 430 B.C., Thucydides fell victim to the plague, which may explain his graphic (and accurate) description of the plague and its effects. In 424 B.C., Thucydides was appointed general, but arrived at the battlefield too late to save a significant Athenian colony. For this, he was exiled for 20 years, returning to Athens only 4 years before his death in 400 B.C.

Thucydides' purpose in writing was simple: "My work is not a piece of writing designed to meet the taste of an immediate public, but was done to last for ever."[6] Some historians contend that while the conflict between Athens and Sparta was important, the lasting historical significance of the Peloponnesian War is due to Thucydides rather than to the events of the war. One of the principal reasons that the *History* has stood the test of time is that it depicts a conflict between two very different societies. Consider the two:

Attribute	Athens	Sparta
Power orientation	Sea-based	Land-based
Type of government	Democratic	Autocratic
Civil-military relations	Civilian-oriented	Militaristic
Ideal leader	Pericles	Archidamus

These two city-states were, in many respects, precursors to modern nation-states, which is another reason that contemporary international relations specialists still read Thucydides. In this sense, Athens, Sparta, and the other Greek city-states were a kind of microcosm of the international system.

In 431, an ally of Sparta—Thebes—attacked an ally of Athens—Plataea—and the two most powerful city-states went to war. Why? The cause of the conflict, according to Thucydides, was quite straightforward: "What made war inevitable was the growth of Athenian power and the fear which this caused in Sparta."[7] The "Archidamian War" (named after the Spartan ruler) lasted from 431 to 421 B.C. Sparta wanted to battle Athens on the land, and Athens and its leader, Pericles, wanted to battle on the sea. The two cities maneuvered to position, and Pericles refused to engage the Spartans. But there were those Athenians who fell in battle, and Pericles' "Funeral Oration" is one of the best known speeches of recorded history—one that has influenced generations of speechwriters, including Abraham Lincoln, since its delivery. Soon after Pericles delivered his oration,

Athens suffered a disastrous plague that killed one-third of its soldiers and its great leader, Pericles.

Following this calamity, the advantage in the war went to Sparta. For its part, Athens abandoned the conservative policy of Pericles and confronted Sparta in a series of battles. An ineffective peace lasted from 421–415 B.C., and two factions vied for the Athenians' support. Nicias favored **appeasement** of Sparta, and Alcibiandes favored a more aggressive approach. In 416 B.C., Athens attacked Melos (see the critical thinking exercise at the beginning of this chapter) and when it was victorious killed all adult males, enslaved the rest of the Melians and gave the island to 500 Athenian colonizers. Athens then decided to attack Syracuse on the island of Sicily. Unfortunately for it, Athens suffered a terrible defeat. Sparta continued fighting and in 404 B.C. finally defeated Athens completely.

During the cold war (see Chapter 7), some observers portrayed the United States as a modern day Athens and the Soviet Union as the contemporary Sparta. Think about the following questions:

To what extent do you think that this comparison was accurate?

If this comparison had validity, then why did the United States and USSR not go to war like Athens and Sparta?

BOX 2.1   Thucydides on War, Government, and Leadership

- Think, too, of the great part that is played by the unpredictable in war: think of it now, before you are actually committed to war. The longer a war lasts, the more things tend to depend on accidents.[8]

- For we must not bolster ourselves up with the false hope that if we devastate their land, the war will soon be over.[9]

- Remember that success comes from foresight and not much is ever gained simply by wishing for it.[10]

- For those who are politically apathetic can only survive if they are supported by people who are capable of taking action. They are quite valueless in a city which controls an empire, though they would be safe slaves in a city that was controlled by others.[11]

And what about the contemporary relevance of Thucydides? In the course of the debate in the U.S. Congress in January 1991 prior to the Gulf War, Senator Wyche Fowler read from Thucydides and noted: "The lesson is first and foremost the uncertainties of war, as true as when the European

Powers plotted a brief, decisive war in 1914, as in 1964 when we sought no wider war in Vietnam, or in 415 B.C. when Athenians dreamed of glory on the far-off battlefield. In none of these cases did those who planned the conflict foresee the ultimate costs, in blood and treasure, of the long-range consequences of their actions."[12]

THE FORERUNNERS TO STATES

Around 3,000 B.C., groups of people in what we now know as the Middle East interacted with one another both cooperatively and competitively. Egyptians, Phoenicians, Semites, Sumerians, Akkadians, Amorites, Hittites, Assyrians, Medes, Persians, and others emerged on the scene at this time. (Those who have read parts of the Old Testament in the Bible will recognize some of these groups because it recounts their history.) In contrast to the cultural heterogeneity of the Middle East, homogeneity characterized ancient China; i.e., it consisted of the same ethnic group. Nonetheless, it was not until China's Zhou (pronounced "Joe") dynasty, which began in 1122 B.C., that the Chinese state began to emerge.[13] Historians have found that there were approximately 200 political entities in China almost 3,000 years ago.[14]

THE GREEK CITY-STATES AND THE ROMAN EMPIRE

As Thucydides and other Greek historians noted, a number of city-states developed on the Peloponnesian Peninsula. These city-states interacted with one another in the ways that modern countries do: they traded with one another, exchanged ambassadors, negotiated with each other, and sometimes even went to war.

Eventually, in 146 B.C. the larger, more powerful **Roman Empire** subjugated the city-states of ancient Greece and thereby underscored the power of larger, well-organized political entities. Unlike the Greek city-states, Rome was a unified power that was able to dominate the then-known world because of its size, power, and organization. Despite its power, however, Rome was not without internal problems. One of the most famous Roman emperors, Caesar, conquered Gaul (the area we now call France) in 51 B.C. and then marched on Rome itself. Caesar was assassinated by one of his own generals, Brutus, an event that ushered in a period of anarchy for two decades. After a prolonged struggle, Octavius wrested control from Anthony and Cleopatra who committed suicide when they were defeated.

International relations scholars refer to large, dominating states such as the Roman Empire as **"hegemons"** or **"hegemonic powers."** The problem of such large empires is that they are difficult to control effectively. An American international relations expert has noted the conditions of the Roman Empire in its last days:

> The absence of central authority was reflected in the deterioration of the roads, bridges, and canals that under the Empire had facilitated commerce between the Empire's cities and the countryside.... The disintegration of the imperial system left households and communities vulnerable to marauders and outlaw bands, as well as to onslaughts from barbarian tribes.[15]

THE DARK AGES AND THE AGE OF SCHOLASTICISM

With the disintegration of the Roman Empire in the fifth century A.D., Germanic tribes overran much of the territory that had been controlled by Rome. The last Roman soldiers left Britain in 436, and in 455, vandals sacked Rome itself. The organization of the Roman Empire was lost, and Europe entered a period that historians have called "the Dark Ages" because little was accomplished.

In 800 a new ruler, Charlemagne, established a new empire. In addition to the secular authority of Charlemagne, the Roman Catholic Church, ruled by the pope, also exercised control over the lives of people. Barbarians continued their attacks on Charlemagne's empire and were eventually successful in overrunning it; rather than rejecting Christianity, many accepted it. By the end of the millennium, authority was in essence shared by the secular Holy Roman Emperor and the pope.

At the turn of the millennium, society was organized according to a system called **feudalism.** This system had a very few lords who owned the land and resources and vassals who were practically slaves of the lords. The economy was predominantly agricultural, and there was very little trade or commerce with other cities. With the growth and expansion of cities and the establishment of village markets (which occurred around 1000 A.D.), trade increased, cities grew in importance and a new class—merchants—began to emerge. All of these developments had profound implications for society and politics. A money-based economy developed, replacing the barter economy of feudal times. Cities grew both in population and in importance, and increasingly these cities needed organization to provide security and order. Modern international relations analysts have compared the rise of village markets and the economic opportunities that they provided to modern multinational corporations. The rise of cities, then, had economic, social, and political consequences.

The eminent University of Chicago historian, William H. McNeill, has pointed out: "The self transformation and expansion of Islam was the most dramatic and conspicuous shift in world history that took place between A.D. 100 and 1500.... By the year 1000 the inhabitants of northwestern Europe possessed a comparatively numerous knightly class whose armament and training gave them man-to-man superiority over any other military force in the world."[16] When these two developments—the rise of Islam and the establishment of western military force—are considered together, we conclude the result was the **Crusades.** Imbued with a desire to recapture the holy sites of Christendom, knights from Europe traveled to the Middle East on various crusades from 1100 to 1300.

The Crusades

The Crusades were a sad, in some cases pathetically tragic, meeting of the Islamic and Christian worlds that continue to have an impact. The Christian knights of Europe wanted to regain control over the holiest shrines of Christendom and fought courageously and brutally to do so. The Muslim defenders fought equally courageously and brutally to defend what they considered to be holy shrines of Islam. The resulting fighting caused the deaths of many Christians and Muslims. To this day, vestiges of the crusades can still be seen in the Middle East. There are, for example, blue-eyed Arabs, descendants of long-ago crusaders. Politically, the crusades established a fear and hatred between the Middle East and the West that has remained in the minds of many today.

In order to defend their kingdoms and to support crusading forays into the Middle East, the kings of Europe needed more and more resources: soldiers, weapons and money. And in order to obtain these resources, kings sought to expand their territory and to conclude alliances with the newly emerging and increasingly wealthy commercial classes. Of course, the merchants demanded something in return for their resources and loyalty. The **"Magna Carta"** (Great Charter) concluded in 1215 between the English King John and nobles illustrated the type of agreement that was concluded. Of course, the other important element of power within society at this time was the church, and the royalty increasingly competed with religious authorities for resources and the loyalty of people. In many cases, the church and kings worked out an agreement to work together. In other cases, the two powerful institutions competed with one another.

THE RENAISSANCE AND REFORMATION

During the fourteenth century, a new movement of intellectual growth and ferment began around the Italian city-state of Florence and spread throughout northern Italy. This **Renaissance** or "rebirth" was marked by a revival of classical scholarship and an emphasis on rationalism. For about a century, the city-states of Florence, Venice, Milan, Rome, Naples, and others dominated the politics of the Italian peninsula. But there were also exernal powers that were interested in the politics of the Italian Peninsula; these included France, Spain, Germany, and the Papacy.

Machiavelli

It was in this environment of political intrigue and competition that **Niccolo Machiavelli** developed his ideas about power and politics. The most famous of his works, *The Prince,* written in 1513 but not published until 1532, was a kind of manual that Machiavelli wrote to try to curry favor with the ruling Medici family. Prior to Machiavelli, philosophers had emphasized the role of God in political affairs. A popular doctrine was the **divine right of kings** which held that a sovereign's right to rule came directly from God. Machiavelli had a very different view: "The chief foundations of all states, whether new, old or mixed, are good laws and good arms."[17] Machiavelli's view of politics, in short, was secular and power-oriented. He was primarily concerned with the survival of his city-state (Florence) and did not address the formation or maintenance of any system or collection of city-states. Thus, according to a later student of the European balance of power system, *The Prince* "is a document for the individual ruler, and not for the state system."[18]

The importance of *The Prince* is hard to overestimate. A respected professor, Max Lerner, has called *The Prince* "one of the half dozen books that have done most to shape Western thought."[19] Because of his separation of the sacred from politics and because of his focus on power, some call Machiavelli the father of modern political science. Some contemporary business-school professors assign their students to read *The Prince* in order to learn how to gain and keep power in the modern corporate world.

The separation of church and state was strengthened further in 1517 in the German city of Wittenberg when Martin Luther posted ninety-five theses on his church's doors attacking what he viewed as the evils of the Catholic Church and challenging the authority of the pope. This action catalyzed the Protestant **Reformation** and further divided the religious and secular worlds. In addition, by emphasizing the "priesthood of all believers" and the view that the relationship between God and people was one that did not require the intercession of a member of the clergy, Luther further liberated individuals.

> ### BOX 2.2 Machiavelli on Laws, Arms, Leadership
>
> - Where the very safety of the fatherland is at stake there should be no question of reflecting whether a thing is just or unjust, humane or cruel, praiseworthy or shameful. Setting aside every other consideration, one must take only that course of action which will secure the country's life and liberty.[20]
>
> - A prince should ... have no other aim or thought, nor take up any other thing for his study, but war and its organization and discipline, for that is the only art that is necessary to one who commands.[21]
>
> - A prince being ... obliged to know well how to act as a beast must imitate the fox and the lion, for the lion cannot protect himself from traps, and the fox cannot defend himself from wolves. One must therefore be a fox to recognize traps, and a lion to frighten wolves.[22]
>
> - ... the best fortress is to be found in the love of the people, for although you have fortresses they will not save you if you are hated by the people.[23]
>
> - Only those defenses are good, certain and durable, which depend on yourself alone and your own ability.[24]

The Thirty Years' War

The Renaissance and the Reformation unleashed a torrent of emotions on the European continent and resulted in a number of religiously based wars, which dominated the sixteenth and seventeenth centuries. One of history's most costly wars was fought over religion and lasted from 1618–1648. It lasted so long that the duration of the war became its name: the **Thirty Years' War.** In Bohemia, 29,000 of its 35,000 villages were destroyed, and the shortages produced by the war were so severe that there were reports of people eating cats, dogs, rats, and even other people![25] In the end, historians estimate that the war reduced the population of Europe by at least one-fourth. Drained by the economic, physical, and human costs of the war, the leaders of 135 principalities agreed in 1648 in the Treaty of Westphalia that rulers should have sovereign power over their jurisdictions and, in particular, that they should be able to determine the religion of the territory under their control. This established the principle of "sovereignty" in international relations, and this became the foundation of the modern state. Significantly, a Dutch jurist by the name of Hugo Grotius published a book entitled *On the Law of War and Peace* in 1625, a book which became the basis of modern international law and which assumed the primacy of states (see Chapter 10).

The outcome of the Thirty Years' War affected the shape of European politics. For example, the decline of Spain began, not with the defeat of the Armada, but with the losses suffered during the war in Germany and the Netherlands. By the end of the war, Sweden, France, and the Netherlands emerged as the most powerful in Europe; however, this dominance was to be short-lived. Great Britain soon replaced the Netherlands as the dominant seapower of Europe, and Russia under Peter the Great defeated and supplanted Sweden in 1709 at the Battle of Poltava.

THE EMERGENCE OF NATION-STATES

What we know as states are relatively recent creations. In fact, they only began to appear about 350 years ago, following the end of the Thirty Years' War.

If NASA had invented a functional "time machine" and we were able to go back in time four centuries, we would discover that the people of that era would think very differently about politics and states. For example, if we were to visit Italy, we would find that people there would not identify themselves as "Italians"; rather they would identify themselves as "Florentines" (people from Florence) or "Venetians" (people from Venice). This was similar to the way in which ancient Greeks had identified themselves: by referring to the city in which they lived. It is estimated that there were approximately 300 independent political units in Europe during the seventeenth and eighteenth centuries.[26] Italy was not unified until 1870. Similarly, Germany was divided into a number of different regions and city-states and was not unified until 1871.

The recognition of the principle of "sovereignty" in the Treaty of Westphalia marked the beginning of the emergence of modern nation-states. There are many definitions of "sovereignty." One scholar has written: "a sovereign state is one that is free to independently govern its own population in its own territory and set its own foreign policy."[27] Essentially, sovereignty gives states the right to do almost whatever their leaders choose to do within their boundaries.

International politics was conducted quite differently during the last part of the seventeenth century than today. Latin was the language of international relations, and diplomats both wrote to and conversed with one another in Latin. The Treaty of Westphalia and other agreements of the seventeenth century were drafted and signed in Latin.[28] During the eighteenth century, the French demanded that their language be used in diplomatic proceedings, and by the mid-eighteenth century French had become established as the language of diplomacy. The Treaty of Aix-la-Chapelle, signed in 1748, was drafted in French, and from that time on agreements were written in French.

The leaders of the seventeenth and eighteenth centuries were mostly aristocrats who shared common traditions and beliefs. They were educated in a similar manner; and many of the leaders were related to one another. For example, Marie Antoinette (the wife of Louis XVI of France) was the daughter of Empress Maria Theresa of Austria-Hungary. Queen Victoria of England was the grandmother of the World War I German ruler, Kaiser Wilhelm II, and his foe, the Russian ruler, Czar Nicholas II, making them first cousins. The degree to which the leaders of nineteenth century Europe were related is indicated by the family tree of Queen Victoria.

The common background of the rulers affected the way in which world politics was conducted during this era. For example, wars were largely fought very differently than during the twentieth century. Military forces were most often hired mercenaries and were smaller in number than later forces. Because nationalism was not particularly strong, mercenaries' loyalties and commitments were fluid. For example, the great Prussian military strategist, **Karl von Clausewitz,** actually fought against French forces for Russia. An officer who lost a battle was unlikely to receive another command; this fact of military life influenced the way that battles were fought. They tended to be exercises in maneuver rather than head-on, decisive battles. Wars were limited and defensive and were fought in order to stabilize the system. For example, if a great power was defeated, vindictive peace terms were avoided, and the great power was restored to its prewar position within the international community. Prior to the eighteenth century, a distinction was made between soldiers and civilians. Much of Western thinking about "just" and "unjust" wars was based on the ability to distinguish between combatants and civilians.

By the last part of the eighteenth century, many of the old norms were breaking down due to the spread of the ideas of the **Enlightenment,** ideas such as equality, liberty, and the separation of church and state. These ideas were reflected in the United States, which one prominent political scientist has called "the first new nation."[29] Following the success of the

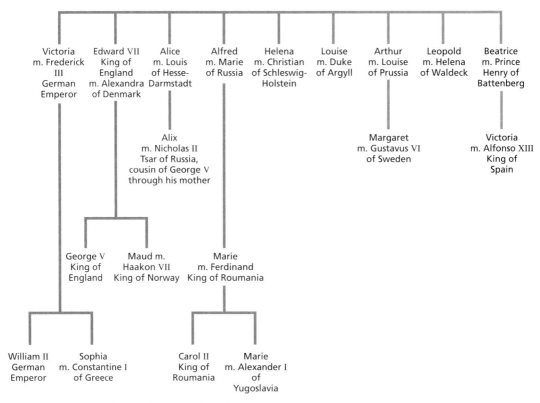

Figure 2.1. Descendants of Queen Victoria
Source: William L. Langer. *An Encyclopedia of World History,* 4th ed. Boston: Houghton Mifflin, 1968, p. 669.

American Revolution, there were attempts at revolution throughout Europe, including France, England, Ireland, Holland, Belgium, Switzerland, Germany, Italy, Hungary, and Poland.

The most significant of these late eighteenth-century revolutions occurred in France. The power and passions released by the **French Revolution** proved to be difficult to restrain and turned violent. In essence, the oppressed became the oppressors.

DISCUSSION QUESTIONS

1. What were the factors that caused the war between Athens and Sparta?
2. What caused city-states to join together to form nation-states?
3. What is the relevance of history to contemporary world politics? For example, are the hatreds caused by the Crusades still evident in the world?

KEY TERMS

American Revolution	Machiavelli, Niccolo
appeasement	Magna Carta
Clausewitz, Karl von	Melian Dialogue
Crusades	Peloponnesian Wars
divine right of kings	Reformation
Enlightenment	Renaissance
feudalism	Roman Empire
French Revolution	Thirty Years' War
hegemon, hegemonic power	Thucydides

KEY DATES IN WORLD HISTORY

The Greek Period

1184 B.C.	Capture of Troy by Greece
c. 850 B.C.	Homer writes his epic poems, *The Iliad* and *The Odyssey*
460–451 B.C.	First Peloponnesian War; Athens vs. Corinth
431–421 B.C.	Great Peloponnesian War; Athens vs. Sparta
414–404 B.C.	Thucydides writes his famous history

The Roman Period

146 B.C.	Rome defeats Greece
58–51 B.C.	Caesar conquers Gaul (what is now France)
44 B.C.	Assassination of Caesar
476 A.D.	End of the Roman period

The Middle Ages

400–800 A.D.	Attacks on Europe from Huns, Goths, and others
771–814	Charlemagne's reign

The Age of Scholasticism

800–1200	Catholic Church dominates
1100–1300	Crusades

Renaissance and Reformation

1513	Niccolo Machiavelli writes *The Prince*
1517	Martin Luther begins the Protestant Reformation
1588	Britain defeats the Spanish armada

Age of Revolution

1618–1648	Thirty Years' War
1776–1783	American Revolution
1789–1799	French Revolution
1799	*Coup d'état* by Napoleon Bonaparte

RECOMMENDED PRINT, MULTIMEDIA, AND INTERNET SOURCES

Print

DIAMOND, JARED. *Guns, Germs, and Steel: The Fates of Human Societies.* New York: W. W. Norton, 1997.

FAIRBANK, JOHN KING. *China: A New History.* Cambridge, MA: Harvard University Press, 1992.

KAGAN, DONALD. *On the Origins of War and the Preservation of Peace.* New York: Doubleday, 1995.

KAUPPI, MARK V. and PAUL R. VIOTTI. *The Global Philosophers: World Politics in Western Thought.* New York: Lexington Books, 1992.

KEEGAN, JOHN. *A History of Warfare.* New York: Knopf, 1994.

MCNEILL, WILLIAM H. *A World History.* New York: Oxford University Press, 1967.

THUCYDIDES. *The History of the Peloponnesian War.* London: Penguin, 1954, 1972.

TOYNBEE, ARNOLD J. *Change and Habit: The Challenge of Our Time.* New York: Oxford University Press, 1966.

WRIGHT, QUINCY. *A Study of War,* abridged edition. Chicago: University of Chicago Press, 1942, 1964.

Video

Charlemagne and the Holy Roman Empire. Princeton, NJ: Films for the Humanities and Sciences, 31 minutes. Covers the life and times of Charlemagne and the conflict between Henry IV and Pope Gregory VII.

Thucydides: The Peloponnesian Wars and Plato: Alcibiados I. Princeton, NJ: Films for the Humanities and Sciences, 72 minutes. A BBC production employing contemporary actors to deliver the speeches contained in Thucydides' great work.

CD-ROM

Britain 1750–1900: Expansion, Trade, and Industry. Princeton, NJ: Films for the Humanities and Sciences. Using documents and pictures, this CD-ROM focuses on life in England during the industrial revolution.

Internet

This site focuses entiely on Machiavelli and includes his major works, his biography and Machiavelli chat rooms: http://www.sas.upenn.edu/~pgrose/mach/

ENDNOTES

[1] Quoted by the *Los Angeles Times*, July 10, 1997, p. 18.

[2] JARED DIAMOND, *Guns, Germs, and Steel: The Fates of Human Societies* (New York: W. W. Norton, 1997).

[3] Thucydides, *History of the Peloponnesian War*, translated by Rex Warner (London: Penguin, 1954).

[4] Ibid., pp. 401–402.

[5] Ibid.

[6] Ibid., p. 48.

[7] Ibid., p. 49.

[8] Ibid., pp. 56–57.

[9] Ibid., p. 83.

[10] Ibid., p. 417.

[11] Ibid., p. 161.

[12] *The New York Times*, January 13, 1991, sec. 4, p. 1.

[13] JOHN KING FAIRBANK, *China: A New History* (Cambridge, MA: Harvard University Press, 1992), p. 39.

[14] QUINCY WRIGHT, *A Study of War*, abridged ed. (Chicago: University of Chicago Press, 1942, 1964).

[15] SEYOM BROWN, *New Forces, Old Forces and the Future of World Politics: Post-Cold War Edition* (New York: HarperCollins, 1995), p. 34.

[16] WILLIAM H. MCNEILL, *A World History* (New York: Oxford University Press, 1967), p. 251.

[17] NICCOLO MACHIAVELLI, *The Prince and the Discourses* (New York: Modern Library, 1950), Chapter XXII. p. 44.

[18] EDWARD VOSE GULICK, *Europe's Classical Balance of Power* (New York: Norton, 1967), p. 43.

[19] MAX LERNER, "Introduction to *The Prince and the Discourses*," p. XXX.

[20] Quoted in GRAHAM EVANS, *Dictionary of International Relations* (London: Penguin, 1998), p. 311.

[21] MACHIAVELLI, *The Prince*, Chapter XIV, p. 53.

[22] Ibid., Chapter XVIII, p. 64.

[23] Ibid., Chapter XX, p. 81.

[24] Ibid., Chapter XXIV, p. 90.

[25] WILL and ARIEL DURANT, *The Age of Reason Begins*, vol. 7 of *The Story of Civilization* (New York: Simon & Schuster, 1961), p. 567, quoted by Brown, *New Forces, Old Forces*, p. 41.

[26] GULICK, p. 9.

[27] MARK W. JANIS, *An Introduction to International Law* (Boston: Little, Brown, 1988), p. 122.

[28] HAROLD NICOLSON, *Diplomacy*, 3rd ed. (New York: Oxford University Press, 1963), p. 223.

[29] SEYMOUR MARTIN LIPSET, *The First New Nation: The United States in Historical and Comparative Perspective* (New York: Basic Books, 1963).

3

The State System and the Balance of Power

CRITEX:

Interpreting Graphical Information: Napoleon's March on Moscow

STATES are one of the most important building blocks of contemporary world politics and have been so for the past three-and-a-half centuries. States are powerful and demand, to a greater or lesser extent, that their citizens support them.

In 1799 **Napoleon Bonaparte** staged a successful *coup d'état* and then crowned himself emperor of France in 1804. He demanded that French citizens support their country with their taxes and their lives. Napoleon was one of the first leaders to draft citizens to fight in the military in a policy that Napoleon called the *levée en masse* (which translates literally as "a gathering or rising in a body").

Napoleon had an ambitious objective: to take over all of Western Europe—and he came close to succeeding. His most difficult campaign, and ultimately one of the major reasons that he fell short of

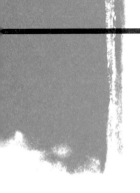

achieving his goal, was the invasion of Russia. The graphic on the following page depicts the losses suffered by Napoleon's army in his attempt to take over Russia in 1812. The artist, Charles Joseph Minard, drew the width of the band to correspond to the number of soldiers who began the campaign (422,000) at Niemen, near the Polish-Russian border. Several contingents of Napoleon's army peeled off from the main force and are indicated by the narrower bands which represents a smaller number of soldiers. As the army advanced toward Moscow, there were many casualties and defections, and by the time the army reached the outskirts of Moscow, only about 100,000 soldiers remained. These soldiers faced brutally cold temperatures, which were recorded by Minard on the scale at the bottom of the graphic. By the time Napoleon's army retreated to its original starting point, only 10,000 of the original 422,000 remained. According to Yale Professor Edward Tufte, this graphic "may well be the best statistical graph ever drawn."[1] As you examine the graphic, list the variables—that is, information—that you see plotted:

1.

2.

3.

4.

5.

6.

NAPOLEON AND THE REVOLUTION IN WORLD POLITICS AND WARFARE

Declaring (without much exaggeration) "I am the revolution," Napoleon Bonaparte became the emperor of France and proceeded to attempt to take over all of Europe. Napoleon used a new, revolutionary means to fight his wars: he drafted ordinary French citizens to fill the ranks of his army previously filled with mercenaries. This innovation had several consequences. First, it made Napoleon's armies bigger and therefore more powerful than other armies due to its sheer size. Second, as citizens filled the ranks of Napoleon's army, French society itself became a legitimate target of opposing militaries. The previous distinction between soldiers and civilians was blurred, and ordinary citizens were no longer immune to attack because they represented a resource of power. Third, wars became less limited in objectives, scope, and destruction, as the Napoleonic Wars first indicated and as the twentieth century devastatingly confirmed.

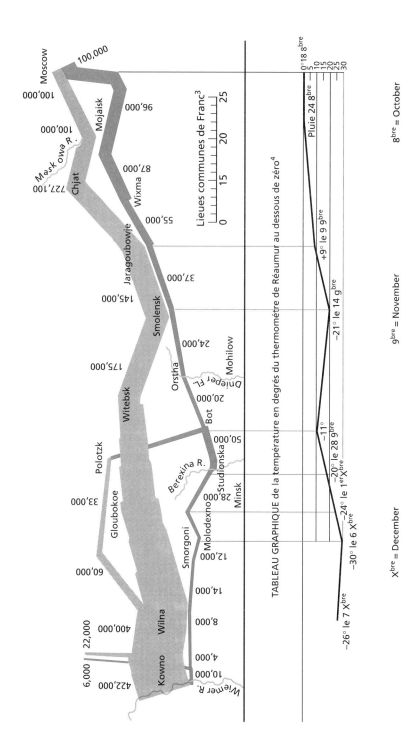

Napoleon's March on Moscow

1 Map showing the successive loss of men of the French Army in the Russian Campaign of 1812–1813
2 Prepared by Mr. [Charles Joseph] Minard, Inspector General of Bridges and Roadways
3 Linear scale in kilometers
4 Graph of the temperature in degrees below zero [in Celsius]

Source: Reprinted in Edward Tufte, *The Visual Display of Quantitative Information* (Cheshire, CT: Graphics Press, 1983), p. 41; used by permission.

Napoleon's attempt to take over Europe lasted from 1793 to 1815. The European powers were finally successful in defeating Napoleon at the Battle of Waterloo in 1815. Napoleon's defeat removed the immediate threat of a French takeover of Europe, but it did not solve the problems created by almost 20 years of war. The foreign minister of the Austro-Hungarian empire, **Klemens von Metternich,** invited the leading European statesmen to Austria for a conference (called the **Congress of Vienna**) to discuss how to put Europe back together again. These leaders met and discussed various plans for providing for peace and stability. After two years of discussions, they agreed that the balance of power would be the best way for them to conduct world politics.

THE BALANCE OF POWER: ITS ORIGIN AND DEVELOPMENT

The statesmen of the seventeenth and eighteenth centuries were very much influenced by scientific developments in their thinking about politics. Just as scientists were discovering that the natural and physical worlds were governed by laws and structures, statesmen concluded that the political world must also be governed by analogous laws. Although the Treaty of Utrecht of 1713 was the first European treaty that specifically mentioned the **"balance of power,"** the practice of states seeking a common equilibrium had been observed for many years. The Italian city-states of the Renaissance had practiced a form of the balance of power.

Statesmen thought of the balance of power as a kind of "clockworks." One can also think of the balance of power as a kind of mobile, the type that parents suspend over the cribs of children. Mobiles can have any number of elements; however, they must be balanced or the structure will be destabilized. Similarly, the balance of power can have two or more elements, but they must remain balanced, no matter how many elements there are, or the system will be destabilized and cease to exist.

The basic elements of the balance of power mobile are called **"great powers"** or, sometimes, **"essential actors."** A system with two great powers is called a **"bipolar"** system, with three members it is a **"tripolar"** system, and with four or more, a **"multipolar"** system. Throughout the seventeenth and into the early eighteenth century, the balance of power was essentially bipolar with France and the Austro-Hungarian Empire constituting the two principal poles of power and Britain occupying a less powerful, but very significant, position as the "balancer" of the system. During the eighteenth century, the mobile became more complex, and five powers emerged as the great powers: Austria-Hungary, France, Great Britain, Prussia, and Russia. The European balance of power worked relatively well; from the end of the Thirty Years' War in 1648 through 1792, there were no great territorial changes in continental Europe with the exception of the first partition of Poland.[2] This century-and-a-half period was characterized by the preservation of the status quo.

The stability of the European status quo was destroyed by Napoleon's attempt to take over Europe starting in 1793 and continuing intermittently until 1815. This attempt to achieve what modern international relations experts would call "hegemony" dominated the politics of Europe and upset the balance of power that had provided almost 150 years of stability.

In the French town of Chaumont, representatives of the Austro-Hungarian, British, Prussian, and Russian governments in March 1814 signed a treaty which the eminent historian of the European balance of power, Edward Gulick, described as "one of the outstanding documents of diplomatic history since the Renaissance."[3] In this treaty, the signatories agreed to decisively defeat Napoleon and to continue their alliance following their victory over France. In part, the treaty stated:[4]

> The present Treaty of Alliance having for its object the maintenance of the balance of Europe, to secure the repose and independence of the Powers, and to prevent the invasions which for so many years have devastated the world, the High Contracting Parties have agreed among themselves to extend its duration for twenty years from the date of signature.

The **Treaty of Chaumont** incorporated many of the principles of the balance of power that had developed over the course of the previous century and a half; it was, in short, "old in theory but new in practice."[5] The theory of the balance was quite simple: it was designed to insure the survival of independent states and to prevent the domination by any one state.

The coalition of forces opposing Napoleon was victorious and sent Napoleon into exile on the island of Elba. The statesmen of Europe met in Vienna beginning in September 1814 to try and reconstruct European political order in the aftermath of the Napoleonic wars. Representatives of the four great powers were present: Klemens von Metternich (foreign minister of Austria-Hungary), Viscount Castlereagh (foreign minister of Great Britain), Talleyrand (French foreign minister), and Tsar Alexander of Russia. The attendees at the Congress of Vienna were concerned with several major questions concerning territorial settlements, the restoration of various European monarchies, and various other outstanding questions that resulted from the defeat of France.

On February 25, 1815, Napoleon escaped from his island exile, Elba, landed soon thereafter in Cannes and marched toward Paris. Along the

> **BOX 3.1   The Contemporary Relevance of History**
>
> **Dr. Henry A. Kissinger** wrote his doctoral dissertation, later his first book, on the Congress of Vienna. On the first page, Kissinger wrote: "Whenever peace—conceived as avoidance of war—has been the primary objective of a power or a group of powers, the international system has been at the mercy of the most ruthless member of the international community. Whenever the international order has acknowledged that certain principles could not be compromised even for the sake of peace, stability based on an equilibrium of forces was at least conceivable."[6] To what extent do you think that the loss of twelve members of Dr. Kissinger's family in the concentration camps of Nazi Germany affected his views of the need for order in world politics?

way, Napoleon gained the support of many French people. Within two weeks of his landing in the south, Napoleon formed a new government in Tuileries. Louis XVIII, who had been restored to his throne by the Congress of Vienna, feared for his future and fled France for Ghent, Belgium.

News of Napoleon's escape from Elba reached Vienna on the night of March 6–7, and the negotiators turned immediately to the question of how to deal with the crisis. They agreed that Napoleon's return to Europe was "incompatible with the peace and security of Europe," and declared him to be "an enemy and disturber of the peace of the world."[7] The statesmen, in effect, put into effect the provisions of the Treaty of Chaumont that they had concluded a year previously. As Napoleon sought to increase the strength of his army, so too did his opponents. On June 15, 1815, Napoleon marched into Belgium seeking to divide the allied armies. Initially successful, Napoleon was confronted by British forces under Wellington on June 18. By 8 o'clock that night, the Battle of Waterloo was over, and Napoleon was defeated.

The statesmen at the Congress of Vienna were successful in creating a stable international system. In 1815, there were 50 members of the European international system: 5 great powers (Great Britain, France, Russia, Prussia, and Austria-Hungary), 4 secondary powers (Spain, Portugal, Sweden, and the Netherlands), 40 lesser powers and 4 "free cities."

The emergence of states and the development of a defined balance of power system created the need for **diplomacy**.[8] Evolving from the interactions of the Italian city-states of the Renaissance, diplomacy involved representatives of one government meeting with representatives of another in order to discuss or negotiate solutions to problems. One British diplomat, Sir John Wotton, defined an ambassador as "an honest man sent to lie abroad for the good of his country," and another diplomat defined his profession as "honorable spying." By the mid-eighteenth century, French was established as the language of diplomacy, and the proceedings of both the Congress of Vienna (1815) and the Congress of Paris (1856) were conducted in French. It was not until the Paris Conference at the end of World War I that English was used in addition to French to conduct the discussions. We will return to the topic of diplomacy in Chapter 11.

The growth of the diplomatic service in Great Britain was characteristic of trends in Europe. Diplomacy at this time was clearly centered on Europe; between 1792 and 1815, Great Britain had 30 overseas missions, and 25 of these were located in Europe. Diplomacy was also conducted by appointees of the sovereign, and there was no bureaucracy to speak of. When William Pitt the Younger was British Prime Minister, he had a permanent undersecretary, 12 clerks, and a "decipherer of letters" to assist him in carrying out the responsibilities of his office, including foreign affairs. Ambassadors were expected to select their own staffs, and it was not until 1822 that steps were taken to create a regular foreign service for overseas diplomatic missions.

In the United States, there has always been a certain ambivalence concerning diplomacy. On the one hand, Americans have had great respect for diplomacy. The Department of State, the agency principally responsible for the conduct of U.S. foreign relations, was the first executive agency established under the Constitution in 1789. Those who served as secretary of state in the early years of the American republic included Thomas Jefferson, John Marshall, James Madison, James Monroe, John Quincy Adams, Henry Clay, and Martin Van Buren. Five members of this group were elected president, and one became chief justice of the Supreme Court. But Americans distrusted aristocracy and sometimes viewed aristocrats and diplomats as one and the same. In order to assure control over diplomacy, Americans demanded democratic checks and balances, and perhaps the most perceptive observer of American culture, the Frenchman Alexis de Tocqueville, noted the dangers of this approach:

> Foreign policy does not require the use of any of the good qualities peculiar to democracy but does demand the cultivation of almost all those which it lacks. Democracy favors the growth of the state's internal resources. It extends comfort and develops public spirit, strengthens respect for law in the various classes of society, all of which things have no more than an indirect influence on the standing of one nation in respect to another. But a democracy finds it difficult to coordinate the details of a great undertaking and to fix on

some plan and carry it through with determination in spite of ob-
stacles. It has little capacity for combining measures in secret and
waiting patiently for the result. Such qualities are more likely to belong to a single man or to an aristocracy.[9]

THE BALANCE OF POWER AND ITS OPERATION

We have seen how the balance of power developed historically; how have
scholars depicted this important mechanism for managing power in international relations? Partly because European statesmen shared common
ideals, language, and goals, they were able to agree on the way in which
international relations should be conducted. The balance of power was
based on the following assumptions.

1. Sovereign states are the primary actors in international relations, and
   other nonstate actors such as international organizations and corporations are not as important as states.
2. Certain states are recognized as more powerful and influential than
   other states and are referred to as "great powers" or "essential actors."
3. States have conflicting goals and will engage in war in order to gain
   as much power, defined as control over territory, as possible.
4. Despite the existence of conflict and, on occasion, war, there nevertheless was a consensus among the great powers on the preservation
   of the international system.
5. No one member of the international system should become dominant.
6. Power must be measurable.
7. Flexibility of alignments was required.

These assumptions need to be explained. First, the balance-of-power
system was what contemporary international relations theorists call **"state
centric";** that is, the basic building blocks of the system were states, not international organizations, multinational corporations, or any other group.
These states possessed "sovereignty," and thus they could do what their
leaders chose to do within their boundaries.

Second, the most powerful states were recognized as the "great powers" of the system. This exalted status was conferred by the possession of
significant power in terms of territory, people, and military capability. In
the nineteenth century, the five great powers were Great Britain, France,
Austria-Hungary, Prussia (Germany), and Russia.

Third, balance-of-power advocates note that states have conflicting goals and will therefore compete with one another for influence and power in international relations. War was an integral part of the classical balance-of-power system, which allowed for the redistribution of power among the great powers.

Fourth, the members of the balance-of-power system recognized that the system itself must be preserved; that this goal was in the selfish interests of each of the members. Thus the major objective of the system was to maintain **stability,** even at the cost of peace if necessary.

Fifth, no individual member of the system could predominate; if any member tried to achieve hegemony, then the other members of the balance-of-power system would ally with one another in order to oppose the state trying to achieve hegemony over the system.

Sixth, if power is to be "balanced," then there must be some way to measure power. During the eighteenth and nineteenth centuries, power was defined in terms of three main variables: territory, population and military strength. In fact, during their negotiations in Vienna, the diplomats consulted with a respected Prussian statistician in order to see how many people Napoleon had defeated and were therefore at the disposal of the Congress for redistribution to other states. This concern over territory and people was related to "compensations," which were the adjustments that were made in order to balance power among the great powers. Often colonies provided a convenient means for a defeated power to provide **compensations** to the victorious powers. Of course, the people within the colonies that served as compensations (and were turned over to the victors) had absolutely no say over their fate.

The final requirement for the balance of power that was very important was **diplomatic flexibility.** The seventeenth and early eighteenth centuries provide many examples of the ways in which states shifted their allegiances from one to another. Historian Edward Gulick outlined the diplomatic flexibility of Great Britain:[10]

starting with participation in the Barrier Treaty (1715) with Austria and Holland against France and an alliance with Austria (1716). This system was then paralleled by a triple alliance (1717) of Britain, Holland, and France, which in turn was elaborated by the inclusion of Austria in a well-known quadruple alliance (1718) created to check Spanish aggression. By 1721, however, we find Britain and France, having dropped out of their earlier alliance structure against Spain, now going into an alliance *with* Spain. By 1725 Britain, France, and Prussia were allies against Austria; in 1725 Britain renewed the earlier triplice with Spain and France; and in the 1730's Britain was back in an Austrian alliance (1731) and later at war (1739ff) with her erstwhile Spanish ally.

Britain's diplomatic flexibility was not unusual; Austria-Hungary, for example, was at war intermittently with France between 1792 and 1809, then became France's ally and assisted in 1812 with the invasion of Russia, her former ally. Prussia, which had been an enemy of France from 1792 and 1795 and again in 1806 began the Russian campaign in 1812 as an ally of Napoleon and then changed sides and fought the French. Such diplomatic vacillation was not viewed by balance-of-power practitioners as treachery; rather, flexibility was a basic characteristic of the system.

In fact, the system created at the Congress of Vienna provided peace in Europe for a century—until August 1914. Perhaps that accomplishment is what caused Henry Kissinger to try to implement some of the ideas of the Congress of Vienna in the contemporary era when he served as the President's Assistant for National Security Affairs and then as U.S. Secretary of State.[11]

Political and Technological Revolutions

Despite the relative peace of the century from 1815–1914, there were some conflicts, events, and developments that had lasting significance and called into question the continued viability of the balance-of-power system. In 1848, German nationalists campaigned for a unified Germany with the king of Prussia as its head. The nationalists' petition was refused, and Germany was not unified until Otto von Bismarck's rule. Also in 1848, a wave of revolution swept the continent of Europe, similar in some respects to the earlier revolutionary period of the late eighteenth century. In addition, **Bismarck** became chancellor of Germany in 1866 and declared war on Austria-Hungary. This war, like the Civil War in the United States, was fought with technologically advanced weapons including breech-loaded rifles, machine guns, railroads for transporting war materiél, and the telegraph for communicating rapidly and secretly. These weapons would change the conduct and face of war, but no one realized the revolutionary character of these weapons until the First World War.

Italy was unified in 1870; the following year Bismarck successfully unified Germany. Throughout Europe, people increasingly identified themselves with the state in which they lived. By the end of the nineteenth century, **nationalism**—the belief in the distinctiveness of a particular group of people sharing a common background and historical experience—was a rallying cry all across Europe. Nationalism made it increasingly difficult for the balance of power to operate effectively because one of the main requirements of the balance of power was flexibility of alliances.

Added to nationalistic fervor was a force in world politics that was becoming increasingly significant: ideology. In 1853, **Karl Marx** and Friedrich Engels published *The Communist Manifesto,* which presented a radical way of viewing societies and conflicts within societies. Communism was one of several ideologies that attracted the allegiances of people in various countries. The growing pull of ideologies also weakened the effectiveness of the balance of power.

When the balance of power began to evolve with the Treaty of Westphalia in 1648, aristocratic elites ruled the states of Europe, and there was little consultation with either members of the public or interest groups. However, as time went by, both public opinion and interest groups became increasingly important. As the balance of power developed so too did a number of democratic countries, most notably the United States. As democratic leaders came to the fore, the norms of behavior supportive of the balance-of-power system became less acceptable. To Woodrow Wilson, the balance of power was anathema, "an old and evil order." In contrast to the secret diplomacy conducted in the palaces of Vienna, Paris, or London, Wilson campaigned for "open covenants, openly arrived at." Wilson was simply the most vocal spokesman for those who favored democratic control of foreign policy and diplomacy (see Chapter 6). This call for increased democratic control hampered the operation of the balance of power.

Changes within the international system also weakened the effective operation of the balance of power in the late nineteenth century. Although some European countries possessed empires on which, as the British writer Rudyard Kipling put it, "the sun never sets," the great powers were running out of room to expand. In addition, many of those in colonies of the great powers began to object to their "second-class status" in international relations. By the late nineteenth and early twentieth centuries, there were some clear competitors in Asia, Africa, and Latin America. In China, a group of nationalists known as the "boxers" because of the martial arts fighting they used, rebelled against western control and domination of China. In South Africa, the Boers—originally from Holland—objected to British domination. And Japan became the first Asian country to defeat a European state when it defeated Russia in the Russo-Japanese War of 1904–1905.

Significantly, technology had enabled the west to defeat Japan in the mid-nineteenth century. Japan learned from its humiliating defeat at the hands of the United States in 1854 and went about copying western technology. A half a century later, it was western technology adapted for Japan's purposes that enabled it to defeat Russia. Beginning with the Civil War in the United States and culminating in the Russo-Japanese War, technology appeared to be an increasingly important element of national power.

By the turn of the century, two main alliances had formed, and the members of each of these alliances were increasingly unwilling to shift from one alliance partner to another. Tsar Nicholas and Kaiser Wilhelm, the leaders respectively of Russia and Germany in 1914, were first cousins. They had grown up together and knew each other well. When war threatened to break out between their two countries, they sent each other telegrams—addressed to "Nicky" and "Willi"—trying to avert conflict. But despite their personal friendship and best efforts, the world's most costly war up until that time began.

YOU IN WORLD POLITICS

So you're interested in teaching political science, history, or international relations? If you have been particularly interested in the last two chapters and are generally interested in political science or history, you might be thinking about a career related to this field. Of course, the first thing to do is to major in history, international studies, or a related field. If after majoring in one of these disciplines you still find you like this field and want to go on, then you will need to go on to graduate school. If you want to teach history at the junior or high-school level, then you will need to earn a teaching credential, and the requirements for these vary from state to state. If you want to teach at the junior college level, then a master's or M.A. (which stands for "master of arts") is sufficient. If you want to teach in a college or university, then a Ph.D. (which stands for "doctor of philosophy"), also called a doctorate, is essential. But be forewarned: the competition for college and university teaching jobs is fierce. In recent years, some history departments inform their incoming graduate students that even if they successfully complete their doctorates, they may not be able to find a job in the academic marketplace. One of the best orientations to graduate school is *Getting What You Came For: The Smart Student's Guide to Earning a Master's or a Ph.D.* (New York: Farrar, Straus and Giroux, 1995).

DISCUSSION QUESTIONS

1. In what ways did the Napoleonic Wars differ from previous wars?

2. How did the balance of power provide for peace and stability?

3. Kaiser Wilhelm and Tsar Nicholas were first cousins, had a good re-lationship and wanted to avoid war between their countries. Despite their desire, war broke out. Why?

KEY TERMS

balance of power
bi-, tri-, and multipolar systems
Bismarck, Otto von
compensations
Congress of Vienna
diplomatic flexibility
essential actors
great powers

Kissinger, Henry
Marx, Karl
Metternich, Klemens von
Napoleon Bonaparte
nationalism
stability
state centric
Treaty of Chaumont

KEY DATES

1799	Napoleon stages *coup d'état* and seizes power in France
1803–1815	Napoleonic Wars
1812	France invades Russia; Napoleon's army defeated
1814–1815	Congress of Vienna
1815	Battle of Waterloo; Napoleon defeated
1837–1901	Queen Victoria rules Great Britain
1848	Revolutions in Bohemia, Germany, France, and Hungary
1853–1856	Crimean War
1870	Unification of Italy
1871	Unification of Germany
1904–1905	Russo-Japanese War

RECOMMENDED PRINT, MULTIMEDIA, AND INTERNET SOURCES

Print

ALBRECHT-CARRE, RENE. *A Diplomatic History of Europe Since the Congress of Vienna.* New York: Harper and Row, 1958.

CRAIG, GORDON A. *Europe Since 1815,* 3rd ed. New York: Holt, Rinehart and Winston, 1971.

——— and ALEXANDER L. GEORGE. *Force and Statecraft: Diplomatic Problems of Our Time,* 3rd ed. New York: Oxford University Press, 1995.

——— and FELIX GILBERT, eds. *The Diplomats 1919–1939,* 2 vols. Princeton, NJ: Princeton University Press, 1967.

GILBERT, FELIX. *To the Farewell Address: Ideas of Early American Foreign Policy.* Princeton, NJ: Princeton University Press, 1961.

GULICK, EDWARD VOSE. *Europe's Classical Balance of Power.* New York: W.W. Norton, 1955, 1967.

KENNEDY, PAUL. *The Rise and Fall of Great Powers: Economic Change and Military Conflict from 1500 to 2000.* New York: Vintage Books, 1987.

KISSINGER, HENRY A. *A World Restored: The Politics of Conservatism in a Revolutionary Age.* New York: Grosset and Dunlap, 1964.

———. *Diplomacy.* New York: Simon & Schuster, 1995.

NICOLSON, HAROLD. *Diplomacy,* 3rd ed. London: Oxford University Press, 1963.

TUFTE, EDWARD. *The Visual Display of Quantitative Information.* Cheshire, CT: Graphics Press, 1983.

Video

The Battle of Waterloo 1815. Princeton, NJ: Films for the Humanities and Sciences, 30 minutes. The events leading to the rise and fall of Napoleon.

Napoleon Bonaparte. Princeton, NJ: Films for the Humanities and Sciences, 12 minutes.

Internet

For internet sites related to Charles Minard's graphic of Napoleon's march on Moscow, see:

http://www.cs.smu.edu/groups/sage/lg.minard/html

http://www.cs.cme.edu/groups/sage/sagewalk2.html

ENDNOTES

[1] EDWARD TUFTE, *The Visual Display of Quantitative Information* (Cheshire, CT: Graphics Press, 1983), p. 41

[2] EDWARD VOSE GULICK, *Europe's Classical Balance of Power* (New York: W.W. Norton, 1964), p. 39.

[3] Ibid., p. 151.

[4] Quoted by GORDON A. CRAIG and ALEXANDER L. GEORGE, *Force and Statecraft: Diplomatic Problems of Our Time,* 3rd. ed. (New York: Oxford University Press,1995), p. 23.

[5] GULICK, p. 156.

[6] HENRY A. KISSINGER, *A World Restored: The Politics of Conservatism in a Revolutionary Age* (New York: Grosset and Dunlap, 1964), p. 1.

[7] Ibid., p. 263.

[8] HAROLD NICOLSON, *Diplomacy,* 3rd. ed. (New York: Oxford University Press, 1963), p. 44.

[9] ALEXIS DE TOCQUEVILLE, *Democracy in America* (Garden City, NY: Anchor Books, 1969).

[10] GULICK, p. 68.

[11] DAN CALDWELL (ed.), *Henry Kissinger: His Personality and Policies* (Durham, NC: Duke University Press, 1983).

Actors, Power, and Interdependence in World Politics

CRITEX:
Who and What Are in the News?

HEN terrorists take captives hostage and want to demonstrate that they are alive, they take a photogaph of the hostage holding a current issue of a newspaper. Because such a photo could not have been taken until the day that the newspaper was published, this provides proof that the hostage is alive on that particular day. In this exercise, I want to demonstrate the importance of international relations by having you read several pages of one of the most respected newspapers in the United States. By having you read the current issue of a newspaper, you will see the actual influence of international issues on politics.

There are many reputable newspapers in the world. A number of these focus only on their local communities; others have a broader scope and focus on events throughout the world. In the United States, only the most prestigious

newspapers in the large metropolitan areas can afford to have reporters stationed overseas at foreign bureaus. Among the most respected newspapers in the United States are *The New York Times, Washington Post, Los Angeles Times, Chicago Tribune, Boston Globe* and *Wall Street Journal.*

Get a copy of *one* of these newspapers and determine the following:

1. How many of the stories on the front page and the editorial pages concern domestic issues?

2. How many of the articles on the front page and the editorial pages concern international issues?

3. What is the single most important story of the day? Does it concern domestic or international issues?

4. Are there articles that concern problems that affect both domestic and international politics? Do some issues make it too difficult to classify the articles as either domestic or international?

5. Are there places, people, and/or problems that you have never heard of before?

You may want to discuss the above questions with other students, or your professor may want you to write a brief essay on these questions and/or to discuss your answers in class. Or you may want to create a file, scrapbook, and/or journal concerning an issue of particular interest to you.

Optional Critexes:

1. Using Non-American Sources of News: If there are members of your class from foreign countries, or if you have access to newspapers or magazines such as *The Times of London, Le Monde, Der Spiegel,* or others, read the non-U.S. accounts of the same news events that are covered in American sources. Are there differences in the U.S. and non-American sources? If so, how would you characterize such differences?

You should not feel badly if you encounter new information or if you do not know some of the things that you read about. Now is the time and this class is the place to learn about international issues that are increasingly important.

2. Using the Internet Undoubtedly a number of people who read this book will be very familiar with the internet; indeed, some readers will get most of the news about the world from the internet. For such individuals, the critex that introduced this chapter will seem archaic, a relic of the past. This exercise is designed to introduce those who may not have ever used the internet to the vast resources of "cyberspace."

Many news organizations maintain internet sites that contain articles, photos, audio reports and even video clips of recent news stories. Check with either your local public or college library or the campus computer center to see how you can access the internet. Once you find this out, then go to the following sites to see the type of news stories you can access.

For CNN stories, photos and videos, type: http://www.cnn.com

For C-SPAN programs and index, type: http://www.c-span.org

To listen to news reports from National Public Radio, type: http://www.npr.org

After you have looked over several U.S. sources of information, then check several of the following foreign news sources:

Weekly Mail & Guardian (Johannesburg, South Africa): http://www.mg.co.za/ mg/

Pana News Agency (information on Africa): http://www.africanews.org/PANA/

News from Taiwan: http://www.talentscout/sinanet.com

Indian Daily: http://www.indiadaily.com

As you use the internet more and more, create "bookmarks" for the websites that you find most useful. What sorts of differences (if any) did you notice between the U.S. and foreign sources of information? If you completed the introductory critex to this chapter, what differences (if any) did you notice between the newspapers and internet sources? Which news source do you prefer? Why?

ACTORS IN WORLD POLITICS

In the critex that you completed at the beginning of this chapter, you undoubtedly identified many different individuals, organizations, and countries that are involved in world politics. These are called the "actors" of international relations. Not so long ago, states were considered to be the only actors on the stage of world politics. Today, in addition to the world's 194 states, there are many different **nonstate actors.** In keeping with the levels of analysis approach described in Chapter 1, nonstate actors will be described as individual, state, and international-system actors.

Individuals can and do make a difference in world politics. Of course, the difference that they make can be good or bad, large, or small. Think of the individuals whom you believe have made a difference to the world. Who are they? Why do you think that they made a difference?

Those who would be on many people's lists would include prominent politicians such as Napoleon Bonaparte, Otto von Bismarck, Slobodan Milosevic, Adolf Hitler, Golda Meir, Margaret Thatcher, and Saddam Hussein. But one need not have been an important politician to have had an enormous impact on the world, as the lives of Mohammed, Buddha, and Jesus Christ illustrate. So too do the careers of Mahatma Gandhi, Nelson Mandela, and Vaclav Havel. Finally, one need not even be connected with a specific political system or country to have an impact on the world, as the late Mother Theresa and Pope John Paul II show.

BOX 4.1   Pope John Paul II and Capital Punishment

During his visit to the United States in January 1999, Pope John Paul II visited St. Louis, Missouri. Darrel J. Mease had been sentenced to the death penalty ten years earlier for murdering three people. The Pope appealed for clemency to the governor of Missouri, who granted the Pope's appeal. One person, particularly the Pope, can make a difference.

In recent years another type of individual has had a significant impact on world politics: terrorists. Examples of such are Abu Nidal and Osama Bin Laden who have become commonly known because of their sponsorship and involvement in terrorism.

At the international level of analysis, there are a number of different actors. Five types will be discussed in this section: (1) intergovernmental organizations, (2) regional organizations, (3) nongovernmental organizations, (4) multinational corporations, and (5) the news media.

Intergovernmental Organizations

Intergovernmental or **international organizations** are formed by states in order to further their particular interests. Some international organizations such as the International Postal Union deal only with one particular issue; others have a broader scope. Some intergovernmental organizations have a limited membership; for example, the **Organization for Economic Cooperation and Development (OECD)** is limited to developed states. The international organization that comes closest to having a universal membership of the world's states is the United Nations. As of 1999, 185 of the world's 194 states belonged to the UN.

Regional Organizations

Some intergovernmental organizations have a regional focus and all in some instances members are from the same geographic area. Like international organizations, **regional organizations** may focus on different issues. For example, the **North Atlantic Treaty Organization (NATO)** was originally founded in 1949 to provide for the defense of Western Europe, Canada and the United States. With the fall of communism in Eastern Europe and the Soviet Union, NATO accepted new challenges and responsibilities, most notably peacekeeping in Bosnia and attacking Serbia to stop the killing of ethnic Albanians in Kosovo.

Perhaps the most prominent regional organization in the world today is the **European Union (EU).** The regional organizations that preceded the EU were the European Coal and Steel Community (ECSC) and the European Economic Community (EEC), also known as the Common Market. The founders of both of these organizations succeeded in creating an integrated system in which all members had a stake in preserving the system. Robert Schuman, one of the founders of the ECSC, was once asked how he had developed an interest in the production of steel, and he replied, "I don't give a damn about steel or coal; what I care about is preventing World War III."

Nongovernmental Organizations

While both international and regional organizations are composed of states, other **nongovernmental organizations (NGO)** are not. NGOs are composed of individuals or groups that are united to further their interests. These interests may be private, such as the International Federation of Airline Pilots, or they may promote "public interests," such as prohibiting torture—one of the central objectives of **Amnesty International.**

No one really knows how many NGOs there are in the world today. One source definitively states that there were 4,646 nongovernmental organizations in 1990,[1] while Dr. Jessica T. Mathews, a respected analyst of international relations and the current president of the Carnegie Endowment for International Peace, cites an estimate of 35,000 NGOs in the developing countries alone.[2] Dr. Mathews concludes, "In fact, it is impossible to measure a swiftly growing universe that includes neighborhood, professional, service, and advocacy groups, both secular and church-based, promoting every conceivable cause and funded by donations, fees, foundations, governments, international organizations, or the sale of products or services."[3]

YOU IN WORLD POLITICS

So you're interested in working for a nongovernmental organization? There are literally hundreds of private, nongovernmental organizations which work in international affairs; they are so important that they have been awarded the distinction of their own acronym, "NGOs." Some NGOs are religious in origin; others are entirely secular. Some are quite large, others are minuscule. They share a lack of direct government control and general concern for humanitarian issues. Prominent examples include World Vision, Crossroads Africa, Oxfam, Catholic Relief Services, and CARE. The American government administers some foreign aid through some of these agencies, and they have been prominent in such issues as famine relief in Africa. The NGOs overlap somewhat with private advocacy organizations such as Amnesty International. Many of these organizations employ small permanent staffs; recruitment is often based on previous performance as a volunteer. Salaries are low, but many people find the work extremely rewarding.

Multinational Corporations

Multinational corporations (MNC) are private businesses that have dealings and transactions in more than one country. They are not new in world politics; for example, the British East India Company was integral to the British Empire and controlled much of South Asia throughout the nineteenth century. So there are historical precedents for the MNCs of today.

What is new about contemporary multinational corporations is their number, scope, and significance. By the mid-1990s there were 38,500 MNCs with more than 250,000 foreign subsidiaries. These generated more than $5.2 trillion in global sales, about one-fifth of the world's total economy of $25 trillion. MNCs employ more than 73 million people, about 10 percent of all employees outside of the agricultural sector.[4]

The economic power of individual MNCs is clear when we examine Table 4.1, which compares state and corporate economic power.

This table shows that Indonesia's gross domestic product is slightly larger than General Motors' sales, but that GM's sales are greater than the GDP of Turkey. Which actor is more powerful: states or multinational corporations?

TABLE 4.1

State and Corporate Power, 1994 (United States $ billions)

State or Corporation	Total GDP or Corporate Sales
Indonesia	$174.6
General Motors	168.8
Turkey	149.8
Denmark	146.1
Ford	137.1
South Africa	123.3
Toyota	111.1
Exxon	110.0
Royal Dutch Shell	109.8
Norway	109.6
Poland	92.8
Portugal	91.6
IBM	72.0
Malaysia	68.5
Venezuela	59.0
Pakistan	57.1
Unilever	49.7
Nestle	47.8
Sony	47.6
Egypt	43.9
Nigeria	30.4

Source: Fortune Magazine, 1996. Used by permission.

The News Media

General Colin Powell has noted a reality of the contemporary era: "For good or for ill, instantaneous visual communication has revolutionized news coverage in our time. Jet travel, satellites, and minicams allow live, around-the-clock coverage, like CNN (Cable News Network), and have removed the old print media filters between the reporter and the audience."[5] The news media are so important that they have become an actor in world politics.

Whenever an international crisis occurs, all of the parties immediately tune in to CNN to get the latest news. Deputy Secretary of State Strobe Talbott recounted watching the attack on the Russian Parliament building, called the "White House," in October 1993. As Russian dissidents attacked, Talbott discussed the incident with his Russian counterpart. Talbott recalled:

> For the next half-hour, Mamedov and I watched transfixed, exchanging occasional impressions as the battle came to its dramatic and bloody denouement. Following a phased assault that gave those

inside the White House several opportunities to surrender, government forces retook the building and arrested the leaders of the opposition. . . . Here was the famous "CNN effect" at its most dramatic. Just as the network had made it possible for Mamedov and me to watch an event unfold in real time as we discussed its implication over an open phone line, so the communications revolution had contributed to the transformation of his country and of our world.[6]

At present there are an estimated 800 million television sets and more than 2 billion radios in the world; these, in addition to magazines, newspapers, movies, and telephones, provide the media through which information travels. Today's leaders are constantly aware that what they say may be broadcast throughout the entire world. Recalling a press conference during the Gulf War, General Powell recalled: "We were talking not only to the press assembled in front of us; we were talking to four other audiences—the American people, foreign nations, the enemy, and our troops."[7] The news media constitute a transnational actor in contemporary world politics.

DOMINANT METAPHORS OF WORLD POLITICS: THE STATE-CENTRIC AND TRANSNATIONAL MODELS

Throughout the years, political scientists and international relations specialists have developed various metaphors of world politics. If you had taken this course three or four decades ago, your professor probably would have compared world politics to a game of billiards with the balls on the table representing nation-states. Such a representation would have fairly accurately represented the realities of international relations because states dominated the system. The **state-centric model** of world politics is represented by the following diagram:[8]

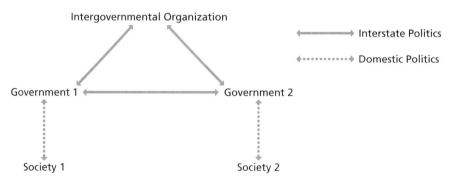

Figure 4.1. The State-Centric Model of World Politics
Source: Adapted from: Robert O. Keohane and Joseph S. Nye, Jr., eds., *Transnational Relations and World Politics.* Cambridge, MA: Harvard University Press, 1971, p. xiii.

There are several problems with this **"billiard ball" model** of world politics. First, all of the balls on a billiard table are the same size, yet in the contemporary world, states vary in size from China, with 1,200,000,000 people, to countries with only a few tens of thousands of citizens. If the "billiard ball" model represented states proportionately, there would be balls ranging from the size of peas to beach balls on the table! Second, there are only balls on a billiard table. What about other actors in international relations such as terrorist groups, multinational corporations, churches, and other nongovernmental organizations? If the billiard ball model were accurate, then there would have to be many different representations of nonstate actors on the table.

In the critical thinking exercise that you completed at the beginning of this chapter, it is probable that you and your fellow students found many different groups and organizations playing a role in contemporary world politics. Nonstate actors have existed for a long time; however, they have become more prominent in recent decades because of advances in communication and transportation. These advances enable subnational groups in one state to communicate with subnational groups in other states.

BOX 4.4   The Power of Large Companies

With control of one-third of the world's gas reserves, one million acres of land, over 365,000 employees, and interests in dozens of other businesses, Gazprom (the company that owns Russian oil and gas reserves) has annual revenues estimated by Western industry analysts at $20 billion to $25 billion and profits of $6 billion. If it were to be ranked by the Global Fortune 500, Gazprom would be second in profits, behind only Royal Dutch Shell. Gazprom is responsible for 5 percent of the entire Russian economy and is the country's biggest taxpayer, pouring $4 billion annually into the state. In fact, Gazprom does not pay nearly the amount of taxes it should.... Gazprom is untouchable and is allowed to avoid or defer billions in tax payment.

From: David Remnick, *Resurrection: The Struggle for a New Russia* (New York: Random House, 1997), p. 178.

Two highly respected American political scientists, Robert Keohane and Joseph Nye, portrayed contemporary international relations as occurring according to the following diagram:[9]

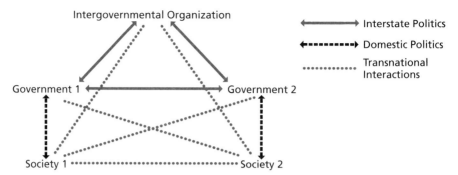

Figure 4.2. Transnational Interactions and Interstate Politics
Source: Adapted from: Robert O. Keohane and Joseph S. Nye, Jr., eds., *Transnational Relations and World Politics.* Cambridge, MA: Harvard University Press, 1971, p. xiii.

This diagram depicts classic interstate politics, domestic politics, and transnational relations. It shows government to government, interstate relations, which is the traditional focus of international-relations scholars. As your reading of a contemporary newspaper shows, there are a number of ties between domestic societies, and these societies also have ties to other governments and even to international organizations. Thus, while this diagram is more complex than figure 4.1, it more accurately reflects the realities of contemporary world politics.

These models or metaphors are useful only to the degree that they help us to better understand world politics. Let's see how they can help. If we try to understand the international politics of the Congress of Vienna, which took place during the early nineteenth century (see Chapter 3), the state-centric framework fairly accurately depicts what was going on: the four great powers of Europe (Austria-Hungary, Great Britain, Russia, and France) met in Vienna to develop arrangements for managing power in international relations. The principal statesmen who met in Vienna—Metternich, Castlereagh and Talleyrand—were free to negotiate with one another without concern about the necessity of achieving public or parliamentary approval of their proposals.

An international agreement from the late twentieth century contrasts markedly with the relatively simple interactions culminating in the Congress of Vienna agreements. For example, consider the **Chemical Weapons Convention,** which was, of course, negotiated by states. Due to the increased power and involvement of the public and parliaments in the treaty-ratification process, the negotiators at this international conference, unlike those at Vienna almost two centuries before, had to keep in mind relative public support for the agreements, the role of interest groups (particularly the manufacturers of chemicals) and the attitude of their respective parliaments toward the agreement. Given the involvement of a whole range of nonstate actors, the transnational model does a much better job of representing what the writer Henry James called the "humming, buzzing confusion of reality."

What, then, are the significant actors in contemporary world politics? The starting place since the end of the Thirty Years' War in 1648 has been states. Today, the 194 states in the world are characterized by great diversity. Table 4.2 describes the characteristics of 12 states. One can readily see that they vary a great deal. Russia is the largest country geographically, and it is almost twice as large as the second largest countries—the United States, China and Canada. The People's Republic of China has 1.2 billion people, about one-quarter of the world's population, and that is more than a million times as large as the small Pacific island state of Tuvalu which has a total population of about 10,000.

POWER, POLITICS, AND ISSUES AREAS

"Power" is one of the most widely used and least understood concepts in both political science and international relations. On the one hand, everyone "knows what power is." On the other hand, power can be quite confusing.

Definitions of Power

Power is most often defined in terms of its attributes; however, such a definition does not really define power, it simply describes the elements that go into making a state powerful. Political scientist Robert Dahl of Yale University defined power as the ability to get others to do what they otherwise would not do. This definition is oriented to actual behavior rather than to a list of elements or attributes. It is closely related to the classical definition of politics as "who gets what, when, how."[10]

Attributes of Power

Although the behavioral definition of power is useful, it does not provide much guidance as to which actor in a given international environment has more power than another actor. To make such an assessment, a consideration of the elements of power can be helpful. Such attributes can be categorized as tangible and intangible. Tangible elements of a state's power include the following factors:

1. Geography: Natural terrain, the resources within a state's territory and geographic size may influence a state's power. For example, Poland has no natural boundaries between two powerful states, Russia and Germany. Consequently, the history of Poland for most of the past 400 years is a tragic history of invasion, occupation, and control by Germany and/or

TABLE 4.2

Attributes of Power for Selected States

State	Land Area (square kms.)	Population (1998)	GDP in billions (1997) of U.S. dollars	GDP per capita (1997) of U.S. dollars	ICBM	SLBM	Bomber	Military Personnel
Bangladesh	144,000	127,567,000	167	1,330	0	0	0	121,000
China	9,596,960	1,236,914,658	4,250	3,460	17	12	0	2,820,000
France	547,030	58,804,944	1,320	22,700	0	64	0	358,800
Italy	301,230	56,782,748	1,240	21,500	0	0	0	298,400
Mexico	1,972,550	98,552,776	694	7,700	0	0	0	175,000
Russia	17,075,200	146,861,022	692	4,700	756	412	66	1,159,000
Saudi Arabia	1,960,582	20,785,955 (Expatriates = 25%)	207	10,300	0	0	0	105,500
Sudan	2,505,810	33,550,552	27	875	0	0	0	94,700
Switzerland	41,290	7,260,357	172	23,800	0	0	0	3,300 (active) 390,000 (reserve)
Tuvalu	26	10,444	0.008	800	0	0	0	Police Force
United Kingdom	244,820	58,970,119	1,242	21,200	0	32	0	210,940
United States	9,629,091	270,311,756	8,083	30,200	680	432	174	1,401,600

Sources: Columns 1–4: Central Intelligence Agency, World Factbook 1998. http://www.odci.gov/cia/publications/factbook Columns 5–8: International Institute for Strategic Studies, The Military Balance 1998/99. London: Oxford University Press, 1998.

Russia. Conversely, Switzerland is surrounded by mountains and can be defended from external land attack by guarding a limited number of mountain passes. That geographic fact is probably the single most important reason that Switzerland has not been attacked and occupied.

2. **Population:** This factor can either confer power or detract from a state's power. China's 1.2 billion people are a source of power, yet they also place enormous demands on the Chinese government. Not just the total population, but demographic characteristics such as the level of education in a particular country are also important. For example, those countries with close to 100 percent literacy are potentially more powerful than those with a less literate population.

3. **Natural resources:** States with significant resources have become increasingly powerful in world politics. For example, consider Saudi Arabia. Just 60 years ago, life in this area had not changed much in centuries. Bedouins roamed the desert, and the politics of the Arabian Peninsula was dominated by interactions among family-based clans. But discovery of oil in Saudi Arabia in 1932 began a transformation. The oil business in Saudi Arabia was initially controlled by the major international oil companies, and it was only after Saudi Arabia joined with other oil producing states to form the **Organization of Petroleum Exporting Countries (OPEC)** that the state of Saudi Arabia became wealthy. At the other end of the spectrum of wealth and poverty lie countries such as Bangladesh.

4. **Economic capacity:** A state's economic strength is often significant in world politics, and the measurements that are most often used are either **gross national product (GNP),** the total value of goods and services produced by the citizens of a state whether in the country or not, or **gross domestic product (GDP),** the total value of goods and services produced by a state domestically. If we were trying to assess the economic power of the states listed in Table 4.2, it would appear that China was very powerful because it has the second largest GDP of those countries listed in the figure. However, this does not tell the whole story. In addition to GNP or GDP, we need to consider how these resources are (theoretically) distributed throughout society. In order to calculate this figure, the GNP or GDP must be divided by population to calculate a per capita (per person) figure. When this is calculated for the countries listed in Table 4.2, China slips from the second-ranked country in GDP to the ninth-ranked country in per capita GDP. A number of valuable sources of information concerning international economics exist; two of the most important are the World Bank's *Global Development Indicators* and the Central Intelligence Agency's *Handbook of International Economic Statistics.*[11]

5. **Military strength:** Throughout history, people have often considered a state's power to be synonymous with its military power. And the measurement of this power has varied over time. For example, during the

nineteenth century, the world's statesmen considered "capital ships" (large ships such as battleships and cruisers) to be the most important attributes of military power. Following World War II, the possession of nuclear weapons became the most important criterion for great power status. Of course, the irony of the late twentieth century was that the world's most powerful states—those that possessed nuclear weapons—were afraid to use the most lethal weapons in their arsenals, knowing that such use could result in the end of civilization. The best single source of information on states' military power is *The Military Balance* published annually by the London-based International Institute for Strategic Studies.[12] The most comprehensive source of data on individual weapons systems can be found in the various publications of the Jane's organization.[13]

These five tangible elements of power, as useful as they are in assessing a state's power, do not tell the entire story. Students of world politics (not to mention world leaders) must be sensitive to *intangible* factors of power, including:

6. The political system and political leadership: A state's political system and its leadership can literally determine whether a state succeeds or fails. A stable political system can last for a long time, and an unstable system results in a decrease of power and sometimes even dissolution, as occurred with the former Soviet Union in December 1991.

7. National morale: The dedication by a group of people to a set of ideals and policies can be enormously powerful. It was that dedication to the ideal of independence that contributed significantly to the creation of a new state, the United States of America, in 1776. The appeal of independence remained a powerful motivating force in world politics throughout the twentieth century, a fact of international life that some have not adequately understood. In the mid-1960s, President Lyndon Johnson dismissed the followers of North Vietnamese leader Ho Chi Minh as "little peasants running around in black pajamas." That derisive dismissal failed to acknowledge the fact that Ho's followers had been fighting for North Vietnamese independence for more than 25 years. They fought first against the French, then against the Japanese in World War II, then against the French (again), and finally against the Americans. Ho's followers were committed to winning independence or to die trying to achieve it.

INTERNATIONAL INTERDEPENDENCE

Power has been the principal focus of international relations specialists since the time of Thucydides two-and-a-half millennia ago. And, as noted above, power has been correlated with various attributes of states. Although commonly referred to, power in the contemporary international system is not well understood; however, it is clear that power partially depends upon time and context. The late Chinese leader, Mao Zedong, once said, "Power comes out of the barrel of a gun." Time and again throughout history, Mao was correct, but during the past several decades, power also came from barrels of oil and bushels of grain.

During the early 1970s, a number of countries enjoyed an unprecedented economic boom. Economic prosperity, coupled with a relaxation of tensions (referred to as "détente" from the French lexicon of classical diplomacy) between the "East" (communist states) and the "West" (anticommunist states), increased the importance of economic issues in world politics. When the Soviet Union suffered a series of crop failures, it turned to the West to purchase grain. Like citizens in advanced industrial states, Soviet citizens increased their consumption of meat as the USSR's level of development increased. This, in turn, increased the consumption and demand for grain.

Another source of feed for cattle is fish meal, and much of the world's supply of fish meal comes from the catch of anchovies off the coast of Peru. In 1972, the catch significantly declined, further increasing the demand on other protein-rich grains such as soybeans. Adverse weather conditions over large parts of the world in the early 1970s decreased grain production in a number of areas and resulted in serious food shortages in parts of Asia and Africa, in particular. Finally, the Arab-Israeli war of October 1973 and the ensuing oil embargo by the Organization of Arab Petroleum Exporting Countries (OAPEC) increased the price of oil to new levels. This development had two major effects: (1) it increased the cost of running farm machinery such as tractors and combines, and (2) it increased the cost of fertilizers, many of which are petroleum based. To a large extent, the remarkable progress of the so-called "green revolution" of the 1960s had depended upon increased mechanization and oil-based fertilizers to dramatically increase crop yields.

The confluence of seemingly unrelated international events had a significant impact. Increased demand drove the price of grain up, and increased demand for oil and petroleum products similarly drove prices up. The average price of a barrel of oil went from $3.00 per barrel in September 1973 to more than $12.00 per barrel in early 1974, an increase of 400 percent. The result of these increases wreaked havoc in many developing countries, which were vulnerable to such increases. Even wealthy, developed countries such as the United States and Japan were sensitive to these price increases, and gasoline was rationed in many areas of the United States.

Dr. Henry Kissinger was a quintessential realist who, in his academic writings, had always emphasized the role of military power in history. In the aftermath of the Arab-Israeli War of October 1973, Kissinger characterized the OPEC decision to raise oil prices as "one of the pivotal events in the history of this century."[14] Following the war, Kissinger did not speak or write about the role of military power, as he had done throughout his career previously; rather, he mentioned the "international fact" of multilateral interdependence in every speech, interview, and article that he delivered or wrote.[15] Characteristic of this approach was the following excerpt from a 1975 speech: "As technology expands man's reach, the planet continues to shrink. Global communications make us acutely aware of each other. Human aspirations and destinies increasingly are intertwined."[16] Why was it that a person who had devoted the whole of his academic work to the analysis of power, diplomacy, and war would call attention to the emerging forces of global communications and technology? Perhaps because they were increasingly important elements of power.

Two of the first political scientists to focus on the importance of modern communications and technology were Robert O. Keohane and Joseph S. Nye, Jr. In an important work published first as a special issue of the academic journal, *International Organization,* and subsequently as a book, Keohane and Nye defined **transnational relations** as "the movement of tangible or intangible items across state boundaries when at least one actor is not an agent of a government or an international organization."[17] In terms of the model of world politics previously presented in this chapter (see Figure 4.2), Keohane and Nye noted that in contemporary world politics people in one society may put pressure on another government directly or people in one society may put pressure on people in another society. These interactions are not depicted in the state-centric model of world politics (see Figure 4.1).

According to Nye, "**interdependence** refers to situations in which actors or events in different parts of a system affect each other. Simply put, interdependence means mutual dependence."[18] By itself, interdependence neither guarantees peace nor conflict, although many have assumed that mutual dependence will have one effect or the other. It may be that in some situations increased trade leads to a decrease in conflict. But, of course, there are many situations in which significant levels of trade have not led to peace. France and Germany traded more with one another than any other two states in the world in 1914, but that fact did not prevent them from going to war against one another.

International interdependence exists in a number of different forms. The two principal types are military and economic interdependence. Military interdependence results from mutual dependence created by military competition between two or more states. Throughout the cold war, the United States and the Soviet Union were dependent upon one another; an increase in the nuclear arsenal of one superpower caused concern in the other superpower, and it was often matched either in kind or with a weapon designed to counter the quantitative or qualitative increase on the other side. One is reminded of the old saw, "The more things change, the more they stay the same!"

DISCUSSION QUESTIONS

1. If one were to prepare a comparison of tangible elements of power for the United States and North Vietnam in 1965, the United States would appear to be much stronger than North Vietnam. How and why, then, did North Vietnam defeat the United States and its ally, South Vietnam?

2. Which are the most powerful actors in each of the following issue areas: military affairs, economics, and cultural affairs?

3. Does international interdependence guarantee peace? Why or why not?

KEY TERMS

Amnesty International
Chemical Weapons Convention
European Union (EU)
gross domestic product (GDP)
gross national product (GNP)
interdependence
intergovernmental
   (or international) organization
   (IGO)
multinational corporation
   (MNC)
nongovernmental organization
   (NGO)

nonstate actor
North Atlantic Treaty
   Organization (NATO)
Organization for Economic
   Cooperation and
   Development (OECD)
Organization of Petroleum
   Exporting Countries (OPEC)
power
regional organizations
state-centric model (also billiard
   ball model)
transnational relations

RECOMMENDED PRINT, MULTIMEDIA, AND INTERNET SOURCES

Print

CALDWELL, DAN. "Food Crises and World Politics." *Sage Professional Papers in International Studies,* vol. V, series no. 02–049 (Beverly Hills: Sage Publications, 1977).

International Institute for Strategic Studies (IISS). *The Military Balance,* published annually. London: IISS.

KEOHANE, ROBERT O. and JOSEPH S. NYE, Jr. (eds.). *Transnational Relations and World Politics.* Cambridge, MA: Harvard University Press, 1970.

———. *Power and Interdependence: World Politics in Transition.* Boston: Little, Brown, 1977.

MATHEWS, JESSICA T. "Power Shift." *Foreign Affairs,* vol. 76, no. 1 (January/February 1997), pp. 50–66.

NYE, JOSEPH S., Jr. *Understanding International Conflicts: An Introduction to Theory and History,* 2nd ed. New York: Longman, 1997.

TALBOTT, STROBE. "Globalization and Diplomacy: A Practitioner's Perspective," *Foreign Policy* 108 (Fall 1997), pp. 69–83.

U.S. Central Intelligence Agency. *World Factbook,* published annually. Washington, DC: Government Printing Office (also available on the internet; see below).

———. *Handbook of International Economic Statistics,* published annually. Washington, DC: Government Printing Office (also available on the internet; see below).

Multimedia

International Institute for Strategic Studies. *The Military Balance and Strategic Survey 1998/99.* Oxford England: Oxford University Press, 1999 (CD-ROM).

"The Terrorist and the Superpower." *Frontline,* originally broadcast on April 13, 1999; focuses on Osama bin Laden.

Internet Sources

Amnesty International: http://www.amnesty.org/

European Union: http://www.europa.eu.int

International Committee of the Red Cross: http://www.icrc.org/

International Federation of the Red Cross: http://www.ifrc.org/

International Institute for Strategic Studies: http://www.isn.ethz.ch/iiss/

Organization for Economic Cooperation and Development (OECD): http://www.oecd.org/

Organization of American States (OAS): http://www.oas.org/

U.S. Central Intelligence Agency: http://www.odci.gov/cia

U.S. Department of Defense: http://www.defenselink.mil/

ENDNOTES

[1] Union of International Associations, *Yearbook of International Organizations 1990/91*, vol. I (Munich: Sauer, 1990), p. 1659.

[2] JESSICA T. MATHEWS, "Power Shift," *Foreign Affairs*, vol. 76, no. 1 (January/February 1997), p. 52.

[3] Ibid., p. 53.

[4] The figures on MNCs in this paragraph are taken from Charles W. Kegley, Jr. and Eugene R. Wittkopf, *World Politics: Trend and Transformation*, 7th ed. (New York: St. Martin's/Worth, 1999), p. 192.

[5] COLIN POWELL, with JOSEPH E. PERSICO, *My American Journey* (New York: Random House, 1995), pp. 528–529.

[6] STROBE TALBOTT, "Globalization and Diplomacy: A Practitioner's Perspective," *Foreign Policy*, no. 108 (Fall 1997), pp. 69–70.

[7] POWELL, p. 529.

[8] ROBERT O. KEOHANE and JOSEPH S. NYE, Jr. (eds.), *Transnational Relations and World Politics* (Cambridge, MA: Harvard University Press, 1970, p. XIV.

[9] Ibid., p. xiv.

[10] HAROLD LASSWELL, *Politics: Who Gets What, When, How* (New York: World Publishing Company, 1958).

[11] Each of these publications is published annually; see World Bank, *World Development Indicators* (Washington, DC: World Bank, 1997) and the U.S. Central Intelligence Agency, Directorate of Intelligence, *Handbook of International Economic Statistics 1995* (Washington, DC: Superintendent of Documents, 1995).

[12] International Institute for Strategic Studies, *The Military Balance 1996/97* (London: Oxford University Press, 1997).

[13] See, for example, *Jane's All the Ships of the World* (London: Jane's, published annually).

[14] HENRY A. KISSINGER, *Years of Upheaval* (Boston: Little, Brown, 1982), p. 885.

[15] DAN CALDWELL, "The Policies of Henry Kissinger," in Dan Caldwell (ed.), *Henry Kissinger: His Personality and Policies* (Durham, NC: Duke University Press, 1983), pp. 122–123.

[16] HENRY A. KISSINGER (Washington, DC: U.S. Department of State, Bureau of Public Affairs, May 12, 1975), p. 3.

[17] Ibid., p. xii.

[18] JOSEPH S. NYE, Jr., *Understanding International Conflicts: An Introduction to Theory and History*, 2nd ed. (New York: Longman, 1997), p. 162.

PART 11

What Is the History of World Politics?

5

The Second Thirty Years' War: World Wars I and II

CRITEX:
The Human Cost of War

WARS have cost the lives of millions of human beings. The Thirty Years' War of 1618–1648 caused great destruction and devastation in Europe. In the critical thinking exercise at the beginning of Chapter 2, the bands on the map represented the size of Napoleon's army. The graphic showed that of the 422,000 French soldiers who attacked Moscow, only about 10,000 of those soldiers made it back to their starting place and, it should be noted, these figures do not reflect the casualties of the Russians opposing Napoleon's army.

Most people expected the war that began in August 1914 to be over by Christmas, in keeping with other conflicts of the late nineteenth and early twentieth centuries. But this war was to be different: enormously more destructive than any previous war, and though the guns fell silent in 1918, the underlying causes

TABLE 5.1

U.S. Casualties in Major Wars

War	Total Deaths	Wounds not mortal	Total Casualties
Civil War	364,511	281,881	646,392
World War I	116,516	204,002	320,518
World War II	405,399	670,846	1,076,245
Korean War	54,246	103,284	157,530
Vietnam War	58,167	153,303	211,470

Source: 1995 Information Please Almanac, 48th edition (Boston: Houghton Mifflin Company, 1994), p. 387.

of the war were not settled, and the "second act" of what can be thought of as the "Second Thirty Years' War" lasted until 1945.

Table 5.1 shows the casualties that the United States has suffered in the wars it has fought.

When one considers the total number of people killed in the two costliest wars of human history, it is hard to comprehend the aggregate numbers: 14 million soldiers and civilians were killed in World War I, and 60 million were killed in World War II. These losses had significance at each of the three levels of analysis discussed in Chapter 1. The magnitude of these losses had an impact on the world at large, on the states fighting (both victors and vanquished alike) and on individual families who lost loved ones. The meaning of these losses is difficult to comprehend.

Poets can help others to see and sense reality more clearly or they can eclipse reality. Following the outbreak of World War I, a number of poets went marching off to war. Early in the war, the theme expressed by many poets was characterized by the following poem, "Happy is England Now" by John Freeman.[1]

There is not anything more wonderful
Than a great people moving towards the deep
Of an unguessed and unfeared future; nor
Is aught so dear of all held dear before
As the new passions stirring in their veins
When the destroying dragon wakes from sleep.

Happy is England now, as never yet!
And though the sorrows of the slow days fret
Her faithfullest children, grief itself is proud.
Ev'n the warm beauty of this spring and summer

That turns to bitterness turns then to gladness
Since for this England the beloved ones died.

How would you characterize the tone of this poem? _____

_____

What do you think that the author felt? _____

_____

As the war continued, a different tone emerged, as the poem, "Rendezvous," by Alan Seeger illustrates:[2]

I have a rendezvous with Death
At some disputed barricade,
When Spring comes back with rustling shade
And apple-blossoms fill the air—
I have a rendezvous with Death
When Spring brings back blue days and fair.

The poet was prescient, for on July 4, 1916, he and all his comrades were mowed down by a German machine gun at the battle of the Somme. There were a million casualties at this battle; the war had become stalemated in the trenches of the Western Front, and the poets reflected the war weariness of the populations of the warring countries. Osbert Sitwell's "This Generation" depicted this:[3]

Their youth was fevered—passionate, quick to drain
    The last few pleasures from the cup of life
Before they turned to suck the dregs of pain
    And end their young-old lives in mortal strife.
They paid the debts of many a hundred year
    Of foolishness and riches in alloy.
They went to death; nor did they shed a tear
    For all they sacrificed of love and joy.
Their tears ran dry when they were in the womb,
For, entering life—they found it was their tomb.

By the end of the war, a sense of total frustration and loss was characteristic of the formerly optimistic young poets. In an imaginary tour of a battlefield, Philip Johnstone captured the feeling of pointlessness of many of those who had fought in the war:[4]

Ladies and gentlemen, this is High Wood,
Called by the French, Bois des Fourneaux,
The famous spot which in Nineteen-Sixteen,
July, August and September was the scene
Of long and bitterly contested strife,
By reason of its High commanding site.
Observe the effect of shell-fire in the trees
Standing and fallen here is wire, this trench
For months inhabit, twelve times changed hands;
(They soon fall in), used later as a grave.
It has been said on good authority
That in the fighting for this patch of wood
Were killed somewhere above eight thousand men,
Of whom the greater part were buried here,
This mound on which you stand being . . .
　　　　Madame, please,
You are kindly requested not to touch
Or take away the Company's property
As souvenirs; you'll find we have on sale
A large variety, all guaranteed.
As I was saying, all is as it was,
This is an unknown British officer,
The tunic having lately rotted off.
Please follow me—this way . . .
　　　　the path, sir, please,
The ground which was secured at great expense
The Company keeps absolutely untouched,
And in that dug-out (genuine) we provide
Refreshments at a reasonable rate.
You are requested not to leave about
Paper, or ginger-beer bottles, or orange-peel,
There are waste-paper baskets at the gate.

What is the tone of this poem? _____
_____

How do you think the author felt? _____

_____
How does this poem compare with "Happy Is England Now" by John
Freeman (quoted at the beginning of this exercise)? _____

_____

WORLD WAR I

At 11:15 on the morning of June 28, 1914, a Serbian nationalist named Gavrilo Princip assassinated the heir apparent to the throne of the Austro-Hungarian throne, Franz Ferdinand, and his wife, during their visit to the Bosnian capital of Sarajevo. This occurred in an international environment of great tensions; all five great powers were locked in an arms race, and a buildup of arms by one state was viewed as a direct threat by other members of the international system.

Reflecting the mores of the classical diplomatic system, the leader of Russia, Tsar Nicholas II, and the leader of Prussia, Kaiser Wilhelm II, were first cousins. They had grown up together and were good friends. Despite this fact, they followed the advice of their respective militaries and prepared for war. The need to prepare for war made it almost inevitable. Even the leaders of the two most powerful countries on the European continent could not prevent war from occurring. Sadly, in contrast to the expectations of most people, when war came, it was not the brief, almost romantic conflict that most people had expected. Rather, it was long, drawn out and enormously costly. You can see the psychic cost of the war in the eyes of the soldiers.

The Archduke Franz Ferdinand and his wife in Sarajevo on the day they were assassinated, June 28, 1914.
Source: Robert Hunt Library; reprinted in Martin Gilbert, *The First World War: A Complete History* (New York: Henry Holt, 1994), photograph no. 1, following p. 72.

The arrest of Gavrilo Princip (being held on the right).
Source: Foto Archiva, Belgrade; reprinted in Martin Gilbert, *The First World War: A Complete History* (New York: Henry Holt, 1994), photograph no. 2, following p. 72.

Following four long years of war, the Axis powers were defeated. But the victorious countries were not in much better condition than the vanquished states. More than 9 million soldiers and 5 million civilians died in the war. The results of **World War I** were threefold: economic, political, and social collapse.

The economic collapse of Europe was devastating. At the end of the war, the Allies decided that Germany was primarily responsible for starting the war and should therefore pay reparations. In the initial years following the war, the German **Weimar government** did its best to keep up the payments, but these crippled the new democratic German government. There was rampant inflation and widespread unemployment. In January 1923, one U.S. dollar was worth 20 thousand Deutschmarks (the German currency); by December 1923, a dollar was worth *billions* of Deutschmarks. Then in 1929 the **Great Depression** hit and caused havoc in Europe as well as the United States. Germany was particularly hard hit. Unemployment went from 1 million in 1929 to 5 million by 1933. The currency was worth so little that American cereal manufacturers even bought Deutschmarks in order to place a Deutschmark bill inside of every pack-

A wounded man with a "thousand yard" stare.
Source: Imperial War Museum, London; reprinted in Martin Gilbert, *The First World War: A Complete History* (New York: Henry Holt, 1994), photograph no. 69, following p. 456.

age of breakfast cereal as a marketing ploy to sell more cereal, on the assumption that American children accompanying their parents to the grocery store would plead with their parents to buy the cereal with the German money!

The war destroyed the old European political order. The four empires that had provided stability in Europe during the previous two centuries disappeared at the end of the war. The Austro-Hungarian (or Habsburg) Empire was divided up into a number of small states. In addition, the Turkish Ottoman Empire and the Hohenzollern Empire in Germany had collapsed. And the **Bolshevik Revolution** in Russia in November 1917 had removed Russia from the war and had established a new force in world politics: **communism.**

The war also destroyed the social stability that had characterized European societies. In the atmosphere of destruction and devastation in post-World War I Europe, some new philosophic movements prospered. **Nihilism,** which can be defined as the denial of the existence of any foundation for truth or knowledge, became the new creed of many Europeans. In short, World War I destroyed the economic, political, and social fabric that had held Europe together for centuries without replacing it with a new fabric.

The statesmen who met at the Versailles Conference at the end of World War I had several options to choose from in attempting to re-create stability on the European continent: the balance of power, the punishment of Germany, and collective security.

The Balance of Power

Many in Europe wanted to return to the system that had provided relative peace and stability during the eighteenth and nineteenth centuries: the balance of power. Metternich, Castlereagh, and Talleyrand had based their strategy at the Congress of Vienna on the balance of power. Despite Napoleon's attempt to take over Europe, the leaders at the Congress of Vienna restored France as a full member of the European balance-of-power system that provided stability during the remainder of the nineteenth century, a period of revolutionary change. With the victory of the Bolshevik communists in Russia, would not the balance of power make sense? Why not return to this tried and true strategy?

Making Germany Pay for the War

At the end of World War I, many felt that Germany had been the sole cause of the war, and that if Germany had not pursued its aggressive policies, then the war would not have occurred. Consequently, many favored making Germany pay for the war. This sentiment was particularly strong in France and Great Britain. Following his election as British prime minister in 1918, Lloyd George promised to make Germany pay **reparations;** in his words, "to squeeze the German lemon until the pip squeaked." The war had been particularly costly to France, where tax collections in 1918 alone covered only one-eighth of the French government's expenditures, which primarily resulted from the war. At the peace conference which met at Versailles, French Premier Clemenceau pressed particularly hard for the demilitarization of Germany.

The League of Nations

The victorious powers wanted to create a political system that would prevent the resumption of another world war. President **Woodrow Wilson** of the United States was highly critical of the balance-of-power system, which he believed had contributed to the outbreak of the the the war. In Wilson's view, the balance of power was "an ugly plan of armed nations, of alliances, of watchful jealousies, of rabid antagonisms, of purposes concealed, running by the subtle channels of intrigue through the veins of people who do not dream what poison is being injected into their systems."[5] Wilson proposed a new system for managing power in world politics: collective security. The basic idea of the system was to outlaw all aggression in international relations; any state that attacked another would be opposed by all of the other members of the international community. Opposition to aggression, it was assumed, would be automatic and immediate (you will see in Chapter 6 a complete description of the assumptions of collective security).

The statesmen at Versailles debated these three strategies and could not agree on any one of them. Ultimately, a grand compromise was reached. France and Britain won acceptance of the vindictive policies toward Germany that they favored in exchange for their begrudging acceptance of collective security, the system for managing power favored by Woodrow Wilson, the president of the single most powerful state to emerge from World War I. This new system was to be embodied in a new organization, the **League of Nations.** The hopes and expectations for this new organization ran high, but were dashed on the rocks of political reality when the United States Senate would not approve the United States entry into the League. So from the beginning, the League was crippled by the failure of the United States to join it. And Germany, as we have seen, was economically crippled by the harsh demands for reparations.

THE INTERWAR INTERREGNUM: THE CALM BEFORE THE STORM

Storm clouds appeared on the horizon of world politics in 1929 when the U.S. stock market collapsed, catalyzing the Great Depression. This had a significant effect on the world economy and not just the United States. In addition to this economic bad news, there were also disturbing reports from Asia. In 1931, Japan attacked Manchuria and took it over; six years later, Japan attacked the Chinese mainland. In both of these cases, the League of Nations did little. In December 1934, Italy attacked the African country of Ethiopia, which had once faught a war with Italy. The emperor of Ethiopia, Haile Salassie went to the League of Nations to request help from other League members. In response, the League voted to impose economic sanctions against Italy, which proved to be ineffective.

Hitler's Rise to Power

In Germany, the news was also disturbing. Reacting to the hyperinflation caused by the reparations forced on them by the Versailles Treaty and blaming the Weimar government, a charismatic, arch-nationalist, **Adolf Hitler,** became chancellor of Germany in January 1933. The year after this, Hitler withdrew Germany from the League of Nations and repudiated provisions of the Versailles Treaty by openly building up the German military. Again, the League stood by and watched—but did nothing to stop Hitler.

Hitler on the March

In 1936, Germany marched into the Rhineland, an area that had been occupied by the allies at the end of World War I and which was supposed to be returned to Germany. Germany's reassertion of control over the Rhineland, however, was a violation of the Versailles Treaty. In 1938, Germany annexed Austria and occupied the Sudetenland, an area that was originally German territory with a majority of German inhabitants, which had been given to Czechoslovakia at the end of World War I. In September 1938, representatives of Britain, France, and Germany met in Munich to discuss the future of Czechoslovakia and agreed to the German occupation of the Sudetenland. The British Prime Minister, Neville Chamberlain, returned to London after signing the **Munich Agreement** and announced that he thought that he and his policy of appeasement had achieved "peace for our time." Hitler, however, was not satisfied with the Sudetenland and then occupied other parts of Czechoslovakia: Bohemia and Slovakia.

　　While Hitler was not very concerned about military threats from France, Britain, and the League of Nations, he was more concerned about the great power to his east: the Soviet Union. Germany and the USSR were the outcasts—the "pariah states"—of the 1930s; they were not accepted by the other great powers which viewed Germany as the cause of the First World War and the USSR as a power bent on revolution. As a result, Germany and the Soviet Union developed a relationship that confirms the old adage: "Politics makes strange bedfellows." One of the more fascinating aspects of this relationship concerned the cooperation between the German and Soviet militaries during the 1930s. The Versailles Treaty prohibited Germany from large-scale training maneuvers. The Soviet Union was an enormous country covering eleven time zones, more than twice as large as the United States, with vast areas that were off limits to foreigners. The Germans and Soviets worked out a mutually beneficial *quid pro quo:* the German military could practice its new strategy and tactics of "lightning war" (**Blitzkrieg**) on Soviet territory, and the Soviet military would be able to learn about the latest in military technology and its application to warfare.

But military cooperation did not resolve the political problem that Hitler faced. To address that problem, Hitler turned to diplomacy. Poland's history during the past 400 years has been one of occupation, partition, and tragedy due to a simple geographic fact: it lies between two great powers—Germany and Russia—with no significant geographic barriers separating them. In order to both gain more territory (what Hitler referred to as more "living room" or *Lebensraum*) and to secure his eastern border, Hitler proposed that Germany and the Soviet Union divide Poland and agree not to attack one another. This deal was negotiated in August 1939 by the German (Ribbentrop) and Soviet (Molotov) foreign ministers and was referred to as the **Nazi-Soviet Pact.**

WORLD WAR II

On September 1, 1939, Germany attacked Poland, and the new mechanized German *Panzer* tanks faced an outgunned but courageous Polish military. (There were cases recorded by Nazi propagandists of Polish cavalry charging German tanks on horseback, and the results were predictable and sickening.) Great Britain and France had concluded alliances with Poland, and following the German attack, declared war on Germany. This began the "second act" of the Second Thirty Years' War, and like the first Thirty Years' War, it was enormously destructive.

The Second World War (World War II) was truly a *world* war; few areas of the world were unaffected by the war and many areas of the world became battle zones. There were two principal fronts: Europe and the Pacific. For about two years—from September 1939 to June 1941—Great Britain and, until their defeat, France, Holland, and Belgium, faced Nazi Germany alone. Once Hitler had defeated and occupied the Western European states (with the exception of Great Britain), he turned his attention to the east. In June 1941, Germany violated the Nazi-Soviet Pact and attacked the USSR. Like Napoleon 129 years before, the Germans made it to the outskirts of Moscow, in the end they were defeated both by the courage and sacrifices of the Soviet people and by the harsh Russian weather. German soldiers had been sent into battle with only summer uniforms, and the winter of 1941 was one of the coldest on record during the previous century.

President Roosevelt was sympathetic to the British (and, following their entry into the war against Germany, the USSR) and sought to assist in their war effort, but he was constrained by American public opinion and the Congress. On December 6, 1941, the first person to fly solo across the Atlantic and a true American hero, Charles Lindbergh, spoke at Madison Square Garden advocating American neutrality in the war in Europe. There was significant support for Lindbergh's isolationist position. However, the next day Japanese forces under the control of Admiral Yamamoto executed a brilliant attack on American forces stationed at **Pearl Harbor,** Hawaii. President Roosevelt called December 7th a "day that would live in infamy," and requested a declaration of war on Japan from the Congress.

The United States Enters the War

The United States' entry into the war created what British Prime Minister Winston Churchill would later call the **"Grand Alliance"** of Great Britain, the United States, and the Soviet Union. In their various wartime meetings, the leaders of these three countries—the "Big Three" of Roosevelt, Churchill, and Stalin—agreed upon a number of principles. The first agreement was to defeat the **Axis Powers** (Germany, Japan, Italy) in Europe first and then to turn attention to the Pacific theater of the war. Second, the Allies agreed that the Axis Powers would have to agree to **"unconditional surrender,"** and that no one would negotiate separately an end to their fight against the Axis states. Third, in 1942, President Roosevelt promised Stalin that the Allies would attack western Europe so that Germany would be forced to move military forces from the eastern front in Russia back to western Europe. Stalin and other Russians believed that the Soviet people had been paying for the war in blood while others, primarily the United States, was paying for the war with matériel. For various reasons, including a shortage of landing craft to move soldiers across the English Channel, the Allies "second front" was not opened until the invasion of Normandy in June 1944.[6]

With the success of the cross-channel invasion, the eventual defeat of Germany was assured, although this took almost a year. In May 1945, the German *Fuehrer* (leader) Adolph Hitler and his mistress committed suicide in a bunker in Berlin, and Hitler's successors surrendered unconditionally to the Allies. That ended the war in the European theater; meanwhile, Japan fought on in the Pacific.

BOX 5.1   The "Boys of Pointe du Hoc" Remembered

On the fiftieth anniversary of the invasion of Normandy, President Reagan delivered a tribute to those who had fought and died: "We stand on a lonely, windswept point on the northern shore of France. The air is soft, but forty years ago at this moment, the air was dense with smoke and the cries of men, and the air was filled with the crack of rifle fire and the roar of cannon. At dawn, on the morning of the 6th of June 1944, 225 [U.S. Army] Rangers jumped off the British landing craft and ran to the bottom of these cliffs. Their mission was one of the most difficult and daring of the invasion: to climb these sheer and desolate cliffs and take out the enemy guns....

Behind me is a memorial that symbolizes the Ranger daggers that were thrust into the top of these cliffs. And before me are the men who put them there.

These are the boys of Pointe du Hoc. These are the men who took the cliffs. These are the champions who helped free a continent. These are the heroes who helped end a war....

Strengthened by their courage, heartened by their valor and borne by their memory, let us continue to stand for the ideals for which they lived and died.[7]

The War in the Pacific

The American strategy in the Pacific was dominated by two military leaders: General Douglas MacArthur and Admiral Chester Nimitz. They favored a strategy of "island hopping" from one Pacific island to the next in order to move closer to the Japanese mainland. Unknown to all but the very highest U. S. government officials, was a top secret project. Called the **"Manhattan Project,"** this massive undertaking had as its objective to develop a new class of weapons based on new principles of physics. Groups of scientists were sent to a remote site at Los Alamos, New Mexico, in order to develop these fearsome new weapons before Germany or Japan. There were many uncertainties, some of which were most disturbing. For example, the Los Alamos scientists believed that a nuclear explosion would not ignite the earth's atmosphere and burn the earth's supply of oxygen, but they were not sure.[8]

In July 1945, the nuclear age began with a test explosion at Alamagordo, New Mexico. The scientists estimated that the explosion would release the equivalent of 100 to 10,000 tons of dynamite; in fact, it released the equivalent of 19 thousand tons.[9] The Manhattan Project scientists had built two nuclear bombs, one using unriched uranium and the other plutonium. In the first hours of August 6, 1945, a lone B-29 bomber named the *Enola Gay* (after the pilot's mother) took off on its deadly mission. It arrived over its target—**Hiroshima, Japan**—at 9 o'clock in the morning. The bomb had the destructive power equivalent to 12,500 tons of TNT. The bomb was detonated 570 meters above ground, and the blast lasted just one second. But in that short amount of time, the explosion produced heat at "ground zero" (the name of the point of detonation) of 3,000 to 4,000 degrees Centigrade, about the same temperature as the surface of the sun. The blast and heat destroyed more than 62 thousand of Hiroshima's 90 thousand buildings, and an estimated 71 thousand people died that day; many more died in the days, weeks, months and years that followed.

Two days after the bombing of Hiroshima, the Soviet Union declared war on Japan. Still the Japanese did not surrender. On August 9, a bomb named "Fat Man" was dropped on **Nagasaki.** This bomb, made from plutonium, had a destructive yield of 22 thousand tons of dynamite. An estimated 35 thousand to 40 thousand people were killed immediately, and 60 thousand were injured.

On August 6, 1945, Hiroshima was bombed. This photo was taken on September 7, 1945.
Source: UPI/Bettmann Newsphotos; reprinted in John Newhouse, *War and Peace in the Nuclear Age* (New York: Alfred A. Knopf, 1989), following page 110.

The bombings of Hiroshima and Nagasaki even today are painful memories for both Japanese and Americans, and questions occur to thoughtful people everywhere. Was the use of nuclear weapons justified? One bomb? Two bombs? How many Americans and Japanese would have died if the United States had invaded the home islands of Japan? Journalists, politicians, philosophers, and historians have considered these thorny questions, and while the answers are not crystal clear, a few facts are. First, more people—135 thousand—were killed in Dresden, Germany, in February 1944. Less than a month later, fire-bombing raids on Tokyo with conventional (i.e. nonnuclear) killed 80 thousand and injured 40 thousand. Thus, more people were killed in Dresden and Tokyo than were killed in Hiroshima and Nagasaki. Second, American officials estimated that a physical invasion of Japan would have resulted in a million American casualties and even more Japanese. Third, the climate of opinion was very different in 1945 than today. Most Americans believed that the Japanese had ruthlessly attacked first and that the United States was justified in using whatever weapons it had to end the war. Harry S Truman, who had become president following the death of Franklin Roosevelt in April 1945, saw the issue directly and simply; when he received a message that Hiroshima had been bombed, Truman told those around him: "This is the greatest thing in history. It's time for us to get home."[10]

The End of World War II

On the morning of August 10, 1945, radio broadcasts from Japan indicated that the Japanese government was prepared to surrender unconditionally. Four days later, representatives of the Imperial Japanese government stepped onto the deck of the *USS Missouri*, met General MacArthur and signed the formal surrender ending World War II, the most costly war in human history. It is estimated that more than 60 million people died in the war; 26 million of these were from the USSR, as many as 15 million Chinese, 6.5 million Germans, 6 million Jews, 4 million Poles, more than 2 million Japanese, almost 2 million Yugoslavs, 600 thousand French citizens, 400 thousand British, and 405 thousand Americans.

The people of the world were relieved that the war had ended, but the world of 1945 was very different from the pre-World War II world, and the editors of *Time* magazine sensed this. In the first issue published after the bombings of Hiroshima and Nagasaki, they wrote:

> The greatest and most terrible of wars ended, this week, in the echoes of an enormous event—an event so much more enormous that, relative to it, the war itself shrank to minor significance. The knowledge of victory was as charged with sorrow and doubt as

with joy and gratitude. More fearful responsibilities, more crucial liabilities rested on the victors even than on the vanquished.[11]

In many respects the war had begun in 1914, had a long intermission of 20 years (1919–1939) and then wound up with 6 years of unprecedented carnage. And though the guns fell silent in 1945, echoes of the pained cries of the wounded, both civilian and military, and the voices of the poets can be heard even now. And despite the end of the war and the unconditional surrender of the Axis powers, a number of outstanding issues remained. What was to be the shape of Europe? Who would control the former Axis powers? What would be the effects of the fearsome new nuclear weapons on world politics? At the end of the war, there was joy, relief, and happiness, but there was a deep sadness for the cost paid for war and an uneasiness about the future.

DISCUSSION QUESTIONS

1. In historical hindsight, what could world leaders have done at the end of World War I, if anything, to prevent the outbreak of another world war?
2. By the end of World War II, in what ways had the world changed since the beginning of World War I?
3. How important were economic conditions in the outbreak of World War II?

KEY TERMS

Allied Powers
Axis Powers
Blitzkrieg
Bolshevik (Communist)
   Revolution
Communism
Grand Alliance
Great Depression
Hiroshima and Nagasaki
Hitler, Adolf
League of Nations

Manhattan Project
Munich Agreement
Nazi-Soviet Pact
nihilism
Pearl Harbor
reparations
unconditional surrender
Weimar Government
Wilson, Woodrow
World War I
World War II

KEY DATES

World War I

June 28, 1914   Archduke Franz Ferdinand and his wife were
                 assassinated in Sarajevo, Bosnia

July 1914	Austria-Hungary declares war on Serbia
August 1914	World War I begins
November 1917	Bolshevik (Communist) Revolution in Russia; led by Lenin
November 11, 1918	World War I ends

The Inter-war Period

1919	Treaty of Versailles
1920	League of Nations founded; United States is not a member
1925	Geneva Protocol outlaws poison gas
1929	U.S. stock market crash; onset of worldwide depression
1930	Smoot-Hawley tariff leads to "beggar-thy-neighbor" policies
1931	Japan invades Manchuria
January 1933	Adolf Hitler becomes chancellor of Germany
December 1934	Italy attacks Ethiopia
1936–1939	Civil War in Spain
1937	Japan invades China
1938	Annexation (*Anschluss*) of Austria by Germany
1938	Munich agreement signed by Hitler and British Prime Minister Chamberlain, an attempt to appease Hitler
1939	Germany occupies Czechoslovakia
August 1939	Germany and USSR sign Nazi-Soviet Pact

World War II

September 1, 1939	Germany attacks Poland; World War II begins
1940	Germany invades France, Belgium, and Holland; Japan occupies much of Southeast Asia
June 1941	Germany attacks the Soviet Union
December 7, 1941	Japan attacks Pearl Harbor; United States enters the war
1942	Axis forces defeated at the battles of Stalingrad (USSR), Midway (Pacific), and El Alamein (North Africa)
June 6, 1944	Allies invade Europe at Normandy
May 1945	Allies defeat Germany; Victory in Europe (VE) Day
August 1945	United States bombs Hiroshima and Nagasaki with atomic bombs
	Japan surrenders; VJ Day

RECOMMENDED PRINT, MULTIMEDIA, AND INTERNET SOURCES

Print

AMBROSE, STEPHEN. *Citizen Soldiers: The U.S. Army from the Normandy Beaches to the Bulge to the Surrender of Germany, June 7, 1944–May 7, 1945.* New York: Simon & Schuster, 1997.

———. *D-Day June 6, 1944: The Climactic Battle of World War II.* New York: Simon & Schuster, 1994.

CRAIG, GORDON and FELIX GILBERT, eds. *The Diplomats 1919–1939,* 2 vols. Princeton, NJ: Princeton University Press, 1967.

GARDNER, BRIAN (ed.), *Up the Line to Death: The War Poets 1914–1918.* London: Methuen, 1964.

GILBERT, MARTIN. *The First World War: A Complete History.* New York: Henry Holt and Company, 1994.

JOLL, JAMES. *The Origins of the First World War,* 2nd ed. London and New York: Longman, 1984.

KEEGAN, JOHN. *The Battle for History: Re-Fighting World War II.* New York: Vintage Books, 1995.

———. *The Second World War.* London: Penguin Books, 1990.

REMARQUE, ERICH MARIA. *All Quiet on the Western Front.* Boston: Little, Brown, 1929.

RHODES, RICHARD. *The Making of the Atomic Bomb.* New York: Simon & Schuster, 1986.

SPECTOR, RONALD. *Eagle Against the Sun: The American War with Japan.* New York: Free Press, 1985.

TAYLOR, A. J. P. *The First World War: An Illustrated History.* London: Penguin Books, 1966.

———. *The Origins of the Second World War.* London: Penguin Books, 1964.

WEINBERG, GERHARD L. *A World at Arms: A Global History of World War II.* Cambridge, England: Cambridge University Press, 1994.

WRIGHT, GORDON. *The Ordeal of Total War 1939–1945.* New York: Harper and Row, 1968.

Video

All Quiet on the Western Front: There are two film versions of Erich Maria Remarque's pacifist novel concerning German soldiers in World War I; the first produced in 1930, and the second in 1979.

The Great War and the Shaping of the Twentieth Century. Alexandria, VA: PBS Video. A magnificent eight-part series that focuses on the military, political, and cultural history of the First World War.

The Longest Day. The 1962 Academy award winning film focusing on the Normandy invasion.

Russia's War: Blood Upon the Snow. Alexandria, VA: PBS Video. A ten-part series focusing on World War II on the Eastern front; draws on previously secret Soviet archives.

Saving Private Ryan. Steven Spielberg's fictional account of a company of soldiers who participated in the invasion of Normandy.

Schindler's List. Steven Spielberg's emotional masterpiece about a German industrialist who saved thousands of Jews from death.

The Thin Red Line. Based on the book by James Jones describing the war in the South Pacific and the invasion of Guadalcanal.

Victory at Sea. The classic series on the naval aspects of the war.

Wilfrid Owen: The Pity of War. Princeton, NJ: Films for the Humanities and Sciences, 58 minutes. Drawn from the poems, letters and diaries of one of the best known World War I poets.

World at War. A series of twenty-six segments produced by the British Broadcasting Corporation in the mid-1960s; contains interviews with veterans, statesmen, and citizen participants in the Second World War.

CD-ROM

Britain Since 1930. Princeton, NJ: Films for the Humanities and Sciences. Focuses on the impact of World War II on British life.

The First World War and Its Consequences. Princeton, NJ: Films for the Humanities and Sciences. Photographs, newreel footage, maps, diagrams, personal accounts, and artists' drawings recount the war from beginning to end.

Internet

United States Institute of Peace: http://www.usip.org/ This site contains information about an institute created by Congress to inform and educate people on how to achieve peace.

Websites concerning the atomic bombing of Hiroshima and Nagasaki:

A-bomb museum: http://www.csi.ad.jp/ABOMB/index.html

The decision to use the bombs:

http://www.dannen.com/decision/index.html

ENDNOTES

[1] JOHN FREEMAN, "Happy is England Now," in Brian Gardner, ed., *Up the Line to Death: The War Poets 1914–1918* (London: Magnum Books, 1977), p. 8.

[2] ALAN SEEGER, "Rendezvous," in ibid., p. 32.

[3] OSBERT SITWELL, "This Generation," in ibid. p. 149.

[4] PHILIP JOHNSON, "Highwood," in ibid., p. 157.

[5] RAY S. BAKER and WILLIAM E. DODD, eds., *The Public Papers of Woodrow Wilson, War and Peace* (New York: Harper, 1927) cited by Inis L. Claude, Jr., *Power and International Relations* (New York: Random House, 1962), pp. 81–82.

[6] JOHN KEEGAN, *The Second World War* (New York: Penguin Books, 1989).

[7] RONALD REAGAN, "Remarks at the U.S. Ranger Monument," Pointe du Hoc, France, in *Speaking My Mind* (New York: Simon & Schuster, 1989), pp. 218–220.

[8] JOHN NEWHOUSE, *War and Peace in the Nuclear Age* (New York: Alfred A. Knopf, 1989).

[9] Ibid., p. 40.

[10] HARRY S TRUMAN, *Memoirs: Year of Decision* (Garden City, NY: Doubleday, 1955), p. 421.

[11] *Time,* August 20, 1945, p. 19.

6 Collective Security

CRITEX:
Influential Leaders

PRESIDENT John Kennedy once said that one person could make a difference in this world. Of course, this is both true and false, depending upon how one thinks about "changing the world." Educational research has shown that teachers have an influence on their students that is inversely proportional to the grade level. That is, your kindergarten teacher in all probability had more of an influence on you than will the professor in this course. Elementary school teachers open up entirely new areas of knowledge and wonder to their students, thus "changing the world," albeit a small corner of it, but an enormously important part to their students.

A small number of individuals throughout history have actually had the opportunity to change the world, for better or worse. Some leaders have grand visions of "the proper place" of their

countries in the world. Leaders such as Julius Caesar of Rome, Otto von Bismarck in Germany, or Napoleon Bonaparte in France have sought to increase the power and wealth of their countries by expanding their territorial holdings and, for better or ill, left their mark on history.

Other leaders are remembered primarily for the calamities that they have brought upon their states' people. Without Adolf Hitler, perhaps World War II and its 60 million fatalities could have been avoided. Josef Stalin in the Soviet Union ordered the deaths of at least 20 million Soviet citizens, and Mao Zedong in China implemented policies that resulted in mass famine and the deaths of an estimated 16 to 20 million Chinese during the "Great Leap Forward" of the late 1950s.[1]

As you think about leaders you have heard and read about, who are the ones who come to mind for the following categories?

Most respected _____

Most feared   _____

Accomplished the most good _____

Perpetrated the most evil _____

Most famous female leader _____

Briefly describe the reasons that you selected each of the above leaders.

WOODROW WILSON

Between 1982 and 1994, on three different occasions the Siena Research Institute has asked historians and political scientists which U.S. presidents they most respect. Table 6.1 provides the results of this survey of expert opinion.

Wilson's high rating may be due to the fact that he is the only former political science professor to have served as president.

Woodrow Wilson may only ring a faint bell in the recesses of your memory, but he was an important figure for both the United States and the rest of the world because he was a person with a vision for a better world, a world free of the devastation created by war and conflict. Although Wilson's vision was never fully realized, it was manifested in two international organizations—the League of Nations and the United Nations—and numerous programs.

Wilson was born in 1856 in Staunton, Virginia, to a stern father and loving mother. Wilson's father was a Presbyterian minister, and this background influenced Wilson for all of his life. He approached problems from

TABLE 6.1

The Ranking of the Most Respected U.S. Presidents

	1982	1990	1994
Franklin Delano Roosevelt	1	1	1
Abraham Lincoln	3	2	2
Theodore Roosevelt	5	5	3
George Washington	4	4	4
Thomas Jefferson	2	3	5
Woodrow Wilson	6	6	6
Harry S Truman	7	7	7
Dwight D. Eisenhower	11	12	8
James Madison	9	8	9
John F. Kennedy	8	10	10

Source of Data: Douglas A. Lonnstrom and Thomas O. Kelly, II, "Rating the Presidents: A Tracking Study," *Presidential Studies Quarterly,* vol. 27, no. 3 (Summer 1997):593.

a highly moralistic orientation and constantly searched for answers to problems that were consistent with his own Christian beliefs.

Wilson's first contact with war and conflict came when he was a young boy. He went to his father's church where wounded Confederate soldiers from the Civil War were cared for. The images that he saw never left him, and they motivated him to work for peace.

As a young boy, Wilson was sick and developed rather late. He dreamed of becoming a statesman. Two social scientists—Alexander George and Juliette George—have written an outstanding biography of Wilson that focuses on Wilson's personality and its effect on policy.[2] According to the Georges, Wilson sought to compensate for his shortcomings by excelling in his academic pursuits. Although he was a below-average student as a boy, he worked hard to develop his academic talents. When it was time for college, Wilson first attended Davidson College, a Presbyterian college in North Carolina then transferred to Princeton, where he did good, but not outstanding, work.

Like many readers of this book, Wilson was attracted to the study of law and upon graduation, he went to law school at the University of Virginia, the institution founded by Wilson's hero, Thomas Jefferson. Wilson worked hard in law school, graduated in 1880 and set up a private law practice in Atlanta, Georgia, with a friend and fellow law school graduate. The two newly minted attorneys assumed that there would be substantial demand for their legal advice and counsel. They were wrong, and after less than a year, they closed their office. Wilson decided to pursue graduate studies in political science at Johns Hopkins University in Baltimore, Maryland.

Even as a boy, Wilson had been attracted to the parliamentary system of government of Great Britain. William Gladstone, the great British politician, was Wilson's political hero. In his doctoral dissertation, subsequently published as his first book entitled *Constitutional Government,* Wilson advocated a parliamentary system of government for the United States. Wilson's book was well received, and he served as a professor at Bryn Mawr College and then Wesleyan University. Wilson's second book, *The State,* was published in 1889 and contributed to his academic reputation. Wilson's dream had always been to return to Princeton to teach, and he was invited to do so in 1890. By the time Wilson returned to Princeton, he had achieved a successful academic career.

Wilson as President of Princeton University

After serving as a professor at Princeton for twelve years, Wilson became president of the university in 1902. In his eight years in this position, he successfully reformed the undergraduate curriculum and then set his sights on building a new graduate school. A later professor-turned-statesman, Dr. Henry Kissinger, once wrote that academic politics are the worst of all kinds because the stakes are so low. Pitched battles over relatively minor issues such as teaching loads, curricular matters, and the "big issues" of the quality of the food in the faculty dining room and the allocation of parking spaces, are fought over as if they are life and death struggles. Wilson found himself in such a conflict. The dean of the graduate school, Andrew Fleming West, wanted to build the new school a mile from the main Princeton campus. Wilson wanted to build the new school on the main campus to facilitate communication and interaction between the undergraduate and graduate students. The battle between Wilson and Dean West served as a precursor to Wilson's later battle with Senator Henry Cabot Lodge over the League of Nations.

Wilson won the battle with West, and consequently the new graduate school was built on Princeton's main campus. Oddly, however, Wilson's victory did not satisfy him; he still longed to be a statesman, his boyhood dream. His opportunity came in 1910 when representatives of the New Jersey political machine came to Wilson and asked him to run for governor. Wilson did so and won. As governor, Wilson pursued policies that were consistent with the domestic agenda of the progressives at the time and had no occasion to become involved with international issues.[3]

Wilson as President of the United States

Wilson was successful as governor of New Jersey and his record as a reformer caused the Democratic Party to name him as its presidential nominee in 1912. Wilson won the election by defeating the Republican incumbent, William Howard Taft, and the Progressive Party's candidate, Theodore Roosevelt. Wilson entered the Oval Office with an ambitious agenda for both domestic and foreign policies. From his first day in office, it was clear that Wilson was going to be an activist; on his inauguration day, Wilson called a special session of Congress, and on April 8, 1913, he went to Capitol Hill and delivered a message to both houses of Congress—the first president to do this since John Adams. Wilson embarked on an ambitious plan of introducing and implementing a number of progressive measures including the support of free trade, the creation of the Federal Reserve banking system, and the establishment of the Federal Trade Commission. According to Wilson's biographer, Princeton political scientist Arthur Link, "Wilson's strengthening and extension of the presidential powers constituted perhaps the most lasting contribution to American political practice."[4] As Professor Link notes, Wilson's accomplishments in the domestic political arena were significant; however, as political storm clouds gathered over Europe, Wilson's views on international politics became more important.

Wilson was not only a member of the Democratic Party; he was also a democrat, one who believed in the legitimate—in Wilson's view, God-given—right of people to choose their own leaders and type of government. This belief in and support for the right of self-determination was central to Wilson's *thinking* about world politics. His *practice* deviated significantly from this theory. Wilson's policies toward Latin America illustrated the gap between his *theory* and his practice of international relations. While espousing **self-determination** for all peoples (presumably including Latin Americans), Wilson ordered more interventions into Latin American countries than any U.S. president before or since.

When war broke out on the European continent in August 1914, Wilson pursued two long-standing American foreign policy objectives: neutrality and free trade. These objectives were challenged when Germany sought to cut off trade between the United States and Great Britain and France by using submarines to attack shipping. On May 7, 1915, the *Lusitania,* a civilian passenger ship with 1,198 people on board (128 of whom were Americans) was sunk. Even in the face of this Wilson supported a neutralist stance:

There is such a thing as being too proud to fight. There is such a thing as a nation being so right that it does not need to convince others by force that it is right.

Former Spanish-American War hero and President, Theodore Roosevelt, reacted characteristically: "Professor Wilson, that Byzantine logothete who was supported by the flubdubs, mollycoddles and flapdoddle pacifists." Despite such criticism, Wilson maintained his support for a neutralist stance throughout 1915 and 1916. In the 1916 presidential campaign, Wilson ran on the slogan, "He kept us out of war."

The United States Enters World War I

In March 1917, two events turned Wilson and the United States around on the issue of entering World War I. At the beginning of the month, Wilson made public the "Zimmerman Telegram," which purportedly was a promise from the German foreign minister to Mexico that Mexico would be given the southwestern United States if it would enter the war on Germany's side.[5] This understandably caused quite a stir in the United States. Later in the month, German submarines attacked and sank four unarmed American merchant ships. These events were too much for the United States to accept, and it declared war on Germany by a vote of 82–6 in the Senate (April 4, 1917) and 373–50 in the House (April 6). The United States, according to President Wilson, entered the war "to make the world safe for democracy." America's involvement came during the last months of the war, and by the end of the war, 117 thousand Americans had died.

As the end of what up to that time had been the most costly war in human history approached, Wilson turned his attention to the structure of the postwar international system. And in keeping with his moralistic approach to world politics, he had a vision of the system that he was confident would keep the peace.

THE IDEAL OF COLLECTIVE SECURITY

Throughout the classical diplomatic era, there were philosophers and statesmen who longed for an alternative to the balance-of-power system. In 1712, Abbé de Saint-Pierre proposed a league of European rulers who would agree to submit disputes to arbitration and who would join against any ruler who would not do this. In short, the threat of force would be used to compel each ruler to settle disputes by arbitration.[6] Frederick the Great of Prussia was sarcastic in his evaluation of the proposal: "The thing is most practicable; for its success, all that is lacking is the consent of Europe and a few similar trifles." Referring to Abbé de Saint-Pierre, the French political philosopher Jean Jacques Rousseau wrote: "This good man saw clearly enough how things would work, when once set going, but he judged like a child of the means for setting them in motion."

The **collective security** ideal lay fallow for two centuries. Following his successful arbitration of the 1904–1905 Russo-Japanese War, Theodore Roosevelt received the Nobel Peace Prize. In his acceptance speech he said: "It would be a master stroke if those great powers honestly bent on peace would form a League of Peace, not only to keep the peace among themselves, but to prevent by force if necessary." The international community did not heed Roosevelt's advice, however, and the ensuing war broke out with devastating results for the victors and the vanquished alike (see Chapter 5).

To some, World War I had resulted from the inherent instability of the balance of power system. President Woodrow Wilson was blunt in his condemnation of the balance of power, which he called "that old and evil order which prevailed before this war began....[7] Wilson and other critics of the balance of power believed that it was not only evil, but that it was incompatible with American ideals. For example, as noted in Chapter 3, balance-of-power advocates believed that war should be waged in order to maintain and preserve the system. Historically, however, Americans have been against using war for such purposes. In addition, the balance of power requires secrecy in order to operate. This was anathema to President Wilson who had called for international agreements negotiated in public. The balance of power required control by a small group of leaders, and such an elitist approach was also unacceptable to those who supported democratic methods. Lastly, the balance of power required ideological flexibility. According to this approach, the United States should be willing—if its national interests so dictated—to break diplomatic relations with Great Britain and to establish an alliance with the Soviet Union. But many of the Soviet Union's basic assumptions about domestic and international politics were simply unacceptable to many Americans, starting with Woodrow Wilson.[8]

Wilson's Proposal—the League of Nations

In order to avoid another catastrophic war, Wilson proposed a new international organization, the League of Nations, which was designed to embody the following principles of collective security:

1. In any case of armed conflict, all states would agree on the originator of the conflict. The identification of the aggressor would be quick and decisive.

2. All states have an interest in stopping aggression.

3. All states are able to join in united action against an aggressor.

4. The combined power of the collective group opposing the aggressor will be great enough to defeat the aggressor.

5. Knowing of the overwhelming power that will be used against it, an aggressor will either settle its disputes peacefully or be defeated.

The Failure of the League

These assumptions proved to be unrealistic and unreasonable. Importantly, the United States Senate chose not to join the League of Nations, which crippled the organization from the beginning. In 1931, Japan invaded Manchuria, and the newly established collective security organization failed to respond with anything other than a torrent of rhetorical denunciations. In December 1934, Benito Mussolini's Italy attacked the African country of Ethiopia in a brutal manner using mustard gas for the first time since World War I. Ethiopian Emperor Haile Selassie went to the headquarters of the League to seek assistance in repelling Italian aggression. Selassie pointed to the blatant nature of the Italian attack and called for the member states of the League to come to the aid of his country as they had promised to do in the Covenant. As in the earlier Manchurian case, the League responded with words and some ineffective economic sanctions but no really effective actions. The League failed to respond to other challenges to peace in the inter-war (1919–1939) period which resulted in the "second act" of the disastrous "play" that had begun in 1914.

Collective security advocates such as Woodrow Wilson believed that individuals and states would—if left to themselves—generally cooperate rather than conflict with one another. Balance-of-power supporters, also called "realists," believed that individuals and states would naturally compete and conflict with one another. The eighteenth-century British political philosopher, Thomas Hobbes, was characteristic of this approach; he wrote that the "state of nature" was hardly pristine or idyllic; rather, life in the state of nature was "nasty, brutish and short."[9] Given this view of human affairs, it is understandable that realists thought that national interests should be the principal guide to policy. When a state's national interests were threatened, the state should act. If those interests were not directly threatened, then no action should be taken.

Collective security advocates believed that there were interests that went beyond the boundaries of any one country. For example, stopping aggression was in the interest of all of the world's states and not simply those states bordering an aggressive, expansionist country. As a consequence of these views, collective-security supporters believed that all states have an interest in stopping aggression, while realists believe that a state should join in opposing aggression only when its own national interests are threatened. Thus, when aggression occurs, neutrality is a very real possibility for realists and is out of the question for collective-security advocates.

The objectives of the international system were very different for balance-of-power and collective-security adherents. For the former, international stability was the central goal of the system. For collective-security supporters, peace was the goal. "Stability" and "peace" were related, but not always synonymous. A stable international system could be peaceful, and a peaceful international system could be stable; however, war might be required to establish stability.

Realists emphasize the tangible elements of power, such as geography, population, natural resources, economic capacity, and military strength (see Chapter 4). Collective-security advocates note that intangible sources of power such as world public opinion, national morale, and international prestige can be important—even decisive on occasion—in world politics and consequently emphasize intangible sources of power.

In essence, the balance-of-power system is a decentralized system for managing power because the members of this system decide for themselves what action (if any) they will take on the international scene. The collective-security system is more centralized; states decide what action the international organization will take. Because states in the balance-of-power system are supposed to follow their own selfish national interests and decide on actions for themselves, balance-of-power advocates reserve the right for states to adopt "self help" solutions to problems. Just as vigilantes in the Old West adopted remedies beyond the law, balance-of-power supporters advocate the same sort of remedies for modern day states. In contrast, collective-security supporters advocate observing and relying on international legal structures and processes. An example will help to clarify the differences of the two approaches. If the members of a terrorist group headquartered in state A attack targets in state B, realists would argue that state B is justified in staging retaliatory attacks on state A. Collective-security advocates would argue that state B should refer the problem to a regional or international organization for investigation and adjudication. These differences are summarized in Box 6.1.

THE FOUNDING OF THE UNITED NATIONS

After six years of war and more than 60 million dead in World War II, the victorious allies wanted to "get it right" and avoid a third global conflict. Fifty-one of the world's states—almost all that existed at that time—sent

---

**BOX 6.1   The Balance of Power
and Collective Security Contrasted**

Balance of Power	Collective Security
1. Conflict is general; cooperation is exceptional.	1. Conflict is exceptional; cooperation is general.
2. National interest is the principal guide to policy.	2. Universal interests should guide policy.
3. A state should join in opposing an aggressor only if its national interests are threatened.	3. All states have an interest in stopping aggression.
4. A state should be neutral unless its interests are threatened.	4. In the event of aggression, no state can remain neutral.
5. Emphasis is on world stability at any price, including war.	5. World peace is the goal, at any price.
6. Tangible power is what matters.	6. Intangible sources of power can be important.
7. The system of managing power is decentralized.	7. The system of managing power is centralized.
8. States may have to adopt "self help" remedies.	8. The emphasis is on international law.

---

representatives to San Francisco where the delegates met to discuss the founding of a new, hopefully effective, collective-security organization called the United Nations.

Essentially, the structure of the United Nations was an amalgam of the balance-of-power and collective-security systems. The UN Charter

---

BOX 6.2   John Kennedy and the United Nations

Included in the ranks of the reporters covering the founding of this new organization was a young U.S. former naval officer who had been wounded in the war. At the end of the war, he got out of the Navy and then had to decide what to do with his life. Growing up in a wealthy family, he was in the fortunate position of not having to work just to earn a living, and he never would have been compelled to work a day the rest of his life. The young war hero decided to go to Stanford Business School, and while there he began covering the proceedings of the United Nations as a journalist. But neither business nor journalism would prove to be this young man's calling; rather, John Fitzgerald Kennedy chose to go into politics.

gave each member a seat in the **General Assembly;** however, only the five victorious Allies of World War II—the United States, the Soviet Union, United Kingdom, France and China—were given permanent seats on the **Security Council.** In a sense, membership on the Security Council was analogous to the five polar balance-of-power system of the nineteenth century. The so-called "**Permanent-Five (Perm-5)**" clearly had more power than other members of the UN because they had the power to veto any proposals that came before the Security Council. In addition to the "Perm-5," there are ten other members of the Security Council, who serve on a rotating basis.

At the end of World War II, in contrast to 1919, the United States joined the collective-security organization. Franklin Roosevelt, who had served in Woodrow Wilson's administration in the Navy Department, supported many of the principles of collective security.[10] This experience and orientation undoubtedly influenced Roosevelt to support the organization of the United Nations. In addition, the Senate supported an activist, international role for the United States in the post-World War II international system.

The heart of the new system was based on Article 2: "All Members shall refrain in their international relations from the threat or use of force against the territorial integrity or political independence of any state...." If a situation threatening peace arose, the threatened state was supposed to report the situation to the Security Council which was made up of the five victorious states—the post-World War II great powers. According to the UN Charter, the Security Council, would then deliberate and decide what action, if any, to take. Such action had to be supported unanimously by the members of the Security Council.

As hostility developed between the western countries and the Soviet Union, unanimous agreement became difficult to achieve in the Security Council. As a result of the paralysis of the Security Council, states were entitled to establish regional security organizations to protect themselves against aggression according to Article 51:

> Nothing in the present Charter shall impair the inherent right of individual or collective self-defense if an armed attack occurs against a Member of the United Nations until the Security Council has taken measures necessary to maintain international peace and security.

It was in this context that the North Atlantic Treaty Organization (NATO) was born. And it was NATO, not the UN, that provided for peace and stability in Europe throughout the cold war (see Chapter 7).

Many people criticize the United Nations on the grounds that it failed in its original purpose of preventing conflict and war and preserving peace. There are certainly legitimate grounds for such criticism; however, it would be unfair to dismiss the many accomplishments of the UN on these grounds. As just one example, most people do not realize that the reason that smallpox has been virtually eradicated from the world is due to the actions of the **World Health Organization (WHO)** , which is an agency of the United Nations. Had the UN or WHO not existed, smallpox would probably still be causing the deaths of many thousands, perhaps even millions, of people.

The Structure of the UN

There are 6 major organizations and 20 associated agencies that make up the United Nations. First, the General Assembly which currently has 185 members, virtually every state in the world with the exception of Kiribati, Nauru, the Republic of China, Switzerland, Tuvalu, Monaco, and four other states. If nothing else (and some criticize the UN on these grounds), the UN is a "talk shop" where the leaders of the world's states can meet and discuss issues of common concern.

The second organization is the Security Council which has five permanent members and ten members elected for two-year rotating terms. Only the five permanent members have the veto power. The Security Council has the responsibility, according to the UN Charter, for organizing collective security and peacekeeping operations. On only two occasions in its more than half century existence has the United Nations sent military forces to intervene on behalf of states that had been attacked; the UN sponsored collective-security operations in South Korea in 1950 and in Kuwait in 1990–1991.

Another very important aspect of the United Nations operations concerns peacekeeping throughout the world. Although the UN was not able, contrary to its founders' hopes, to stop all war, it has been able to serve as a valuable intermediary in a number of conflicts. Beginning in 1948 with deployments in the Middle East, UN forces have been deployed throughout the world. Since 1948 the United Nations has conducted 36 peacekeeping operations, and a number of these have been very significant operations, including those in the Suez Canal/Sinai Peninsula area (1956–1967), the Congo (1960–1964), and more recent operations in Somalia, Haiti, and Rwanda. Not all of these operations have been successful, but on the whole UN peacekeeping operations have contributed to international peace and stability. In recognition of this fact, UN peacekeeping forces were awarded the prestigious Nobel Peace Prize in 1988. A graphic summary of the principal UN peacekeeping operations, as well as a depiction of the growth in UN membership and its budget are presented in Figure 6.1.

Third is the **Secretariat** which is the UN's principal administrative body and is headed by the **Secretary-General** of the United Nations, who is elected to a five year term. The Secretariat is staffed by 15,000 international civil servants, 11,000 of whom are stationed around the world and 5,000 at UN headquarters in New York City. Since its founding in 1945, seven people have served as Secretary General.

BOX 6.3 The United Nations' Secretaries General		
	Home Country	*Term of Office*
Trygve Lie	Norway	1946–1953
Dag Hammarskjold	Sweden	1953–1961
U Thant	Burma	1961–1972
Kurt Waldheim	Austria	1972–1982
Boutros Boutros-Ghali	Egypt	1992–1997
Kofi Annan	Ghana	1997–present

Beginning in the mid-1990s, some members of the U.S. Congress became disenchanted with Secretary General Boutros Boutros-Gali, and the Clinton Administration concluded that it could not support him for a second five-year term. Consequently, another secretary general was chosen to succeed him: **Kofi Annan.**

The **International Court of Justice (ICJ),** more commonly known as the World Court, is headquartered in The Hague in the Netherlands. Fifteen jurists are selected from around the world to serve nine-year terms.

BOX 6.4   Staffing the United Nations, Disneyland and McDonald's

- 52,280 people work for the UN, which includes the Secretariat and 29 other organizations such as UNICEF.

- Disneyland and Disney World employ almost as many people— 50,000.

- More than three times as many (150,000 people) work for McDonald's.

For other facts about the UN, go to the United Nations Website:
http://www.un.org/news/facts/setting.htm

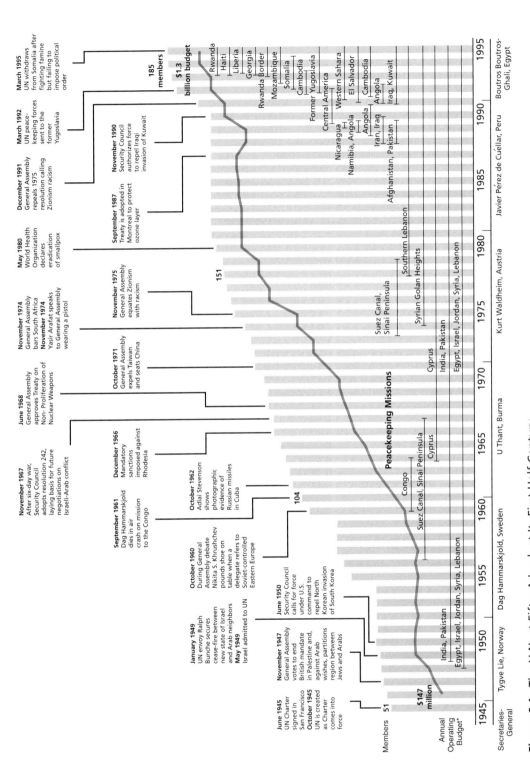

Figure 6.1. The U.N. at Fifty: A Look at Its First Half Century.

* Adjusted for inflations, in 1994 dollars. Starting in 1974, the U.N. adopted two-years budgeting. Data after 1973 are the annual average for the corresponding two-year period.

Source: The New York Times, October 22, 1995, p. 8. Copyright © 1995 by The New York Times. Reprinted by permission. Data from United Nations and Margaret P. Karns and Karen A. Mingst, *The United Nations in the Post-Cold War Era.* Boulder, CO: Westview, 1995.

This is the closest analog to an "international supreme court," but there are significant problems with this analogy because states decide whether or not they will submit cases to the ICJ and, even if they do, whether or not they will abide by the ICJ's rulings.

A fourth UN organization is the **Economic and Social Council (ECOSOC)** which is responsible for coordinating the United Nations' specialized agencies and organizations such as the World Health Organization (WHO), the UN Children's Emergency Fund (UNICEF), and the Food and Agricultural Organization (FAO). ECOSOC consists of 54 members which serve three-year terms, and it meets twice a year, once in New York and the other time in Geneva, to discuss issues related to commodity agreements, debt burden, "sustainable development," and the coordination of the various other social and economic organizations and activities of the UN.

More than 20 different specialized agencies in the United Nations deal with many different problems. The **World Health Organization (WHO)** is perhaps the most prominent of these specialized agencies; others include the UN High Commissioner for Refugees (UNHCR) and the UN Children's Fund (UNICEF), which sponsors many programs designed to improve the health and welfare of children, particularly those in poorer countries. Another of the specialized agencies, the Food and Agricultural Organization (FAO), is dedicated to increasing the world food supply. Many of the developments in the 1960s that resulted in dramatically improved crop yields—what some referred to as the "green revolution"—had been sponsored by FAO.

A fifth UN organization, the **Trusteeship Council,** was originally founded to oversee the administration of UN trust territories that carried over from the League of Nations' mandate system. In November 1993, the people of the Trust Territory of the Pacific Islands voted to join with the United States. This ended the need for the Trusteeship Council, although it still exists on paper in order to avoid the requirement to amend the UN Charter.

Cost of UN Operations

The operations of the 6 major organizations and 20 specialized agencies of the United Nations, of course, cost money; in absolute terms, the cost is high. In 1998, the budget for the UN's core functions was $1.25 billion. When compared to other organizations, this amount of money may not be as much as it initially appears to be. For example, this is about 4 percent of New York City's annual budget, a billion dollars less than the yearly cost of Tokyo's fire department, and about equal to the cost of one B–1 bomber.

The cost of UN peacekeeping forces is about equal to the core functions budget: $1.3 billion for 1998. This covered the cost of peacekeeping in 13 different operations, including those in the former Yugoslavia. This also is a lot of money in absolute terms, but not so much when compared to other organizations. For example, $1.3 billion is the equivalent of one-half of 1 percent of the U.S. military budget.

How does the United Nations pay its expenses? Not surprisingly in a world of sovereign states, the UN depends upon the contributions of its member governments to pay its expenses. These contributions were set and periodically reviewed so that they would be proportional to a state's income and ability to pay. This was a kind of international analog to the progressive income tax in the United States. Currently, the UN has assessed the United States 25% of the core operations of the UN, which in 1998 equaled $298 million, about $1.11 per American. The UN assessed the United States 31 percent of the cost of peacekeeping operations, equal to approximately $400 million in 1998. Some members of the U.S. Congress have been quite critical of the UN and have called for either not paying U.S. dues or dramatically reducing U.S. contributions. In 1995, for example, the Congress unilaterally reduced the amount that the United States would contribute to support UN peacekeeping operations from 31 percent to 25 percent.

Cost is only one of the criticisms that have been raised concerning the UN. Some in the United States argue that the UN does not promote U.S. national interests and is sometimes even opposed to U.S. interests in the world. Some critics on the left argue that the UN does not operate the way that it was designed to: as a collective-security organization of the type that Woodrow Wilson envisioned many years ago. And, of course, whenever there is a case of waste, fraud, or abuse, critics are quick to condemn the entire UN organization for the wrongdoing of a few.

Some critics argue that things are so bad that the United States should get out of the UN. Consider, however, the type of world that we would have without the United Nations. First, there would be no organization or place for virtually the entire international community to discuss important issues of the day such as Bosnia, Kosovo, global warming, AIDS, and so on. Second, there would be no forum in which to discuss international wrongdoing. When Iraq invaded and occupied Kuwait in 1990, the UN passed eleven different resolutions calling initially on Iraq to withdraw from Kuwait and then authorizing the coalition of 32 countries to force Iraq to withdraw. With the disintegration of the Soviet Union in 1991 and the demise of the cold war, it may be that the UN will no longer be crippled by the ideological fissures of the past cold war and may be able to function more effectively. But how?

The United Nations' Problems: Calls for Reforms

Like any other organization, the United Nations cannot function without financial resources. Therefore, a place to start in thinking about the reform of the UN is to provide it with resources that are adequate to meet its requirements. Records indicate that 111 of the 185 member of the UN are behind in their dues.[11] As of September 1998, $2.5 billion is owed to the United Nations by its member states. The largest debtor is the United States, which owes somewhere between $819 million (U.S. Congress's estimate) to $1.6 billion (UN's estimate). The Clinton administration and the Congress worked together to develop a compromise that would allow the United States to pay $819 million in exchange for the UN adopting a number of reforms.

In July 1997, Secretary General Kofi Annan announced a number of reforms designed to make the UN more efficient and effective. One thousand jobs out of a total of 53,333 would be eliminated. Administrative overhead would be reduced from 38 percent to 25 percent, and activities such as procurement and storage of archives would be consolidated. The result of these reforms would be to hold the budget of the core activities of the UN to $1.3 billion per year into the next century. Initially, the reforms were not particularly welcomed in the U.S. Congress. Senator Rod Grams (R-Minn.), chairman of the Senate Foreign Relations Subcommittee on International Operations, called the secretary general's reforms "meager" and "unacceptable."[12]

Mr. Annan's reforms focused primarily on the operations of the United Nations and not on the structures of the organization. A number of prominent observers, for example, raised important questions about the membership and operation of the Security Council. As noted previously, at the time of the founding of the UN, the Security Council consisted of the five victorious allies from World War II: the United States, USSR, United Kingdom, France, and China. (At the time the UN was founded, there was only one China. From the victory of the Communists over the Nationalists in 1949 until 1971, the Republic of China on Taiwan held China's seat on the Security Council. When the Communist People's Republic of China was admitted to the UN, it became China's representative on the Security Council.)

The UN at 50

On the occasion of the 50th anniversary of the founding of the UN in 1995, some observers asked whether it was not time to make some structural changes in the organization that had been founded in a very different international environment. Many thought that it was time to include the second and third largest contributors to the UN—Japan and Germany—as members of the Security Council. But if this were done, the Council would become even more dominated by the advanced industrial states than previously. Another proposal was to include permanent regional membership from large regional powers such as India, Brazil, Nigeria, and South Africa. In July 1997, the U.S. ambassador to the UN, Bill Richardson, announced that the United States supported membership on the Security Council for Japan and Germany, plus as many as three developing countries.[13]

CONCLUSION

As a boy, Woodrow Wilson saw first hand the ravages of war when he saw wounded Confederate soldiers being cared for at his father's church. Perhaps it was these images or perhaps it was the devastation witnessed, experienced, and written about by the poets of World War I that caused him to seek to develop a system for managing power in international relations that would be an alternative to the balance of power. Wilson fought courageously for a new organization that embodied the principles of collective security—the League of Nations—but ultimately failed to persuade the Congress that the United States should join. Partially because the United States was not a member, the League failed to stop various acts of aggression in the inter-war period, and the "second act" in the world's two most costly wars ensued.

At the end of World War II, the victorious allies were determined to right the mistakes of their predecessors from World War I, and the United States not only joined, but was the principal supporter of the new United Nations for most of the cold war. But as the membership of the new organization shifted to the newly independent states of Asia, Latin America, and Africa, the UN reflected less the interests of the United States and more the interests of the international community. As a result, some in the United States criticized the United Nations and called for the United States to withdraw from the UN.

As you think about the type of world that you want to see in the decades ahead, do you think that your preferred world would be better off with or without the United Nations?

YOU IN WORLD POLITICS

So you're interested in working for the United Nations? Employment at the United Nations is done by the different organizations that make up the UN. The United Nations Secretariat employs 14,800 staff members from 160 different countries. Jobs at the UN are in a number of different fields, including administration, economics, finance, translation, law, public information, and development. In keeping with General Assembly directives, the UN currently gives preference to women who are equally qualified with men. Entry level professionals are chosen through competitive examinations, and an applicant for such positions should have a college degree and be 32 years old or younger. Those interested in working for the Secretariat should write:

United Nations
Examinations and Tests Section
Division for Staff Development and Performance
Policy and Specialist Services
Office of Human Resources Management
Room S-2590
New York, NY 10017

The UN sponsors an internship program that is restricted to students who are currently enrolled in a master's degree program. (Anyone who has already earned a master's degree will not be considered.) Interns are not paid and the costs of travel, accommodations and living expenses are the responsibility of interns or their sponsoring organizations. For further information on the UN internship program, write:

Coordinator of the Internship Program
Room S-2570
United Nations
New York, NY 10017
Telephone: 212/963-4437

For the most recent information on UN employment opportunities, see the UN website: http://www.un.org.

DISCUSSION QUESTIONS

1. In what ways did Woodrow Wilson's personal experiences lead him to favor collective security?

2. The balance of power and collective security are both systems for managing power in world politics. How are the two systems similar? How do they differ?

3. In what ways do you think the United Nations could be strengthened?

KEY TERMS

Annan, Kofi
collective security
Economic and Social Council
 (ECOSOC)
General Assembly
International Court of Justice
 (ICJ)
Permanent-Five (Perm-5)

Secretariat
Secretary-General
Security Council
self-determination
Trusteeship Council
World Health Organization
 (WHO)

RECOMMENDED PRINT, MULTIMEDIA, AND INTERNET SOURCES

Articles and Books

GEORGE, ALEXANDER L. and JULIETTE L. GEORGE. *Woodrow Wilson and Colonel House: A Personality Study.* New York: The John Day Company, 1956.

LINK, ARTHUR S. *Wilson the Diplomatist: A Look at His Major Foreign Policies.* Chicago: Quadrangle Books, 1957.

———. *Woodrow Wilson and the Progressive Era 1910–1917.* New York: Harper & Row, 1954.

MAYER, ARNO J. *Wilson vs. Lenin: Political Origins of the New Diplomacy 1917–1918.* New York: World Publishing Company, 1967.

MINGST, KAREN A. and MARGARET P. KARNS. *The United Nations in the Post-Cold War Era.* Boulder, CO: Westview Press, 1995.

YODER, AMOS. *The Evolution of the United Nations System.* 3rd ed. Washington, DC: Taylor and Francis, 1997.

Video

No Place to Hide: The UN's Peacekeeping Efforts. Princeton, NJ: Films for the Humanities and Sciences, 50 minutes. Hosted by long-time UN official Sir Brian Urquhart; a United Nations production.

Internet Sources

Academic Council on the United Nations System: http://www.yale.edu/acuns
United Nations internet sites include:
    UN home page: http://www.unic.org/
    UN system: http://www.unsystem.org
    Department of Public Information: http://www.un.org
    Food and Agricultural Organization (FAO): http://www.fao.org
    Peacekeeping operations: http://www.un.org/depts/dpko
    UNIFEM: UN Development Fund for Women: http://www.undp.org/unifem
    U.N. Development Program: http://www.undp.org
    World Health Organization (WHO): http://www.who.ch/
U.S. Mission at the UN: http://www.un.int/usa/

ENDNOTES

[1] JOHN LEWIS GADDIS, *We Now Know: Rethinking Cold War History* (New York: Oxford University Press, 1997), p. 216.

[2] ALEXANDER L. GEORGE and JULIETTE L. GEORGE, *Woodrow Wilson and Colonel House: A Personality Study* (New York: Dover Publications, 1964).

[3] ARTHUR S. LINK, *Wilson the Diplomatist: A Look at His Major Foreign Policies* (Chicago: Quadrangle Books, 1957), pp. 10–11.

[4] ARTHUR S. LINK, *Woodrow Wilson and the Progressive Era 1910–1917.* New York: Harper & Row, 1954.

[5] REINHARD R. DOERRIES, *Imperial Challenge: Ambassador Count Bernstorff and German–American Relations*, 1908–1917 (Chapel Hill, NC: University of North Carolina Press, 1989).

[6] JAMES F. DOUGHERTY and ROBERT L. PFALTZGRAFF, Jr., *Contending Theories of International Relations: A Comprehensive Survey*, fourth edition (New York: Longman, 1997), pp. 7–8.

[7] Quoted by INIS CLAUDE, Jr., *Power and International Relations* (New York: Random House, 1962), pp. 81–82.

[8] ARNO J. MAYER, *Wilson vs. Lenin: Political Origins of the New Diplomacy 1917–1918* (New York: World Publishing Company, 1967).

[9] THOMAS HOBBES, *Leviathan.* Edited by C.B. Macpherson. Baltimore, MD: Penguin Books, 1968.

[10] ALEXANDER L. GEORGE, "Domestic Constraints on Regime Change in U.S. Foreign Policy: The Need for Policy Legitimacy," in Ole R. Holsti, Randolph M. Siverson, and Alexander L. George, eds., *Change in the International System* (Boulder, CO: Westview, 1980), pp. 233–262.

[11] CRAIG TURNER, "UN Chief Offers Overhaul Plan to World Body," *Los Angeles Times*, July 17, 1997, p. A 3.

[12] Ibid., p. A 8.

[13] "U.S. Backs 5 New Permanent Posts on UN Security Council," *Los Angeles Times*, July 18, 1997, p. A 20.

7

The Rise and Demise of the Cold War

CRITEX:
What is worth risking your life for?

t HROUGHOUT history, people have fought wars. Prior to the Napoleonic Wars, these were fought primarily by mercenaries. Wars since the early 1800s have been fought by regular citizens, many of whom were drafted into their country's military. The human costs of wars rose dramatically in the twentieth century, as you learned in Chapter 5. Think about a fundamental question in this critical thinking exercise: What is worth risking your life for? Indicate several of the things that you thought of:

_____ Nothing; I am opposed to the use of force under any circumstances.

_____ I would be willing to risk my life defending the territory of my country.

_____ I would be willing to risk my life defending an ally of my country.

_____ I would be willing to risk my life while serving in a U.N. peace-keeping mission.

_____ I would be willing to risk my life helping to assist refugees who are homeless.

Discuss your responses with your professor and other members of your class.

INTRODUCTION TO THE COLD WAR

The United States by itself spent $5 trillion—that's $5,000,000,000,000—on national defense during the cold war and lost 100,000 of its citizens, the dearest resource of any country, to conflicts during the cold war. Given the expenditure of these resources, clearly American leaders thought that something significant was at stake. In retrospect, the post-World War II period can be divided into six periods:

1945–46: Post-World War II transition;

1947–62: Acute cold war;

1963–68: Limited détente;

1969–79: Détente;

1980–88: Renewed cold war;

1989–91: End of the cold war.

In this chapter, we will review these periods both historically and analytically.

THE ORIGINS OF THE COLD WAR
AND THE POST-WORLD WAR II TRANSITION

Throughout World War II, the leaders of the United States (President Franklin Roosevelt), Great Britain (Prime Minister Winston Churchill), and the Soviet Union (General Secretary Josef Stalin) met to discuss the strategy and conduct of the Allied war effort and various plans for the post-World War II era. Churchill and Stalin supported the reestablishment of the balance of power, and wanted particularly to delineate and recognize **spheres of influence.**

Roosevelt had served in Woodrow Wilson's administration and was a supporter of Wilson's collective security concept and therefore rejected Churchill and Stalin's attempt to reinstitute the balance-of-power system. But Roosevelt realized that the concept of collective security had been sullied by the events prior to the Second World War. Therefore he proposed what he called his "Great Design" for four powers—the United States, USSR, United Kingdom, and eventually China—to become the "Four Policemen" of the world.[1] These four powers would have a monopoly of military power and would settle international disputes among themselves. It was, in essence, based on the European balance-of-power Concert system of the early nineteenth century. For various reasons largely related to the lukewarm response of the public to Roosevelt's "Four Policemen" idea, the "Big Three" (the United States, USSR, and Great Britain) turned their attention to other possibilities for managing power in the post-World War II international system.

A reinvigorated collective security organization, the United Nations, was founded in San Francisco in April 1945. In contrast to the League of Nations, the United States, which had emerged from the war in 1945 as the single most powerful country in the world, was a member. As noted in Chapter 6, advocates of collective security thought that the Security Council of the United Nations would be able to define and unanimously oppose aggression in the international system. In the event of aggression, the attacked state was supposed to report the aggression to the Security Council, and it would take action against the aggressor. If unanimous agreement was not reached, then states could resort to regional organizations for support.

In February 1946, several events occurred that caused concern about the future of the international system. Josef Stalin, the dictatorial ruler of the USSR, delivered a speech in which he announced an ambitious five-year plan and indicated that his country would maintain its military at its wartime strength; in short, there would be no immediate return to a peacetime footing. Concerned, U.S. officials in Washington sought an explanation for Stalin's decision. The *chargé d'affaires* in Moscow, **George Kennan,** composed a 6,000-word telegram focusing on the sources of Soviet foreign policy. Kennan argued that Soviet leaders were essentially defensive and that the United States needed to buy time so that the Soviet system would eventually expire of its own contradictions.[2] This telegram, a version of which was later published anonymously in the influential journal *Foreign Affairs,* was immediately grasped by President Truman and his advisors because it provided a readily understandable explanation of the Soviet foreign policy. Several weeks after Kennan had sent his "long telegram" analyzing Soviet foreign-policy behavior, Winston Churchill, who had been voted out of office at the end of the war, visited Fulton, Missouri, and announced: "From Stettin in the Baltic to Trieste in the Adriatic, an iron curtain has descended across the continent...." He then asked rhetorically how the West should respond: "I am convinced that there is nothing they [Soviet leaders] admire so much as strength, and there is nothing for which they have less respect than weakness." With Stalin's, Kennan's and Churchill's statements on the record, the rhetorical foundation of the cold war was in place; only a spark was needed to ignite the fires of East-West conflict.

THE ACUTE COLD WAR, 1947–1962

In early 1947, Great Britain, exhausted from fighting two horrendously costly wars in the first half of the twentieth century, announced that it was going to discontinue its military assistance for Greece and Turkey. There were numerous reports that in both of these countries, communists were actively working to take control. In response to the British announcement, President Truman requested $400 million in aid from the U.S. Congress. Many members of Congress reflected the traditional American belief in isolationism: that the United States should go back to a "Fortress America" position and let the rest of the world deal with their own international problems. This isolationist position was particularly supported by Republican members of Congress. Secretary of State George Marshall went to the Congress to testify on behalf of the $400 million that President Truman had requested. According to Marshall's deputy, Dean Acheson, things were not going well, and it did not appear that Marshall was convincing many Congressmen. Acheson's turn to testify came and, as he recalled in his memoirs,

> No time was left for measured appraisal. In the past eighteen months, I said, Soviet pressure on the Straits, on Iran, and on northern Greece had brought the Balkans to the point where a highly possible Soviet break-through might open three continents to Soviet penetration. Like apples in a barrel infected by one rotten one, the corruption of Greece would infect Iran and all to the east. It would also carry infection to Africa through Asia Minor and Egypt, and to Europe through Italy and France....[3]

Acheson's analogy of rotten apples in a barrel—closely related to the predominant cold war analogy, the domino theory—convinced Congress to support U.S. aid for Greece and Turkey, and when President Truman went to Congress on March 12, 1947, his request for aid was approved over-whelmingly. The **Truman Doctrine,** also known as the **containment doctrine,** was born.

The Marshall Plan

Several years after World War II had ended, Europe was still in shambles from the destruction and devastation wrought by the war. The political, economic, industrial, commercial, and agricultural institutions of all of the European states—victors and vanquished alike—had been destroyed. President Truman and his advisors believed that unless the United States provided European democracy with help, communist movements would take over.

In June 1947, less than two months after President Truman had announced the policy of containment, Secretary of State George Marshall delivered the commencement address at Harvard University. This graduation speech was very different from the average "go out into the world and succeed" type of graduation address; in it Secretary Marshall invited the European states to submit a plan to the United States for the reconstruction of Europe. The United States did not limit participation in the program to any particular countries, and initially several Eastern European states—Poland and Czechoslovakia—indicated that they would like to participate. Stalin intervened and vetoed participation by any Eastern bloc country. The Western European governments submitted their plan to the United States, and in the ensuing years, the United States provided an estimated $13 billion in aid. This was in "1947 dollars"; if one were to calculate the value of this money today, it would be somewhere in the neighborhood of $150 billion!

The **Marshall Plan** stands as one of the great success stories of American foreign policy and international relations. The Western European countries were able to recover economically, politically, and socially, and remained noncommunist. This is one time that American altruism and self-interest merged in a single program. The governments of several of the countries that benefited from the Marshall Plan commemorated their appreciation with special scholarship programs: Great Britain established the Marshall Scholars Program for recently graduated American undergraduates and the German government established a fellowship program for American professors.

By the end of 1947, it was clear that the cooperation among the members of the "Grand Alliance" that had defeated the Axis powers was not going to continue, and the two most powerful states in the post-World

War II era—the United States and the Soviet Union—seemed to be on a collision course. Throughout the eighteenth, nineteenth, and twentieth centuries, the central part of Europe has been pivotal in world politics. Thus, Western leaders grew very concerned when Czechoslovakia's communist party took over the government.

To a great extent, the crucible of the cold war was Germany, and in particular, Berlin, which was located 110 miles (180 kilometers) inside of East Germany, the sector controlled by the Soviet Union. Because Berlin had been the capital of Nazi Germany, it was divided into four sectors among the victorious allies. The French, British, and American sectors were combined to form West Berlin. The agreement among the Allies called for unfettered access to Berlin via the freeway (in German *Autobahn*); however, on June 20, 1948, the Soviets cut off electrical power to West Berlin and then closed all road, rail, and barge traffic into the city. West Berlin had also received food products and petroleum from the Soviet sector, and these shipments were also stopped. By the end of June, a complete blockade of Berlin had been implemented.[4]

The Berlin Airlift

Broadly speaking, President Truman faced a spectrum of choices between two extremes: he could accept the Soviet actions and do nothing, or he could insist on exercising American access rights to West Berlin by ordering the U.S. Army to drive tanks through the Soviet barricades. Both of these options were unacceptable, but for different reasons. The first option smacked of appeasement, and the second option could have resulted in escalation to world war. After meeting with his advisers, Truman decided on a middle course: to resupply West Berlin with the basic necessities of life via air. For almost a year, West Berlin's lifeline was provided by flights from West Germany. The **Berlin airlift** record was set on Easter Sunday of 1949 when 1,398 flights transporting 12,941 tons of goods were made.[5] Eventually, the Soviets recognized that the West was not going to abandon West Berlin, and they discontinued the blockade.

The Founding of NATO

The western response to the takeover of Czechoslovakia and the Berlin blockade was to establish in 1949 a "collective self-defense" organization under Article 51 of the United Nations Charter. This new organization was called the **North Atlantic Treaty Organization,** also known by its acronym, **NATO.** It was founded principally to deter a military attack on Western Europe. The NATO treaty is called a "self-executing treaty" because it defines an attack on one member as equivalent to an attack against all the members. NATO was and remains one of the most important treaties for each of its members.

The year 1949 witnessed several other significant events. In August, the Soviet Union exploded its first atomic bomb, several years ahead of what American scientists had predicted. The following month, the Chinese communists under Chairman Mao Zedong successfully defeated their Nationalist opponents. With this, the communists ruled the world's largest state.

The Korean War

On June 25, 1950, North Korea attacked South Korea and overran its capital, Seoul, within 72 hours. In keeping with the provisions of collective security contained in the United Nations Charter, South Korea reported North Korea's aggression to the UN Security Council. The Soviet Union was boycotting Security Council meetings to protest the failure of the UN to replace the Republic of China (Taiwan) with the newly established People's Republic of China. Therefore, when the Security Council voted on a resolution on whether or not to assist South Korea, the resolution was approved; the **Korean War** had begun. Although 15 countries committed themselves to oppose the North Korean aggression, the majority of the military forces in South Korea were from South Korea and the United States. General Douglas MacArthur was put in charge of these forces, and he ordered a daring, amphibious assault behind North Korea's forces at Inchon. North Korean forces retreated to the north of the thirty-eighth parallel. UN forces continued their advance with the goal of uniting Korea. When UN forces approached the North Korean border with China in November 1950, 300 thousand Chinese soldiers counterattacked and drove UN forces to the south. Sporadic fighting continued, but the war became a stalemate. Only with the death of Stalin in March 1953 and the election of a new president, Dwight Eisenhower, in the United States was the stalemate broken and a ceasefire agreement reached. More than 3 million Koreans, an unknown number of Chinese, 54 thousand Americans and 15 thousand combatants from other UN member states died in the war.

The United States and its allies in the West viewed the Korean War as blatant aggression inspired by the Soviet Union and possibly the prelude to an invasion of Western Europe. Recent scholarship based on declassified documents in Russia and the United States has concluded that, while the North Korean attack on South Korea "was not Stalin's brainchild," nevertheless, "Stalin's calculations, as well as Kim's [Il Sung], were responsible for this tragedy."[6]

Throughout the 1950s and early 1960s, the United States and the Soviet Union continued to interact with one another throughout the world. Over time, certain patterns were evident in these interactions. In Figure 7.1, the elements of the **grand design and grand strategy** of American cold war policy are summarized. Grand design refers to the ends or long-term goals of a country, while grand strategy refers to the means for achieving those goals.

A central objective of U.S. cold war policy as indicated in the grand design that follows was to "stop the spread of communism while at the same

---

Grand Design:

● Accept the emergence of a bipolar structuring of the international system into two opposing hostile camps; maintain the stability and unity of the "free world" bloc.

● Stop the spread of communism but also avoid World War III.

Grand Strategy:

● Strive to maintain U.S. military superiority.

● Contain the spread of communism through deterrence of military aggression and through political, economic, and military measures to reduce the vulnerability of small, weak countries to internal or external subversion.

● Form a "free world" network of collective-security alliances led by the United States.

● Employ careful, presidentially controlled crisis management of confrontations and limited wars to prevent escalation to a world war.

● Avoid *de facto* as well as *de jure* recognition of Soviet postwar territorial acquisitions and Soviet sphere of influence in Eastern Europe.

Figure 7.1. The Grand Design and Grand Strategy of U.S. Cold War Policy
Source: Adapted from Alexander L. George, "The Role of Cognitive Beliefs in the Legitimation of a Long-Range Foreign Policy: The Case of F. D. Roosevelt's Plan for Post-War Cooperation with the Soviet Union." Paper presented to the conference on Approaches to Decision-Making, August 9–12, 1977, Oslo, Norway.

time avoiding World War III." This objective was tested most seriously in 1948 when the Soviets closed the ground access routes to Berlin. In 1961–1962, it would be tested again in Berlin and in Cuba. The crises over Berlin in 1948 and 1961 and Cuba in 1962 were the three most serious crises of the entire cold war because they threatened direct, military confrontations between the two most powerful states in the system at the time, the United States and the USSR.

In 1961, refugees were leaving East Germany in record numbers. The Soviet embassy in Berlin had calculated that during the 1950s, 1.2 million people had left the German Democratic Republic.[7] This immigration constituted a significant "brain drain"—many of those who left were the most educated. In addition, the stability of the East German currency was threatened. In response, Soviet and East German authorities began to erect temporary barriers between East and West Berlin to close off the escape route of oppressed East Germans to the west. Within several days, these temporary barriers were strengthened and the **Berlin Wall** became perhaps the most visible and recognizable symbol of the cold war.

The 1961 Berlin crisis heightened tensions between the two superpowers. Of great concern to the leaders of both countries was the military balance. In the 1960 election, John Kennedy charged that the Eisenhower-Nixon administration had allowed a "missile gap" to develop between the United States and the Soviet Union. At this time, there were two types of ballistic missiles: **Intercontinental ballistic missiles (ICBMs),** which had a range of 3,000 miles or more and were therefore capable of going from one continent to another, and **Intermediate** or **medium range ballistic missiles (IR/MRBM)** which had a range of 600 to 3,000 miles. In fact, there was a "missile gap": the United States had more ICBMs than the USSR and the USSR had more IR/MRBMs than the United States. No matter where the Soviet leaders deployed the missiles in their country, they could not reach the United States. Therefore, the Soviets tried to catch up to the United States in the summer of 1962 by attempting to secretly deploy nuclear weapons to Cuba where they would be able to reach most of the continental United States. When the American government obtained evidence of Soviet actions, the **Cuban missile crisis,** the most serious crisis of the cold war period, developed.[8] During a tense thirteen-day period, the Soviet and American leaders discussed, threatened, and cajoled one another. In the end, the United States publicly promised not to sponsor, either directly or indirectly, any invasions of Cuba and privately promised to remove American IRBMs from Turkey. For its part, the Soviets agreed to remove their nuclear weapons from Cuba. After the crisis

BOX 7.1   Supplementary Critex: To the Brink and Back

In October 1962, the United States and the Soviet Union came very close to going to war. The incident, dubbed the "Cuban Missile Crisis," was caused by an attempt by the Soviet Union to secretly send missiles armed with nuclear weapons and install them on the island of Cuba. If war had occurred, it could have ended civilization as we know it.

Throughout the first half of 1962, Soviet leader Nikita Khrushchev assured President Kennedy that his country was not and would not send missiles that could be used to attack the United States to Cuba. There were, however, an increasing number of indicators that Khrushchev was not telling the truth.

On October 15, 1962, an American U-2 spy plane took photographs of several Soviet missile bases in Cuba. The evidence was presented to President Kennedy, and he had his assistant for national security affairs, McGeorge Bundy, call together a group of men to advise him. This group was called the "Executive Committee" or "ExCom." Among the members were the following: Secretary of State Dean Rusk, Secretary of Defense Robert McNamara, Secretary of the Treasury Douglas Dillon, Director of the Central Intelligence Agency Robert McCone, the president's brother who was the Attorney General, Robert Kennedy, Presidential advisor Theodore Sorensen, and Joint Chiefs of Staff Chairman General Maxwell Taylor.

Looking back on the Cuban missile crisis, President Kennedy had said that the probability of direct Soviet-American conflict had been "between one out of three and even." In the words of Secretary of State Rusk, "We were eyeball to eyeball, and the other fellow just blinked."

While "going to the brink" may have made sense to President Kennedy, his advisors, and most Americans in 1962, younger Americans such as yourself often have a difficult time understanding the justification for nearly blowing up the world. In a word—or rather two—the United States and the Soviet Union almost went to war because of the "cold war." What was this? How did it start? How was it waged and what did it cost? Was it worth it?

After the disintegration of the USSR, a number of interesting histories of the Cuban missile crisis were published based on the accounts of actual participants. For one of the best, see Alexander Fursenko and Timothy Naftali, *One Hell of a Gamble* (New York: W.W. Norton, 1997).

was resolved, President Kennedy estimated that the chances of direct U.S.-Soviet conflict had been "between one out of three and even."[9] You need not have taken probability and statistics to know that the latter probability is equivalent to the flip of a coin: heads we have nuclear war, tails we don't. Fortunately the coin came up tails.

THE LIMITED DÉTENTE ERA, 1963–68

It was as if Kennedy and Khrushchev had gone to the precipice and peered over the edge into the abyss that would have been nuclear war. Neither leader liked what he saw, and in the aftermath of the Cuban missile crisis, the two superpowers negotiated several agreements to "lessen tensions," a process which in the language of classical diplomacy was called **détente.** The first of the agreements was the **Hot-Line Agreement** calling for a cable link between Washington and Moscow in order to provide direct, secure, rapid communications between the two capitals. The second agreement was negotiated by American, Soviet, and British diplomats in a matter of weeks. The **Limited Nuclear Test Ban Treaty (LTBT)** prohibited nuclear tests from being conducted in the atmosphere. Prior to this agreement, nuclear tests were conducted in the atmosphere, releasing substantial radioactive material that then entered the human food chain through mothers' or cows' milk. If nothing else, the LTBT was a significant "clean air act."

Following the conclusion of these two agreements, it appeared that the United States and the Soviet Union had begun a new relationship, marked by both competition and cooperation. In November 1963, President Kennedy was assassinated, and in October 1964, Khrushchev was removed from office. Also in that year, the United States became more involved in the conflict in Vietnam. In February 1965, the United States began bombing North Vietnam's capital city, Hanoi, for the first time, and this began the escalation of conflict for the United States. Ultimately, the United States would have 548 thousand military personnel in Vietnam. In 1968, an average of 278 Americans per week were being killed in the war, and draft calls for males were 30 thousand per month. As the cost of the war rose, the American public became increasingly alarmed and critical about U.S. involvement. The escalating American commitment to the defense of South Vietnam and the support of North Vietnam by the USSR meant that the détente that appeared so promising in 1963 did not develop beyond the two agreements described above.

THE DÉTENTE ERA, 1969–1979

When President Richard Nixon and his advisor for national security affairs, Dr. Henry Kissinger, entered office in January 1969, they faced a nation more divided than at any time in U.S. history since the Civil War. They wanted to disengage the United States from the **Vietnam War,** but were not willing to do so at the cost of American "credibility." They believed if the United States, as Nixon put it, "bugged out" of Vietnam, then neither American allies or potential enemies would believe American threats or promises in international affairs. Consequently, Nixon and Kissinger devised a new, complex grand design and grand strategy for the United States.

The Nixon-Kissinger Grand Design and Grand Strategy

Nixon and Kissinger recognized that the People's Republic of China was emerging as one of the world's great powers. Consequently, they sought to open a dialogue with the Chinese government. The initial, official contacts between Chinese and Americans were made not by diplomats but by athletes. The first Americans to visit China were ping pong players, who broke the ice in the long, chilly relationship between the United States and the People's Republic of China. Once the athletes thawed the Sino-American deep freeze, the statesmen became involved. In July 1971, Henry Kissinger made a secret visit to China via Pakistan in order to lay the groundwork for a presidential visit, and in February 1972, Nixon visited mainland China and signed the Shanghai Communiqué which called for the eventual normalization of Sino-American relations.

Nixon's visit to China caused great concern in the Soviet Union because Soviet leaders feared that the normalization of Sino-American relations would place them at a diplomatic disadvantage. Consequently, the Soviets invited Nixon to visit the USSR, which he did in May 1972. During this visit called the Moscow Summit, American and Soviet officials signed more than 12 different agreements calling for cooperation in various endeavors such as housing, space exploration, and trade. Perhaps most important, President Nixon and Leonid Brezhnev signed two agreements to limit their offensive and defensive, strategic nuclear weapons. The negotiations that resulted in these agreements were called the **Strategic Arms Limitation Talks** also known by the acronym "**SALT.**"

Nixon's visits to China and the USSR were designed to encourage the Chinese and Soviet governments to support a moderate international system and to assist the United States in extricating itself from its painful foreign-policy involvement in Vietnam. In fact, Nixon and Kissinger would not even begin the SALT negotiations without an assurance from Soviet leaders that they would help the United States withdraw from Vietnam.

To be sure, Nixon and Kissinger remained committed to stopping the spread of communism, but in their grand design and grand strategy for American foreign policy they had a more complex, differentiated view of communism and the U.S. policy designed to meet it. Figure 7.2 summarizes the principal elements of this policy.

Grand Design:

- Accept the emergence of a tripolar configuration of power in the security issue area and a multipolar international economic system.

- Encourage the development of a moderate international system supported by the United States, USSR, and People's Republic of China.

- Stop the spread of communism to areas of the world in the traditional Western sphere of influence, but avoid direct military confrontations with the USSR.

Grand Strategy:

- Accept Soviet achievement of nuclear parity; strive for the limitation of strategic arms (SALT).

- Contain the spread of communism through deterrence of military aggression, the use of positive incentives, mixed strategies employing positive and negative sanctions, and covert operations.

- Maintain firm collective-security commitments with NATO and Japan; other alliance commitments should be more flexible.

- Employ careful, presidentially controlled management of crises and limited wars to prevent escalation; communicate and consult with other states during crises.

- Encourage ties between the United States and USSR through the conclusion of a number of cooperative projects in the economic, scientific, cultural, and technological areas.

- Maintain U.S. foreign-policy commitments despite reduced public and congressional support.

Figure 7.2. The Grand Design and Grand Strategy of U.S. Détente Policy
Source: Adapted from Dan Caldwell, *American-Soviet Relations: From 1947 to the Nixon-Kissinger Grand Design* (Westport, CT: Greenwood Press, 1981).

During the acute cold war, American leaders developed a simple calculus for Americans to understand international relations: Communist states were bad and anticommunist states were good. The only information that Americans needed in order to determine whether a state was good or bad was whether it was communist or anticommunist. Of course, such a simplistic key to international relations was subject to misinterpretation. By the late 1950s, several different varieties of communism existed (e.g., Soviet, Chinese, and several national variants such as Yugoslavian and Vietnamese). Within the anticommunist, "Free World" bloc were some rather antidemocratic, brutal governments such as Iran, which contained some secret-police organizations (e.g., SAVAK) similar to those in some communist countries.

Nixon and Kissinger's approach was far more difficult for Americans to understand. In essence, Nixon and Kissinger noted that the United States had to deal with communist states and that to do so was not wrongheaded or evil. But the cold-war belief system had a powerful pull for many Americans. Also, the Nixon-Kissinger approach was more complicated and harder to understand: communist countries such as the People's Republic of China or the Soviet Union could be the friend or enemy of the United States—depending upon the circumstance. For the year and a half following the May 1972 Moscow Summit meeting, the United States and the Soviet Union seemed to have entered a new era of relations; journalists and academics wrote about "the end of the cold war" and "a new era of peace."

The Yom Kippur War

In early October 1973, Egypt and Syria attacked their sworn enemy, Israel, on the holiest day of the Jewish calendar, Yom Kippur. The resulting war placed great demands on the military inventories of all of the combatants, and very soon the Arab countries' principal ally, the USSR, was resupplying them with military materiél, and the United States sent military equipment to its ally, Israel. Paraphrasing the German strategist Karl von Clausewitz, one journalist asked if détente was not simply the "cold war carried on by other means."[10] During this war, called the **October** or **Yom Kippur War,** the Arab members of the Organization of Petroleum Exporting Countries (OPEC) announced that they would not export oil to any country supporting Israel. This embargo had three main results. First, decreased supply and increased demand drove the price of oil from $3.00 per barrel in September 1973 to $12.00 per barrel by January 1974, a 400 percent increase. Second, as a result of oil-price increases, oil-exporting countries became very wealthy. And third, a new force in world politics emerged.

While there was some question about the extent to which the Soviet Union encouraged their Arab allies to attack Israel, there was no doubt that the USSR was active in various areas of the world, including the Horn of Africa and southern Africa. Many Americans, particularly conservatives, were concerned by Soviet activities throughout the world. To some, it appeared as if Nixon and Kissinger had made the same error that British Prime Minister Neville Chamberlain had made a generation earlier: appeasement. Criticism was so strong of the Nixon-Kissinger détente policies that President Gerald Ford, who had succeeded Nixon following his resignation in August 1974, banned the use of the word "détente" by members of his administration. But this semantic change was not enough, and a hitherto little known, southern governor, Jimmy Carter, was elected president in 1976.

President Jimmy Carter: From Election to Defeat

President Carter entered office with an ambitious agenda for both domestic and foreign policy. He was the first president to publicly declare that nuclear **disarmament,** as opposed to **arms control,** would be his objective as president.[11] Carter continued the SALT negotiations, but these negotiations had become more difficult because of the increasingly sophisticated technology of the weapons. In a sense, the negotiators were racing the weapons designers. The SALT I agreements took two and a half years to negotiate; the SALT II Treaty took seven-and-a-half years and was signed in June 1979. The U.S. Senate held hearings on the treaty during the summer. In August, American intelligence agencies "discovered" a Soviet combat brigade in Cuba, delaying consideration of the treaty. In November, Iranian militants took over the U.S. embassy in Teheran and took 52 Americans hostage. Even though these events were only tangentially related to the SALT II Treaty, they raised questions in the minds of the public about the foreign policy competence of the Carter administration.

On Christmas eve of 1979, the Soviet Union, concerned about the spread of Islamic fundamentalism, invaded, occupied, and installed a puppet leader in Afghanistan. Shaken by this blatant aggression, President Carter sent Brezhnev "the sharpest message" of his presidency telling him that the invasion of Afghanistan was "a clear threat to the peace" and "could mark a fundamental and long-lasting turning point in our relations."[12] The Soviet invasion had two immediate effects: (1) it caused Carter to withdraw the SALT II Treaty from Senate consideration; and (2) it ended the decade-long attempt to moderate the competition of the cold war.

THE "NEW" COLD WAR, 1979–1991

President Carter's 1980 State of the Union address reflected the mood of his administration and, more broadly, the rest of the country; the president noted that the '80s "have been born in turmoil, strife, and change." Carter backed up his rhetoric with significant increases in the defense budget and military programs. But his conversion to cold warrior was too late. Ronald Reagan, the former governor of California and one of the most conservative politicians of the late twentieth century, had almost achieved the impossible in 1976; he had come close to taking the Republican nomination away from the incumbent president, Gerald Ford. In 1980, many of the things that Reagan had spoken of for years had come to pass, and his conservative, militant rhetoric resonated with the American people. At the end of the campaign, the incumbent president, Jimmy Carter, won only 49 electoral votes compared to Reagan's 489.

President Ronald Reagan and the Cold War

In his first press conference as president, Ronald Reagan sounded the alarm and warned that the Soviets "reserved unto themselves the right to lie, cheat, commit any crime." Building on the military increases that President Carter had begun, Reagan called for even greater increases, which the Congress approved. In March 1983, Reagan called for the U.S. research community to turn its attention to develop a defense against Soviet missile attack. The president called this the "**Strategic Defense Initiative**" **(SDI);** his critics referred to it as "**Star Wars.**" From the memoirs of former Soviet decision makers and declassified Soviet documents, we now know that Soviet leaders thought that the United States was preparing to attack the USSR preemptively and thought that SDI was simply one step toward preparing for such an attack. The stability of the new cold war was even more fragile than people at the time thought.

    In March 1985, the leader of the communist party of the Soviet Union, Konstantin Chernenko, died. For a decade, the Soviet Union had been ruled by a series of older, sick men: Leonid Brezhnev, Yuri Andropov, and Chernenko. With the passing of Chernenko, the ruling body of the party, the Politburo, decided to hand the mantle of leadership to its youngest member, Mikhail Gorbachev. Assuming power at a time of economic, political, and military crisis, Gorbachev can be compared to a physician who is confronted with a patient made sick by a serious infection. Clearly, in 1985, the Soviet body politic was very sick, and "Dr." Gorbachev was confronted with two choices: he could treat the symptoms of the patient ("Go home, drink lots of fluid, take some aspirin, and get lots of rest"). This is the strategy that Brezhnev and his successors had chosen, and the "patient" showed no signs of recovering. Gorbachev opted for the more radical strategy: to amputate the infected limb in hopes that such action would lead to full recovery. Gorbachev announced and implemented four new policies: (1) *glasnost*, which translated means "openness," (2) *perestroika*, which means restructuring, (3) democratization, and (4) "new thinking" in foreign policy. In keeping with the latter policy, Gorbachev announced a unilateral reduction of 500,000 Soviet troops, the Soviet withdrawal from Afghanistan, and he then began meeting with his American nemesis, Ronald Reagan. Much to the surprise of both Reagan and Gorbachev, the two men got along well and met more times than any of their predecessors. And over the course of several years, the cold war came to an end during their administrations.

WHY DID THE COLD WAR END?

Like the Holy Roman Empire or ultra-nationalist Russian politician Vladimir Zhironovsky's Liberal Democratic Party, the "cold war" is a misnomer; at times it was very "hot." Yet, it was not *a* war as traditionally understood. The cold war was enormously costly for its participants; the United States lost 100 thousand of its citizens and spent $5 trillion on defense during the four-and-a-half decades of the cold war. Many times as many Koreans and Vietnamese died in the wars fought in their countries. When the cold war came to an end in the late 1989–1991 period, its end was unanticipated, unpredicted, and unplanned for by statesmen and analysts alike. What were the factors that caused the end of the cold war?

First, many people understand history as a study of the "great men" who have acted forcefully. In the accounts published to date, some historians have emphasized the role, albeit unintentional, that Mikhail Gorbachev played in the demise of communism, the disintegration of the USSR, and the end of the cold war. Others have emphasized that Ronald Reagan, and particularly his SDI program, played a role in the cold war endgame.

Second, some argue that changes in Eastern Europe forged the way for changes in the Soviet Union. A few political scientists had the acumen to recognize the significance of the Polish workers' revolt in the early 1980s. The union, Solidarity, was, to borrow from Abraham Lincoln, a true proletariat creation by the workers and for the workers. Karl Marx would

So you're interested in working for the U.S. Government? Most people working in international affairs in Washington work for agencies other than the State Department. Unfortunately, there is no single recruiting device such as the Foreign Service exam for these organizations. The biggest employers are the Defense Department (both military and civilian) and the intelligence organizations, particularly the Central Intelligence Agency and the National Security Agency. Civilians hired by the Defense Department tend to be people with particular specialties; advanced degrees are usually required. Given the informal hiring process, actual job experience, which in practice means internships, is very important.

Intelligence careers can be divided into analysts (people who work with secret material trying to decide its significance) and clandestine operatives or spies. Anyone interested in such positions should look at the book *Careers in Secret Intelligence* by David Atlee Phillips, a former C.I.A. officer. Tim Weiner's article, "Spies Wanted," *The New York Times Magazine,* January 24, 1999, is also useful. The Central Intelligence Agency and the National Security Agency both hire junior-level career people on the basis of exams; you should contact each agency separately to see what their current needs and procedures are. They also hire a lot of people with particular skills for analysis, usually with advanced degrees. They seem to be particularly interested in exotic languages, geographic area specializations, economics, political science, international relations, mathematics, computer science, engineering, and physical science. Again internships are particularly useful here. For further information, write: CIA Employment Center, P. O. Box 12727, Arlington, VA 22209-8727. There is also a great deal of information about the CIA at http://www.odci.gov.cia

Many "domestic" executive agencies have international activities or offices; these are often small, but sometimes they offer interesting opportunities. The Department of Commerce, for example, is concerned with foreign trade; the Department of Agriculture with farm exports; and the Department of Justice with international legal issues. Smaller organizations include the Export-Import Bank and the Office of the Special Trade Representative.

The number of people on Congressional staffs concerned with international affairs is substantial. There is no single recruiting process for such jobs; people are selected on the basis of contacts, past experience, and educational qualifications, roughly in that order. Internships are crucial for anyone interested in these sorts of positions. Jobs on Capitol Hill are most often filled by being at the right place at the right time, and unpaid internships will sometimes result in full-time job offers.

have been pleased with the membership of Solidarity; the only problem is that it was founded to protest the policies of a communist government, which supposedly represented the interests of the "people." But over time, these interests were either forgotten or intentionally ignored, and the interests of the privileged *elite* of the communist party took precedence over those of the vast majority of the Polish people. Once Solidarity succeeded, the days of communist control in other countries were numbered.

Third, as argued in the best-selling book, *The Rise and Fall of Great Powers,* by Yale historian Paul Kennedy, great powers decline when they overextend their international commitments.[13] It is this process of "imperial overstretch," Kennedy avers, that leads to decline. When applied to the cold war, Kennedy's thesis seems to be relevant to the decline of the USSR; it is less applicable to the United States.

Fourth, economists and political scientists, most notably Charles Kindleberger and Kenneth Waltz, have argued that international peace and stability result from the presence of a dominant (or "hegemonic") power.[14] According to Waltz's theory of **structural realism,** as the dominance of the United States became evident to the USSR, it decided to opt out of the cold-war competition, and this is what caused the end of the cold war.

Fifth, some argue that the end of the cold war resulted from the fusion of the old and new: namely, the diffusion of the old, but seductive, ideas of freedom, individual liberty, and democracy. These ideas were propagated by new communications technology. For example, East Germans watching West German television were told that the advertisements were simply propaganda, but East Germans reached the obvious conclusion—there were many more and higher-quality goods in the West than in the East. In this view, it was the ideas of the Enlightenment, liberalism, and western democratic capitalism that ultimately won the cold war.

A NEW WORLD ORDER?

Following the Gulf War in early 1991 and the disintegration of the Soviet Union at the end of 1991, President Bush often spoke of a "new world order." He did not, however, clarify the parameters of what he had in mind. A series of crises characterized this new international system, and there was no central structure for dealing with these crises. Thus, the United States, as the world's last remaining superpower, dealt with some of these (Somalia, Rwanda, Haiti); the United Nations dealt with others; NATO dealt with some (Kosovo); and ad hoc collections of states dealt with others, most notably Bosnia. By the end of the 1990s, questions remained: What would be the characteristics of the future international system, and how would politics be conducted within this system?

While the classical diplomatic system was composed of multiple great powers (see Chapter 3), the cold war was dominated by only two powers: the United States and the USSR. With the implosion of the Soviet Union, only one superpower remained.

DISCUSSION QUESTIONS

1. What were the principal causes of the cold war? Could American or Soviet leaders have done anything differently in order to avoid the cold war?

2. During the Berlin crises of 1948 and 1961 and the Cuban missile crisis of 1962, there was a very real possibility of direct, military conflict between the United States and the Soviet Union. Was the threat of war justified to force the USSR to remove its missiles from Cuba?

3. What was the turning point in the cold war, and which level of analysis (individual, state, international) best explains this?

KEY TERMS

arms control	Limited Nuclear Test Ban Treaty
Berlin crises of 1948 and 1961	(LTBT)
Berlin Wall	Marshall Plan
containment	North Atlantic Treaty
Cuban missile crisis	Organization (NATO)
détente	October (or Yom Kippur) War
disarmament	spheres of influence
grand design and grand strategy	Strategic Arms Limitation Talks
Hot-Line (Agreement)	(SALT)
Intercontinental ballistic missiles	Strategic Defense Initiative (SDI)
(ICBM)	(also called Star Wars)
Intermediate or medium range	structural realism
ballistic missiles (IR/MRBM)	Truman Doctrine
Kennan, George	Vietnam War
Korean War	

KEY DATES

February 1946	Stalin's speech; Kennan's "long telegram"
March 1946	Churchill's "iron curtain" speech
March 1947	Truman (or containment) Doctrine announced

June 1947	Marshall Plan for the recovery of Europe announced
June 1948	The first Berlin crisis; *Autobahn* blocked and airlift instituted
April 1949	North Atlantic Treaty Organization (NATO) founded
August 1949	USSR explodes its first atomic bomb
October 1949	People's Republic of China founded
June 1950	Korean War begins with North Korean attack on South Korea
November 1952	First hydrogen (H-bomb) exploded by United States
March 1953	Stalin died
August 1953	First Soviet H-bomb test
1954	Vietnamese communists defeat French forces at Dien Bien Phu
October 1956	Hungarian Revolution; USSR intervenes
August 1957	USSR launches first intercontinental ballistic missile (ICBM)
October 1957	USSR launches first earth-orbiting satellite (Sputnik)
January 1959	Fidel Castro takes over Cuban government
April 1961	Failure of the Bay of Pigs invasion
August 1961	Second Berlin crisis; Berlin Wall is built
October 1962	Cuban missile crisis
1963	Hot-Line Agreement and Limited Test Ban Treaty are signed
February 1965	United States begins bombing campaign against North Vietnam
June 1967	Arab-Israeli "Six Day" War
July 1968	Nuclear Non-Proliferation Treaty (NPT) signed
August 1968	USSR invades Czechoslovakia
February 1972	Nixon visits the People's Republic of China
May 1972	Nixon visits Moscow and signs the SALT I and other agreements
October 1973	Arab-Israeli Yom Kippur War
April 1975	North Vietnam defeats South Vietnam
June 1979	Carter and Brezhnev sign SALT II Treaty
November 1979	Iranian militants take over U.S. embassy in Tehran with 52 American hostages
December 1979	USSR invades Afghanistan
1980–1988	Iran-Iraq War with more than 1 million casualties

March 1983	Reagan announces the "Strategic Defense Initiative" (SDI)
March 1985	Gorbachev becomes leader of the USSR
December 1987	Reagan and Gorbachev sign the Intermediate Nuclear Forces (INF) Treaty
November 1989	Berlin Wall falls
August 1990	Iraq attacks and occupies Kuwait
January 1991	Coalition of 32 states attacks Iraq and forces it to withdraw from Kuwait
July 1991	START I Treaty signed
December 1991	USSR disintegrates and ceases to exist
1993	START II Treaty signed
December 1997	120 states sign the Land-Mine Treaty

RECOMMENDED PRINT, MULTIMEDIA, AND INTERNET SOURCES

References

Because this chapter focuses on contemporary world politics, there are a number of interesting memoirs by the leaders who participated in the decisions described in this chapter. Therefore, the first section lists some of the most interesting of these.

ACHESON, DEAN. *Present at the Creation: My Years at the State Department.* New York: W.W. Norton, 1969.

BAKER, JAMES A., III. *The Politics of Diplomacy: Revolution, War and Peace, 1989–1992.* New York: G. P. Putnam's Sons, 1995.

BRZEZINSKI, ZBIGNIEW. *Power and Principle: Memoirs of the National Security Adviser, 1977–1981.* New York: Farrar, Straus, Giroux, 1983.

CARTER, JIMMY. *Keeping Faith: Memoirs of a President.* New York: Bantam Books, 1982.

GORBACHEV, MIKHAIL. *Memoirs.* New York: Doubleday, 1995.

KISSINGER, HENRY A. *White House Years.* Boston: Little, Brown, 1979.

———. *Years of Upheaval.* Boston: Little, Brown, 1982.

———. *Years of Renewal.* New York: Simon & Schuster, 1999.

KHRUSHCHEV, NIKITA. *Khrushchev Remembers.* Boston: Little, Brown, 1970.

———. *Khrushchev Remembers: The Last Testament.* Boston: Little, Brown, 1974.

———. *Khrushchev Remembers: The Glasnost Tapes.* Boston: Little, Brown, 1990.

NIXON, RICHARD M. *RN: The Memoirs of Richard Nixon.* New York: Grosset and Dunlap, 1978.

REAGAN, RONALD. *An American Life.* New York: Simon & Schuster, 1990.

SHULTZ, GEORGE P. *Turmoil and Triumph: My Years as Secretary of State.* New York: Charles Scribner's Sons, 1993.

VANCE, CYRUS. *Hard Choices: Critical Years in America's Foreign Policy.* New York: Simon & Schuster, 1983.

Secondary Sources:

ALLISON, GRAHAM T. and PHILIP ZELIKOW. *Essence of Decision: Explaining the Cuban Missile Crisis*, 2nd ed. New York: Longman, 1999.

CALDWELL, DAN. *American-Soviet Relations: From 1947 to the Nixon-Kissinger Grand Design.* Westport, CT: Greenwood Press, 1981.

FURSENKO, ALEKSANDR and TIMOTHY NAFTALI. *"One Hell of a Gamble": Khrushchev, Castro, and Kennedy, 1958–1964.* New York: W.W. Norton, 1997.

GADDIS, JOHN LEWIS. *The United States and the Origins of the Cold War.* New York: Columbia University Press, 1972.

———. *Strategies of Containment: A Critical Appraisal of Postwar American National Security Policy.* New York: Oxford University Press, 1982.

———. *We Now Know: Rethinking Cold War History.* New York: Oxford University Press, 1997.

GARTHOFF, RAYMOND. *Détente and Confrontation: American-Soviet Relations from Nixon to Reagan.* Washington, DC: The Brookings Institution, 1985.

———. *The Great Transition: American–Soviet Relations and the End at the Cold War.* Washinton, DC: The Brookings Institution, 1994.

MURPHY, DAVID E., SERGEI A. KONDRASHEV, and GEORGE BAILEY. *Battleground Berlin: CIA vs. KGB in the Cold War.* New Haven: Yale University Press, 1997.

TALBOTT, STROBE and MICHAEL BESCHLOSS. *At the Highest Levels: The Inside Story of the End of the Cold War.* Boston: Little, Brown, 1993.

ZELIKOW, PHILIP and CONDOLEEZZA RICE. *Germany Unified and Europe Transformed: A Study in Statecraft.* Cambridge, MA: Harvard University Press, 1995.

ZUBOK, VLADISLAV and CONSTANTINE PLESHAKOV. *Inside the Kremlin's Cold War: From Stalin to Khrushchev.* Cambridge, MA: Harvard University Press, 1996.

CD-ROM

Seven Days in August: The Cold War's Defining Moment. An interactive CD-Rom focusing on the 1961 Berlin Crisis, produced by Time Warner.

Video

The Cold War, an excellent, twenty-four part series on the entire cold war produced by CNN in 1998. Released by Warner Home Video.

Topaz: A 1969 Alfred Hitchcock-produced movie based on Leon Uris's best-selling book about the Cuban missile crisis. (The laser disc video version has two alternative endings for the movie.)

Missiles of October, a play produced by ABC.

Internet

CNN website to accompany above video series: CNN.com/ColdWar
Cuban missile crisis websites:
    http://library.advanced.org/11046
    http://hyperion.advanced.org/11046/
    http://lcweb.loc.gov/exhibits/archives/colc.html
National Security Archive: http://www.seas.gwu.edu/nsarchive
North Atlantic Treaty Organization (NATO): http://www.nato.int
U.S. Department of State, Foreign Relations Series:
    www.state.gov/www/about_state/history
U.S. Library of Congress (documents and data on U.S.–USSR relations):
    http://lcweb.loc.gov/exhibits/archives.intn.html
World Governments Archive, Declassified Documents Reference System-US:
    www.psmedia.com/ddrs.htm

ENDNOTES

[1] ALEXANDER L. GEORGE, "Domestic Constraints on Regime Change in U.S. Foreign Policy," in Ole R. Holsti, Randolph M. Siverson, and Alexander L. George, eds., *Change in the International System* (Boulder, CO: Westview, 1980).

[2] "X" [George Kennan], "The Sources of Soviet Conduct," *Foreign Affairs* (July 1947).

[3] DEAN ACHESON, *Present at the Creation: My Years in the State Department* (New York: W.W. Norton, 1969), p. 293.

[4] See the fascinating history based on recently declassified documents and coauthored by former CIA and KGB officers: David E. Murphy, Sergei A. Kondrashev, and George Bailey, *Battleground Berlin: CIA vs. KGB in the Cold War* (New Haven, CT: Yale University Press, 1997).

[5] Ibid., p. 63.

[6] VLADISLAV ZUBOK and CONSTANTINE PLESHAKOV, *Inside the Kremlin's Cold War: From Stalin to Khrushchev* (Cambridge, MA: Harvard University Press, 1996), pp. 54–55.

[7] ZUBOK and PLESHAKOV, pp. 248–249.

[8] For a fascinating account of the Cuban missile crisis, see Graham T. Allison and Philip Zelikow, *Essence of Decision: Explaining the Cuban Missile Crisis,* 2nd ed. (New York: Longman, 1999).

[9] JOHN F. KENNEDY quoted in Robert F. Kennedy, *Thirteen Days: A Memoir of the Cuban Missile Crisis* (New York: W. W. Norton, 1969).

[10] THEODORE DRAPER, "From 1967 to 1973: The Arab-Israeli Wars," *Commentary* (December 1973).

[11] DAN CALDWELL, *The Dynamics of Domestic Politics and Arms Control: The SALT II Treaty Ratification Debate* (Columbia, SC: University of South Carolina Press, 1991).

[12] HAROLD H. SAUNDERS, "Diplomacy and Pressure, November 1979–May 1980," in Warren Christopher, ed. , *Americans Hostage in Iran: The Conduct of a Crisis* (New Haven, CT: Yale University Press, 1985), pp. 90–91.

[13] PAUL KENNEDY, *The Rise and Fall of Great Powers: Economic Change and Military Conflict from 1500 to 2000* (New York: Random House, 1987).

[14] KENNETH WALTZ, *Theory of International Politics* (Reading, MA: Addison-Wesley, 1979).

What Are the Significant Issues of World Politics?

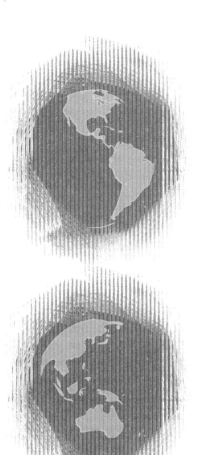

PART III

War, Peace, and International Security

CRITEX:
The Doomsday Clock: How Many Minutes to Midnight?

A T THE END of World War II, a number of the scientists who had been involved with the development of nuclear weapons in the **"Manhattan Project"** wanted to do what they could to prevent the further use of nuclear weapons. As a result, they founded a journal called *The Bulletin of the Atomic Scientists.*

From its founding in 1947 to the present, the editors of *The Bulletin* have maintained a "clock" to indicate how close the world is to "midnight," i.e., blowing up the world. According to Dr. Eugene Rabinowitch, one of the founders of the journal, "*The Bulletin*'s clock is not a gauge to register the ups and downs of the international power struggle; it is intended to reflect basic changes in the level of continuous danger in which mankind lives in the nuclear age, and

143

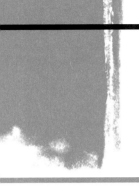

will continue living, until society adjusts its basic attitudes and institutions to the challenge of science."

Figure 8.1 summarizes the time set by the editors of *The Bulletin* and the events that caused them to set the clock ahead or back.

Based on the world situation when you read this, at what time do you think the clock should be set? Why?

INTRODUCTION

The twentieth century may well be remembered by future generations as the "century of total war"; indeed, the combined costs of World Wars I and II in human lives are staggering: more than 74 million people died in the two global conflagrations. Ironically, it was in the radioactive ashes of Hiroshima and Nagasaki that the causes of the "long peace" of the last half of the twentieth century were to be found. Nuclear weapons made the hitherto high costs of war almost incomprehensible. But the "self-deterrent" aspects of nuclear weapons applied only to those states with nuclear weapons; the use of military force and even war remained a tool of statecraft for almost all of the members of the international system.

THE USE OF MILITARY FORCE

War of Attrition

States have used military force in four different ways throughout history. First, states have employed military force in order to achieve victory through attrition—that is, by simply wearing out one's opponent. The best example of **war of attrition** was World War I. Of course, the danger of using this strategy is that one's own forces, as well as one's opponents, will be worn out by the war. This was what occurred in the trenches of the Western Front during World War I, and those who had fought in the war remembered and called attention to the barbarity of war. Erich Maria Remarque's novel, *All Quiet on the Western Front,* was typical of the realistic, rather than romantic, portrayal of war. In one scene, Remarque wrote:

> Bertrick has a chest wound. After a while a fragment smashes away his chin, and the same fragment has sufficient force to tear open Leer's hip. Leer groans as he supports himself on his arm, he bleeds quickly, no one can help him. Like an emptying tube, after a couple of minutes he collapses. What use is it to him now that he was such a good mathematician at school.[1]

1947

Seven minutes to midnight

The clock first appears on the Bulletin cover as a symbol of nuclear danger.

1949

Three minutes to midnight

The Soviet Union explodes its first atomic bomb.

1953

Two minutes to midnight

The United States and the Soviet Union develop hydrogen bombs.

1960

Seven minutes to midnight

The cold war begins to thaw.

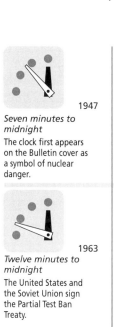

1963

Twelve minutes to midnight

The United States and the Soviet Union sign the Partial Test Ban Treaty.

1968

Seven minutes to midnight

The nuclear weapons "club" now has five members: France, China, Britain, the United States, and the Soviet Union.

1969

Ten minutes to midnight

Ratification of the Nuclear Non-Proliferation Treaty.

1972

Twelve minutes to midnight

Strategic Arms Limitation Talks (SALT) lead to the first nuclear arms control agreement between the United States and Soviet Union.

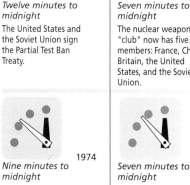

1974

Nine minutes to midnight

SALT at an impasse; India joins the nuclear club.

1980

Seven minutes to midnight

Deadlock in US–Soviet arms talks continues; nationalistic wars and terrorist acts increase; the gulf between rich and poor states grows.

1981

Four minutes to midnight

Presidential Directive 59 asserts that nuclear war is feasible; the superpowers develop weapons for war-fighting.

1984

Three minutes to midnight

The arms race intensifies; arms control negotiations are suspended.

1988

Six minutes to midnight

The United States and the Soviet Union sign a treaty to eliminate intermediate-range nuclear forces (INF); super-power relations improve; more nations actively oppose nuclear weapons.

1990

Ten minutes to midnight

The clock, redesigned in 1989, reflects democratic movements in Eastern Europe, which shatter the myth of monolithic communism; the Cold War ends.

1991

Seventeen minutes to midnight

The United States and the Soviet Union sign the long-stalled Strategic Arms Reduction Treaty (START) and announce further unilateral cuts in tactical and strategic nuclear weapons.

1995

Fourteen minutes to midnight

Further arms reductions are stalled while global military spending continues at Cold War levels. Greater risks of nuclear "leakage" from poorly guarded former Soviet facilities.

Figure 8.1. The "Clock" of *The Bulletin of the Atomic Scientists*
Source: The Bulletin of the Atomic Scientists.

Blitzkrieg

Modern technology has created several revolutions of military affairs. The first of these revolutions was brought on by the steamship, the second, by the machine gun, the third, by aircraft. It is possible that we are witnessing a fourth revolution today in the form of digital information.[2] The German General Staff recognized the potential of land and air forces working together in combined attacks, and during the period between World Wars I and II, the German military developed *Blitzkrieg* tactics (see Chapter 5). This new form of warfare was metaphorically as quick and deadly as lightning because it employed the coordinated use of aircraft and armored vehicles such as tanks. *Blitzkrieg* was the prototype of a second use of military force—the quick, decisive, overwhelming use of force. The Soviet Union employed this strategy in its invasions of Hungary in 1956 and Czechoslovakia in 1968.

The Limited Probe

A third type of military force was the limited probe in order to test an opponent. A state wishing to challenge another may take an action that places the onus of reacting on another power, which may choose to meet the challenge, back down, or escalate the conflict. Two examples of this use of military force by the United States occurred in Berlin in 1948, when the United States responded to the closing of the access routes to West Berlin by implementing an airlift to resupply Berlin. A second case concerned the Quemoy crisis of 1958, when the United States chose to back the Chinese Nationalists' resupply of its forces on the island of Quemoy.

Use of Coercive Diplomacy or Compellence

The fourth use of military force envisioned the use of diplomacy and military force in tandem and is called **coercive diplomacy** or **compellence.** According to professors Gordon Craig and Alexander George, this strategy "employs threats or limited force to persuade an opponent to call off or undo an encroachment—for example, to halt an invasion or give up territory that has been occupied."[3] Many countries have attempted to implement coercive diplomacy. For example, the United States sought to pressure Japan in 1939–1941, Cuba and the Soviet Union during the missile crisis of 1962, and Saddam Hussein prior to the Gulf War of 1990–1991.

With the advent of nuclear weapons, statesmen were less interested at the end of World War II in the uses of nuclear weapons than in *avoiding* the use of nuclear weapons, and they turned their attention to devising plans to avoid the use of force.

ATTEMPTING TO DO AWAY WITH NUCLEAR WEAPONS: THE BARUCH AND GROMYKO PLANS FOR NUCLEAR DISARMAMENT

Clearly and tragically, the bombings of Hiroshima and Nagasaki had ushered in a new era of warfare (see Chapter 5 for the effects of the bombings of these cities). Of course, it would have been just as possible to kill as many people with conventional (i.e., nonnuclear weapons), but the time factor had changed dramatically; it was now possible to kill tens of thousands of people in minutes rather than in weeks or months.

Several days following the bombing of Hiroshima, Stalin told a group of Soviet scientists, "Hiroshima has shaken the whole world. The balance has been broken. Build the bomb—it will remove the great danger from us."[4] As Soviet scientists proceeded with their efforts to develop their own nuclear weapons, American and Soviet diplomats began to discuss the need to limit or even eliminate nuclear weapons.

In December 1945, President Truman appointed a committee chaired by Undersecretary of State Dean Acheson to study the control of nuclear energy. The following month a group of consultants headed by David Lilienthal was appointed to assist Acheson's committee. After three months of work, the Acheson-Lilienthal report was completed and released to the public. It called for the creation of an international authority to own and exercise control over all nuclear research and development. The proposed International Atomic Development Authority (IADA) would also be granted the power to manage, inspect, and license all nuclear facilities. The proposal called for the implementation of an agreement banning all nuclear weapons and the termination of U.S. nuclear weapons production and development to be deferred until the IADA was established.

The principal provisions of the **Acheson-Lilienthal Plan** were adopted by Bernard Baruch, whom President Truman had appointed as U.S. ambassador to the United Nations. The **Baruch Plan** specified that if a member of the UN Security Council were charged with violating the agreement, the alleged violator would not be allowed to exercise its veto power. The Soviet Union rejected this provision and presented a counterproposal—the **Gromyko Plan**—calling for a ban on the use or fabrication of nuclear weapons and for the destruction of existing stockpiles of nuclear weapons. At the time it was presented, only the United States had nuclear weapons; the USSR did not test its first nuclear weapons until August

1949. The Gromyko Plan did not contain provisions for the effective verification of the implementation of the agreement, and American policymakers were concerned about this omission.

The Baruch and Gromyko plans were the first efforts by the United States and the Soviet Union to achieve nuclear disarmament, and they failed for two main reasons: the USSR did not want to be frozen into a perpetual inferior position relative to the United States, and the United States did not trust Stalin to implement the provisions of the Gromyko Plan without adequate verification.

DETERRENCE: "IF YOU WANT PEACE, PREPARE FOR WAR"

The rejection of the Baruch and Gromyko plans meant that the United States and the Soviet Union would not be able to eliminate nuclear weapons and would therefore have to do something with them—but what?

Deterrence is a concept as old as humanity, and one that has contributed to human survival. In all likelihood, you are alive, and therefore, able to read this book because you were a target of deterrent threats. Parents tell their children, "Don't go in the street without looking both ways, or you will be punished." Fortunately, such threats usually work, and children survive.

Following the detonation of a nuclear weapon by the USSR in August 1949, Soviet and American leaders told one another, "Don't invade the territory of my country or its allies, or if you do, you will have to suffer greatly." More formally, two respected scholars have defined deterrence as consisting of "an effort by one actor to persuade an opponent not to take action of some kind against his interests by convincing the opponent that the costs and risks of doing so will outweigh what he hopes to gain thereby."[5] Deterrence existed before the advent of nuclear weapons; it simply took on a more fearsome character following the invention of nuclear weapons.

Deterrence is based on several fundamental assumptions. First, it is assumed that if the threat to a state is sufficiently great and is credible (i.e., believable), that the resort to war will be excluded from consideration. Second, decisionmakers are assumed to be "rational problem-solvers," meaning that they select goals, examine the alternatives for achieving those goals, and select an alternative on the basis of cost-benefit analysis; that is, they choose the option that maximizes benefits and minimizes costs. Third, threat is seen to be a function of destructive capability; the greater destructive capability, the greater the threat.

While the essential idea of deterrence is simple, as the concept developed during the cold war, it became increasingly complicated. The mission of deterrence focused on the types of wars that were deterred and various targets were considered in order to threaten potential aggressors. A whole new vocabulary developed to describe various deterrence strategies (see Box 8.1)

BOX 8.1   Deterrence Concepts

As strategists developed the concept of deterrence, they also developed a new lexicon, including the following terms:

Superiority

Parity

Sufficiency

Massive retaliation

Flexible response

Controlled response

Minimal deterrence

Extended deterrence

Gradual deterrence

Assured destruction

Damage limitation

Counterforce targeting

Countervalue targeting

The last policy referred to aiming nuclear weapons at cities in order to kill the maximum number of people. To what extent do you think the vocabulary of deterrence was developed in order to shield its practitioners from the devastating, potential consequences of what they were doing?

Strategists, policymakers, and members of the public came to think of nuclear weapons as having several possible purposes. Of course, some people think that nuclear weapons have *no* appropriate mission because their use would result in enormous devastation. People who think this way would reject nuclear deterrence in all forms and call for the abolition of nuclear weapons by all states that have them.

Others believe that nuclear weapons have the single mission of preventing a nuclear attack on the United States or its closest allies by threatening a nuclear response for such an attack. Those who believe in this minimal or fundamental form of nuclear deterrence favor developing and deploying only the nuclear weapons that are needed for the single purpose of deterring a nuclear attack.

Some believe that nuclear weapons serve two purposes: to prevent a nuclear attack and to prevent the use of conventional (i.e., nonnuclear) forces against the United States or its allies. Such a policy—called **extended deterrence**—requires the development and deployment of a greater number and more types of weapons than fundamental deterrence.

A last group believes that in addition to preventing nuclear and conventional attack on the United States and its allies by threatening a nuclear response, nuclear weapons can be used for multiple missions to increase political power, discourage undesirable actions by other states and possibly to "fight and win" a nuclear war. This is essentially going beyond deterrence and using nuclear weapons for purposes of compellence (see next section).

Nuclear deterrence was paradoxical: in order to successfully deter, threats had to be credible, and to be credible, threats had to be backed up with actual military forces. But once developed and deployed, those forces were used only rarely due to the fear that, if used, the military forces of the superpowers would result in possible escalation to nuclear war and the annihilation of those states that used nuclear weapons.

As noted in the last chapter, American and Soviet military forces came close to confronting one another directly on three occasions: Berlin in 1948 and 1961 and in Cuba in October 1962. In the aftermath of the Cuban missile crisis, both President Kennedy and Chairman Khrushchev realized that nuclear war was not simply a hypothetical possibility; it could really happen, and it almost did in October 1962. What could be done to lessen the danger faced by the superpowers?

During the first years of the 1960s, several analyses of arms control were published by civilian strategists. These analysts believed that arms control could supplement defense policies and increase the security of the United States. According to two of the early theorists, arms control had three major objectives: (1) to reduce the risk of war, (2) to reduce damage should war occur, and (3) to reduce the economic costs of preparing for war.[6] These writings on arms control were viewed by many policymakers as interesting, but somewhat removed from the real world of day-to-day international security. The Cuban missile crisis changed that; following the crisis, nuclear war was viewed as a very real, and frightening, possibility.

Khrushchev referred to the danger of escalation to more serious conflict in a letter that he wrote to President Kennedy at the height of the Cuban missile crisis:

> An even more dangerous case occurred on 28 October [1962], when your reconnaissance aircraft invaded the northern area of the Soviet Union, in the area of the Chukotski Peninsula, and flew over our territory. One asks, Mr. President, how should we regard this? What is this—a provocation? ... an intruding aircraft can easily be taken for a bomber with nuclear weapons, and that can push us toward a fatal step.[7]

During the Cuban missile crisis, there had been no quick, direct, secure means for the leaders of the two most powerful countries in the world to communicate with one another. Former long-time Soviet Ambassador to the United States Anatoly Dobrynin recalled how he communicated with Moscow:

> When I wanted to send an urgent cable to Moscow about my important conversation with Robert Kennedy, it was coded at once into columns of numbers (initially this was done by hand and only

YOU IN WORLD POLITICS

So you're interested in joining the military? Some college students consider joining the military when they finish college, and there are a number of things to think about when considering this option. Few entry-level positions offer young people as much responsibility as entry-level military jobs. For example, the lowest ranking naval officers are often responsible for issuing orders for ships at sea and are, therefore, responsible for the lives of all of the sailors on their ship.

The military services are staffed by two levels of personnel: enlisted and officers. To become an officer, one generally needs to have graduated from college. In fact, the military services sponsor "Reserve Officer Training Corps" (ROTC) programs at many colleges, and these programs offer a good entry into the military for college students. In addition, the Marines offer a summer officer training program (Platoon Leader Class) and all of the services, depending upon the recruitment needs of the service, offer "Officer Candidate Schools" (OCS). If interested in serving in the military, contact the local recruiter of the service in which you are interested.

later by machine). Then we called Western Union. The telegraph agency would send a messenger to collect the cable. Usually it was the same young black man, who came to the embassy on a bicycle.[8]

Apparently both Soviet and American leaders found such rudimentary arrangements unsatisfactory, and following the resolution of the crisis, the two countries moved to establish a direct communication link—the so-called "hot-line"—between Moscow and Washington, D.C. Hollywood filmmakers portray this as a red telephone on a desk; it is actually a teletype-like machine.

The Cuban missile crisis and other crises stimulated research on **coercive diplomacy** and the variables that contributed to success. After many years of painstaking research, Alexander George and his colleagues found that the following eight variables were significant.[9]

1. Clarity of the objectives is sought through the use of coercive diplomacy.
2. Strength of motivation: a state employing coercive diplomacy must perceive its interests as threatened.
3. Asymmetry of motivation: the more strongly motivated party will tend to prevail.
4. A sense of urgency on the part of a state's leaders contributes to success.
5. Strong leadership of the states involved in coercive diplomacy is important.
6. Adequate domestic and international support are needed.
7. Unacceptability characterizes the threatened escalation.
8. Clarity concerning the precise terms of settlement of the crisis is significant in reaching an agreement.

Deterrence and coercive diplomacy are related in approach as can be seen in Table 8.1. The objective of deterrence is to "persuade an opponent not to undertake an action," and the objective of coercive diplomacy is to persuade an opponent to undo a previous action of some sort, to undo a particular action, or to introduce changes in the government.[10]

As is clear from this diagram, deterrence and coercive diplomacy are closely related. In addition, coercive diplomacy and crisis management are also related. In fact, many of the operational requirements for managing crises affect the way in which coercive diplomacy is implemented.

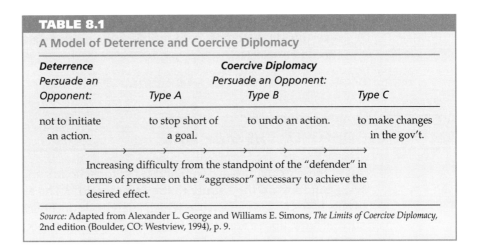

TABLE 8.1

A Model of Deterrence and Coercive Diplomacy

Deterrence *Persuade an* *Opponent:*	*Coercive Diplomacy* *Persuade an Opponent:*		
	Type A	*Type B*	*Type C*
not to initiate an action.	to stop short of a goal.	to undo an action.	to make changes in the gov't.

Increasing difficulty from the standpoint of the "defender" in terms of pressure on the "aggressor" necessary to achieve the desired effect.

Source: Adapted from Alexander L. George and Williams E. Simons, *The Limits of Coercive Diplomacy,* 2nd edition (Boulder, CO: Westview, 1994), p. 9.

THE REQUIREMENTS FOR CRISIS MANAGEMENT

In earlier studies, seven operational principles that contribute to the effective **crisis management** have been identified:[11]

1. Each side's political leaders must maintain control over military options such as alerts and troop movements.

2. The tempo and momentum of military movements must be slowed down and pauses created to provide enough time for each side to exchange diplomatic signals and communications and to provide enough time to give each side time to assess the situation, make decisions, and respond to proposals.

3. Movements of military forces must be carefully coordinated with diplomatic actions as part of an integrated strategy for terminating the crisis acceptably, without war or escalation to higher levels of violence.

4. Movements of military forces and threats of force intended to signal resolve must be consistent with limited diplomatic objectives—that is, "noise" must be avoided or minimized.

5. Military moves and threats that give the opponent the impression that one is about to resort to large-scale warfare, thereby forcing him to consider preemption, should be avoided.

6. Diplomatic-military options should be chosen that signal, or are consistent with, a desire to negotiate a way out of the crisis rather than to seek a military solution.

7. Diplomatic proposals and military moves that leave the opponent a way out of the crisis, compatible with his fundamental interests, should be selected.

A CASE STUDY ON DIPLOMACY AND THE USE OF FORCE: *THE GULF WAR*

All of these principles are well and good for scholars and academic analysts, but how do they apply to the "real world"? The analysis of actual events helps to see the ways in which analytical concepts and frameworks such as those above are useful. In this section the concepts presented above are used to analyze U.S. decisions and actions prior to and during the 1990–1991 Gulf crisis.

Iraq is a country with a long history; one tradition is that the Garden of Eden was located in Mesopotamia, at the junction of the Tigris and Euphrates rivers. The ancient city of Babylon was located in Iraq, and **Saddam Hussein** has sponsored the rebuilding of the city. Saddam has had the bricks used in the rebuilding project inscribed "The Babylon of Nebuchadnezzar was reconstructed in the era of Saddam Hussein." Muslims first conquered the territory that is now Iraq in the seventh century A.D. A millennium later in 1638, Baghdad became a frontier post of the Ottoman Empire. This lasted until the disintegration of the Ottoman Empire in 1917, and Iraq then became a British mandate territory. In 1932 Iraq declared its independence and became part of the Hashemite kingdom, which was ruled by the ancestors of the late King of Jordan, King Hussein, who is not related to Saddam. During World War II, Iraq first flirted with Nazi Germany and then declared war on the Axis powers in 1943. In 1968 a group of Iraqis, including then 31-year-old Saddam, took over the government. These revolutionaries were members of the Baath Party ("Baath" translates as "renaissance.")

Saddam Hussein was born in Tikrit, a small town in northern Iraq on April 28, 1937. Saddam's father died before he was born, and his stepfather abused him. Although he applied to go to the Baghdad Military Academy, Saddam failed the entrance examination and never served in the military. The uniform that he wears is that of his political party.

When he was twenty-one years old, Saddam participated in an unsuccessful assassination plot to kill the ruler of Iraq. Those who have known Saddam characterize him as ruthless, unpredictable, and arrogant. These characteristics undoubtedly contributed to the reasons that Saddam

PLO Chairman Yasser Arafat with Saddam Hussein
Source: Sygma; reprinted in Lawrence Freedman and Efraim Karsh, *The Gulf Conflict 1990–1991: Diplomacy and War in the New World Order* (Princeton: Princeton University Press, 1993), photograph no. 2, following page 218.

waged a costly war with Iran from 1980 to 1988. In this war it is estimated that 120 thousand Iraqis died and 300 thousand were wounded. Iran suffered similar casualties. Altogether, there were more than a million casualties (wounded, killed, and missing in action) in this Gulf war.

At 2 A.M. on the morning of August 2, 1990, Iraqi military forces moved across the border and took over neighboring Kuwait. This was very disturbing to many of those in the advanced industrial world because Iraq possessed 10 percent of the world's known oil reserves, Kuwait had another 10 percent, and Saudi Arabia possessed 25 percent. Were Iraq to continue its forward movement and takeover Saudi Arabia, then Saddam would control almost half of the world's proven oil reserves. This was a frightening prospect to the leaders of economies that almost literally "ran on oil."

Prior to the Iraqi invasion of Kuwait, the Western countries had sought to deter such an invasion. After the invasion and occupation of Kuwait, the

Western states sought to deter an invasion of Saudi Arabia. They did this by sending military forces almost immediately. These forces demonstrated Western support for the continued independence of Saudi Arabia and demonstrated this commitment in a very tangible way. In the early days of the Gulf crisis, there was one case of unsuccessful deterrence (deterring an Iraqi attack on Kuwait) and one successful case (deterring an Iraqi attack on Saudi Arabia).

Once the coalition of countries opposing Iraq had achieved deterrence, they then sought two objectives via coercive diplomacy. First, the international community sought to achieve "type B" coercive diplomacy (see Table 8.1 on p. 153): to force Iraq to withdraw from Kuwait. Second, the international community also sought to achieve the more difficult "type C" coercive diplomacy: to restore the preinvasion government of Kuwait, headed by the Al-Sabah family, to power. Initially, the international community sought to achieve these objectives by means of an economic embargo of Iraqi imports and exports. More than 90 states participated in this embargo, which had significant effects on Iraq including a drastic reduction in oil exports from Iraq and the freezing of Iraqi assets. But these effects did not hurt either Saddam or his loyalist followers in the Republican Guard. After four months Iraq still occupied Kuwait, and the Al-Sabah family was in exile in foreign countries.

Events in other parts of the world had an effect on the Gulf crisis. The progressive Soviet leader, Mikhail Gorbachev, announced in September 1990 that his country—the Soviet Union—supported the coalition opposing Saddam and called on Iraq to withdraw from Kuwait and restore the preinvasion government to power. On November 29, 1990, the foreign ministers of the 15 member states of the United Nations Security Council approved a resolution calling, once again, for the withdrawal of Iraq from Kuwait and approving the use of military force if Iraq would not withdraw.

There were several significant reasons that some members of the coalition wanted to act sooner rather than later. Each year Muslims the world over observe a month of fasting during a period called Ramadan. The timing of this period is determined by the lunar calendar and in 1991 Ramadan was going to be in March, and the pilgrimage to Mecca—called the "Haj"—was going to be in June. In addition, there were climatic factors to consider. Dust storms typically kick up during the spring in the Middle East, and during the summer, the temperature is brutally hot.

For all of these reasons, the United States issued a classic **ultimatum** to Saddam containing three elements: (1) a demand that Iraq withdraw from Kuwait and restore the Al-Sabah family to power, (2) a time limit re-

> **BOX 8.1   Optional Critex: The Expansion of NATO
> to Estonia, Latvia, and Lithuania**
>
> In 1998, the members of the North Atlantic Treaty Organization
> (NATO) invited three former members of the Warsaw Pact—Poland,
> Hungary, and the Czech Republic—to join NATO. This invitation
> caused great concern in Russia because many Russians considered
> this to be an affront.
>
> Other former members of the former Soviet/Eastern European
> bloc also expressed interest in joining NATO. Among those that most
> wanted to join were the three Baltic republics of Estonia, Latvia, and
> Lithuania. Assume that you are an advisor to the Secretary General
> of NATO. Would you advise to extend membership to the Baltic Re-
> publics or not? Why?

quiring these actions be accomplished by January 15, 1991, and (3) a statement threatening U.S. action to achieve these objectives if not performed
by Iraq. When Iraq failed to comply with these demands, the coalition attacked Iraq, according to General Colin Powell, "suddenly, massively and
decisively." In essence, coercive diplomacy had failed, and the use of military force was employed in order to achieve the coalition's objectives.

Wars, like love affairs, are much easier to start than to end. Once the
coalition had attacked Iraq with devastating air raids, military and civilian leaders began thinking about how the war should end. The problem
of **war termination**—ending a war—is a vitally important subject, but one
that has not received the academic attention of deterrence, coercive diplomacy, arms control, or crisis management.

Professors Craig and George have noted that in considering the subject of war termination, "one must distinguish between a mere cessation
of hostilities and a peace agreement that attempts to resolve the conflicting aims over which the battle has been waged. Hostilities may end with
a cease-fire or armistice that leaves the issues at stake unsettled and defers
their consideration to a later peace conference."[12] In this case, American
decision makers were concerned about the "public relations" aspects of the
end of the war; specifically, they were concerned that the United States
would be accused internationally of "butchering the Iraqis." After the war
was over, General Powell recalled that "press reports about the 'Turkey
Shoot' on the 'Highway of Death' were an important consideration...."[13]

In the end, the United States observed the resolutions passed by the United Nations and left Saddam Hussein in power. The irony of the war is that within seven years of its end, almost all of the leaders of the victorious coalition, including President Bush and Prime Minister Thatcher, were out of power, while Saddam remained in power.

THE NEW FACE OF CONFLICT: INFORMATION WARFARE

Successful leaders throughout history have recognized the crucial importance of information and communications in achieving their objectives whether in commerce or in war. For example, in the Second Punic War, Hannibal's skillful use of mirrors to send signals to his forces concerning the movements of Roman forces enabled him to launch effective surprise attacks on the Roman units.[14] Genghis Khan, whose conquests are legendary, also employed information and communications to his advantage. According to RAND Corporation analysts John Arquilla and David Ronfeldt, "Clearly the key to Mongol success was superior command, control, communication, and intelligence. Scouts and messengers always took along three or four extra horses, tethered, so that they could switch mounts and keep riding when one grew tired. This gave the horsemen, in relative terms, something approximating an ability to provide real-time intelligence, almost as from a satellite, on the enemy's order of battle and intentions."[15]

One of the most significant uses of information in the twentieth century was the Allies' breaking of Germany's and Japan's codes, which enabled the Allies to know a great deal about the location, strength, and plans of enemy forces.[16] Franklin Roosevelt and Winston Churchill made extensive use of the Axis powers' decrypted messages; however, Churchill refused to rely on intelligence reports that had been "sifted and digested" and insisted on seeing the "authentic documents … in their original form."[17]

The Chinese character for "crisis" has two meanings: "danger" and "opportunity." Similarly, the information revolution of the past several decades represents both danger and opportunity to contemporary decision makers. The principal dangers are twofold: (1) the possibility of information overload, and (2) the possibility of information and information technology being used for hostile purposes.

Illustrating information overload, it would be impossible for a contemporary leader to review even a small percentage of the raw "unsifted and undigested" information received by a country or large corporation in a single day. In commenting on the crisis in Lebanon in July 1982, George Shultz, who was U.S. secretary of state-designate at the time, commented: "I became aware of an acute problem with the State Department's system of crisis management: the pace of events had outstripped the traditional methods of receiving cabled messages from overseas and responding with written instructions to our posts. There simply was not time to draft, type, code, transmit, decode, process and read written telegraphic traffic."[18] Eight years later, the situation that Shultz described had only become worse; during the first 30 hours of the Gulf War, American troops received 1.3 million electronic messages.[19] Even Churchill, one of the greatest leaders of the twentieth century, would have been overwhelmed.

These examples demonstrate that a contemporary information problem is not *obtaining* information; rather, it is storing, processing, accessing, and presenting information so that it is usable by the leader to make decisions. Confronted with "information overload," decision makers resort to the path of least resistance: CNN.

The Gulf War dramatically illustrated a second danger (or opportunity, depending upon one's view) of the information revolution, that is, using information technology for hostile purposes. Anyone who watched television during either the Gulf War or bombing of Kosovo remembers the dramatic use of precision-guided munitions—so-called "smart bombs." The increased effectiveness of these weapons was made possible by the miniaturization of electronics and increased information about targets. There were other effective uses of information in the war. According to *U. S. News and World Report,* the United States was able to disrupt Iraq's air-defense computers by surreptitiously placing several microchips containing a computer virus into computers smuggled into Iraq.[20]

In the opening days of NATO's bombing of Yugoslavia in 1999, Serbian computer users were able to temporarily disable NATO's World Wide Web site by overloading NATO's computer server with more queries than it could handle. NATO responded by adding an additional server and a filter to block out disabling queries. This provides a recent example of what some aspects of war might look like in the future.

As Hannibal's and Genghis Khan's previously cited uses of information demonstrate, information warfare is "virtually as old as warfare itself."[21] However, it has taken on new significance given two factors: (1) the dependence of individuals, corporations, and countries on computer networks, and (2) the vulnerabilities of these networks to attack and disruption. Whereas information was previously a means of waging war more effectively, it is now—as the Gulf War and Yugoslavian examples illustrated—a means of actually executing war.

Growing Dependence and Growing Security Concerns

Both civilian and military organizations have shown great interest in and concern over their vulnerability to information warfare. A review of the references at the end of this chapter, will reveal the concern over the threat of information warfare and related subjects that both civilian and particularly military organizations in the United States currently have. Various U.S. organizations in both the private and public sectors have sponsored conferences and symposia on this subject.[22] Clearly, there is much concern about the possibility of information warfare.

The growth of information in today's world is staggering. The amount of information in the world is reported to be doubling every eighteen months.[23] An estimated 85 percent of all the scientists who have ever lived are alive today. Computers have contributed to the exponential growth of information. According to Dr. Carver Mead of the California Institute of Technology, "The entire Industrial Revolution enhanced production by a factor of about a hundred. The microelectronic revolution has already enhanced productivity in the information-based technology by a factor of more than a million—and the end isn't in sight yet."[24] If another high-tech industry—the aircraft industry—"had undergone similar progress during the last three decades, a trip from Tokyo to Washington, D.C., would take less than five minutes, would cost $2, and would all be done on less than half a gallon of gas."[25]

This is the good news, but there is a downside as well. With a relatively small investment, someone can purchase a computer system that could provide the capability to disrupt various national infrastructures. The principal investigator of a U.S. General Accounting Office report has stated: "Countries today do not have to be military superpowers with large standing armies, fleets of battleships or squadrons of fighters to gain a competitive edge. Instead, all they really need to steal sensitive data or shut down military computers is a $2,000 computer and modem and a connection to the internet."[26] The widespread propagation of computer viruses confirms this point.

The dependence on and threat to contemporary organizations is both real and substantial. Consider, for example, the U.S. Department of Defense which "has a vast information infrastructure of computers and networks to protect including over 2.1 million computers, 10,000 local networks, 100 long-distance networks, 200 command centers, and 16 central computer processing facilities or MegaCenters. There are over 2 million Defense computer users and an additional two million non-Defense users that do business with the Department."[27] There are many different ways that an individual or organization, such as the Department of Defense, can use information technologies both offensively as well as defensively.

Figure 8.2 presents a typology of illustrative offensive (left side) and defensive (right side) techniques and hardware. The sections of the "pyramid" represent the various components of the international system. Most

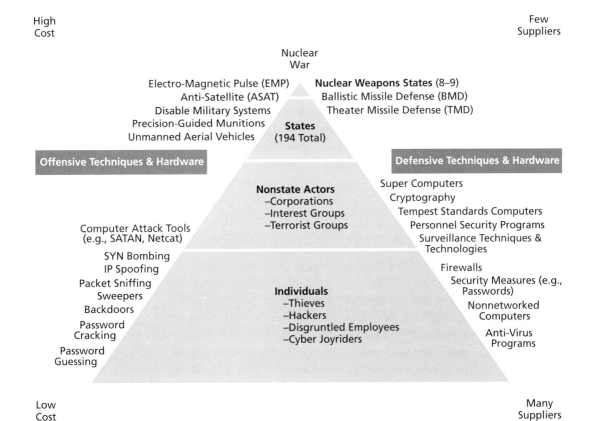

Figure 8.2. Information Operations and Warfare Typology

numerous, of course, are individuals. A conservative estimate is that there are currently 40 million internet users in almost all of the world's 194 countries. Some of these users are simply curious to see if they can "get into" an organization's computer system; these can be thought of as cyberspace joyriders. Unfortunately, there are more malevolent groups who have more hostile intentions. The U.S. Defense Information Systems Agency (DISA) estimates (although no one knows for sure) that in 1994 DOD computers were broken into by unknown persons more than 300 thousand times.[28]

As Figure 8.2 notes, there are a number of defensive techniques that individuals, corporations, and countries can employ to decrease their vulnerability to infowar attacks. Almost everyone who uses a computer today uses an "anti-virus" program.[29] A simple solution to "hacker vulnerability" is to dedicate a single computer to internet communications and to not connect this machine to the organization's network. Of course, this means that the organization's members cannot take advantage of the communications advantages that the internet offers. Security measures, such as passwords, "firewalls," and "tempest-standard" computers are some of the other defensive techniques and hardware widely available, but at increasing cost. Only those organizations willing and able to devote substantial resources to security can afford cryptography and the supercomputers that make encryption secure.

There are many ways that **information warfare** can be waged offensively. Almost anyone who uses a computer has, at one time or another, engaged in "password guessing," perhaps to use a friend's computer. "Password cracking" and outright theft are techniques that attackers use to steal passwords to obtain unauthorized access to accounts. Computers can easily scan a dictionary to search for possible passwords. Alphanumeric characters are more difficult to crack, but computers can compare all possible combinations of numbers and letters.

Beyond "hacking" and "cracking," attackers can employ a wide variety of tools and techniques, many of which are freely available on the internet. For example, the "Security Administrator Tool for Analyzing Networks" (acronym: "SATAN") was originally designed to assist network administrators test their computers for security weaknesses. Attackers have discovered, however, that SATAN is a useful tool to launch automated attacks.

Of course, the information revolution has contributed to the increased effectiveness of a number of weapons systems, including precision-guided munitions and remotely piloted vehicles. These systems were used extensively and effectively, as any television viewer knows, during the Gulf War and the NATO bombing of Serbia and Kosovo in 1999.

Francis Bacon was correct; "Knowledge itself is power." And modern technologies have made information readily available to individuals, corporations, international and transnational organizations, and states. Information may be used for benign or malign purposes. There are many uncertainties concerning the possible uses of military force and information, but one thing is certain: contemporary decision makers must consider how their organizations may both use and be threatened by military force and information.

DISCUSSION QUESTIONS

1. German Chancellor Otto von Bismarck once said that it was "blood and iron" that decided the issues of international relations. To what extent is that still true? Or is it silicon and transistors that increasingly decide the issues of world politics?

2. To what extent have international crises in recent times been dealt with according to the principles of coercive diplomacy and crisis management described in this chapter?

3. If we had a crystal ball and were able to look 100 years into the future, what would war look like? Will war exist a century from now?

KEY TERMS

Acheson-Lilienthal Plan	Gromyko Plan
Baruch Plan	Gulf War
coercive diplomacy	information warfare
compellence	Saddam Hussein
crisis management	ultimatum
deterrence	war of attrition
extended deterrence	war termination

RECOMMENDED PRINT, MULTIMEDIA, AND INTERNET SOURCES

Print

CRAIG, GORDON and ALEXANDER L. GEORGE. *Force and Statecraft: Diplomatic Problems of Our Time,* 3rd ed. New York: Oxford University Press, 1995.

FREEDMAN, LAWRENCE. "The Revolution in Strategic Affairs. *Adelphi Paper 318.* London: Oxford University Press for the International Institute for Strategic Studies, April 1998.

GEORGE, ALEXANDER L. and WILLIAM E. SIMONS. *The Limits of Coercive Diplomacy,* 2nd ed. Boulder, CO: Westview, 1994.

GEORGE, ALEXANDER L. and RICHARD SMOKE. *Deterrence and American Foreign Policy: Theory and Practice.* New York: Columbia University Press, 1974.

NEWHOUSE, JOHN. *War and Peace in the Nuclear Age.* New York: Alfred A. Knopf, 1989. A well-written and researched book to accompany the video series listed below.

SCHELLING, THOMAS C. *The Strategy of Conflict.* New York: Oxford University Press, 1960.
———. *Arms and Influence.* New Haven, CT: Yale University Press, 1966.

Print Sources on the Gulf War

FREEDMAN, LAWRENCE and EFRAIM KARSH. *The Gulf Conflict, 1990–1991: Diplomacy and War in the New World Order.* Princeton, NJ: Princeton University Press, 1993. This is the best overview and analysis of the Gulf War.

GORDON, MICHAEL R. and BERNARD E. TRAINOR. *The Generals' War: The Inside Story of the Conflict in the Gulf.* Boston: Little, Brown, 1995. Focuses on the way that U.S. strategy for the war developed.

GRAUBARD, STEPHEN. *Mr. Bush's War: Adventures in the Politics of Illusion.* New York: Hill and Wang, 1991. A very critical account of the events leading up to and including the Gulf War.

JENTLESON, BRUCE. *With Friends Like These: Reagan, Bush and Saddam, 1982–1990.* New York: W. W. Norton, 1994. A critical account of U.S.-Iraqi relations in the eight years prior to the war.

KHALED BIN SULTAN. *Desert Warrior: A Personal View of the Gulf War by the Joint Forces Commander.* New York: HarperCollins, 1995. The view of the war by the Saudi commander; addresses (and disputes) some of General Schwarzkopf's points.

MILLER, JUDITH and LAURIE MYLROIE. *Saddam Hussein and the Crisis in the Gulf.* New York: Times Books, 1990.

SCHWARZKOPF, H. Norman with Peter Petre. *It Doesn't Take a Hero: The Autobiography.* New York: Bantam Books, 1992. The story from the commander of U.S. forces.

CD-ROM

Desert Storm: The War in the Persian Gulf. New York: Time Warner, 1991.

Video

Dr. Strangelove or: How I Learned to Stop Worrying and Love the Bomb. The classic 1964 film directed by Stanley Kubrick and starring Peter Sellers.

The Gulf War. Princeton, NJ: Films for the Humanities and Sciences, a three-part series with each program lasting 60 minutes. Includes interviews with Jordan's King Hussein, Iraqi foreign Minister Tariq Aziz, General Norman Schwarzkopf, and former Secretary of State James Baker.

The Gulf War. PBS video.

The Road to War: American Decision Making During the Gulf Crisis. Princeton, NJ: Films for the Humanities and Sciences, 2 hours, 27 minutes. Focuses on how decisions were made in the United States.

War and Peace in the Nuclear Age. Boston: WGBH/PBS, 1989. A magnificent series that covers the period from the development of nuclear weapons through the Reagan administration; 13 one-hour segments.

Internet

Arms Sales Monitoring Project: http://www.fas.org/asmp/

Carnegie Endowment for International Peace: http://www.ceip.org/   Provides information related to international security affairs and a link to the journal *Foreign Policy.*

Henry L. Stimson Center: http://www.stimson.org   A think tank that focuses on international security issues.

Heritage Foundation: http://www.heritage.org/   A policy research organization that contains materials and links to foreign policy and security affairs.

Hoover Institution on War, Revolution and Peace (Stanford University): http://www-hoover.stanford.edu

International Relations and Security Network: www.isn.ethz.ch/

Military Spending Clock: The Center for Defense Information, a private nongovernmental organization maintains this site that records how much the United States spends on defense: http://www.cdi.org/sc/javaclock.html

National Defense University: http://www.ndu.edu/

North Atlantic Treaty Organization (NATO) Integrated Data Service: http://www.nato.int/structur/   Provides information about NATO, including issues of the *NATO Review.*

RAND Corporation: http://www.rand.org/   One of the oldest and most respected think tanks in the United States; contains descriptions of RAND's research and publications.

Stockholm International Peace Research Institute (SIPRI): presents data on military spending around the world: http://sipri.se/

ENDNOTES

[1] ERICH MARIA REMARQUE, *All Quiet on the Western Front* (London: G. P. Putnam's, 1929).

[2] See Alvin Toffler and Heidi Toffler, *War and Anti-War: Survival at the Dawn of the 21st Century* (Boston: Little, Brown, 1993).

[3] GORDON CRAIG and ALEXANDER L. GEORGE, *Force and Statecraft: Diplomatic Problems of Our Time,* 3rd ed. (New York: Oxford University Press, 1996), p. 196.

[4] Quoted by JOHN LEWIS GADDIS, *We Now Know: Rethinking Cold War History* (New York: Oxford University Press, 1997), p. 96.

[5] CRAIG and GEORGE, p. 124.

[6] THOMAS C. SCHELLING and MORTON H. HALPERIN, *Strategy and Arms Control* (New York: Twentieth Century Fund, 1961).

[7] Letter from Nikita Khrushchev to John F. Kennedy (official translation), October 28, 1962, printed in *Department of State Bulletin,* November 19, 1973, p. 653.

[8] ANATOLY DOBRYNIN, *In Confidence: Moscow's Ambassador to America's Six Cold War Presidents* (New York: Times Books, 1995), p. 96.

[9] This list is adapted from ALEXANDER L. GEORGE, WILLIAM SIMONS, and DAVID K. HALL, *The Limits of Coercive Diplomacy: Laos, Cuba, Vietnam,* 2nd ed. (Boulder, CO: Westview, 1994), pp. 280–286.

[10] Ibid.

[11] ALEXANDER L. GEORGE, ed., *Avoiding War: Problems of Crisis Management* (Boulder, CO: Westview, 1991), p. 25.

[12] CRAIG and GEORGE, p. 229.

[13] MICHAEL R. GORDON and BERNARD E. TRAINOR, *The Generals' War: The Inside Story of the Conflict in the Gulf* (Boston: Little, Brown, 1995), pp. 414–415.

[14] Example taken from JOHN ARQUILLA, "The Strategic Implications of Information Dominance," *Strategic Review,* (Summer 1994), p. 25.

[15] See JOHN ARQUILLA and DAVID RONFELDT, "Cyberwar Is Coming!" *Comparative Strategy,* vol. 12 (1993).

[16] F. W. WINTERBOTHAM, *The Ultra Secret* (New York: Dell, 1994); Ronald W. Clark, *The Man Who Broke Purple* (London: Weidenfeld and Nicholson, 1977).

[17] ALVIN TOFFLER, *Powershift: Knowledge, Wealth, and Violence at the Edge of the 21st Century* (New York: Bantam Books, 1990), p. 270.

[18] GEORGE P. SHULTZ, *Turmoil and Triumph: My Years as Secretary of State* (New York: Charles Scribner's Sons, 1993), p. 44.

[19] WILLIAM MATTHEWS. "U.S. Forms Warfare School to Fight Information Overload," *Defense News,* May 16–22, 1994, p. 22.

[20] *U. S. News and World Report, Triumph Without Victory: The Unreported History of the Persian Gulf War* (New York: Times Books, 1992).

[21] ABE SINGER and SCOTT ROWELL, "Information Warfare: An Old Operational Concept With New Implications," *Strategic Forum,* no. 99 (Washington, DC: Institute for National Strategic Studies, National Defense University, December 1996), p. 1.

[22] "Serbs' Revenge: NATO Web Site Zapped," *The New York Times,* April, 1999, p. A14.

[23] JOHN H. PETERSEN, "Info Wars," *U.S. Naval Institute Proceedings* (May 1993), p. 89.

[24] Quoted by WALTER B. WRISTON, *The Twilight of Sovereignty: How the Information Revolution Is Transforming Our World* (New York: Charles Sribner's, 1992, p. 103.

[25] SINGER and ROWELL, *Information Warfare,* p. 2.

[26] JACK L. BROCK quoted in PHILLIP SHENON, "Defense Department Computers Face a Hacker Threat, Report Says," *The New York Times,* May 23, 1996, p. A11.

[27] U.S. General Accounting Office, *Information Security: Computer Attacks at Department of Defense Pose Increasing Risks,* GAO/AIMD-96-84 (Washington, DC: Government Printing Office, May 1996), p. 10.

[28] "The Pentagon's New Nightmare: An Electronic Pearl Harbor," *Washington Post,* July 16, 1996, p. C 3.

[29] Ibid., p. 12. "A virus is a code fragment that reproduces by attaching to another program. It may damage data directly, or it may degrade system performance by taking over system resources which are then not available to authorized users."

9

Arms Control and Disarmament

Interpreting Political Cartoons

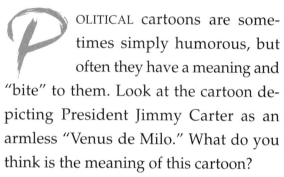 OLITICAL cartoons are sometimes simply humorous, but often they have a meaning and "bite" to them. Look at the cartoon depicting President Jimmy Carter as an armless "Venus de Milo." What do you think is the meaning of this cartoon?

Another attempt to make light of a very heavy subject, in this case nuclear proliferation, is depicted on page 171. What meaning do you think that the cartoonist was trying to convey in this cartoon?

As you read newspapers and news magazines, look for political cartoons and think about the meaning of them.

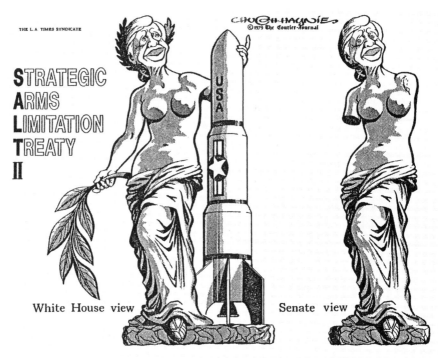

STRATEGIC
ARMS
LIMITATION
TREATY
II

White House view   Senate view

Jimmy Carter as Venus de Milo

THE WEAPON TO END THE WORLD

A new weapon that many people believed would result in the end of the world had been invented. There was great concern that Armageddon was rapidly approaching—so much concern that the Pope called a major, international conference to discuss the possible means of controlling the fearsome new weapon. This new threat to the future of the world was not nuclear weapons, chemical or biological weapons, or a new weapon based on an advanced, esoteric technology; it was the crossbow. Pope Innocent II organized the conference in 1139.

This example usually brings smiles to the faces of people who hear it for the first time. How could people be so naive to believe that a weapon as simple as the crossbow could threaten the future of the world? The crossbow was, of course, a marked technological improvement over the long bow and was capable of inflicting many more casualties per unit of time. It would be theoretically possible for millions of people to be killed by the arrows from crossbows; of course, such a slaughter would require years and years.

THE FAR SIDE   By GARY LARSON

"Wouldn't you know it! Now the Hendersons have the bomb."

Proliferation

Today, millions of people could be killed in a matter of hours by what scientists call **"weapons of mass destruction,"** meaning nuclear, chemical, and/or biological weapons. It is the relatively short period of time in which death and destruction can be wrought that distinguishes our era from all others that have preceded it.

Because of the actual death and destruction caused by small arms and the enormous destructive potential of modern weapons of mass destruction, many people throughout the world favor various means of controlling, limiting, and eradicating certain types of weapons. In this chapter, a typology of various types of weapons and the means to limit them is presented.

Although the terms "arms control" and "disarmament" are often used as synonyms, they are not. Arms control refers to the *limitation* of numbers and/or quality of certain types of weapons. Disarmament refers to the *elimination* of certain types or even all weapons. Thus, disarmament is more comprehensive than arms control. In an important, early essay on arms control, Thomas Schelling and Morton Halperin identified three objectives of arms control: (1) to reduce the risk of war, (2) to reduce the destructiveness should war occur, and (3) to reduce the economic cost of preparing for war.[1] There have been attempts to achieve both arms control and disarmament agreements, and both will be reviewed in this chapter.

HISTORICAL ATTEMPTS TO ACHIEVE ARMS CONTROL AND DISARMAMENT

For almost as long as they have fought, human beings have sought to control and limit conflict. Table 9.1 lists some of the efforts over the past 3,000 years to ameliorate conflict and its destructiveness.

Following World War I, the United States took the initiative and convened a conference in Washington, DC, with the purpose of limiting naval weapons. U.S. Secretary of State Charles Evans Hughes made a dramatic proposal to reduce the American battleship fleet in concert with the other

TABLE 9.1

Chronological List of Arms Control and Disarmament Agreements (The following is an illustrative, but not exhaustive, listing of various arms control and disarmament agreements.)

Date Signed	Agreement	Purpose
Premodern Agreements:		
1100 B.C.	Israelite-Philistine term of peace	Limited Israel's use of iron
448 B.C.	Athens-Persia Accord	Demilitarized Aegean Sea
201 B.C.	Rome-Carthage Treaty	Limited military forces, including a prohibition on war elephants
989 A.D.	Peace and Truce of God	Established noncombatant status
1787	Anglo-French Pact	Limited navies
1815	Declaration of Swiss Neutrality	Neutralized Switzerland
1817	Rush-Bagot Agreement	Demilitarized the Great Lakes
1868	St. Petersburg Declaration	Prohibited "dum-dum" bullets
1899/ 1907	Hague treaties	Prohibited use of poison gas and codified rules of war
1919	Treaty of Versailles	Limited German military forces
1922	Washington Treaty	Limited major navies
1925	Geneva Protocol	Prohibited the use of chemical and biological weapons
Post-World War II Agreements:		
1959	Antarctica Treaty	Prohibited the deployment of all weapons in Antarctica
1963	"Hot-Line" Agreement	Established direct communications link between United States and USSR
1963	Limited Test Ban Treaty	Prohibited nuclear tests in the atmosphere
1967	Outer Space Treaty	Prohibited the deployment of nuclear weapons in space
1967	Latin American Nuclear Free Zone (Treaty of Tlatelolco)	Prohibited deployment of nuclear weapons
1968	Non-Proliferation Treaty (NPT)	Designed to prevent the spread of nuclear weapons
1971	Seabed Arms Control Treaty	Prohibited the deployment of weapons of mass destruction on the seabed
1971	"Accidents Measure" Agreement	Confidence building measures
1971	Hot-Line Modernization Agreement	Provided for satellite communications circuits between Washington and Moscow
1972	Biological Weapons Convention	Prohibited the development, production, and stockpiling of biological weapons
1972	"Incidents at Sea" Agreement	Reduced the risks of dangerous activities
1972	Anti-Ballistic Missile (ABM) Treaty	Limited the deployment of ABMs to two sites
1972	Interim Agreement on Offensive Arms	Limited the deployment of ICBMs and SLBMs
1973	Prevention of Nuclear War Agreement	Confidence-building measures

Date Signed	Agreement	Purpose
TABLE 9.1 (continued)		
Post-World War II Agreements:		
1974	Threshold Test Ban Treaty	Limited underground nuclear tests
1976	Peaceful Nuclear Explosions Treaty	Prohibited the use of nuclear explosions for "peaceful purposes," such as excavation
1977	Environmental Modification Convention	Prohibited modifying the environment for military purposes
1979	Strategic Arms Limitation Treaty (SALT II)	Placed limits on strategic offensive weapons
1980	Nuclear Material Convention	Physical protection of nuclear materials
1986	Conference & Security-Building Measures	Provided for confidence-building measures
1987	Nuclear Risk Reduction Centers	Provided for U.S. and USSR risk-reduction centers
1987	Intermediate Nuclear Forces (INF) Treaty	Eliminated U.S. and USSR intermediate- and short-range missiles
1988	Ballistic Missile Launch Notification	Provided for the notification of any ballistic-missile launch
1990	Conference on Forces in Europe	Limited conventional weapons in Europe
1991	Strategic Arms Reduction Treaty (START I)	Reduced ICBMs, SLBMs, and bombers
1992	Treaty on Open Skies	Provided for unencumbered overflights
1993	START II	Further reduced ICBMs, SLBMs, and bombers
1996	Comprehensive Test Ban Treaty (CTBT)	Prohibited all nuclear tests

great powers of that time. Within a matter of months, the negotiators reached agreement to place a freeze on the building of naval fortifications in the Pacific and to limit their capital ship (i.e., battleships and cruisers) tonnage to the following limits: 500 thousand tons each for the United States and Great Britain; 300 thousand tons for Japan; and 175 thousand for France and Italy. The **Washington Naval treaties** actually required the signatories to scrap a total of 68 capital ships. A second naval arms control conference held in London in 1930 resulted in several other controls. However, in 1934 Japan announced its intention to withdraw from the 1922 Washington Naval Treaty, and within a few years all of the major powers had embarked on significant naval construction programs.

There were several other attempts during the period between World Wars I and II to achieve arms control and disarmament. The United States introduced the **"Geneva Protocol"** in 1925 to prohibit the use of poison gas and bacteriological weapons. Although the United States signed this agreement in 1925, it was not ratified until 1975 because American officials were concerned that signing the treaty would prevent the United States from using riot control chemicals such as tear gas.

The interwar efforts to achieve arms control and disarmament were not able to prevent the outbreak of the Second World War in September 1939. New and fearsome weapons were used, most notably at the end of the war, on Hiroshima and Nagasaki. Since the initial use of nuclear weapons, experts and lay persons alike have debated whether these weapons have altered the nature of war itself or whether they are simply extensions of previous weapons. During the cold war if the United States and the USSR had used only a small percentage of the nuclear weapons in their stockpiles, the resulting death and destruction would have exceeded that caused by any previous international conflict.

Both the United States and the Soviet Union presented proposals at the United Nations in 1946 to attempt to put the "nuclear genie" back in its bottle: the Baruch Plan and the Gromyko Plan discussed in Chapter 8. These proposals failed for two basic reasons: the Soviet Union did not want to foreclose its option of developing nuclear weapons, and the United States wanted to have confidence that any agreement would be verifiable. The USSR was unwilling to accept on-site verification within the Soviet Union, which precluded effective verification throughout the late 1940s and the 1950s. This in turn precluded any substantive progress in achieving arms control and disarmament.

In August 1949, the Soviet Union detonated its first nuclear explosion, and thus became the second member of the "nuclear club." In January 1952, the UN General Assembly established the UN Disarmament Commission to investigate the possibility of negotiating the control of nuclear and conventional weapons. No real progress was made in this forum, and following the death of Joseph Stalin in 1953 and the election of President Dwight D. Eisenhower, in 1954 the United Nations created a new forum, the Subcommittee on Disarmament. From 1954 through 1957, the United States, the Soviet Union, Great Britain, France, and Canada met to discuss a number of substantive proposals. Although these negotiations were significant in some respects, they failed to produce any formal agreements and the Soviet Union withdrew from the talks in 1957.[2]

In August 1957 the Soviet Union tested the first intercontinental ballistic missile (ICBM) and the following October launched the first earth-orbiting satellite, *Sputnik.* At the same time, the United States was developing similar systems. The development and deployment of the ICBM marked a revolution in modern warfare. Prior to the development of ICBMs, the geographic location of the United States shielded it from attack. The flight time of an ICBM going from the Soviet Union to the United States or vice versa is 30 minutes. Thus, ICBMs made the United States vulnerable to attack as never before in its history. During the 1960 presidential campaign, John F. Kennedy called attention to the "missile gap" that he felt existed between the United States and the Soviet Union, and he emphasized the need for the United States to "catch up with" the Soviets. As a result, when he was inaugurated, President Kennedy called for the United States to build up its conventional and nuclear forces.

This was not the result that Nikita Khrushchev had intended. Indeed, through his boasting about Soviet military strength, Khrushchev had hoped to gain political leverage vis-à-vis the United States. By 1961, however, he was faced with an embarrassing situation: a missile gap in ICBMs favoring the United States. President Kennedy and his advisors recognized this fact following the deployment of the first reconnaissance satellite in early 1961. As of October 1962, the military forces of the United States and Soviet Union were as follows:[3]

	United States	U.S.S.R.
ICBM launchers	179	30–50
SLBM launchers	144	97
Strategic bombers	1,450	155
MR/IRBM launchers	105	750 (24 in Cuba)
Warheads/bombs	3,000	250

Note: The above figures include operational, test, and training weapons.

As one can see from this table, the United States had a significant superiority in the number of strategic intercontinental nuclear weapons (i.e., the first three categories of weapons yielded an advantage of 1,773 to approximately 300), while the Soviet Union had a substantial lead in medium- and intermediate-range ballistic missiles (750 to 105). These MR/IRBMs had been designed and deployed for possible use in a European conflict and could not be used against the United States if deployed in the Soviet Union because of their limited range. However, if deployed in Cuba, they could easily reach most of the continental United States. Thus, by clandestinely deploying MR/ICBMs in Cuba, the Soviet Union could move substantially closer to the achievement of nuclear parity with the United States. The temptation for a "quick fix" of Soviet strategic inferiority was too great to resist, and during the summer of 1962 the Soviet Union began its secret deployment of MR/IRBMs to Cuba.

The United States discovered the Soviet missiles in mid-October at about the time that they were becoming operational. The Kennedy administration felt that the missiles had to be removed, and the resulting confrontation was the most serious of the post-World War II period. Once the Soviet Union agreed to remove its missiles, the crisis was resolved, but the probability of a Soviet-American war (as estimated by President Kennedy once the crisis was over) had been between one out of three and even.

Following the Cuban missile crisis, Kennedy and Khrushchev moved to lessen the risk of nuclear war by concluding the Hot-Line Agreement and the Limited Nuclear Test Ban Treaty in 1963. These agreements, along with the **Antarctica Treaty** of 1959, were the initial building blocks of the contemporary arms-control regime.

A TYPOLOGY OF ARMS CONTROL AND DISARMAMENT AGREEMENTS

In the following section, contemporary arms-control agreements according to their principal purpose are described. The typology of arms-control agreements presented here complements the chronological description of the agreements that is presented in Table 9.1.

Nuclear Weapon-Free Areas

In 1957, scientists from around the world cooperated in a number of studies of the earth as a part of the International Geophysical Year. Some of these studies concerned Antarctica, and the scientists involved concluded that Antarctica should be off limits for military deployments. At the United States' initiative, an international conference on Antarctica was called that resulted in a 1959 Antarctica Treaty that prohibited the testing and deployment of conventional and nuclear weapons and the disposal of radioactive waste in Antarctica. In addition, the signatories of the agreement agreed to suspend their territorial claims to Antarctica for a 30-year period. This treaty was the first post-World War II arms control agreement and set a precedent for prohibiting the deployment of nuclear weapons to certain areas.

Just as the village green was regarded in the past as the common property of the village, outer space and the oceans are similarly regarded today as the "common heritage of humankind." In an attempt to avoid an arms race in space, the UN General Assembly unanimously adopted a resolution in 1963 urging all states to refrain from deploying nuclear weapons in outer space. This resolution constituted the basis of the **Outer Space Treaty** that was signed in 1967. The Seabed Arms Control Treaty signed in 1971 prohibited the deployment of nuclear weapons and other "weapons of mass destruction" (such as biological weapons) on the seabed. These two agreements are attempts to assure that the global commons of the contemporary era will remain demilitarized.

During the Cuban missile crisis, a number of Latin American leaders became concerned that their countries would suffer great harm should war between the United States and the Soviet Union occur. Their fear, of course, was justified. Following the resolution of the crisis, Bolivia, Brazil, Chile, Ecuador, and Mexico announced that they were prepared to renounce the manufacture, storage, deployment, and testing of nuclear weapons on their territory. The UN General Assembly supported this statement, and in 1967 the **Treaty of Tlatelolco** was signed calling for the creation of a nuclear-free zone throughout Latin America.

Nuclear Testing Restrictions

Several events in the 1950s and early 1960s called public attention to atmospheric nuclear testing and its effects on humans and the environment. In 1954, fallout from an American 15-megaton hydrogen-bomb test conducted in the South Pacific contaminated a Japanese fishing boat, the *Lucky Dragon*. Indian Prime Minister Nehru and the British Parliament requested that the United States cease testing. Scientists in the 1950s detected an increasing incidence of radioactive isotopes in the bone marrow of children due to the ingestion of these isotopes through milk. If this trend continued, many doctors and scientists believed, the incidence of leukemia and other forms of cancer would increase. Furthermore, many believed that the major source of these isotopes, such as strontium 90, came from nuclear tests conducted in the atmosphere. Consequently, many in the scientific community, as well as ordinary citizens, called for the cessation of nuclear testing in the atmosphere. In the 1956 presidential election, Adlai Stevenson called for a nuclear test ban, and within a year the Pope, the German Bundestag, and the British Labour party made similar appeals to the United States and the Soviet Union.

The test-ban issue was discussed at the UN Disarmament Subcommittee negotiations, but, as noted previously, these negotiations ended with no agreements being reached. In 1958, the United States and the Soviet Union agreed to conduct a series of meetings of experts to discuss various arms-control issues, including a nuclear test ban. Although there were a number of technical and political differences between the Soviet and American experts, they nevertheless agreed to open negotiations among the three powers that possessed nuclear weapons at that time: the United States, the Soviet Union, and the United Kingdom. Following the opening of these negotiations in Geneva in November 1958, the three negotiating states observed a moratorium on nuclear testing until September 1961 when the Soviet Union tested an enormous weapon with an estimated yield equal to the destructive power of 58 million tons of TNT.

There was great concern over the Soviet decision to resume testing. In addition, France exploded its first nuclear weapon in 1960. Many people feared that as more and more states developed nuclear weapons the problem of atmospheric nuclear pollution would grow increasingly serious. The Cuban missile crisis made clear that nuclear war was not just a hypothetical possibility; it really could happen. Following the crisis, President Kennedy warned in a commencement address at American University in June 1963: "Today should total war ever break out...no matter how ...our two countries would become the primary targets.... All we have built, all we have worked for, would be destroyed in the first 24 hours." Kennedy went on to speak of the need for a new approach in Soviet-American relations, and he proposed a treaty to outlaw nuclear tests. According to Kennedy, "The conclusion of such a treaty...would check the arms race in one of its most dangerous areas.... It would increase our security—it would decrease the prospects of war."[4]

The Soviets broadcast President Kennedy's speech in its entirety and, in July, Khrushchev indicated that the Soviet Union would be willing to engage in negotiations to limit nuclear testing. During the summer of 1963, American, Soviet, and British representatives met; by August they had drafted and agreed upon the Limited Test Ban Treaty, which prohibited nuclear tests in the atmosphere, outer space, and under water. This treaty was important for three principal reasons. First, at the very least it was a significant "clean air act" that resulted in a substantial reduction of atmospheric nuclear pollution. Second, and more important, the Limited Test Ban Treaty was a first step toward controlling the testing of nuclear weapons. Third, the treaty, along with the "hot line" agreement, constituted the cornerstone of modern arms control.

Despite its value, however, the Limited Test Ban Treaty did not stop nuclear testing. France and the People's Republic of China continued to test in the atmosphere, and the United States, the Soviet Union, and the United Kingdom conducted extensive testing underground. Since the signing of the Limited Test Ban Treaty (LTBT), world leaders cited a comprehensive test-ban treaty as their goal. For instance, in the preamble of the LTBT the signatories promise "to achieve the discontinuance of all test explosions of nuclear weapons for all time." And in Article VI of the **Nonproliferation Treaty,** the signatories promise "to pursue negotiations in good faith on effective measures relating to cessation of the nuclear arms race at an early date." The long-held objective of concluding a **Comprehensive Test Ban Treaty (CTBT)** was achieved in 1996 when a CTBT was signed.

Crisis Management and Crisis Prevention

Soon after World War II, it became clear that the United States and the Soviet Union were going to be competitors, rather than collaborators, in the post-1945 international system. However, even during the height of the

Cold War, Soviet and American leaders recognized that there were limits to the competition between their two countries. Leaders of both states realized that threats against the homeland of the other power threatened dangerous escalation and, consequently, neither state threatened the homeland of the other. In addition, leaders of both countries avoided direct confrontations between the military forces of the other power. The most serious crises since 1945 were precisely those in which these rules for avoiding crisis escalation were violated. Historians and political scientists generally agree that the three most serious crises were the Berlin crises of 1948 and 1961 and the Cuban missile crisis of 1962.

The United States and the Soviet Union generally communicated by deed rather than by word during the Cold War. Both countries used military forces, deployments, and maneuvers to send signals to the other side. Actions usually do speak louder than words, although they do not always convey as clear a meaning. For instance, during the Cuban missile crisis, a U.S. Air Force plane strayed off course and headed toward the USSR. Soviet leaders could have plausibly interpreted this to be the vanguard of an American attack. Fortunately, Khrushchev recognized the incident for what it was and did not order a retaliatory attack.

Following their brush with nuclear war, Kennedy and Khrushchev decided that it would be good for American and Soviet leaders to have a means of communicating with one another quickly, reliably, accurately, and secretly. As noted previously, the United States and USSR agreed to install a "hot line" between Washington and Moscow, and it was first used during the Arab-Israeli war of June 1967, when Israeli forces mistakenly attacked and sank a U.S. Navy ship, the *U.S.S. Liberty.* The hot line has been used subsequently during a number of foreign-policy crises involving the United States and Russia. In September 1971, the Hot-Line Modernization agreement was signed, and today the hot line is a state-of-the-art satellite link.

Soviet and American leaders recognized the need to develop procedures to lessen the probability of accidental nuclear war. At the same time that the Hot-Line Modernization Agreement was signed, the **Accidents Measures Agreement** was also signed. This agreement called for the United States and the Soviet Union to notify each other (1) immediately in the event of an accidental, unauthorized, or any other unexplained incident involving a possible detonation of a nuclear weapon which could create a risk of outbreak of nuclear war, (2) in the event of detection of unidentified objects, and (3) in the event of a planned missile launch beyond the territory of the launching party in the direction of the other party. The agreement calls for notification via the hot line. While this agreement did not call for the reduction of the arsenals of the United States or the Soviet

Union, it provides an important means of building confidence, increasing crisis stability, and thereby decreasing the danger of crisis escalation.

Nonproliferation Agreements

The spread of nuclear weapons became a major concern of many leaders during the 1950s and 1960s. In the late 1950s, a number of states presented resolutions calling for nonproliferation. In 1960, France tested its first nuclear device, an event that heightened public concern. In 1963, President Kennedy noted that it was possible that 10 states would develop nuclear weapons by 1970, perhaps 15 to 20 by 1975. Kennedy regarded the latter possibility as "the greatest possible danger."[5] The "nuclear club" was further expanded in 1964 with the first Chinese nuclear explosion.

The French and Chinese detonations dramatized the potential dangers of nuclear proliferation and represented direct threats to the Soviet Union, but Soviet policymakers refused to discuss nonproliferation as long as the United States was considering a plan called the **Multilateral Force (MLF)** to equip naval vessels in Europe with nuclear weapons and to man these ships with crew members drawn from North Atlantic Treaty Organization (NATO) countries. Proponents of this plan argued that it was a means of advancing European integration while simultaneously avoiding proliferation. Opponents of the proposal in the West contended that the MLF clouded the issues of NATO defense and precluded serious arms control. Soviet leaders were particularly critical of the plan since they felt that the United States was simply attempting to provide West Germany with nuclear weapons. In 1965, however, the United States abandoned the MLF proposal, opening the way for negotiations on the problem of nuclear proliferation.

As a result of discussions at meetings of the Eighteen Nation Disarmament Committee from 1965 to 1967 and informal meetings between Secretary of State Dean Rusk and Foreign Minister Andrei Gromyko in 1967, the United States and the Soviet Union were able to agree on the text of a draft nonproliferation treaty. The nonnuclear weapons' states were particularly concerned about three issues: safeguards, balanced obligations, and security assurances. In regard to the second issue—balanced obligations—the nonnuclear weapons' states believed that their renunciation of nuclear weapons should be accompanied by a commitment by the nuclear weapons states to seek a reduction in their nuclear arsenals. This concern resulted in the addition of Article VI to the treaty, calling for parties to the treaty "to pursue negotiations in good faith on effective measures relating to cessation of the nuclear arms race at an early date."

On July 1, 1968, the Nonproliferation Treaty (NPT) was opened for signature, and 62 states, including the United States and Soviet Union, signed. The treaty contained provisions for the nontransfer of nuclear weapons by signatories possessing nuclear weapons and for the continued nonacquisition of nuclear weapons by the other signatories. West Germany was therefore effectively prevented from acquiring nuclear weapons under its independent control, a matter of utmost importance to the Soviet Union. The treaty contained international safeguards to guarantee that material from peaceful nuclear programs was not diverted into weapons production. The nuclear states also promised to assist with the development of peaceful uses of nuclear energy in the nonnuclear weapons' states. In essence the NPT resulted in a quid pro quo: the nonnuclear weapons' states promised to forego the acquisition of nuclear weapons in exchange for a promise by the nuclear states to assist the nonnuclear states with their peaceful nuclear programs and to seek an end to the arms race.

The explicit objective of the NPT was to halt completely the spread of nuclear weapons. With the spread of technology and knowledge, however, that goal has proved to be impossible to achieve, as indicated by the test of a "peaceful nuclear device" by India in May 1974 and of several nuclear weapons in 1998. Most experts believe that Israel has secretly produced a limited number of assembled or nearly assembled nuclear weapons.[6] Following the 1998 Indian nuclear tests, Pakistan also tested several nuclear weapons. In addition to these three states, there are about twenty nonnuclear weapons' states that have nuclear reactors capable of producing enough plutonium or enriched uranium to produce nuclear weapons. These states include a number that are in crisis-prone areas of the world.

Since the proliferation of nuclear weapons has proved impossible to halt completely, the emphasis since the mid-1970s has been to attempt to slow the pace of proliferation. The Indian and Pakistani explosions of 1998 served as reminders that proliferation is still a problem, despite the existence of the NPT.

As the number of states with nuclear facilities has grown, so too has concern about the protection of nuclear material. At present there are over 240 commercial nuclear-power reactors in operation in 22 countries.[7] All of these, of course, require nuclear fuel in order to operate and a number of these produce plutonium as a byproduct. It takes approximately ten pounds of plutonium and a basic knowledge of nuclear physics to produce an atomic bomb. A U.S. intelligence report estimated that 31 countries, many of which are engaged in long-standing regional disputes, will have the ability to produce nuclear weapons by the year 2000. While there was hope at one time to halt all nuclear proliferation (this was, in fact, the objective of the NPT), that goal is no longer possible to achieve.

Disarmament Agreements

As noted in the introduction to this chapter, "arms control" refers to the quantitative and/or qualitative limitation of weapons, while "disarmament" refers to the elimination of certain types or all weapons. According to these definitions, all of the agreements discussed thus far are arms *control*, rather than *disarmament*, agreements. However, two agreements—the **Biological Weapons Convention** and the Intermediate Forces Treaty—call for the elimination of certain weapons.

Soon after entering office, President Nixon renounced the first use of chemical weapons and in addition stated that the United States unconditionally renounced all forms of biological warfare. Chemical weapons are produced by inorganic subelements, whereas biological weapons, such as anthrax, are produced by biological processes. Toxins act like chemical agents but are produced by biological processes. In 1970, President Nixon indicated that the United States would extend its ban to toxins as well as the two other categories of chemical-biological weapons.

President Nixon's unilateral decision to disarm the United States' biological weapons capability was not simply a magnanimous or idealistic gesture on his part. Indeed, during World War I poison gas was used extensively with devastating results. Part of the reason that it was so destructive was that its effects often could not be controlled; a shift in wind, for instance, could make the attacking party the victim of its own attack. Chemical and biological weapons do not observe boundaries. Nixon and his advisors reasoned that if biological weapons were ever used by the United States, the ultimate result could be as devastating for the United States as for the state or states we were attacking. This reasoning, coupled with the inherent horror associated with biological weapons, led to the unilateral American decision to eliminate biological weapons from the U.S. arsenal.

Discussion of an international convention prohibiting biological weapons took place at the Conference of the Committee on Disarmament, and in 1971 the United States and the Soviet Union presented identical texts of an agreement. The UN General Assembly urged acceptance of the convention, and it was opened for signature in April 1972. Within a short time, more than 100 states signed the convention.

In December 1987, Gorbachev visited Washington and signed the **Intermediate Nuclear Forces (INF) Treaty,** which eliminated nuclear missiles based in Europe with ranges of 600 to 3,500 miles, as well as those with ranges of 300 to 600 miles.

Environmental Protection

In a sense, any agreement to control nuclear arms or other weapons of mass destruction, such as biological or chemical weapons, are environmental protection agreements. If weapons of mass destruction were ever extensively employed, their effects on the world's environment would be horrific. Scientists do not know what the exact physical effects of a general nuclear war would be; most agree, however, that the world's physical environment would be profoundly affected. Three agreements have been explicitly concerned with environmental protection: the Antarctica Treaty, the Limited Test Ban Treaty, and the **Environmental Modification Convention.**

As previously discussed, the Antarctica Treaty prohibited the deposit of nuclear waste and the deployment of conventional and nuclear weapons to Antarctica. The Limited Test Ban Treaty, which prohibits nuclear testing in the atmosphere, resulted in a significant decrease in atmospheric pollution caused by radioactive isotopes such as strontium 90. Both of these treaties thus accomplish, among other things, the preservation and protection of the physical environment.

If a state were able to control certain physical phenomena such as earthquakes or rainfall, it would have a powerful weapon at its disposal. Of course, all of the consequences of meddling with nature would be difficult, if not impossible, to predict. The unintended results of tinkering with the environment could be both significant and negative for the state seeking to modify the environment for its own purpose. If there is a principal law of ecology, it is that an action taken to influence an ecological system can often have substantial and unforeseen results.

In July 1972, the United States renounced the use of environmental modification techniques for military purposes. The House of Representatives and the Senate passed resolutions in 1973 urging that an international agreement prohibiting environmental modification be negotiated. In 1974 and 1975 the United States and the Soviet Union held discussions on this subject, and in August 1975 the Soviet and American representatives to the Conference of the Committee on Disarmament (CCD) presented identical drafts of a convention prohibiting military or other hostile uses of environmental modification techniques. This draft agreement was discussed extensively in the CCD throughout 1976, and in May 1977, 34 states, including the United States and the Soviet Union, signed the agreement.

The convention prohibits the use of environmental modification techniques designed to cause physical phenomena such as earthquakes, tidal waves, and/or changes in weather patterns, climate, ocean currents, the ozone layer, or the ionosphere. The agreement calls for the establishment of a "Consultative Committee of Experts" to meet on an ad hoc basis to discuss any questions concerning compliance with the agreement.

Strategic Nuclear Arms Limitations and Reductions

The negotiations between the United States and the Soviet Union to limit strategic nuclear weapons have been the most important of the post-World War II era. These negotiations can be divided into three phases: SALT I (an acronym that stands for Strategic Arms Limitation Talks), which lasted from November 1969 to May 1972; SALT II, which lasted from November 1972 until June 1979; and START, the Strategic Arms Reductions Talks conducted by the Reagan and Bush administrations from 1982–1991.

SALT I   During the mid-1960s, President Johnson made several overtures to the Soviet Union to begin negotiations to limit strategic nuclear weapons. Soviet leaders, however, were uninterested for several reasons. First, the Soviet Union had far fewer strategic weapons than the United States. In 1965, the arsenals of the two sides contained the following weapons:[8]

	U.S.	USSR
ICBMs	854	270
SLBMs	496	120
Long-range bombers	630	190
Total	1980	580

As is readily apparent from this table, the United States had a four-to-one advantage in strategic weapons in 1965. If the Soviet Union had agreed to a freeze in weapons as President Johnson had proposed in 1964, the Soviet Union would have been frozen into a position of inferiority. Second, the Soviets were unwilling to accept on-site inspection, also called for in Johnson's proposal, and there were no commonly accepted means of verification. Third, Soviet leaders did not want to begin negotiations to limit nuclear weapons until they received firm assurance that West Germany would not develop nuclear weapons of its own.

Several developments occurred that made strategic arms negotiations more attractive to the Soviet leadership. In early 1967, President Johnson requested authorization to begin deployment of an **antiballistic missile (ABM)** system and stated that he would deploy the new missile defense system unless the Soviets indicated a genuine willingness to open negotiations to limit strategic nuclear arms. Within several months, Premier Kosygin expressed an interest in beginning the negotiations. In July 1968 the Nonproliferation Treaty (NPT) was signed by 62 states. West Germany accepted the NPT in principle in 1968 and formally signed it in November 1969. Finally, throughout the 1960s, both the United States and the Soviet Union developed and deployed sophisticated satellites and electronic equipment to gather intelligence data, making verification easier. Thus, by 1969 the time was right to begin the negotiations to limit strategic nuclear weapons.

On November 17, 1969, the **SALT I** negotiations began in Helsinki, Finland. Meeting alternately in Helsinki and Vienna, the Soviet and American delegations held seven formal negotiating sessions over the next 30 months.

The major topics of discussion at the SALT I negotiations were the limitation of defensive (ABM) and offensive (ICBM and SLBM) missile systems. These negotiations touched upon important issues such as inspection and verification, and could not be conducted in isolation from other major defense and military issues. Each area of discussion involved painstaking negotiations to reach positions on with which both sides could agree politically as well as militarily. During this period, the Vietnam war escalated, putting additional pressure on the Soviet-American relationship.

The most significant achievements of the Moscow summit were the two SALT I agreements: the ABM Treaty and the Interim Agreement on Offensive Missiles. In the ABM Treaty, the United States and the Soviet Union agreed not to deploy more than two ABM sites, one at the national capital and the other at a site at least 1,300 kilometers from the first site. Each side was limited to no more than 100 interceptor missiles and launchers. To assure compliance, the treaty called for "national technical means of verification," an official euphemism for satellite reconnaissance and the monitoring of electronic signals. The signatories promised neither to interfere with satellite verification procedures nor to deliberately conceal any ABM components. Either party had the right to withdraw from the treaty on six months' notice. The ABM Treaty was a truly remarkable agreement, since each side in essence agreed not to defend itself against an attack from the other side.

The Interim Agreement placed a quantitative limit on both international ballistic missiles and submarine-launched ballistic missiles (SLBMs). The United States was limited to 1,054 ICBMs, the Soviets to 1,618. Each side had the right under the agreement to deploy SLBMs in exchange for the dismantling of ICBMs. This was the so-called "one-way freedom to mix" (from land-based to sea-based forces) provision of the agreement. The Interim Agreement had a duration of five years (1972–1977), and both states stated that they intended to replace it with a permanent agreement.

In summary, the agreement placed quantitative limitations on Soviet and American missile launchers without restricting qualitative improvements such as multiple independently targeted reentry vehicles (MIRV).

Because the ABM agreement was a treaty, the Nixon administration was required by the Constitution to submit it to the Senate for advice and consent. The Senate approved the treaty relatively quickly and near unanimously by a vote of 88–2. Although it was not a treaty, the Interim Agreement also had to be submitted to the Congress for approval according to the terms of the 1961 law that established the Arms Control and Disarmament Agency. There was considerable debate about whether the Soviet Union was granted superiority over the United States by the Interim Agreement.

At the time they were signed, Henry Kissinger contended that the SALT I agreements were "without precedent in the nuclear age; indeed, in all relevant modern history," and that "nothing this administration had done has seemed to it more important for the future of the world than to make an important first step in the limitation of strategic arms." President Nixon stated that neither side won or lost by the agreement; rather, "both sides won, and the whole world won."[9] Thus, to Nixon and Kissinger the signing of the SALT I agreements marked a mutual step by the United States and the Soviet Union toward increased strategic stability and a significant improvement in Soviet-American relations.

SALT II   The second phase of the Strategic Arms Limitation Talks (SALT II) began on November 21, 1972, in Geneva, where all subsequent interdelegation negotiating sessions were held. By early 1973, the United States completed the process of appointing new delegation members, and the two sides got to work. Whereas SALT I imposed quantitative limitations on weapons, the major task of SALT II was to develop qualitative limitations. Most experts agree that the latter task is far more difficult to achieve for many reasons. For example, verification of qualitative limitations is problematic. Satellites can readily verify the number of missile launchers that a country has; however, given present technology, they cannot determine whether the missiles are equipped with "multiple, independently targetable re-entry vehicles" (MIRVs).

Throughout the last half of 1973 and 1974 criticism of the Nixon administration as a result of the Watergate affair became intense. Hoping to conclude a SALT II agreement and to divert the public's attention from Watergate, President Nixon visited Moscow in June 1974. He and Brezhnev signed a protocol to the ABM Treaty limiting each side to one ABM site. They also signed a communiqué stipulating that a SALT agreement covering the period from 1974 to 1985 and dealing with both quantitative and qualitative limitations should be completed prior to the 1977 expiration date of the Interim Agreement. These modest agreements were not enough to stem the tide of domestic criticism and on August 8, 1974, President Nixon resigned from office.

Anxious to reestablish the credibility of the presidency both domestically and internationally, President Gerald Ford ordered the U.S. SALT delegation to press forward with the achievement of a long-term strategic arms control agreement. In November 1974 President Ford met Secretary Brezhnev at Vladivostok to sign an "agreement in principle" which constituted a list of objectives to be achieved in the SALT II negotiations. The two leaders agreed that each of their countries should be limited to 2,400 strategic delivery vehicles (long-range bombers, ICBMs, plus SLBMs), and of this total a maximum of 1,320 could be MIRVed delivery vehicles. The new agreement was supposed to cover the period from October 1977, the date the Interim Agreement expired, through December 1985.

When the terms of the Vladivostok *aide memoire* were made public, neither the proponents nor the opponents of SALT were satisfied with the results. From the perspective of the supporters of arms control, the total aggregate number of strategic nuclear vehicles as well as the MIRV sublimit were set too high. And even though the agreement set equal limits for both the United States and Soviet Union, Senator Jackson was displeased with it since the Soviets would be able to threaten the survivability of the American ICBM force if they deployed all 1,320 warheads allowed by the agreement.

As the negotiators returned to Geneva they were faced with the problem of how to deal with new weapons systems. Somehow, negotiators had to decide in which of the SALT I categories these new weapons belonged and what existing weapons were to be eliminated to maintain the agreed weapons' ceilings. The Soviet Union began to deploy a new bomber, the Backfire, which had a range that would enable it to reach the continental United States from bases within the Soviet Union and to land in neutral territory (presumably Cuba) for refueling. The United States was also working on a number of new weapons' systems, including the MX ("Missile Experimental"), a new large ("heavy") ICBM, the Maneuverable Reentry Vehicle (MARV), the B-1 bomber, the Trident submarine, and the cruise missile.

In addition to the technological problems standing in the way of a SALT II agreement, U.S. domestic politics constituted a further obstacle to reaching an agreement. Ronald Reagan attacked the détente and arms-control policies of the Ford administration and came very close to wresting the Republican nomination away from an incumbent president. Even though Ford received the nomination, he was forced to accept a party platform that in many respects was a repudiation of his administration's policies toward the Soviet Union, thus weakening his SALT II bargaining position.

In his inaugural address, Jimmy Carter indicated a desire to move toward the ambitious goal of nuclear disarmament and not simply arms control. Within several weeks of assuming office, Carter said that he wanted to conclude a SALT II agreement quickly and to move on to further limitations. Along with his support for arms control and disarmament, the president expressed his support for human-rights activists in the Soviet Union by writing personal letters and receiving Soviet dissidents at the White House. Soviet leaders were greatly disturbed by Carter's actions and indicated that a SALT II agreement would be impossible to conclude if such "interference in domestic affairs" continued.

Over two years passed before the United States and the Soviet Union were able to negotiate a SALT II Treaty; however, on June 18, 1979, President Carter and General Secretary Brezhnev, meeting in Vienna, signed the SALT II agreement, which consisted of three parts: a treaty, a protocol, and a statement of principles, designed to remain in effect from the time it entered into force until 1985.

In support of the SALT II agreement, the Carter administration argued that the agreement would: (1) establish limits on building new types of weapons and the improvement of existing strategic arms; (2) set equal ceilings on all major intercontinental strategic nuclear-delivery systems; (3) impose an upper limit on the number of warheads that could be placed on ICBMs and SLBMs; (4) limit the expansion of the arms race; (5) place significant limits on programs that the Soviet Union might develop in the absence of SALT; (6) require the reduction of approximately 250 Soviet missiles and/or bombers; (7) forbid any interference with efforts to verify compliance with the agreement; (8) continue the process of improving relations with the Soviet Union; and (9) enable the United States to save as much as $30 billion over the decade that followed.

Opponents of the SALT II agreement argued that, if ratified, the agreement would: (1) grant the Soviet Union important military advantages in categories of weapons such as heavy ICBMs; (2) restrict the development of significant U.S. strategic arms designed to rectify the Soviet-American strategic imbalance; (3) not result in any substantial monetary savings for the United States; (4) reduce the stability of the strategic nuclear balance; (5) be unverifiable; (6) increase the Soviet drive for expansion of its influence; and (7) mark a significant decline in American power.

The Senate held hearings on the SALT II agreement during the summer of 1979. On November 9, 1979, the Senate Foreign Relations Committee voted 9 to 6 to recommend that the treaty be ratified. The Senate

Select Committee on Intelligence found that the agreement "enhances the ability of the United States to monitor those components of Soviet strategic weapons forces which are subject to the limitations of the Treaty." Only the Senate Armed Services Committee was critical of the treaty, and it appeared that the treaty would be approved by the Senate.

Events seemingly unrelated to arms control and disarmament can have a significant effect on arms limitation negotiations and the congressional consideration of such agreements. Senator Frank Church (D-ldaho) dramatically announced in August that U.S. intelligence agencies had identified a Soviet "combat brigade" in Cuba and that these troops would have to be withdrawn before the treaty could be approved. The Soviet Union repeatedly stressed that the unit had been in Cuba for a number of years and was a *training*, as opposed to combat, unit. Furthermore, the Soviets refused to consider the U.S. demand that the unit be removed from Cuba. The author of an excellent case study of the Cuban brigade crisis and SALT has concluded that if a Senate vote on SALT had been taken in August, the treaty would probably have passed; however, after the Cuban brigade became a public issue, passage of the agreement became doubtful.

In November 1979, a group of anti-American Iranian militants took over the U.S. Embassy in Teheran, and American personnel were taken hostage. The ensuing crisis, although unrelated to SALT, caused many to conclude that the United States could not compromise with the Soviet Union in any way, including the conclusion of the SALT II Treaty.

The final blow to SALT II came in December 1979 when the Soviet Union invaded Afghanistan. Because of this action, President Carter asked the Senate to delay indefinitely consideration of the SALT II Treaty. Despite the fact that the treaty was withdrawn from consideration, it was not forgotten. During the 1980 presidential campaign, Ronald Reagan claimed that the treaty was "fatally flawed" and that it "legitimized the arms race." Following his election, however, President Reagan indicated that the United States would observe the SALT II limitations as long as the Soviet Union did so.

START   In May 1982, in a commencement address to his alma mater, Eureka College, President Reagan announced that the United States and the USSR would resume negotiations on strategic weapons. But the new negotiations would be designed to achieve deep cuts in the strategic nuclear forces of both sides and would hence be renamed the "Strategic Arms Reduction Talks" (START). The first set of the new talks was held from June 1982 to December 1983 in Geneva. There was little agreement between the two sides concerning which forces would be reduced and how reductions would be verified. But the talks did indicate that the Reagan administration was trying to do something to control—even reduce—the number of nuclear weapons.

In keeping with the concerns that Reagan had expressed during the 1980 presidential campaign, the U.S. negotiators at the START talks sought to reduce Soviet capabilities that were viewed as most threatening to the United States, particularly Soviet advantages in heavy missiles and throw weight. In SALT I, the United States and USSR had used launchers as the basic accounting unit; in START, the United States sought to use missiles, throw weight, and warheads as the accounting units. This approach discriminated against the Soviet arsenal which consisted mostly of intercontinental ballistic missiles. Just as the SALT I Interim Agreement had sought to encourage the Soviets to deploy sea-based rather than land-based nuclear forces in the one-way freedom to mix (from ICBMs to SLBMs) provision, the American START proposal sought to encourage the Soviets to depend more heavily on submarines, bombers, and cruise missiles.

For their part, the Soviet Union sought to build on the SALT II Treaty and proposed percentage reductions from the SALT II limits on strategic nuclear delivery vehicles. In addition, the Soviets called for new sublimits on MIRVs and on the total number of nuclear warheads allowed each side. Soviet negotiators rejected the U.S. proposal on the grounds that it was asymmetrically disadvantageous to the USSR; that it called for disproportionate reductions precisely in those weapons categories in which the USSR had an advantage and called for few or no limits on those weapons, such as cruise missiles and bombers, in which the U.S. had an advantage.

The INF Deployments   In November 1983, the United States began deploying intermediate-range nuclear forces (INF) to Europe in keeping with NATO's two-track decision. These deployments deeply concerned the Soviets because one of the systems being deployed, the **Pershing II,** was the most accurate intermediate or long-range nuclear weapon in the American inventory. In addition, the Pershing IIs deployed in West Germany would be able to reach the Soviet Union in five minutes, giving the United States a potential first-strike capability against the USSR, possibly even against Moscow itself. Once the American INF deployments began and the fifth round of the START negotiations ended in December, the Soviets refused to set a date for the resumption of the negotiations. START had stalled.

Arms control analysts Michael Krepon and Alton Frye have summarized the events of 1984: "The year 1984 appears as a blank page in the history of nuclear-arms control. For the first time since SALT began in 1969, an entire year passed without any negotiations between the superpowers over the control and reduction of nuclear armaments."[10] American and Soviet spokespersons tried to place the blame on the other party for the impasse in negotiations. By the end of 1984, Reagan agreed to meet for the first time with Foreign Minister Gromyko. He also gave an address to the United Nations that indicated a possible change in his attitude and approach to the Soviet Union. After a hiatus of 15 months, in January 1985, Secretary of Sate George Shultz and Foreign Minister Gromyko signed an agreement to resume arms control negotiations on three separate but related issues: intermediate nuclear forces, strategic weapons, and defense and space weapons. The Nuclear and Space Arms Talks were to be conducted by a single delegation with three negotiating groups for each side. The first round of the negotiations began in March 1985, and neither the United States nor the USSR had significantly changed their START positions. However, the same month that the talks opened, a new leader was named in the Soviet Union.

Mikhail Gorbachev and "New Thinking" in Soviet Foreign Policy   The Politburo, the ruling body of the Soviet communist party, selected its youngest member, **Mikhail Gorbachev,** to succeed the three elderly leaders who had died in office since November 1982. In his book, *Perestroika,* Gorbachev wrote: "We believed, and still believe, that, as the eighties loomed up, major accords were just a stone's throw away for such areas as anti-satellite weapons, the arms trade, reductions in military activity in the Indian Ocean and the Middle Eastern settlement issues. Ten years ago! How much time and how many resources have been wasted on the arms race, and how many human lives have been lost!"[11] While part of Gorbachev's purpose in writing these words was undoubtedly rhetorical, he backed up his words with actions. He announced a unilateral moratorium on nuclear testing and followed this by announcing a unilateral cut of 500,000 troops from the Soviet military. By the autumn of 1985, the Soviets presented a proposal that responded to many of the points in the American proposal of the previous March and opened the door for further negotiations.

In November 1985, President Reagan and General Secretary Gorbachev met in Geneva for their first summit meeting. According to former arms-control negotiator Paul Nitze, "arms control was a primary topic of discussion. No significant progress was achieved on any of the major arms-control issues, but the two leaders were able to explain to each other directly and thoroughly their views on these issues and thus reach a level of understanding that could facilitate progress in the future."[12] The two leaders agreed that "a nuclear war cannot be won and must never be fought"; they affirmed that the two sides should continue to work toward an INF agreement and a 50 percent reduction in the strategic nuclear arsenals of their countries. And the two leaders agreed to meet again in 1986 and 1987.

In January 1986, Gorbachev made a dramatic announcement calling for a three-stage plan to achieve total nuclear disarmament by the year 2000. Gorbachev proposed that the United States and his country begin the process by reducing 50 percent of their strategic nuclear weapons and, for the first time, agreeing on zero intermediate nuclear forces in Europe. Although Gorbachev called for a different path, he and President Reagan shared a vision of the same destination, nuclear disarmament. Despite this shared goal, the Soviet Union continued to link reductions in strategic nuclear arms with limitations on space-based weapons.

The INF Treaty and Resumption of the START Talks   In mid-1987, American and Soviet negotiators presented proposals based on the less dramatic aspects of the discussions from the 1985 summit meeting, and incremental progress was made. In December 1987, Gorbachev visited Washington and signed the Intermediate Force (INF) Treaty which eliminated nuclear missiles based in Europe with ranges of 600 to 3,500 miles, as well as those with ranges of 300 to 600 miles. In addition, the United States and USSR issued a statement indicating the agreed framework of the START Treaty, which called for a ceiling of 6,000 total warheads on 1,600 launchers with a sublimit of 4,900 warheads on ballistic missiles. At the end of the Washington summit, Soviet and American spokespersons indicated that the two sides were very close to concluding a START agreement and that only a few outstanding issues remained, the most important of which was strategic defense.

At their 1988 summit meeting in Moscow, Gorbachev and Reagan were not able to narrow the U.S. and Soviet differences on the START Treaty that remained. Although negotiations continued after the summit meeting, no further progress was made during Reagan's term of office.

By the time that George Bush entered office in January 1989, the START negotiations had been conducted for six-and-a-half years, about the same amount of time that had been required to conclude the SALT II Treaty. The broad outline of the framework for a START Treaty remained the same as it had been under the Reagan administration, but there were several issues, in addition to SDI, that remained contentious. In addition, the two sides had not worked out the final provisions for the verification of the START Treaty. Although significant new provisions for verification—including on-site inspection, surprise inspections, and a ban on coded telemetry—were part of the INF Treaty, the two sides had difficulty working out the final verification procedures for the START agreement.

In July 1991, the U.S. and USSR signed the first START Treaty (START I), which called for a reduction of the number of long-range nuclear warheads and bombs held by each country by about one-third. In late 1991, the Soviet Union disintegrated. Nuclear weapons remained in four Soviet republics: Russia, Belarus, Ukraine, and Kazakhstan. The leaders of these independent states agreed to ratify START and to turn over their nuclear weapons to Russia by 1999.

A second START Treaty was signed in 1993 by the United States and Russia. This agreement called for a reduction in the total number of long-range nuclear warheads and bombs to less than half of the limitations called for in START I. When START II was implemented, the United States and Russia would be left with 3,000 to 3,500 long-range strategic nuclear weapons.

MICRODISARMAMENT: THE CAMPAIGNS TO BAN LAND MINES AND SMALL ARMS

In recent years, researchers in the security field have noted that since the end of World War II the greatest number of people have been killed and wounded by conventional weapons, such as land mines and small arms. In some countries, the toll has been devastating. There are an estimated 100 million land mines in the world today, and many of these have been deployed in areas of recent conflict. In Angola, an estimated 40 percent of the country's population is made up of amputees due to land mines.[13] A coalition of nongovernmental, public-interest groups called attention to this significant international problem and called for an agreement to ban the deployment of landmines. In 1998, more than 100 states signed an international treaty banning the production and deployment of landmines; the United States did not sign the treaty because it wanted to maintain the right to deploy landmines on the border between North and South Korea. The Nobel Peace Prize for 1997 was awarded to the campaign to ban landmines.

The effort to ban landmines was followed by a campaign to ban small arms, which have been responsible for most of the deaths of civilians. In July 1998, 21 states began meeting to discuss ways that the proliferation of small arms could be curbed. The governments of Norway and Canada have taken the lead in this effort, and meetings of interested countries have been held. To date, no international agreement controlling small arms has been reached, but discussions continue.

"Butterfly" landmine
Source: Arms Control Today, July 1996, page 11.

CONCLUSION

The end of the most costly war in human history presented a vision of future war that was even more horrific than the world had witnessed previously: the specter of nuclear war. Initially, the United States and the Soviet Union sought to control nuclear weapons but were unsuccessful for both political and military reasons. The two "superpowers" then developed, produced, and deployed tens of thousands of nuclear weapons—in order to deter the other side from using them.

Other states believed that they, too, needed nuclear weapons, and Great Britain, France, China, India, and Pakistan openly tested nuclear weapons and joined the "nuclear club." There were additional "secret members," including Israel, that were widely assumed to possess nuclear weapons. Efforts made to limit the proliferation of nuclear weapons were partially successful.

Following the Cuban missile crisis, the United States and USSR moved to stabilize their relationship and to reduce the nuclear danger that they faced. Initally, they installed a direct communications link between Washington and Moscow—the "hot line"—and agreed along with Great Britain to cease testing nuclear weapons in the atmosphere.

Only after the Nonproliferation Treaty was signed and USSR achieved nuclear parity with the U.S. did the two superpowers agree to try and limit their strategic nuclear arsenals. Beginning in 1972 and continuing for the next two decades, the two sides negotiated and concluded impressive agreements calling for the reduction of their strategic arsenals.

With strategic nuclear arms agreements in place, many people turned their focus to landmines and small arms by the late 1990s. A treaty calling for a halt in the production and deployment of landmines was concluded, and conferences focusing on the problems of small arms' proliferation were held.

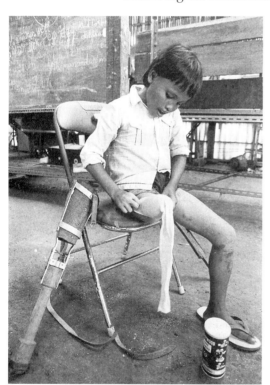

Child amputee
Source: Arms Control Today, July 1996, page 14.

DISCUSSION QUESTIONS

1. Some international relations experts contend that nuclear weapons actually contributed to the "long peace" of the last half of the twentieth century. Do you think that the world would have been more or less peaceful had nuclear weapons not been invented?

2. To what extent is a focus on the need to control nuclear weapons a vestige of the past? Are nuclear weapons still a threat?

3. How can the weapons that have actually killed the most people since the end of World War II (small arms and landmines) be most effectively controlled?

KEY TERMS

Accidents Measures Agreement
Antarctica Treaty
Biological Weapons Convention
Geneva Protocol
Intermediate Nuclear Forces
   Treaty (INF)
Multilateral Force

Nonproliferation Treaty (NPT)
Outer Space Treaty
Sputnik
Treaty of Tlatelolco
Washington Naval treaties
weapons of mass destruction

RECOMMENDED PRINT, MULTIMEDIA, AND INTERNET SOURCES

 Print

BLACKER, COIT D. and GLORIA DUFFY. *International Arms Control: Issues and Agreements*, 2nd ed. Stanford, CA: Stanford University Press, 1984.

BURNS, RICHARD DEAN, ed. *Encyclopedia of Arms Control and Disarmament*. New York: Charles Scribner's Sons, 1993. A comprehensive, three-volume collection of articles.

CALDWELL, DAN. *The Dynamics of Domestic Politics and Arms Control: The SALT II Treaty Ratification Debate*. Columbia, SC: University of South Carolina Press, 1991.

LARSEN, JEFFREY A. and GREGORY J. RATTRAY, eds. *Arms Control: Toward the 21st Century*. Boulder, CO: Lynne Rienner, 1996.

NEWHOUSE, JOHN. *War and Peace in the Nuclear Age*. New York: Alfred A. Knopf, 1989.

SCHELLING, THOMAS C. and MORTON H. HALPERIN. *Strategy and Arms Control*. Washington, DC: Pergamon-Brassey, 1985.

Multimedia

War and Peace in the Nuclear Age. A dated, but still excellent, thirteen-part series on the development of nuclear weapons, doctrines, and policies; complements the book by John Newhouse cited above.

Plague Wars. Frontline (originally broadcast October 13, 1998). Public Broadcasting System.

The Problem of Landmines, NOVA production. Public Broadcasting System.

Internet

Arms Control Association: http://www.armscontrol.org/

Bulletin of the Atomic Scientists: http://www.bullatomsci.org   Contains information related to this important journal and the "Doomsday clock."

Council for a Liveable World: http://www.clw.org/pub/clw/welcome/html

Federation of American Scientists: http://www.fas.org   This public interest group provides information about international security issues.

International Committee of the Red Cross, landmine information: www.icrc.org

Organization for Security and Cooperation in Europe: http://www.osceprag.cz/

United Nations:

> Conference on Disarmament: http://www.unog.ch/frames/disarm/disdoc.htm
>
> Demining Database: http://www.un.org/Depts/Landmine/index.html
>
> Institute for Disarmament Research: http://www.unog.ch/unidir
>
> Peace and Security home page: http://www.un.org/peace

U.S. Department of State, Arms Control and International Security: http://www.state.gov/www/globul/arms/index.html   Provides much information related to arms control and disarmament including the texts of treaties, speeches, and historical documents.

ENDNOTES

[1] THOMAS C. SCHELLING and MORTON H. HALPERIN, *Strategy and Arms Control* (Washington, DC: Pergamon-Brassey, 1985).

[2] For a comparative history of the London Subcommittee and SALT I negotiations, see Chapter 5 of Dan Caldwell, *American-Soviet Relations: From 1947 to the NixonKissinger Grand Design* (Westport, CT: Greenwood Press, 1981), pp. 145–180.

[3] "Table 1: U.S. and Soviet Strategic Forces, October 31, 1962," in RAYMOND L. GARTHOFF, *Reflections on the Cuban Missile Crisis,* revised ed. (Washington, DC: Brookings, 1989), p. 208.

[4] JOHN F. KENNEDY, "Commencement Address at American University, Washington, DC, June 10, 1963," in *Pubic Papers of the Presidents of the United States: John F Kennedy, 1963* (Washington, DC: U.S. Government Printing Office, 1964), pp. 459–464.

[5] "Press Conference of President JOHN F. KENNEDY, March 21,1963," in *Pubic Papers of the Presidents: John F. Kennedy,* op. cit., p. 273.

[6] LEWIS A. DUNN, *Controlling the Bomb: Nuclear Proliferation in the 1980s* (New Haven, CT: Yale University Press, 1983), pp. 48–49.

[7] WILLIAM C. POTTER, *Nuclear Power and Non-Proliferation: An Interdisciplinary Perspective* (Cambridge, MA: Oelgeschlager, Gunn, and Hain, 1982), p. 1.

[8] *The Military Balance, 1972–1973* (London: The International Institute for Strategic Studies, 1972), p. 67.

[9] President Nixon's briefing of congressional leaders, in U.S. Congress, Senate Committee on Foreign Relations, *Strategic Arms Limitation Agreements,* Hearings on S.J. Res. 242, 92nd Cong., 2nd sees., 1972, p. 392.

[10] MICHAEL KREPON and ALTON FRYE, "Arms Control," in Joseph J. Kruzel, ed., *American Defense Annual 1985–1986* (Lexington, MA: Lexington Books, 1985).

[11] MIKHAIL GORBACHEV, *Perestroika: New Thinking for Our Country and the World* (New York: Harper and Row, 1987).

[12] PAUL NITZE, "Arms Control," in Joseph J. Kruzel, ed., *American Defense Annual 1986–1987* (Lexington, MA: Lexington Books, 1986).

[13] HUMAN RIGHTS WATCH, *Landmines: A Deadly Legacy* (Washington, DC: Human Rights Watch, 1993), pp. 148–156.

International Law

CRITEX:

You Decide an International Law Case

MAYOR Rudolph Giuliani of New York City has scored major points with his constituents by attempting to crack down on the diplomatic "scoff-laws" who refuse to abide by the city's parking laws or to pay fines for violating these laws in his city. The reason that New York's diplomats are able to avoid arrest, conviction, and jail sentences for refusing to abide by the city's laws is **diplomatic immunity.** The theory behind this concept is that diplomats should not be subject to arbitrary regulations and laws. Therefore, by exempting diplomats from the jurisdiction of the country in which they are sent, diplomats are protected. This sounds good—but how does it work in practice?

In the early morning hours of January 3, 1997, a car traveling an estimated 80 miles per hour through the city streets of Washington, D. C., slammed into another car stopped at a red light. The impact

was so great that it forced the second car into the air, and it crashed into three other cars. Tragically, a sixteen-year old woman was killed. When the District of Columbia police arrived on the scene, they questioned the driver of the first car, George Makharadze, who at the time of the accident was a diplomat in the Embassy of the Republic of Georgia. Because of his diplomatic status, the police did not administer a blood-alcohol test to Mr. Makharadze; however, the police noted that it appeared that he had been drinking. In normal circumstances when a diplomat commits a crime, he or she is expelled from the host country. In this case, Mr. Makharadze had acted so egregiously that a number of Americans, including the dead woman's mother, called for the waiving of diplomatic immunity, something that is rare but not unheard of.

If you were deciding whether or not to waive Mr. Makharadze's diplomatic immunity what would you decide? Why?

WHAT IS INTERNATIONAL LAW

When people think of international law, they often think of the war tribunals in Nuremberg or The Hague or of debates in the United Nations. These certainly concern issues of international law, but this subject is far more extensive than these "high profile" cases. The following seemingly different events all involve the application of international law:

- an international agreement to ban particular types of weapons, from nuclear weapons to landmines;
- one multinational corporation sues another charging patent infringement;
- a prominent dissident seeks asylum in the embassy of another country;
- an author, musician, or actor requests protection of his or her "intellectual property rights" (copyright) throughout the world;
- atmospheric pollution from one country is blown over a neighboring country causing an increase in acid rain.

Although these represent a wide variety of activities, they all concern international law.

International law may be defined as the system of rules that aims to organize the behavior, of international actors. In this definition, there are three key elements: rules, behavior, and actors. Rules are the norms that are developed or established to guide or constrain the actions or decisions of the various actors of world politics. As noted in Chapter 4, these actors include states and nonstate actors such as individuals, nongovernmental and international organizations.

Broadly speaking, there are two types of international law: public and private. **Public international law** mostly concerns the interactions of states and laws including recognition of governments, boundaries, and territory, laws of war, and treaties in issue areas from arms control to trade. **Private international law** concerns the legal aspects of international trade, commerce, and finance and includes the laws of tariffs, quotas, and lending.

THE DEVELOPMENT OF INTERNATIONAL LAW

Modern international law evolved over many centuries from several different sources. One of the principal sources was moral or religious codes. More than three millennia ago in 2100 B.C., King Hammurabi of Babylon said, "I establish law and justice in the land." The Old Testament of the Bible describes a number of rules that were applicable to the behavior of groups of people as well as to individuals. The Koran, the sacred book of Islam, also describes norms that are applicable to intergroup behavior.

An example of international law deriving from religiously based norms concerns the principles of **just war theory.** Some of those in the early Christian church refused to support earthly kingdoms, but if Christians, considering themselves to be part of the "kingdom of God" on earth, did not give their support to the kingdoms of the world and if the civilized world became converted to Christianity, then who, asked Celsus, a pagan critic of Christianity living in the second century A.D., would protect civilization from "wild and lawless barbarians?"[1] To Celsus (and balance-of-power realists of two millennia later), "peace" was defined in fundamentally different ways than the "peace" of the early Christian church. According to a latter-day realist:

> Peace presupposes order. Order presupposes power. And power, if it does not actually presuppose force, at least presupposes the capacity to prevent the use of force, which usually comes to the same thing.[2]

When confronted with the threat of barbarian invasion, Christians increasingly viewed their divinely inspired "peace of God" as dependent upon the *Pax Romana.* With the accession of Constantine to the Roman throne and his subsequent conversion to Christianity, theologians reasoned that the *Pax Romana* and the Christian peace were one and the same.

By the fifth century the pacifistic practice of the early Christians had deteriorated to such an extent that membership in the church became a prerequisite for enlistment in the Roman military.

Theological justifications were presented concurrent with the shift from abstention to participation in military activity. The Christian ethic of war was first presented by St. Ambrose, who saw little conflict between church and state since he had been the praetorian prefect of northern Italy prior to becoming the bishop of Milan. To Ambrose, the defense of Christianity and the Roman Empire were one and the same. Ambrose stipulated two conditions for Christians to participate in war: the war must be "just" as determined by the civil authority, and priests must abstain from participating in war.

While Ambrose laid the foundations for Christian just-war theory, St. Augustine developed the concept more fully. The kingdom of God, what Augustine called the "City of God," was simply not a realistic possibility in the kingdom of the world. War, as Plato and Cicero had argued, must only be waged with the intent to restore peace, and by "peace," Augustine meant the maintenance of justice through law and order. Augustine postulated that war is only justified if: (1) all peaceful means of settlement have been exhausted; (2) if the injuries from the war do not outweigh the injustices created by the war; (3) if a properly constituted political authority approves the war; and (4) if the only motives of the authority are based on the restitution of justice.[3] Augustine's conception of the just war became the accepted doctrine of the Catholic Church and broader Christian community. How does this apply to twentieth century world politics?

Another major source of modern international law is **diplomacy.** As political entities interacted with one another, they found that certain rules facilitated their interaction. For example, representatives from one state to another needed to be protected from arrest, imprisonment, and/or execution. The custom of not arresting foreign representatives evolved over time into the practice of diplomatic immunity, the principle of international law on which the introductory critex in this chapter focused. This custom was codified into formal, explicit legal language in the 1961 Vienna Convention on Diplomatic Relations.

Diplomats, called "Foreign Service Officers" in the United States, are supposed to represent the interests of their country. There are several different types of diplomats. An ambassador is the representative of one country sent to the capital of another to represent the interests of his or her country. Before the advent of modern communications, ambassadors were granted the freedom to interpret and negotiate on behalf of the leaders they represented. For example, when Benjamin Franklin was the American ambassador to France in the late eighteenth century, it took a sailing ship several months to travel between the United States and Europe. As a result, the president granted Franklin significant power so that he could negotiate on behalf of the United States. With near-instantaneous communications today, diplomats no longer have the independence and leeway in decision making enjoyed by their predecessors. Outside the capital cities of states, they are represented by **consuls** or **consuls-general.** These officials issue visas, deal with problems that citizens of their countries encounter and are responsible for other tasks, such as the promotion of trade and issuing trade documents. Many of the tasks dealt with by diplomats are regulated by international law.

The development of modern international law is credited to a Dutch jurist by the name of **Hugo Grotius (1583–1645),** who published his most influential work, *The Law of War and Peace,* in 1625. You will recall that the Thirty Years' War lasted from 1618 to 1648. Therefore, Grotius's book was published in the midst of the war. With the signing of the Treaty of Westphalia in 1648, modern states began to emerge. In his book Grotius argued that there were principles that bound the states that were emerging at the very time that he was writing. The French political philosopher, Baron de Montesquieu, summarized the legal principle underlying the state system: "Nations ought to do one another in peace, the most good, and in war, the least evil possible."[4] This is a rather good objective to keep in mind even today!

THE SOURCES OF INTERNATIONAL LAW

If you have ever been at sea or even watched ships passing one another, you may have noticed that they always pass left side to left side, or in nautical language, "port to port." Have you ever wondered why ship captains act in this way and how they know they should pass port to port? The Geneva Convention on the Law of the Sea, signed in 1958, stipulates that this is the way ships are supposed to operate, but for centuries—perhaps even millennia—ships had passed one another port to port. In order to avoid collisions, ships captains developed the *custom* of passing port to port. Over time custom was enshrined in a formal, written agreement. **Custom** is therefore the first source of international law and is recognized as such in Article 38 of the Statute of the International Court of Justice, which was the judicial body established by the League of Nations. Diplomatic immunity is another practice of international law that evolved from custom.

The second source is international conventions and agreements. **Treaties** are explicit, binding agreements that create mutual rights and obligations under international law. Since the inception of the Westphalian state system in 1648, more than 25,000 treaties have been concluded. They govern a wide variety of issues from political-military issues of war and peace, arms control and disarmament, to economic issues such as trade, quotas, and taxation to transnational issues such as the environment, communications, and intellectual property rights. It is no exaggeration to state that the contemporary international system could not operate without treaties to regulate international issues.

A third source of international law is "general principles of law recognized by civilized nations." International law had evolved from the interactions of Western, Christian communities which shared a number of common morals and mores. These common values were assumed to be shared by all "civilized nations," despite the fact that many of these same states engaged in some very *uncivilized* actions, such as trading in slaves and war. Despite this glaring contradiction, the authors of the Statute of the International Court of Justice included this phrase as a source of modern international law. Many of those from developing countries objected to this phrase, and more broadly to international law, because it dramatically illustrated the bias that international law had for developed states. The legal principles to which this article referred were principles such as equity (justice by right) and comity (voluntary courtesy).

The fourth source of international law consists of the judicial decisions and teachings of leading authorities. In the United States, the judicial principle of *stare decisis* (Latin words which mean "let the decision stand") is followed; this means that the decision of a court is followed until it is overturned. The principle of *stare decisis* is not observed in international law. Consequently, international courts may consult the decisions of other courts and the teaching of leading authorities in the field in order to assist with reaching decisions.

One other point should be noted: international law, unlike France's Napoleonic Code or the United States Code, has no written, comprehensive body of statutes or laws.

HOW INTERNATIONAL AND DOMESTIC LAW DIFFER

Simplistically speaking (and as every American school child is taught), the legislative branch makes the laws; the executive branch implements the laws; and the judicial branch interprets the laws. Let us apply this threefold organizational framework to international law.

Who makes international law? There is no international equivalent of the United States Congress to pass laws that are binding on all international actors. The General Assembly of the United Nations is the closest analog to an international parliament; however, few of its resolutions are legally binding. In a world of sovereign states, it is states that make laws, and states decide if they will abide by a particular international agreement. In some cases, however, the international community feels so strongly that a particular agreement should be followed that it requires all states to abide with it. For example, both slavery and genocide have been outlawed by international agreements.

Who implements international laws? States decide what to do and what not to do in their international relations. The late, respected international law authority J. L. Brierly wrote: "Each state remains free to take such action as it thinks fit to enforce its own rights." In keeping with this approach, states often take **"self-help"** actions; that is, they take it upon themselves to enforce international law and include such actions as diplomatic protests, reprisals, the threat or imposition of economic boycotts, and the use of military force. "Self-help" includes doing to another state what it has done to you. For example, since its creation in 1948, the state of Israel has adopted a policy of immediate retaliation for any attack on it. Critics of Israel contend that it is following "vigilante justice" and taking law into its own hands. Israel's defenders respond by pointing out that there is no comprehensive international judicial system and that the best way to deter attacks on Israel is to retaliate swiftly and disproportionately.

Who interprets international laws? For any judicial system to operate effectively, it must possess three characteristics. First, it must have compulsory jurisdiction. Assume that you were late leaving your home or dorm for class today, and you went over the speed limit. If the police pull you over, you do not have an option whether or not you will be subject to the court system that will determine what your punishment is for speeding. In international law, states decide whether they will be subject to jurisdiction. For example, in the early 1980s the United States government was hostile toward the communist, Sandinista government of Nicaragua and sought to pressure it by mining three of its harbors in 1984. Seven Nicaraguan vessels and six from other states were damaged, and the Nicaraguan government, understandably infuriated by this action, went to the International Court of Justice—also called the "World Court"—in The Hague, Netherlands, and sued the United States.

The case went through two phases. In the first phase, the United States argued that the ICJ had no jurisdiction because the issues involved were political and not legal. The court found that it did, in fact, have jurisdiction and announced its intention to proceed to a second phase. In response to this ruling, the United States withdrew from the case in January 1985. The U.S. government chose not even to send a defense team to The Hague. Not surprisingly under these circumstances, the court found in favor of

Nicaragua. And what happened to the United States? Not a thing—because there is no enforcement mechanism in international law.

A second essential characteristic for any effective judicial system is an accepted hierarchy of judicial decisions. In international relations there is no hierarchy of decisions. Therefore, there is no way to decide if the decision of a Spanish court, for example, should take precedence over that of an Italian court. In domestic law, typically, national courts' decisions take precedence over those of municipal courts. In international law, large, powerful states' courts do not take precedence over courts of smaller, less powerful states.

Lastly, there must be a recognized "supreme court," and all other courts must be subordinate to its findings. This recognition of a supreme court makes the system work; there is a court of last resort. Presently in the United States, the findings of the International Court of Justice are not superior to the U.S. Supreme Court.

PUBLIC INTERNATIONAL LAW COURTS

Arbitration Tribunals

There are several courts in the international system in which disputes can be argued and judgment reached. One type of international court is an arbitration tribunal, which hears cases and then issues findings based on the facts of the particular case presented. There are a number of such panels, commissions, and tribunals, and they appear to be playing an increasingly significant role in resolving international disputes.

Regional Courts

A second type of international court consists of regional courts, such as the Inter-American Court of Human Rights, the Andean Court of Justice, and the Community Tribunal of the Economic Community of West African States. In addition to these are the European Court of Justice (ECJ) and the European Court of Human Rights. Since its founding in 1952, the ECJ has heard more than 8,500 cases. It used to be that only states could be parties to disputes heard by international courts; this is no longer the case. For example, in the European Court of Human Rights, individuals may initiate cases. The demand was so great on the ECJ that it established a Court of First Instance that hears cases from nonstate actors (individuals, corporations and other organizations).[5]

International Court of Justice

The third type of international court is the International Court of Justice (ICJ) headquartered in The Hague, the Netherlands. The ICJ has fifteen members elected by the UN General Assembly and Security Council for nine-year terms. Typically, each of the members of the UN Security Council has one member and the other ten members are selected from other UN member states. From 1946 to 1997 the ICJ heard 96 cases and issued 60 judgments and 23 advisory opinions. States are often unwilling to submit cases to the ICJ because once submitted, findings in cases by the court are final; they cannot be appealed. This is one reason for the relatively small number of cases. Despite this, the number of cases considered by the ICJ has increased in recent years. Between 1996 and 1998, the court heard an average of 14 cases each year. Unlike the regional international courts, only states may bring cases before the ICJ.

International War Tribunals

A fourth type of court are **international war tribunals**. At the end of World War II, the victorious allies decided to hold the leaders of the Axis Powers accountable for their actions, and trials were held in both Nuremberg, Germany, and Tokyo, Japan. Of course, these trials were possible only because the Allies had achieved complete victory over Germany and Japan which had surrendered unconditionally. In Tokyo 28 Japanese officials were indicted, and 7 were sentenced to be hanged. In Nuremberg, there were 24 defendants, including Hitler's closest advisors and Germany's top military leaders. Most of these sought to defend their actions by noting that they had been following orders of superiors. If this defense had been accepted, then there would only have been one possible guilty party: Adolf Hitler. The War Crimes Court rejected the "following orders" defense and sentenced 12 of the defendants to be hanged. Eventually, 10 were executed; Martin Bormann was tried *in absentia* and Hermann Goering avoided the hangman's noose by committing suicide. In addition to these most powerful German and Japanese officials, more than 3,500 others were indicted and tried. Eventually, the courts imposed the death sentence on more than 1,000 of those indicted, but not all of these were executed.

Many assumed that the Nuremberg and Tokyo trials would serve as both a warning and a deterrent to future potential perpetrators of genocide and other crimes against humanity, but, tragically, that did not prove to be the case, as events in Bosnia, Rwanda, and Kosovo demonstrated.

To what extent should the Nuremberg Principles be applied to Bosnia?

On the afternoon of July 10, 1995, elements of the Bosnian Serb army entered Srebrenica, a city in which the United Nations said refugees could seek refuge and be protected from harm. More than 40,000 had sought refuge in the town. As the Bosnia Serb soldiers entered the city, a UN officer frantically typed a message to his superiors in Geneva:

> Urgent urgent urgent. B.S.A. [Bosnian Serb Army] is entering the town of Srebrenica. Will someone stop this immediately and save these people. Thousands of them are gathering around the hospital. Please help.[6]

Tragically, no one came to help, and within several days reports of horrific acts of brutality were becoming known.

Many thought that acts such as these died with the last shots fired in World War II and the obscenities performed by the Nazis. But the reports from Bosnia were tragically reminiscent of the Holocaust. What is the role of law in the face of such brutality?

In May 1993, the International War Tribunal was convened for the first time since the Nuremberg trials in The Hague, the Netherlands. The court indicted a number of Serbs, Croats, and Muslims from the former Yugoslavia. Of course, there were significant differences between these trials and the Nuremberg trials; the most significant was that there was no clear victor and no unconditional surrender in the Bosnian case.

To what extent should the principles developed in the Nuremberg trials be applied to the Bosnian case? Of course, actions in international relations, as in other human endeavors, often cost something. In this situation many of those who have been indicted bear arms and are protected by armed supporters. Is it worth risking the lives of NATO soldiers in order to arrest those allegedly responsible for the killing of thousands of innocent civilians?

Acting as an advisor to the secretary general of the United Nations, write a memo indicating whether and why you think the principles established at Nuremberg should be applied in the Bosnian case.

Unfortunately, Bosnia was not the only place in the contemporary world where genocide was perpetrated. In Rwanda (see Chapter 14) hundreds of thousands of innocent people were killed, and an international war crimes tribunal was established to indict and prosecute those responsible for these crimes.

The Nuremberg Trial
Source: New York Times, November 19, 1995.

PRIVATE INTERNATIONAL LAW

Consider the following transactions: Japanese automobile manufacturers sell cars to American consumers; the U.S. grain companies sell wheat to Russia; the British distillers sell whiskey to Japan; the Arabian-American Oil Company (Aramco) sells oil to the rest of the world. International commerce in a wide variety of commodities and goods is a defining characteristic of the contemporary world. Indeed, even prior to the Treaty of Westphalia and the development of states, the city-states of Europe developed rules for regulating trade and commerce, referred to as *lex mercatoria* (translation: the law of merchants).[7] In order to promote trade, a number of states adopted the same rules, and as a consequence, the commercial rules of many of the world's states are similar. For example, the Uniform Code of the United States and the Sale of Goods Act in Great Britain are similar.

States, as realists in international relations are fond of pointing out, seek to exert control over the activities in their territory, and one of those activities is international trade. States seek this control through several means, including tariffs and quotas.

So you're interested in becoming a lawyer? Many senior international affairs officials are lawyers but, on balance, law school is probably not the most efficient way to start a career in international relations. Law school is three years of a curriculum which is mostly irrelevant to international affairs. It is hard to get into good law schools, and there is usually no financial aid except for loans. The current surplus of lawyers means that law-school graduates are now having serious trouble getting jobs. It's true that you may be able to get an interesting nonlegal job with a law degree, since employers figure you must be reasonably intelligent if you have survived law school, but there are other alternatives. If you want to be a lawyer, go to law school. If you don't, think seriously about the alternatives.

There is a good deal of confusion about international law as a career. As noted in this chapter, it is convenient to divide international law into public and private. Public international law concerns whether or not the behavior of governments corresponds with international law. This is what the term "international law" means to most people, but there are very few institutions which will pay people to do such analysis. The State Department keeps about 80 lawyers on its staff for this purpose, but most of the other people in the field teach in universities (probably as many in political science departments as in law schools).

Most international lawyers are concerned with private international law—how individuals and corporations can carry on transactions within different and sometimes conflicting legal systems. If an oil tanker ship registered in Liberia and owned by a company in the Cayman Islands carrying a load of oil owned by an American corporation hits a British submarine and dumps its oil onto French beaches, who pays what to whom? Private international law is popular because people and organizations will

A **tariff** is "a levy payable to a state at the place of import of a foreign good."[8] There are two results of tariffs. First, they produce income for the state, and second, they increase the cost of foreign goods and stimulate the sales of competing, domestically produced products (see Chapter 11 for examples of this). A **quota** is a restriction placed on the quantity of foreign goods that may be imported, and the intent is to protect domestic markets from foreign competition. Both tariffs and quotas are implemented by laws passed by states, and international law provides the means by which trade and commerce are made possible.

Another area of major activity of private international law is financial transactions. Each day, currency valued at more than $1.5 trillion is exchanged by individuals, corporations, international organizations, and governments. This could not be accomplished without the rules and procedures provided by international law.

pay money to get answers to these sorts of questions. This kind of work in turn sometimes leads to other things; international lawyers often serve as representatives for multinational corporations to the public and governments, a kind of business diplomatic corps. Nonetheless, international law is a fairly minor branch of law, and this is reflected in law-school curricula; if you get two international law courses in three years, you'll be doing well.

Law school, then, is the best alternative for anyone who wants to practice private international law, but you must remember that you have to be a lawyer first and an international lawyer second. If you want to study public international law, you may actually do better in a Ph.D. program in political science specializing in international law, although there are very few places in the United States where this is a serious alternative; your career will presumably involve working in a university as a teacher-researcher, either in political science or, less likely, in law school.

There is no recognized prelaw curriculum in the United States; essentially law schools will take you regardless of your major if your grade point average and law school admission test scores are high enough. Inasmuch as curriculum makes a difference, they prefer students with broad interests in the liberal arts and tend to frown on preprofessional degrees. In particular, they recommend that you do not take law courses before you get to law school, arguing (probably correctly) that "others" will just teach you incorrectly and that they will have to undo all the damage caused by pre-law school studies. However, anyone interested in law school should take at least one course which requires intensive reading of cases, just to see if you can tolerate it for three years, since that is what you do in law school. Such courses can be found in the political science and philosophy departments at the upper-division level.

SEVERAL APPLICATIONS OF INTERNATIONAL LAW PRINCIPLES

Public international law concerns subjects such as recognition of newly established states, nationality, law of the sea, and control of resources.

Recognition is the act by one state of formally acknowledging the existence of another, and states use recognition in both positive and negative ways. A state may recognize another in order to indicate its approval of the establishment of the new state. When the state of Israel was founded in 1948, the Soviet Union recognized it within minutes, and the United States recognized it within hours. Such quick recognition indicated to the rest of the world that the two most powerful states at that time supported the establishment of a Jewish state. Recognition can also be used to indicate disapproval. The Bolsheviks (communists) staged a successful revolution in 1917 and proclaimed a new government, the Union of the Soviet

Socialist Republics (USSR), also called the Soviet Union. Most of the Western European states and the United States were hostile toward this new government, and several withheld diplomatic recognition. The United States, for example, did not formally recognize the USSR for 16 years—until 1933. Communists in China, under the direction of Mao Zedong, defeated the Nationalists and proclaimed a new government in 1949. As in the Soviet case, the U.S. government demonstrated its hostility toward this new government by withholding formal diplomatic recognition—in China's case for more than 29 years (from 1949 to 1978).

Nationality may be defined as "the legal tie between states and firms or persons, deciding to which states duties and rights are owed or held by such persons or firms."[9] As applied to people, nationality is another word for citizenship and is conferred via three means: (1) when a person is born in a state (*jus soli*), (2) via a person's parents, which is called *jus sanguinis* (nationality by blood or parents), and (3) via naturalization, which involves certain residency and knowledge required by the country in which one wishes to become a citizen. Citizenship confers both benefits and responsibilities on its holder. For example, citizens are usually required to pay taxes to their home states; they may also be required to serve in the military.

Some individuals are citizens of more than one country and therefore possess dual nationality. This can occur in several different ways. Typically, a child born in state A where its parents, who are citizens of state B, are working. If state A applies the rules of both *jus soli* and *jus sanguinis*, then the child may be a citizen of both state A and B. Some countries require children to choose their citizenship, and accept the corresponding responsibilities, at age 18 or 21. Finally, some individuals may seek out dual citizenship for financial or personal reasons. When Hong Kong was returned to the People's Republic of China in 1997, a number of wealthy citizens of Hong Kong were concerned about what would happen under the Chinese communist government. The government of Canada issued passports to Chinese who agreed to invest a minimum of $250,000 in Canadian businesses. Dual citizenship can be advantageous or disadvantageous. Most dual citizens are subject to taxes in both of their "home" countries, although tax treaties limit the amount of tax owed. Students of Irish descent will be interested to learn that the government of Ireland will issue an Irish passport (which is tantamount to a "green card" work permit throughout the European Union) to any person with at least one Irish grandparent.

Law of the Sea.   Another area of growing importance to the international community concerns the control of the world's oceans and resources. For most of recorded history, people assumed that the resources of the world's oceans were inexhaustible; fish and shellfish were so plentiful that there were enough for all. With the growth of population came increasing demand and with technological developments came more efficient means of harvesting the resources of the sea, and it became clear that these resources—not only fish, but also oil, gas, and hard minerals such as manganese, copper, cobalt and nickel—were both valuable and depletable. Most states initially claimed a territorial limit of three miles because this was the distance that a cannonball could be fired. In 1945, the United States asserted sovereign jurisdiction over the oil and gas beneath the continental shelf of the United States which extended hundreds of miles out to sea in some areas. Following suit, Chile then claimed a 200-mile territorial sea, arguing that it was entitled to the fish resources of its adjacent ocean. By 1970, Argentina, Brazil, Chile, Ecuador, El Salvador, Nicaragua, Panama, and Peru claimed a 200-mile territorial limit. A number of conflicts over control of fisheries ensued, including the so-called "Tuna War" between the United States and Peru and the "Cod War" between Great Britain and Iceland.[10]

As the technological means of recovering minerals from the deep seabed increased, interest in these resources correspondingly increased. Wealthy individuals were interested in tapping these resources; multinational corporations wanted to mine them, and states wanted to assert control over the resources in the territory that they claimed. The United Nations argued that the resources of the seabed were "the common heritage of mankind," and that any income from the mining and sale of these resources should be fairly distributed, and perhaps even used to assist development of poor, developing countries. A series of conferences focusing on the law of the sea have been held under the auspices of the United Nations, and the third of these conferences met from 1973–1982. The Third United Nations Conference on the Law of the Sea (UNCLOS III) declared that the deep seabed resources belong to all of humankind, called for the establishment of an international seabed authority, and called for the creation of an intergovernmental mining company to exploit the mineral resources of the seabed. More than 150 states have signed this agreement, and it entered into force in 1993.

CONCLUSIONS

Some people dismiss international law as ineffective and point to examples such as the Kellogg-Briand Pact (also called the Pact of Paris) which was signed in 1928 and had the objective of outlawing war. Of course, neither this nor any other agreement has outlawed war, as the 60 million people killed in World War II demonstrated. But it was this very same agreement under which the Nazi German officials were tried at Nuremberg. So even the Kellogg-Briand Pact has had some utility.

And what about the case presented in the Critex at the beginning of this chapter? What did you decide should be done? Here is what actually happened: The decision went all the way to the president of Georgia, former Soviet foreign minister, Eduard Shevardnadze, who decided to waive Mr. Makharadze's immunity. He was tried in the Washington, DC courts, convicted, and sentenced to many years in prison. This seems like a reasonable outcome, but what will happen when an American diplomat accidentally kills a citizen of another country? Won't there be increased pressure to waive diplomatic immunity?

One can legitimately conclude that public international law has been ineffective in achieving broad, grandiose objectives, such as the elimination of all warfare; however, private international law has been absolutely essential for international trade, commerce, and financial transactions. As the world grows more and more interdependent, private international law will become more and more important.

DISCUSSION QUESTIONS

1. What are the main reasons that the international legal system differs so much from domestic legal systems?
2. Some cynics dismiss international law as a waste of time. How would you defend international law in the face of such criticisms?
3. To what extent are international war tribunals such as those for Bosnia and Rwanda important? Why?

KEY TERMS

consul, consul-general	international war tribunals
custom	just-war theory
diplomacy	quota
diplomatic immunity	recognition
Grotius, Hugo	self-help
International Court of Justice	tariff
international law	treaty

RECOMMENDED PRINT, MULTIMEDIA, AND INTERNET SOURCES

Print

BECK, ROBERT, ANTHONY CLARK AREND, and ROBERT VANDER LUGT, eds. *International Rules: Approaches from International Law and International Relations.* New York: Oxford University Press, 1996.

BRIERLY, J. L. *The Law of Nations: An Introduction to the International Law of Peace,* 5th ed. Oxford: Clarendon Press, 1955.

BROWNLIE, IAN. *Principles of Public International Law,* 4th ed. Oxford, England: Clarendon Press, 1990.

———. *Basic Documents in International Law,* 4th ed. Oxford: Clarendon Press, 1995.

CLARK, ROGER and MADELEINE SANN, eds. *The Prosecution of International Crimes: A Critical Study of the International Tribunal for the Former Yugoslavia.* New Brunswick, NJ: Transaction Books, 1996.

DAMROSCH, LORI FISLER and DAVID SCHEFFER, eds. *Law and Force in the New Internation-al Order.* Boulder, CO: Westview Press, 1991.

EPPS, VALERIE. *International Law for Undergraduates.* Durham, NC: Carolina Academic Press, 1998.

FRIEDMAN, WOLFGANG, OLIVER J. LISSITZYN, and RICHARD C. PUGH, eds. *Cases and Mate-rials on International Law.* St. Paul, MN: West Publishing Company, 1969.

JANIS, MARK. *An Introduction to International Law,* 2nd ed. Boston: Little, Brown, 1993.

JOYNER, CHRISTOPHER, ed. *The United Nations and International Law.* Washington, DC: American Society of International Law, 1997.

RATNER, STEVEN and JASON ABRAMS. *Accountability for Human Rights Atrocities in Inter-national Law.* Oxford: Clarendon Press, 1997.

SLOMANSON, WILLIAM R. *Fundamental Perspectives on International Law,* 2nd ed. St. Paul, MN: West, 1995.

Video

Judgment at Nuremberg. A classic film focusing on the issues and drama surrounding the trial of Nazi officials.

The Legacy of Nuremberg. Princeton, NJ: Films for the Humanities and Sciences, 50 min-utes. Focuses on the moral and ethical issues related to war crimes trials.

Internet

International Court of Justice: Homepage: http://www.icj-cij.org/
    Opinions: www.law.cornell.edu/icj

International Crimes Tribunal: www.un.org/icty/   www.cij.org/tribunal

Rules of War Database, Fletcher School of Law and Diplomacy, Tufts University: www.TUFTS.EDU/fletcher/multilaterals.html

University of Chicago Foreign and International Law:
    http://www.lib.uchicago.edu/LibInfo/Law/intl.html
    UN international law websites: Principal laws: www.un.org/law/
    Treaty database: www.un.org/Depts/Treaty/

War Crimes Tribunal for the Former Yugoslavia, see the United Nations home page on human rights: http://www.un.org/rights

ENDNOTES

[1] ROLAND BAINTON, *Christian Attitudes toward War and Peace* (New York: Abington Press, 1960), p. 68.

[2] MICHAEL HOWARD, "Power Politics—Raymond Aron's Theory of Peace and War," *Encounter* (February 1968), p. 55.

[3] QUINCY WRIGHT, *A Study of War,* 2 vols. (Chicago: University of Chicago Press, 1942), p. 158.

[4] MARK W. JANIS, *An Introduction to International Law* (Boston: Little, Brown, 1988), p. 2.

[5] MARK R. AMSTUTZ, *International Conflict and Cooperation: An Introduction to World Politics* (New York: McGraw-Hill, 1999), p. 318.

[6] STEPHEN ENGELBERG and TIM WEINER, "Srebrenica: The Days of Slaughter," *The New York Times,* October 29, 1995, p. 1.

[7] M. JANIS, *Introduction to International Law,* see Chapter 8.

[8] Ibid., p. 205.

[9] CATHAL J. NOLAN, *The Longman Guide to World Affairs* (New York: Longman, 1995), p. 256.

[10] See JANIS, *Introduction to International Law,* p. 205.

International
Political Economy

CRITEX:
Country Risk Analysis

*M*ANY banks and international corporations analyze the risks that they face investing in various countries around the world. In conducting country risk studies, analysts examine a great deal of economic data concerning the countries in which they are considering investing. Table 11.1 contains economic data on 12 different countries.

Assume that you work for a large, U.S.-based multinational corporation. Furthermore, assume that your supervisor has asked you in which country the corporation should invest $50 million? Which country would you recommend and why?

You might be interested in analyzing other countries' economic data; if so, check in the CIA's *World Factbook* and see if there are any countries that you think would be better investments than those listed in Table 11.1. Discuss your investment recommendations with other members of the class.

TABLE 11.1

Economic and Political Forecast for Selected Countries

	Political Stability	GDP (billion $)	GDP per Capita	GDP Growth Rate	Inflation Rate	Unemployment Rate	Exports (billion $)	Imports (billion $)	External Debt (billion $)	Industrial Growth Rate	Economic Aid (million $)
Argentina	High	$348	$9,700	8.4%	0.3%	13.7%	$25.4	$30.3	$115	8.7%	NA
Botswana	Medium	5	3,300	6.0	10	30	2.3	1.6	619	4.6	189
Brazil	Medium	1,040	6,300	3.0	4.8	7	53	61.4	193	4.5	107
Bulgaria	Medium	35.6	4,100	-7.4	1.0	14	4.9	4.5	10	-7.4	NA
Croatia	Medium to Low	22.7	4,500	4.4	3.7	16	4.3	9.1	6	0	300
Ireland	High	60	18,600	6	1.6	12	54.8	45	14	10.1	81
Ivory Coast	Medium	26	1,700	6.5	3.4	NA	4.2	3.2	16.1	9	552
Jordan	Medium	21	4,800	5.3	3	20	1.5	3.7	7.3	-3.4	424
Kazakhstan	Medium	50	3,000	2.1	12	2.6	5.6	6.0	3.3	3	10
Lebanon	Medium	15.2	4,400	4	9	18	1.0	7.6	2.3	25	700
Pakistan	Medium	344	2,600	3.1	12	NA	8.2	11.4	33	3.3	2,200
Thailand	Medium	525	8,800	-0.4	5.6	3.5	51.6	73.5	90	-15	624

Source: Central Intelligence Agency, *World Factbook 1998*, http://www.odci.gov/cia/publications/factbook

INTRODUCTION

Economics has been important to states since their development at the end of the Thirty Years' War; yet, many observers of international relations have not recognized the significance of economic issues. Today, it is not possible to ignore the importance of economic issues. The front page of a major newspaper on almost any day contains articles related to trade, international monetary relations, and other economic topics. Indeed, it is no exaggeration to note that one simply cannot adequately understand contemporary international relations without some understanding and appreciation of the role that economics plays.

In this chapter, we will cover: (1) historical approaches to the production of wealth, (2) the evolution of the international economic system, and (3) the actors and issues in the international economic system today.

HISTORICAL APPROACHES TO THE PRODUCTION OF WEALTH

Mercantilism and Protectionism

During the past three-and-a-half centuries, three dominant economic explanations of international political economy have emerged. The first of these, **mercantilism,** evolved concurrently with the rise of nation-states. Mercantilists believed that economic power could be maximized through the promotion of exports and by acquiring as much gold and silver as possible. Both of these means to maximize economic power required a robust fleet of merchant ships and a strong navy to protect them. Spain and Portugal in the fifteenth and sixteenth centuries based their policies on mercantilistic assumptions and, because of this, sponsored explorations to the "new world," in an attempt to increase the gold and silver in their treasuries. In essence, mercantilism was a policy of economic nationalism that viewed the world economic system as a zero-sum game: one state's gains were viewed as another state's losses. The prototype of the mercantilistic state was Great Britain of the nineteenth century.

During the 1980s, two political economists, David Blake and Robert Walters, pointed to the emergence of a new form of mercantilism, which they termed **neo-mercantilism:** "trade policy whereby a state seeks to maintain a balance-of-trade surplus and to promote domestic production and employment by reducing imports, stimulating home production and promoting exports."[1] Although it is different in some respects, mercantilism lives on in **protectionist** thinking in the contemporary era. The prototype of the mercantilist or protectionist kind of state was, of course, Japan.

Liberalism

The second way of thinking about the production of wealth in the international system is **liberalism.** At the outset, readers should be aware that this term is used in a specialized *economic sense* and that it does not refer to a left-of-center political orientation. In the nineteenth century, several British thinkers wrote about the theoretical basis for free trade. These writers included Adam Smith, John Stuart Mill and David Ricardo and are now referred to as the **classical liberal economists.** Smith published his important book, *The Wealth of Nations,* in 1776, the same year as the beginning of the American Revolution. That coincidence makes it easy for American students to remember the publication date of one of the most important foundations of the **free enterprise** economic system, but it has other significance. Smith, Mill, and Ricardo laid the foundation for free trade among states.

Smith argued that states have distinctive **absolute advantages** due to their climate, geography, and resources and that each state is "led by an invisible hand to promote an end which was no part of his intention.... By pursuing his own interest he frequently promotes that of the society more effectively than when he really intends to promote it."[2] Ricardo pointed out that because of their natural attributes, Great Britain was well suited to the production of textiles, and Portugal to growing grapes and the production of port, sherry, and wine.

Mercantilists would advise each country to produce each of these products indigenously; to buy them from another country would require the expenditure of gold and silver, an action that is counter to the objective of minimizing imports. The classical liberal economists argued that each country should specialize in the products that it could best produce, and they then should trade with one another in order to obtain what they needed or wanted. Ricardo noted that Portugal could have invested the resources to develop its own textile industry and that Great Britain could have, through the use of greenhouses, irrigation, and illumination, grown its own grapes and produced its own sherry, port, and wine.

But such an expenditure of resources would have been inefficient, and Smith, Ricardo, and Mill contended that each state should specialize in the products it could best produce. This is called the principle of

BOX 11.1   The Principle of Comparative Advantage Illustrated

The classical economists measured the costs of products in terms of labor time and effort. For example, let us assume that a liter of wine would take one hour of labor to produce in State A and two hours in State B, while a bolt of cloth would take two hours to produce in State A and six hours in State B, as depicted in the following table:

Cost of Production (in hours of labor)

	State A	State B
1 liter of wine	1 hour	2 hours
1 bolt of cloth	2 hours	6 hours

Compared with state A, state B is inefficient because its workers need more time to produce both wine and cloth. In short, A has an *absolute* advantage in the production of *both* wine and cloth; however, B does not have as great a disadvantage in wine as cloth. Therefore, A should specialize in the production of cloth and B in wine.

comparative advantage, and it is the foundation on which free international trade rests.

Marxism

The third way of thinking about the production of wealth is **Marxism** or communism. In 1848, Karl Marx and Friedrich Engels published *The Communist Manifesto,* a document that would cast its shadow over most of the twentieth century.[3] In this document, Marx described his view of the world and the place of economics in it. Marx believed that the economic order determined the political order and that the "means of production" were owned by the upper classes. To Marx, history was a constant struggle between the upper class (called the bourgeoisie) and the lower class (called the proletariat). Marx contended that the capitalists exploited the wage earners and showed little, if any, concern for the devastating human effects of the industrial revolution. It should be noted that Marx called attention to some very real inhumane working conditions perpetrated in the name of capitalism, as other writers such as Charles Dickens, noted.

Radicals in Europe read and were attracted to Marx's and Engels's writings, but the nineteenth century ended without a successful revolution.

World War I, however, created the conditions that made revolution possible. However, when revolution came, it was not, paradoxically, in one of the industrialized Western European states; rather, communism came first to Russia, a backward, predominantly agrarian state. In Russia, the socialist party, which opposed the tsarist government, was divided into two factions: the Mensheviks and the Bolsheviks (also called communists). World War I had devastating effects on Russia, and the many Russian people wanted out of the war. In 1917, **Vladimir Ilich Lenin,** a brilliant political theoretician who was also a brilliant politician, led a revolution that successfully toppled the tsarist government. Communism had arrived on the world scene.

Lenin had spent most of his adult life either in internal or external exile because of his activities opposing the Russian government. When World War I broke out, it posed a major theoretical problem for Lenin and other leftists who had vowed not to go to war against one another ... unless their country was attacked by another. Self-defense would be the only legitimate reason for socialists to take up arms on behalf of their respective states. Their allegiance to the cause of international socialism was supposed to transcend their loyalties to their respective countries.[4] When war came, however, German socialists said that France had started the war; French socialists said that German socialists had started the war and so on. An explanation of this breakdown was needed. In 1916, Lenin published his book *Imperialism: the Highest Stage of Capitalism.* In it Lenin argued that the giant, capitalist monopolies competed with one another for markets; this led to fierce competition which, in turn, led to **imperialism**—the takeover of developing countries. It was the drive to dominate and exploit these areas that caused World War I. In short, it was capitalism that caused what up to that time was history's most costly war.

HISTORICAL EVOLUTION OF THE INTERNATIONAL ECONOMIC SYSTEM

As previously noted, from the fifteenth through the mid-seventeenth centuries the major powers based their international economic policies on the basis of mercantilism. In the last quarter of the eighteenth century, the effects of the industrial revolution came to be evident internationally, and the state that had most taken advantage of industrialization—Great Britain—became the dominant actor in the international system. At the same time, the British classical liberals advanced their theory of comparative advantage and free trade. The growth of British economic, political, and diplomatic power occurred concurrently and was complementary. To guarantee free trade and protect its sea lines of communication with the countries with which it traded, Great Britain built the most powerful navy in the world. It also established colonies throughout the world and built an empire.

For Britain to exercise its power, however, colonies were not necessary; free trade was. Because of the industrial revolution, British manufactured goods were very often the highest quality and the cheapest, and free trade enabled the British to ship their goods all over the world. Often instead of establishing colonies, the British would simply try to open the door to trade in various areas. By the mid-nineteenth century, Britain was clearly the dominant economic and political power in the world, what political economists call a hegemon. The rise and dominance of Great Britain marked the ascendancy of liberalism and the eclipse of mercantilism, but strains of mercantilist thinking remained and continued periodically to reemerge.

The **"Open Door" trade policy** favored first by Great Britain and later by the United States clearly benefited the most powerful state in the international system. Communists were quick to condemn the open door, free trade policies supported by hegemonic powers; to them free trade represented a form of imperialism, i.e., exploitation of the poor by the rich.

Even before World War I, governments often used economic policy as an instrument of foreign policy. During the half century prior to the war, the developed states would trade manufactured products for the primary products or commodities from the developing countries. In order to finance their purchases, developing countries would issue bonds, and the developed countries would purchase these, precluding borrowing from other countries. Over time, dependence became complete, and as the late economist Jacob Viner pointed out, bonds "paved the way for bayonets."[5] In addition to buying bonds, developed states would often invest in the ownership or management control of enterprises in developing countries, and they were not above bribing government officials in pursuit of achieving economic objectives. Using these techniques, the United States, prior to World War I, was able to achieve significant economic and financial penetration in the Caribbean and Central America. During the mid 1930s, Nazi Germany achieved a high degree of penetration in Hungary, Bulgaria, Romania, and parts of South America.[6]

In Chapter 4, we examined the concept of international interdependence. Some of those associated with this approach in international relations believe that a greater level of trade among states will lead to a more peaceful world. The slogan of IBM International is "World Peace through World Trade." Most people—unless they have studied international relations—believe this, but it is not necessarily true, as the international economic system in 1914 demonstrates. The two countries with the largest

trade turnover (exports plus imports) in the world just prior to the outbreak of World War I were Germany and France, and yet they went to war. So much for slogans and popular wisdom!

In Chapter 5, we reviewed the enormous costs of World War I, and they will not be repeated here. Suffice it to note that following the war, the allies adopted harsh, vindictive policies against Germany. The Dow Jones industrial average fell to 198 from 381 in early September.[7] On October 3, 1929, the New York Stock Market began sliding faster, leading to a panic on "Black Thursday," October 24. The results were disastrous both domestically and internationally; massive unemployment and hyperinflation were the results. In June 1930, the U.S. government responded to the economic crisis by passing the **Smoot-Hawley Tariff Bill,** which significantly raised tariffs on foreign goods imported into the United States by an average of 53 percent. This legislation catalyzed "a wave of retaliation" on the part of other countries.[8]

Very shortly following passage of the Smoot-Hawley bill, Spain, Switzerland, Italy, Cuba, Mexico, France, Australia, and New Zealand passed tariffs. These actions represented an end to the era of free trade and the "open door" and the beginning of "beggar-thy-neighbor" policies. The United States tried to correct the damage done by the Smoot-Hawley tariff by enacting the **Reciprocal Trade Agreements** of 1934. This action was not effective at the time, but it did lay the groundwork for the free-trade policies adopted after World War II. The downward spiral continued, and the economic effects of the interwar policies should not be underestimated in assessing the causes of World War II.

At the end of World War II, policymakers were determined "to get it right" politically, economically, and diplomatically. The United Nations with the United States as a member was the political solution. American policymakers sought to re-create a liberal, international economic system of capitalist states following World War II, and they attempted to do this with several programs. American policymakers' over-riding concern was that Western Europe remain noncommunist. In the view of General Lauris Norstad, it was not a question of *if* the Soviet Union would attack Western Europe; it was only a question of *when.* In order to prevent the European states from becoming communist and to help them to recover economically, the United States invited the European states to submit a plan for their recovery. This invitation was made by Secretary of State George Marshall and was therefore dubbed the Marshall Plan.

Although the American invitation was issued to the Soviet and Eastern European states as well as the Western European states, Stalin prohibited any Eastern European state from participating. In the end 16 states participated and received a total of $13 billion from the United States during the period of 1948 to mid-1952 (see Map 11.1)

BOX 11.2 The Soldier Statesman*

The son of a coal merchant and a relative of Chief Justice John Marshall, George Catlett Marshall, Jr., knew at an early age that he wanted to become a soldier. Born in December 1880 in Uniontown, Pennsylvania, he spent his boyhood near areas associated with George Washington's early military career. His later exposure to the traditions of Robert E. Lee and Stonewall Jackson, as well as the outbreak of the Spanish-American War, strengthened his inclinations,

He graduated from the Virginia Military Institute in 1901 and was commissioned a second lieutenant in the U.S. Army. In the years before World War I, he served two tours of duty in the Philippines between several home assignments. As chief of operations of the First Army during World War I, he gained widespread recognition for his role in preparing the Meuse-Argonne offensive. Between the wars perhaps his most influential assignment was his tour as Assistant Commandant of the Infantry School at Fort Benning, Georgia, where he instituted changes in the instruction which influenced many World War II commanders.

By the time Hitler had launched the Second World War by his invasion of Poland in September 1939, Marshall had risen to the position of Army Chief of Staff, a post which he held throughout the war. He exerted enormous influence over policy during the war years, successfully insisting upon a cross-channel assault in 1944 instead of Churchill's plan for a Balkan campaign. Marshall recommended his protegé, Dwight D. Eisenhower, to lead the invasion of Europe, after Roosevelt had decided that Marshall was too indispensable in Washington to take command himself. Hailed after the war as "the architect of victory" and the "first global strategist," General Marshall assumed key civilian posts in the Truman Administration. The President first selected him to arbitrate the bitter civil war in China in 1946 before choosing him to be his Secretary of State in 1947. Obliged to resign in early 1949 because of impending surgery, Marshall had recovered sufficiently by 1950 to serve a year as Secretary of Defense. In 1953 he was awarded the Nobel Peace Prize, the first professional soldier in history to receive it.

Marshall died in Washington, DC, on October 16, 1959.

*This summary was derived from the work of Forrest C. Pogue, whose fourth and final volume of his biography, *George C. Marshall* was published in 1987.

Source: U.S. Department of State, Bureau of Public Affairs, *The Marshall Plan: Origins and Implementation,* April 1987, p. 2.

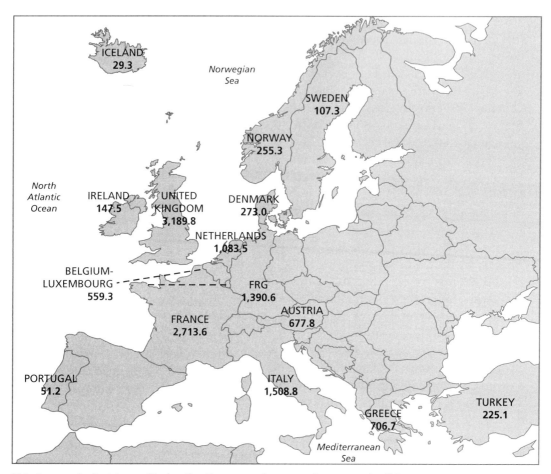

U.S. Economic Assistance Under the European Recovery Program: April 3,
1948–June 30, 1952 (Total Amount in Millions of U.S. Dollars)
Source: U.S. Department of State, Bureau of Public Affairs, *The Marshall Plan:
Origins and Implementation,* April 1987, p. 12.

Of course, this is a significant amount of money, but one must recall that this is in "1947 dollars" and to convert this to current dollars would require us to multiply by a factor of ten. Thus, expressed in "buying power," American contributions to Western Europe equaled about $150 billion, the value of dollars in 1999. This was one of the great success stories of economic recovery and U.S. foreign policy and included some moving personal stories (see box 11.3).

At the end of World War II, the United States was the hegemonic power; the United States' gross national product (GNP), which is the total value of all goods and services produced in a state in a given year, was 50 percent of the world's GNP. The United States alone among both the vic-

> **BOX 11.3   A Personal View of Foreign Aid**
>
> At the time no one could predict what the effect of U.S. aid would be on one young boy who later recounted: "One of the first CARE Packages sent to Europe in the summer of 1946 gave this young refugee his first taste of peanut butter, his first mouthful of that exotic fruit, raisins, and most importantly, his first glass of powdered milk. What terrific memories! For years afterward, even to today, CARE Packages have been 'America' to me and millions like me." The "young refugee" immigrated to the United States, joined the military and worked his way up the chain of command to become the Chairman of the Joint Chiefs of Staff, General John Shalikashvili.[9]

torious and defeated states had not been significantly harmed by the war. In fact, some economic historians argue that it was the war that ended the depression in the United States. Perhaps the most significant power of the hegemon is the power to set the international agenda, and in international economic relations, American policymakers had three goals: (1) to lower trade barriers, (2) to eliminate discrimination in trade, and (3) to establish currency convertibility.[10] Three agreements were reached to further these objectives.

Even before the entry of the United States into World War II, President Roosevelt and Prime Minister Churchill met in August 1941 at sea near Newfoundland to draft a set of principles called the Atlantic Charter. Free trade, self determination, economic cooperation, and freedom of the seas were among the principles that were enumerated in the Charter. It also stipulated that there should be equal access to trade and raw materials, which was a negation of the British Imperial Preference System that gave trade preference to members of the British Commonwealth.

In July 1944, a conference was held in Bretton Woods, New Hampshire, and at this meeting the framework for the post-World War II international economic system was laid. Because of its meeting place, this system is often referred to as the **Bretton Woods System.** Two institutions were established: the **International Monetary Fund (IMF)** and the **International Bank for Reconstruction and Development (IBRD),** more commonly called the **World Bank.** These organizations were dedicated to the promotion of market economies, free trade, and high rates of growth.

The IMF was founded as a global lending agency, in order to aid the recovery of the industrial states from the depression and the devastation of World War II. Its programs were designed to assist countries with balance-of-trade problems and to encourage international monetary cooperation and the expansion of international trade.

The IBRD ("World Bank") was designed to provide international liquidity—that is, loans to countries to assist with their recovery. The member states of the IBRD initially provided $10 billion for loans; however, by mid 1947 its funds were nearly exhausted, and the member states provided another infusion of capital. Once the developed states had made steps in the direction of economic recovery, the World Bank turned its attention to developing states. In 1956 the International Finance Corporation was created, in order to cofinance private investments in member countries, particularly in developing states, where private capital was difficult to attract. In 1960, the World Bank created the International Development Association as an affiliate to provide loans to developing countries, on terms lower than market rates with a lenient repayment schedule.

A third organization was created in 1947 as part of the Bretton Woods System called the **General Agreement on Tariffs and Trade (GATT).** The purpose of this organization was to reduce tariffs and nontariff, protectionist barriers. GATT sought to support the establishment of a liberal international economic order by emphasizing reciprocity and nondiscriminatory trade.

Reciprocity simply refers to the mutual lowering (or increasing) of tariffs or other trade barriers. The principle of nondiscriminatory trade is embodied in **most-favored-nation (MFN)** status. This term is somewhat confusing because MFN simply means that the same terms of trade are applied to all states that are granted this status by a trading partner. An example will help to clarify this concept and its application. Following the massacre of hundreds, perhaps up to several thousand, demonstrators by Chinese government forces in Tiananmen Square in May 1989, the United States threatened to withdraw MFN status from China. This meant that the United States would no longer grant China the same terms of trade as its other trading partners. Let us assume that an American computer corporation was going to buy hard disks for its machines, and it obtained the following pricing information for disks with equivalent capabilities:

Price of One Hard Disk from:

People's Republic of China company	$150
South Korean company	170

It would appear that China would be the best source of hard disks; however, following the Tiananmen Square killings and the U.S. withdrawal of MFN from China, let us assume that a 20 percent tariff on Chinese computer goods was implemented. This would increase the price of the Chinese hard disks to $180 ($150 plus 20 percent tariff), and American purchasers would buy from South Korea because the price of its disks would be less expensive.

One other foundation of the Bretton Woods system should be explained: the **gold standard.** First introduced by Great Britain in 1821, the gold standard fixed the value of a currency to the price of gold. The gold standard was abandoned at the beginning of World War I and had a rocky history during the inter-war period; however, it was reestablished in 1945. The value of the U.S. "key currency," the dollar, was set at $35 per ounce of gold. The system worked relatively well as long as the international community remained confident that the U.S. economy was strong and that the U.S. government would convert foreign dollar holdings to gold upon request. As political economists David Blake and Robert Walters point out, "Over the course of the 1960s it became clear that the United States was incapable of honoring *en masse* its gold conversion obligations. By 1971 official dollar holdings abroad exceeded U.S. gold stocks by over 300 percent."[11]

In addition to this problem, in 1971 the United States ran a big **balance-of-payments deficit** (a situation in which imports exceed exports). During the 1966–1970 period, the United States had deficits of $1.9 to $3.8 billion; in 1971 the U.S. trade deficit soared to $10.6 billion.[12] In August 1971, President Nixon announced—without prior consultations with U.S. allies—a series of measures that ended the Bretton Woods System and transformed the international economic system. Nixon took the United States off the gold standard, imposed a 10 percent surcharge on imported goods, and imposed wage and price controls.

THE CONTEMPORARY INTERNATIONAL ECONOMIC SYSTEM

Perhaps the most notable feature of the post-Bretton Woods international economic system is **flexible exchange rates,** which means that *the dollar has no set value* in relation to gold or any other currencies.

Several issues have dominated the agenda of contemporary international economic relations and include: oil prices, development, international debt, and the move toward economic integration. Each of these topics will be addressed.

Oil was first discovered in the Middle East region in Saudi Arabia in 1932.[13] The oil industry was dominated by a group of seven large oil companies, sometimes referred to as the "seven sisters," that had agreements with the oligarchic governments in the region. Oil was both relatively cheap ($2–$3 per barrel) and plentiful. (Saudi Arabia alone has 25 percent of the world's proven oil reserves.) In 1960, the major oil producers came together to form the **Organization of Petroleum Exporting Countries (OPEC),** essentially an oil cartel. But half of the members of OPEC were colonies of larger, more powerful countries.

In October 1973, Egypt and Syria launched a simultaneous, coordinated attack on Israel, and within several weeks the Arab members of OPEC announced that they would boycott shipments of oil to any countries that supported Israel. The result was panic; countries bought as much oil as they could to build up their stockpiles in anticipation of oil price rises. And rise they did! In 1971 one barrel of oil cost $1.80; just prior to the October War, a barrel cost $3.00. By early 1974 following the OPEC embargo, the price of a barrel was $12.00. When one considers the degree to which modern, advanced industrial states are based on petroleum, this 400 percent increase in the price of oil in a matter of months had enormous impacts on the international economic system.

And if this shock were not enough, added shocks occurred in late 1979 when the Shah of Iran was replaced by the Ayatollah Khomeini. In anticipation of antiwestern policies of the Ayatollah, oil prices skyrocketed for a second time in the 1970s, going from $12 per barrel to $36 per barrel by 1980.

These two events—the OPEC embargo and the fall of the Shah—had at least three very significant international effects. First, the increased price of oil almost overnight turned the Middle Eastern oil-producing countries into the world's bankers. Just as the City of London had been the capital of international finance in the nineteenth century, the Middle East became the locus of capital in the 1980s. Second, because of the importance of oil to all advanced industrial states, the Middle East and Persian (or Arab) Gulf region became an important strategic area to the United States and to the other developed states that depended on the region for oil. This level of dependence varied significantly from the United States which imported 25 percent of its oil from the region to Japan which imported 98 percent of its energy sources. A third effect was on developing countries. During the 1960s, scientists worked to develop plant strains that were more productive and resistant to disease, and the results were dramatically increased yields. Much of the gains of this so-called Green Revolution had been fueled and fertilized by petroleum-based products. When oil prices increased, it made it difficult for developing countries to buy the gasoline to power machinery and fertilizer to feed the new seeds. In many cases, the entirety of foreign earnings went simply to pay for the increased price of oil.

The issue of development has preoccupied world leaders for much of the post-World War II era. Photos and more recently videos of malnourished children have filled the pages of newspapers and magazines and television screens. Despite the attention lavished on the developing states, what has actually been accomplished? In the 1960 presidential campaign, the Democratic Party Platform called for a rethinking of U.S. aid programs, and following the election of John Kennedy, the new administration embarked on an ambitious development agenda. Within the government itself, a new organization, the Agency for International Development (AID), was established to oversee U.S. aid efforts. In addition, the Peace Corps was created for idealistic Americans of all ages to spend several years in a developing country. (When she was in her seventies, President Carter's mother served as a Peace Corps volunteer in India.) An aid program tailored specifically for the needs of Latin America, the Alliance for Progress, was established. In short, the United States seemed to be attempting to extend the social-welfare programs of the New Deal and the Great Society to developing countries. But despite good intentions and some limited benefits, these programs did not achieve their ambitious objectives.

The United Nations also emphasized the need for development and called for a contribution of 1 percent of gross domestic product by the developed states for development programs. Only several states met this goal, and most contributed far less than the target 1 percent. The United States, for example, contributed only a small fraction of 1 percent—about .15 percent—of its GDP to development assistance.

The international development record, however, was not entirely bleak. Some countries with significant resources were able to achieve impressive growth rates. These **Newly Industrializing Countries (NIC),** such as the "four tigers" of Asia—Taiwan, South Korea, Singapore, and Hong Kong—were able to achieve double-digit economic growth rates throughout the 1970s. This led some in the developed countries to look to the developing areas as good potential places to invest. Banks, no one will be surprised to read, are in business to make money.

Bank officers in the 1970s looked longingly at the economic growth rates in many developing countries and encouraged their loans officers to make loans in promising developing countries. The total debt of developing countries in 1982 was $830 billion; by 1988 that had increased to $1.3 trillion and by 1993 to $1.8 trillion. Most of this debt was owned by commercial banks, which obviously do not want to write off their loans resulting in substantial losses to them. The LDC **debt crisis** shook the foundations of the international economic system in the 1980s. Developing, debtor states had four basic ways to finance their debt: (1) to export primary products, such as oil, coffee, and timber; (2) to attract foreign investment; (3) to borrow more hard currency from commercial banks; and/or (4) to borrow from governments. By 1989, most of the World Bank's loans were used to service existing debt.

The largest banks in the world in 1996 were as follows:

Rank	Banking Company	Country	Assets ($billions)
1	Bank of Tokyo-Mitsubishi	Japan	$648
2	Deutsche Bank	Germany	557
3	Credit Agricole	France	480
4	Dai-ichi Kangyo Bank	Japan	434
5	Fuji Bank	Japan	433
6	Sanwa Bank	Japan	428
7	Sumitomo	Japan	426
8	Sakura	Japan	423
9	HSBC Holdings	Hong Kong	405
10	Norinchukin Bank	Japan	375
16	Chase Manhattan Bank (Largest U.S. bank)	United States	334

Source: American Banker, cited by *The New York Times,* December 9, 1997, page C 8.

Beginning in the 1970s, Asian countries enjoyed a spectacular economic boom; growth rates in many of these countries were in double digits, and multinational corporations and banks flocked to Asia. As journalist Thomas Friedman has noted, "Germany's Dresdner Bank told its managers in Asia, 'Lend, lend, lend, otherwise we will lose market share.' Banks make money by lending and each one assumed that Asia was a no-brainer. So they shoved money out the door, just like drug dealers expanding their client base. Their message to the developing world was: 'C'mon kid. Just try a little of this cash. The first loans's free.' "[14] When Asia experienced a severe economic crisis—which some called the "Asian flu"—in 1998, many of the banks and MNCs with significant investments in Asia lost a great deal of money. As noted in the list above, seven of the world's ten largest banks in 1996 were Japanese banks, and these were hard hit by the Asian economic crisis. The long-term effects of this crisis are still not fully known; however, it is clear that Asia is no longer the stable investment that it was the mid-1990s.

Another significant development with both substantial political and economic ramifications was the move toward greater integration. In 1957, the Rome Treaty was signed creating the **European Economic Community (EEC),** also called the **Common Market.** Over time, this collection of states has taken on more members and has called for greater and greater eco-

YOU IN WORLD POLITICS

So you're interested in working for a multinational corporation or a bank? Multinational corporations play a prominent role in current international affairs. Most Americans tend to think in terms of working abroad for an American corporation, but in fact there may well be better opportunities working in the United States, for an American or perhaps even a foreign firm (of course, that may not be what you think of as an international job).

Americans who are sent abroad are often a trial for corporations. They are expensive, have a high failure rate (perhaps as high as 50 percent), don't want to stay long, don't know the language, and sometimes get into trouble. Thus most multinationals are moving toward developing *indigenous* managers (Norwegians to run Exxon Norway, Nigerians for the Coca Cola branch in Nigeria, etc.) and sending abroad only indispensable Americans, usually those with particular technical expertise. This will deprive American business of its major training ground for managers with international sophistication, which in the long run may be a problem for American competitiveness. More important, from your point of view, you will probably not be sent abroad by an American company.

The other side of the coin, of course, is that foreign companies doing business in the United States hire lots of Americans. Moreover, an increasing percentage of American corporations do business abroad, so much "normal business" in the United States involves international issues. In general, if you want to go into business, you need a Master of Business Administration (MBA) degree from the best business school you can get into. If you're interested in working for a foreign company, knowledge of its language and culture can be invaluable, but it is no substitute for business training. Nobody is going to hire you just because you know the appropriate language; they also have to think you will raise their profits.

Among businesses, international banks have been the most willing to hire people without business degrees; they expect to have to train you regardless of your background. Another alternative is analyzing the political risks of investments in particular countries (see the critex at the beginning of this chapter). There are some jobs here within corporations and at consulting firms. However, relatively few people have been hired (most use consultants), and it's not clear that they will be able to move up to other jobs within the organizations.

nomic and political cooperation. The **Maastricht Treaty** signed in December 1991 called for the establishment of a completely integrated common market with free trade and free movement of labor and capital. It further called for a European Monetary Union (EMU) for those countries which had: (1) low inflation and longer-term interest rates; (2) budget deficits not exceeding 3 percent of gross domestic product (GDP); (3) stable exchange rates for two years prior to joining; and (4) total government expenditures no larger than 60 percent of GDP. In January 1999, the first operational step toward the EMU was taken when European markets began using the euro as the common currency.

The eleven members of the EMU represent significant economic power: their combined GDP in 1997 was $6.5 trillion, compared to the United States' $8.1 trillion. The "euro-11's" share of international trade outside of the euro area was 19 percent, slightly larger than the United States' 17 percent share. These figures indicate that the EMU will be a significant actor in the international economic system of the future.

The next step in the evolution of the EMU will be the implementation of a common currency for its members by 2002. Once this occurs, people going from one EMU member country to another will not have to change their money from one currency to another because it will be identical. That will make it easier for tourists, but rougher on poets and romantics!

CONCLUSION

It used to be—not so long ago—that political and military issues were considered to be the realm of "high politics," and economic issues were considered to be "low politics." That has changed, as the OPEC oil embargo made dramatically clear in 1973–1974. Today, economic issues affect virtually every person living in the world whether that is Nairobi, Caracas, Moscow, or Beijing. And that trend is likely to continue.

DISCUSSION QUESTIONS

1. It used to be that political and military issues were referred to as "high politics" and economic and trade issues were viewed as "low politics." Do you think that is the case any longer? Why or why not?

2. What are the trends toward greater economic integration? Do you think that greater economic integration will make the world a more peaceful place?

3. What are the major economic problems in the world today?

KEY TERMS

absolute advantage
balance-of-payments (deficit)
Bretton Woods System
classical liberal economists
comparative advantage
debt crisis
European Economic Community
   (EEC) (or Common Market)
flexible exchange rates
free enterprise
General Agreement on Tariffs
   and Trade (GATT)
gold standard
imperialism
International Bank for
   Reconstruction and
   Devlopment (IBRD) or World
   Bank

International Monetary Fund
   (IMF)
Vladimir Ilyich Lenin
liberalism
Maastricht Treaty
mercantilism
most-favored-nation
neo-mercantilism
Newly Industrializing Countries
   (NIC)
Open Door trade policy
protectionism
Reciprocal Trade Agreement
Smoot-Hawley Tariff Bill
trade turnover

RECOMMENDED PRINT, MULTIMEDIA, AND INTERNET SOURCES

Print

BLAKE, DAVID H. and ROBERT S. WALTERS, 4th ed. *The Politics of Global Economic Relations.* Englewood Cliffs, NJ: Prentice-Hall 1992.

DESTLER, I. M. *American Trade Politics,* 3rd ed. Washington, DC: Institute for International Economics, 1995.

FRIEDEN, JEFFREY A. and DAVID A. LAKE, eds. *International Political Economy: Perspectives on Global Power and Wealth,* 3rd ed. New York: St. Martin's Press, 1995.

JACKSON, JOHN and ALAN SYKES. *Implementing the Uruguay Round.* Oxford, England: Clarendon Press, 1997.

KINDLEBERGER, CHARLES P. *The World in Depression 1929–1939.* Berkeley, CA: University of California Press.

SPERO, JOAN E. and JEFFREY A. HART. *The Politics of International Economic Relations,* 5th ed. New York: St. Martin's Press, 1997.

YERGIN, DANIEL. *The Prize: The Epic Quest for Oil, Money and Power.* New York: Simon & Schuster, 1991.

Video

Battle of the Titans: Problems of the Global Economy. Distributed by Filmakers Library, New York. Focuses on the growth of urbanization in developing countries; features an interview with historian Paul Kennedy; $75 rental.

The Debt Crisis—New Perspectives. Distributed by Filmakers Library, New York. Focuses on the causes and possible solutions to the developing countries debt problem; $75 rental.

Internet

Asian Development Bank: http://www.asiandevbank.org

Far Eastern Economic Review: http://www.feer.com

Institute for International Economics: http://iie.com

International Monetary Fund: http://www.imf.org

International Political Economy Network: http://csf.colorado.edu/ipe/

Organization for Economic Cooperation and Development: Home page:
http://www.oecdwash.org
Trade statistics: http://www.oecd.org/daf/cmis/fdi/statist.htm

U.S. Agency for International Development (AID): http://www.info.usaid.gov

U.S. Census Bureau trade statistics: www.census.gov/foreign-trade/www/

U.S. Department of Commerce, International Trade Administration: www.ita.doc.gov

U.S. International Trade Commission: http://www.usitc.gov/tr/tr.htm

U.S. national debt "clock:" http://www.brillig.com/debt_clock

U.S. National Economic Council:
http://www.whitehouse.gov/WH/EOP/nec/html/

U.S. Trade Representative: http://www.ustr.gov/ Provides access to important international trade agreements.

The World Bank: http://www.worldbank.org/

World Trade Organization (WTO): http://www.wto.org

ENDNOTES

[1] DAVID H. BLAKE and ROBERT S. WALTERS, *The Politics of Global Economic Relations*, 3rd ed. (Upper Saddle River, NJ: Prentice-Hall, 1987), p. 20.

[2] ADAM SMITH, *The Wealth of Nations* (1776).

[3] KARL MARX, *The Communist Manifesto,* edited by Frederic L. Bender (New York: W. W. Norton, 1988).

[4] For a masterful account, see Kenneth Waltz, *Man, the State and War* (New York: Columbia University Press, 1959).

[5] JACOB VINER, *International Economics* (Glencoe, IL: Free Press, 1951), p. 346.

[6] ALBERT O. HIRSCHMAN, *National Power and the Structure of Foreign Trade* (Berkeley, CA: University of California Press, 1945), p. 53.

[7] CHARLES P. KINDLEBERGER, *The World In Depression 1929–1939* (Berkeley, CA: University of California Press, 1973), p. 118.

[8] Ibid., p. 132.

[9] "Remarks by General John Shalikashvili, Chairman of the Joint Chiefs of Staff, CARE 50th Anniversary Symposium," Washington, DC, May 10, 1996.

[10] STEPHEN D. KRASNER, "US Commercial and Monetary Policy," *International Organization* (Autumn 1977).

[11] BLAKE and WALTERS, p. 67.

[12] *International Economic Report of the President* (Washington, DC: Government Printing Office, 1975), p. 137.

[13] DANIEL YERGIN, *The Prize: The Epic Quest for Oil, Money and Power* (New York: Simon & Schuster, 1991).

[14] THOMAS L. FRIEDMAN, "A Manifesto for the Fast World," *The New York Times Magazine*, March 28, 1999, p. 70.

[15] *The Economist* periodically publishes a "Eurobrief" on the implications of the European Monetary Union; see "The Merits of One Money," *The Economist*, October 24, 1998, pp. 85–86; "The International Euro," *The Economist*, November 14, 1998, pp. 89–90.

12

Ethics,
Human Rights, and
Democratization

CRITEX:
The Man Who Stopped the Tanks

 ODAY'S human rights abuses are tomorrow's refugee movements.

U.N. High Commissioner for Refugees[1]

In the spring of 1989, Chinese students demonstrated in the central square in the capital city of Beijing. Stimulated by the ideas of freedom and liberty and the changes introduced in the Soviet Union by Mikhail Gorbachev, these students called for democratic reforms in their own country. By late May, there were several thousand student demonstrators camping out in Tiananmen Square, and the government felt that it had to act to quell the growing unrest.

In the USSR, Gorbachev was attempting simultaneous political and economic reforms. The most powerful Chinese leader, Deng Xiaoping, had sought only economic reforms and had decided not

to reform the political system of the People's Republic of China. The students in Tiananmen clearly wanted comprehensive reforms, not piecemeal reform.

On June 2, Chinese governmental leaders ordered the People's Liberation Army to move into Beijing, and as the Army tanks rolled into the city, a lone Chinese man stepped into the middle of the street and blocked a long line of tanks. Tense moments ensued. Would the tanks simply run over this demonstrator (as tragically occurred several days later), or would the tanks be stopped by this lone man's protest? For a short time, the tanks stopped while the tank commanders decided what to do. Meanwhile, the protester's friends realizing that he was in mortal danger, ran to him and pulled him away from the threatening situation. This man's image lives in the minds of all who witnessed his courageous protest.

Imagine that the Chinese governmental authorities had captured this man. What case would the government present against him? With what "crimes" could he be charged? What would the man's defense be? Either discuss these questions or write a brief essay on them, depending on the instructions from your professor.

This man's protest served as a kind of metaphor of the power of the state *vis à vis* the individual. What is the legitimate power of states? Does sovereignty give states the right to violate human rights?

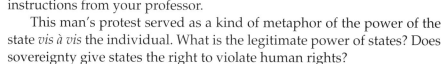

INTRODUCTION

The act of the "man who stopped the tanks" was both simple and courageous: to stand in the way of repression. The tank commanders' choice was simple: to stop or to continue. They chose to stop, and for the minutes that the tanks were halted—until his friends risked their lives and pulled the man who stopped the tanks to safe anonymity—one person had challenged the power of the world's most populous state.

This dramatic event raised questions that are as old as politics:

- What should be the power of the state?
- Should certain principles govern the treatment of individuals by the state? If so, what are those principles and under what conditions do they apply?
- How would you act under similar circumstances?

In this chapter, we will: (1) review the role of ethics in world politics, (2) examine the place of human rights in international relations, and (3)

The Man Who Stopped the Tanks

review the trend toward democratization in the world today. In keeping with one of the central objectives of this book, we will also examine the ways in which you can become involved in these issues, should you choose to do so.

ETHICS IN WORLD POLITICS

When we consider the extent of competition, conflict, and war in world politics, many of us are drawn to the conclusion that "ethics" and "world politics" go together as much as "military" and "music" or "justice." Though understandable, such a view ignores centuries of thinking concerning the acceptability of various acts between or among political actors.

Two eminent professors, historian Gordon Craig and political scientist Alexander George, have noted that "since the emergence of war as a feature of relations between communities," thoughtful people have placed their hopes on five different means to prevent conflict: (1) agreements to restrict or abolish certain kinds of weapons; (2) agreements to limit military operations; (3) doctrines to make war more efficient and therefore to avoid unnecessary destruction; (4) political systems designed to reduce conflict between or among groups; and (5) religious and moral codes forbidding the resort to force.[2] Thus far in this book, we have examined several of these means, including two political systems for managing power in world politics (the balance of power and collective security), arms

control and disarmament agreements to reduce the probability, destructiveness and/or cost of war, and international law. In this chapter, we will
focus on ethical, moral, and religious codes to reduce conflict and govern
international relations.

In perhaps no other area of world politics does the levels of analysis
(see Chapter 1) problem play a more important role. The dilemma was
stated most clearly by Professor Arnold Wolfers in a classic essay:

> Throughout the ages moralists have expressed horror at the way
> princes and sovereign states behave toward one another. Behavior
> that would be considered immoral by any standard can obviously
> be detected in all realms of life; but nowhere does the contradiction
> between professed ethical principles and actual behavior appear so
> patent and universal as in the conduct of foreign affairs.[3]

Professor Wolfers' point becomes crystal clear if we consider an actual
case. "Thou shalt not kill" is not only one of the ten commandments of
the Old Testament, it is also about as close as we get to a universal norm
in human relations; however, most states and individuals suspend the applicability of this commandment when it comes to orders given by the
state. In fact, almost as universal as the individualistic belief in the prohibition against killing is the practice of the state to reward killing in its
name. Virtually every state has awards that are given to the members of
its military who act in a courageous manner. (Please note, this comment
is most certainly not meant to criticize, minimize, and/or demean the re-
cipients of such awards.) Thus, behavior that is close to absolutely prohibited for individuals is rewarded by states. How is one to make any
sense of this seeming contradiction?

Harvard political scientist Joseph Nye suggests that there are three
possible responses to this question: (1) the skeptic who "says that moral
categories have no meaning in international relations because there are
no institutions to provide order,"[4] (2) the state moralist who "stresses a just
order among a society of states," and (3) a cosmopolitan who "stresses the
common nature of humanity." Each of these positions reflects beliefs concerning duties, values, and central concepts. In addition, each view im-
plies a particular view concerning intervention (see Table 12.1).

The skeptical realist believes that ethics and morality do not apply to
world politics. Thucydides was perhaps the first and most influential
member of this group; recall his account of the Melians' plea to the Athenians (see Chapter 2), which fell on deaf ears. Thucydides' lesson of this
episode was characteristic of the skeptics' view of the role of ethics in international relations: "The strong do what they will, and the weak suffer

TABLE 12.1

Three Views of International Ethics

	Duties	*Key Value*	*Central Concept*	*Intervention?*
Skeptical Realist	None to minimal	National interest	Balance of power	Pursue advantage
State moralist	Limited	Self-determination	Society of states	Nonintervention
Cosmopolitan	Large	Justice	Society of persons	Create justice

Source: Adapted from Joseph S. Nye, Jr., *Nuclear Ethics* (New York: Free Press, 1986), p. 35.

what they must." The seventeenth-century British political philosopher Thomas Hobbes was greatly influenced by Thucydides' view of human nature, conflict, and war. In Hobbes's view, the "state of nature" was not some idyllic, pristine Garden of Eden, but rather was "nasty, brutish and short." To Hobbes, the only law is "the command of the sovereign." Later realists such as Hans Morgenthau, Henry Kissinger, and Richard Nixon built their policies on the realist philosophic foundation of Thucydides and Hobbes. Because there is no overarching organization to guarantee order, power is what primarily matters in world politics, and states should not adopt policies for reasons other than the maximization of power.

The **state moralist** believes that the rightness or wrongness of an action in world politics is determined by whether it is approved by a state. There is perhaps no clearer statement of this position than in a toast delivered in 1816 by American naval officer Stephen Decatur: "Our country! In her intercourse with foreign nations, may she always be in the right; but our country, right or wrong!"[5]

The **cosmopolitan** believes that ethics should play a role in world politics, and that there are some transnational beliefs and values that take precedence over the particular values of individual states. As Nye points out, "Many citizens hold multiple loyalties to several communities at the same time. They may wish their governments to follow policies that give expression to the rights and duties engendered by other communities in addition to those structured at the national level."[6] One example of such transnational loyalty would be the Catholic Church; members of this religious denomination seek to follow the dictates of its leader, the Pope, as well as their particular national leader. Many times, the two sources of authority do not conflict. What happens, however, when the Pope recommends one course of action, and the national leader recommends a different course? The individual must then decide whom he or she is going to follow.

Throughout history, philosophers, religious leaders, and politicians have offered a number of ethical guides to policymaking. The problem, of course, is that the guidelines that have been used for centuries for individual decision making may not be applicable to state decision making. In his memoirs, Winston Churchill brought this point out clearly (see box 12.1).

BOX 12.1   Winston Churchill on the Sermon on the Mount

The Sermon on the Mount is the last word in Christian ethics. Everyone respects the Quakers. Still, it is not on these terms that [government] Ministers assume their responsibilities of guiding states. Their duty is first so to deal with other nations as to avoid strife and war and to eschew aggression in all its forms, whether for nationalistic or ideological objects. But the safety of the State, the lives and freedom of their own fellow countrymen, to whom they own their position, make it right and imperative in the last resort, or when a final and definite conviction has been reached, that the use of force should not be excluded. If the circumstances are such as to warrant it, force may be used…. There is no merit in putting off a war for a year if, when it comes, it is a far worse war or one much harder to win. These are the tormenting dilemmas upon which mankind has throughout its history been so frequently impaled.

Source: Winston S. Churchill, *The Gathering Storm* (Boston: Houghton Mifflin Company, 1948), p. 320.

HUMAN RIGHTS IN WORLD POLITICS

If one believes that ethics and morality have some applicability to world politics, then the question becomes what principles apply under which circumstances. The answer to this question is not simple—because ethical principles vary from state to state, region to region, culture to culture. Are there rights of human beings that are universally recognized?

Americans who have taken an elementary civics class would immediately answer, "Of course, there are universal human rights!" The U.S. Declaration of Independence states: "All men are created equal, that they are endowed by their Creator with certain inalienable Rights, that among these are Life, Liberty, and the pursuit of Happiness." In the view of the American founding fathers, the "natural law" of the universe gave human be-

> **BOX 12.2   Are There Universal Human Rights?**
>
> As Professor R. J. Vincent has pointed out, "Human rights might be taken as merely a portmanteau for African rights, American rights, Chinese rights, and so on, so that the term is general but the rights are specific. In Java, according to Clifford Geertz, it is said that: 'To be human is to be Javanese.' Being human is not being Everyman, Geertz goes on, but being a particular kind of man. Thus if there are human rights, they are the rights of a particular people."
>
> *Source:* R. J. Vincent, *Human Rights and International Relations* (Cambridge, England: Cambridge University Press, 1986), pp. 38–39.

ings certain rights that temporal authorities could not take away, and if the state did, in fact, attempt to take away humans' "natural rights," then this violation of the natural order justified revolution against the authorities.[7]

Human Rights
Source: Foreign Policy, 105 (Winter 1996–1997)

It was the seventeenth- and eighteenth-century philosophers—particularly John Locke, Jean-Jacques Rousseau, Montesquieu, and Voltaire—who emphasized the "natural rights of men." The basic rights that these philosophers and the revolutionaries in America and France called for were freedom (or liberty) and equality.

With the rising power of nationalism and the industrial revolution during the nineteenth century, natural rights were eclipsed by the drive for power, and often in this process rights were forgotten. Some conceived of rights in communal rather than individualistic terms. Karl Marx and European idealists believed that the welfare of communities, rather than individuals, should be the goal. As a result of the attention on rights abuses, some progress was made: slavery was abolished; labor laws were enacted; child labor was restricted; women were given the right to vote; and labor unions were established.

Perhaps the greatest stimulus to passing formal human rights agreements was Adolf Hitler and the obscenity of Nazism. The world was both astonished and ashamed by the haunting photographs of the dead and the living dead of the Nazi concentration camps. Following the selection of Hitler as chancellor of Germany in January 1933, laws concerning the discrimination and eventually the execution of Jews, gypsies, and Slavs were passed. In addition, Germany passed laws allowing for arbitrary search and seizure, torture, arbitrary imprisonment, and other violation of rights that had previously been considered, in many states, as "inalienable." But Germany had exercised its rights of sovereignty as a state and had withdrawn these fundamental rights. At the end of World War II, many asked whether state sovereignty should have some limits.

The victorious Allied Powers determined that there were, in fact, limits to what a state could do within its boundaries and that Nazi leaders should be held accountable for their actions prior to and during World War II, and the Nuremberg War Crimes Trials were the result of this determination. As noted in Chapter 10, 24 Nazi officials were charged with committing "crimes against humanity"; that is, crimes committed against civilians even if in accordance with the domestic laws of Germany. Ultimately 12 Nazi officials were convicted and executed.

The Covenant of the League of Nations contained no reference to human rights. In contrast, the preamble of the Charter of the United Na-

Concentration Camp
John Keegan, *The Second World War* (New York: Penguin, 1989), p. 287.

tions stated that one of the purposes of the Charter was "to reaffirm faith in fundamental human rights, in the dignity and worth of the human person, in the equal rights of men and women and of nations large and small." The Charter further stated that one of the main objectives of the United Nations was to encourage "respect for human rights and for fundamental freedoms for all without distinction as to race, sex, language, or religion...." Although the Charter referred to "human rights" in several places, it did not define what those rights were. In addition, the Charter specifically stipulated that nothing in it "shall authorize the United Nations to intervene in matters which are essentially within the domestic jurisdiction of any state...."

The UN and Human Rights

Since its founding in 1945, the United Nations has worked to define and protect human rights. In December 1948, UN General Assembly voted in favor of the **Universal Declaration of Human Rights.** Of the then 55 members of the UN, only 8 states abstained on this vote and the remaining 47 states voted in favor. The Declaration was a resolution, not a legally binding treaty, of the UN General Assembly, but over time it has become a part of customary international law.[8] The Universal Declaration was supplemented by two international treaties, both signed in 1966: (1) the **International Covenant on Civil and Political Rights,** and (2) the **International Covenant on Economic, Social and Cultural Rights.** The three documents above are referred to collectively as the **International Bill of Rights,** and they establish an impressive list of rights that the international community has judged to be necessary for a life of dignity.

The International Bill of Rights calls on states to observe basic standards of human rights for their people; however, these agreements did not contain provisions for monitoring, compliance, and/or enforcement. Throughout the late 1960s and 1970s, the United Nations passed a number of resolutions calling for compliance with UN agreements.

Other Important Human Rights Efforts

In the last half of the 1970s, three developments called international attention to human rights. First, in 1976 the International Covenant on Civil and Political Rights (ICCPR) entered into force—meaning that it went into operation. In accordance with the agreement, a Human Rights Committee, consisting of 18 people elected by the signatories of the covenant, was established and given jurisdiction over the issues arising under the provisions of the ICCPR.

TABLE 12.2

Internationally Recognized Human Rights

The International Bill of Human Rights recognizes the rights to:

Equality or rights without discrimination (D1, D2, E2, E3, C2, C3)

Life (D3, C6)

Liberty and security of person (D3, C9)

Protection against slavery (D4, C8)

Protection against torture and cruel and inhuman punishment (D5, C7)

Recognition as a person before the law (D6, C16)

Equal protection of the law (D7, C14, C26)

Access to legal remedies for rights violations (D8, C2)

Protection against arbitrary arrest or detention (D9, C9)

Hearing before an independent and impartial judiciary (D10, C14)

Presumption of innocence (D11, C14)

Protection against ex post facto laws (D11, C15)

Protection of privacy, family, and home (D12, C17)

Freedom of movement and residence (D13, C12)

Seek asylum from persecution (D14)

Nationality (D15)

Marry and found a family (D16, E10, C23)

Own property (D17)

Freedom of thought, conscience, and religion (D18, C18)

Freedom of opinion, expression, and the press (D19, C19)

Freedom of assembly and association (D20, C21, C22)

Political participation (D21, C25)

Social security (D22, E9)

Work, under favorable conditions (D23, E6, E7)

Free trade unions (D23, E8, C22)

Rest and leisure (D24, E7)

Food, clothing, and housing (D25, E11)

Health care and social services (D25, E12)

Special protections for children (D25, E10, C24)

Education (D26, E13, E14)

Participation in cultural life (D27, E15)

A social and international order needed to realize rights (D28)

Self-determination (E1, C1)

Humane treatment when detained or imprisoned (C10)

Protection against debtor's prison (C11)

Protection against arbitrary expulsion of aliens (C13)

Protection against advocacy of racial or religious hatred (C20)

Protection of minority culture (C27)

Note: This list includes all rights that are enumerated in two of the three documents of the International Bill of Human Rights or have a full article in one document. The source of each right is indicated in parentheses by document and article number. D = Universal Declaration of Human Rights. E = International Covenant on Economic, Social, and Cultural Rights. C = International Covenant on Civil and Political Rights.

Source: Jack Donnelly, *Human Rights and World Politics* (Boulder, CO: Westview Press), 1993, p. 9.

Second, in January 1977, Jimmy Carter was inaugurated president of the United States. During the presidential campaign, Carter had emphasized human rights as the centerpiece of American foreign policy. According to Carter: "Our policy is based on a historical vision of America's role. Our policy is derived from a large view of global change. Our policy is rooted in our moral values, which never change. Our policy is reinforced by our material wealth and by our military power. Our policy is designed to serve mankind."[9] Carter's emphasis of human rights was characteristic of the distinctive American approach to foreign policy, and many from conservatives on the right to liberals on the left supported Carter's emphasis.

Third, **Amnesty International,** a **non-governmental organization (NGO)** founded in 1961 to call attention to violations of fundamental human rights, received the Nobel Peace Prize in 1977. This called increased attention to both the organization and its central objectives, which include to "free all prisoners of conscience ..., ensure fair and prompt trials for political prisoners; abolish the death penalty, torture, and other cruel treatment of prisoners; and end extrajudicial executions and 'disappearances.'"[10] Amnesty International grew dramatically; by 1997 it had more

---

BOX 12.3   Amnesty International and Children

Mr. Mike McClintock, the former Deputy Head of Research of Amnesty International, recalled his experience in Peru: "I first visited the highlands of Peru when a pattern of 'disappearance' and extra-judicial execution began to appear there suddenly in the early 80s. The relatives of the 'disappeared' had set up a hot lunch project which Amnesty International had partially financed.... The project was for the children of 'disappeared' parents.... There had been about a thousand 'disappearances' in the region in the past year; most of them were under eighteens.... Alex, a 12 year old, volunteered to translate from Quechua, the Indian language, into Spanish. For hours he translated tales of terror. Then he asked the Amnesty representative if he could tell his own story. He told us about his older brother who had 'disappeared' a year before. He had seen his fourteen-year old brother chased, slashed with a machete, and dragged off by a civil defense patrol. About 4000 people have 'disappeared' in Peru since 1981. Many of them are young people."

Source: Amnesty International, *Childhood Stolen: Grave Human Rights Violations against Children* (London: Amnesty International British Section, 1995), pp. 1–2.

than 1 million members with 4,273 chapters in 162 countries. Just as important, AI was not alone; other NGOs were founded to promote human rights around the world. For example, other human rights NGOs included Americas Watch, the Lawyers Committee for International Human Rights, and Human Rights Watch, which was founded to conduct regular, systematic investigations of human rights abuses in more than 70 countries.

In the 1980s, the Reagan administration deemphasized human rights and embarked on a new campaign, reminiscent of the cold war, against communism. Because the United States was one of the largest and most powerful countries in the world, this deemphasis had some impact on international human rights; however, the presence and power of nongovernmental organizations focusing on human rights issues maintained the salience of the issue internationally.

Within the human rights movement, there was some controversy concerning the definition of human rights. One of the best known commentators, Maurice Cranston,[11] argued that "economic, social and cultural human

---

TABLE 12.3

Principal Human Rights Conventions

Convention on the Prevention and Punishment of the Crime of Genocide, 1948*

Convention for the Suppression of the Traffic in Persons and of the Exploitation of the Prostitution of Others, 1949

Convention Relating to the Status of Refugees, 1951*

Slavery Convention of 1926, Amended by Protocol, 1953*

Convention on the Political Rights of Women, 1953*

Convention on the Nationality of Married Women, 1957

Convention on Consent to Marriage, Minimum Wage for Marriage, and Registration of Marriages, 1962

Convention on the Reduction of Statelessness, 1961

International Covenant on Economic, Social, and Cultural Rights, 1966

International Covenant on Civil and Political Rights, 1966*

International Convention on the Elimination of all Forms of Racial Discrimination, 1966*

Convention on the Non-Applicability of Statutory Limitations to War Crimes and Crimes Against Humanity, 1968

International Convention on the Suppression and Punishment of the Crime of Apartheid, 1973

Convention on the Elimination of All Forms of Discrimination Against Women, 1979

Convention Against Torture and Other Cruel, Inhuman or Degrading Treatment, or Punishment, 1984*

Convention on the Rights of the Child, 1989

Convention on the Rights of Migrant Workers and the Members of Their Families, 1990

---

*The US has ratified this convention.

Note: date refers to the year the UN General Assembly adopted the convention.

Source: Amnesty International

rights were impractical, of minor importance, and qualitatively different from true (civil and political) human rights."[12] Others, most notably Professor Henry Shue, argued that there was no difference between civil and political and economic, social, and cultural rights.[13] By the late 1990s, there were many international convenants concerning human rights in force.

With the collapse of communism in Eastern Europe and the disintegration of the Soviet Union, the world entered a new era in the 1990s. Some pronounced the "end of history" and others predicted the "clash of civilizations" (see Chapter 15). The conflicts in Bosnia and Kosovo raised unsettling questions about human rights in world politics. These conflicts also called international attention to the treatment of women and refugees.

GENDER ISSUES IN WORLD POLITICS

An important issue in contemporary world politics concerns gender issues.[14] Robert Keohane has argued that a feminist perspective provides the basis for reanalyzing power, sovereignty, and reciprocity, and that it provides a basis for a critique of realism in international relations theory.[15] In a less theoretical way, all one needs to do is to open the newspaper and the importance of this issue is clear. Among the topics that are frequently mentioned in the news are domestic violence, rape, "wife beating," abortion of female fetuses, and female genital mutilation. Beyond these issues are questions concerning the role of women in politics and international relations.

In his analysis of "Women and the Evolution of World Politics," Dr. Francis Fukuyama has concluded that world politics has been "gradually feminizing over the past century" and that a "truly matriarchal world would be less prone to conflict than the one we now inhabit."[16] But the world will still have male despots such as Saddam Hussein and Slobodan Milosevic, so that "masculine policies will still be essential even in a feminized world." One way for women to become more involved in world politics is through internships.

DEMOCRATIZATION IN THE WORLD TODAY

In 1941, there were 12 democratic states out of a total of 50. A little more than half a century later, approximately 75 of the world's 194 states were democratic.[17] In statistical terms, the percentage of democratic countries increased from about 25 percent in 1941 to almost 40 percent in 1996. If one adds the states that Freedom House considered to be "partially free," the percentage increases to 75 percent in 1996. Many observers—academic and nonacademic alike—have commented on this remarkable increase.

YOU IN WORLD POLITICS

So you're interested in an internship? Internships can be a critical supplement to any sort of educational background to get interesting jobs in international affairs. Because of the informal hiring processes, personal contacts can be indispensable. Most students don't have a close relative high up in these organizations; internships are the next best thing. Internships give students direct experience in job situations. Students learn for themselves whether they like this sort of work and what is required to make a career in it. Often they also get direct job offers. If not, they make personal contacts and get recommendations from job supervisors; if nothing else, they have something on their record which distinguishes them from the thousands of other people who will graduate with undergraduate degrees at the same time. The State Department sponsors an excellent, but highly competitive, internship program; if interested, apply early *in the fall* and write to: U.S. Department of State, Student Employment Programs, P.O. Box 9317, Arlington, VA 22219, Telephone: (703) 875–7490.

Two general rules of internships: any internship is better than none, and the longer the internship the better. Summer internships are the most common, and if that's all you can get, take it. However, you should be aware of some limitations of summer internships. You will not be in Washington long. Moreover, summer interns are so numerous that they are often used by offices as clerical labor, people to run copy machines, address envelopes, etc. Many students use the experience for socializing, which is fine—but it detracts from the image of those with more serious interests. Finally, so many students take summer internships now that employers are less impressed than previously. One other thing to remember about internships: apply early. Begin looking for a summer internship in January and don't just send an application; follow it up with phone calls to get yourself known.

The American Political Science Association publishes an excellent guide to finding internships, *Storming Washington: An Intern's Guide to National Government,* which is available for $5.00 from the American Political Science Association, 1527 New Hampshire Avenue, NW, Washington, DC 20036, telephone: (202)483–2512.

For example, in his 1996 presidential victory speech, President Bill Clinton noted that for the first time in human history a majority of people lived under governments that were democratically elected. What caused this "democratic revolution" and what are the implications for world politics?

Generations of democrats (note, that's a lower case "d," not a reference to the political party) have believed that a government, to quote Thomas Jefferson, "of the people, by the people and for the people" is the best form of government. (Or, as Winston Churchill put it, democracy is a bad form of government, but all other forms are even worse!) The events of the late twentieth century provide evidence that when given the opportunity to choose their own form of government, they will choose democracy. In both North and South America, the only nondemocratic government as of 1998 is Cuba. Since 1989, most of the autocratic governments of Eastern Europe have been replaced with more democratic regimes. People have been drawn by the attractions of self-determination. Or as one U.S. political scientist put it, the cold war ended and democracy was ascendant because democracy was "the *geist* whose *zeit* had come" (the idea whose time had come).[18]

A second reason for the victory of democracy was leadership. In January 1981 Ronald Reagan became president of the United States. The oldest man ever inaugurated president, Reagan was in many ways an anachronism in the late twentieth century. He held fast to the beliefs of the first half of the twentieth century, and one of those beliefs was an unshakable belief in the truth, power, and ultimate victory of democracy. When President Reagan spoke to the British House of Parliament, he called for communism to be thrown "on the ash heap of history," and when he spoke in Berlin, he called on the Soviet leaders to "tear down that [Berlin] wall." To the surprise of probably everyone but the President, by the end of 1989 the wall had come down, and by the end of 1991 the USSR was no more. But Reagan does not deserve all of the credit for the end of the cold war and the victory of democracy; someone else played an unwitting role.

In March 1985, the Soviet ruling political body, the Politburo, selected its youngest member, Mikhail Gorbachev, for the most important political position in the USSR, the head of the Communist Party. Gorbachev faced enormous problems, and he knew about all of these since he had been involved in party affairs his entire adult professional career. When he took office, the Soviet Union was in terrible economic shape, and Gorbachev realized this and moved to reform the communist system.

Gorbachev's reforms took four different manifestations. First, he introduced the policy of *glasnost* (translation: "openness"), which allowed artists, writers, and others to express themselves more openly and honestly. In particular, non-Russian nationalists in various parts of the Soviet Union called for greater national autonomy and in some cases independence from the USSR. Second, Gorbachev called for *perestroika,* which referred to the restructing of the Soviet economy from a centrally planned economy to a mixed economy with some elements of free enterprise capitalism. Third, Gorbachev called for the democratization of the Soviet political system which had previously been characterized by the complete autocratic control by the communist party. Fourth, Gorbachev called for "new thinking" in foreign policy, and added meaning to his rhetoric when he concluded arms control agreements with the United States, called for a unilateral cut in Soviet military forces of half a million men, and announced the Soviet withdrawal from Afghanistan. Gorbachev's four policies had the unintended result of contribuiting to the demise of the Communist Party and the disintegration of the Soviet Union, the defining events in the ending of the cold war.

A third attraction of democracy is economics. Many people assume that democracy and capitalism go together. The U.S. pledge of allegiance says that freedom is "indivisible." If that is the case, then political and economic freedom—democracy and capitalism—are indivisible. While the two philosophies do appear to be compatible, if not complementary, one is not a necessary ingredient for the other, as a number of capitalistic, autocratic governments in Asia clearly demonstrate; think of the People's Republic of China and Singapore. As historian Arthur Schlesinger, Jr., has noted, "Democracy requires capitalism, but capitalism does not require democracy, at least in the short run."[19]

Does Democracy Make a Difference?

So what? What difference in world politics does the victory of democracy make? During the past several years, political scientists have focused on the implications of the prevalence of democratic states for the international system. More than 200 years ago, the German philosopher Immanuel Kant wrote a book entitled *Perpetual Peace.*[20] In it he argued that democracies are less apt to go to war because democratic leaders had to answer to their constituents who, because they would be the ones to have to pay for and fight the war, therefore opposed it. Kant predicted that as democracies spread throughout the world, international conflict would decrease and peace would become more common. Kant's theory remained just that until the late twentieth century, but then events developed allowing political scientists to test Kant's propositions in the real-life "laboratory" of the international system.

The controversy over **democratic peace** has been joined by a number of analysts.[21] While it is true that democratic states have generally not gone to war against one another, there are problems with this hypothesis. First, there have been relatively few wars so the number of test cases is not large. Second, it appears that states making the transition to democracy are particularly war prone.[22] A third caveat is that states that are democratic can engage in aggressive behavior; after all, the German people allowed Adolf Hitler to become chancellor in 1933.

Lest one be swept away on a wave of democratic euphoria, two warnings must be made. Boston University political scientist Walter Clemens, Jr., has noted, "Democracies value the individual; markets treat individuals as tools to make money."[23] The danger to democracies from markets is clear: people will opt for their selfish interest at the expense of the common, democratic good. The other danger relates to the character of the democratic countries in the world today.

As noted at the beginning of this section, 75 percent of the world's 194 states are classified by Freedom House as either "free" or "partially free." That is the good news. The bad news is that 35 percent of the world's states are only "partially free," and are characterized as fragile democracies, at best. The managing editor of the influential quarterly *Foreign Affairs*, Fareed Zakaria, has noted the disturbing rise of "illiberal democracies."[24] According to Zakaria: "Illiberal democracy is a growth industry. Seven years ago only 22 percent of democratizing countries could have been so categorized; five years ago that figure had risen to 35 percent. And to date few illiberal democracies have matured into liberal democracies; if anything, they are moving toward heightened illiberalism. Far from being a temporary transitional stage, it appears that many countries are settling into a form of government that mixes a substantial degree of democracy with a substantial degree of illiberalism."[25] Thus it is not just democracy that democrats and human-rights advocates desire; it is *liberal* democracy, reflecting the classical "natural rights" of the Enlightenment, most notably freedom and equality.

CONCLUSION

Ethics, human rights, democratization—these are subjects that have each commanded thousands of articles and books. Our consideration of these subjects has simply scratched the surface, but even that superficial investigation allows us to conclude that these subjects have been important in world politics for a long time and are becoming even more so given the recent seismic events in international relations as the war over Kosovo demonstrated.

DISCUSSION QUESTIONS

1. What is the relationship among ethics, human rights, and democratization? In what ways does one area affect the other two?

2. Democrats since at least the time of Woodrow Wilson have believed that the expansion of democracy will lead to a more peaceful world. What is the evidence of this in the twentieth century?

3. What ethical principles, if any, should be applied to evaluate the correctness of actions by individuals, multinational corporations, states, and international organizations?

KEY TERMS

Amnesty International
cosmopolitan
democratic peace
International Bill of Rights
International Covenant on Civil
    and Political Rights

International Covenant on
    Economics, Social and
    Cultural Rights
state moralist
Universal Declaration of Human
    Rights

RECOMMENDED PRINT, MULTIMEDIA, AND INTERNET SOURCES

Print

Amnesty International. *Report 1997.* New York: Amnesty International, 1997.

BROWN, MICHAEL E., ed. *Debating the Democratic Peace: An International Security Reader.* Cambridge, MA: MIT Press, 1996.

CLAUDE, RICHARD PIERRE and BURNS WESTON, eds. *Human Rights in the World Community: Issues and Action,* 2nd ed. Philadelphia, PA: University of Pennsylvania Press, 1992.

DONNELLY, JACK. *Universal Human Rights in Theory and Practice.* Ithaca, NY: Cornell University Press, 1989.

———. *International Human Rights,* 2nd ed. Boulder, CO: Westview Press, 1998.

FORSYTHE, DAVID P. *The Internationalization of Human Rights.* Lexington, MA: Lexington Books, 1991.

———. *Human Rights and World Politics,* 2nd ed. Lincoln, NE: University of Nebraska Press, 1989.

HOFFMANN, STANLEY. *Duties Beyond Borders: On the Limits and Possibilities of Ethical International Politics.* Syracuse, NY: Syracuse University Press, 1981.

LAUREN, PAUL GORDON. *The Evolution of International Human Rights.* Philadelphia, PA: University of Pennsylvania Press, 1998.

NYE, JOSEPH S., Jr. *Nuclear Ethics.* New York: The Free Press, 1986.

RUSSETT, BRUCE. *Grasping the Democratic Peace.* Princeton, NJ: Princeton University Press, 1993.

STEINER, HENRY and PHILIP ALSTON, eds. *International Human Rights in Context.* Oxford, England: Clarendon Press, 1996.

VINCENT, R. J. *Human Rights and International Relations.* Cambridge, England: Cambridge University Press, 1986.

WALZER, MICHAEL. *Just and Unjust Wars: A Moral Argument with Historical Illustrations.* New York: Basic Books, 1977.

Multimedia:

Amnesty Interactive CD-ROM. Minneapolis, MN: Human Rights USA Resource Center.

Internet

Amnesty International (organization that monitors the rights of prisoners of conscience): http://www.amnesty.org

Human Rights USA (a consortium of four groups, including Amnesty International, to provide information about human rights): http://www.hrusa.org

Human Rights Watch (an organization that monitors human rights abuses in more than 70 countries around the world): http://www.hrw.org

Human Rights Web (contains information on human rights around the world and how individuals can get involved in addressing human rights issues): http://www.hrweb.org

IGC Issue Pages, Womensnet: http://igc.org/igc/womensnet/

National Endowment for Democracy: www.ned.org

Organization of American States: http://www.oas.org/

Relief Web: http://www.reliefweb.int/

Save the Children: http://www.savethechildren.org/scf/

United Nations High Commissioner for Refugees (the UN organization responsible for assisting refugees throughout the world): http://www.unhcr.ch

United Nations home page on human rights (includes information on the UN High Commissioner for Human Rights and the text of the Universal Declaration of Human Rights): http://www.un.org/rights

U.S. Department of State annual human rights reports on selected states: www.state.gov/www/global/human-rights/index.html

U.S. Institute of Peace, Religion, Ethics and Human Rights Program: www.usip.org/research/rehr.html

World Vision (a Christian hunger relief organization): http://www.wvi.org/

ENDNOTES

[1] U.N. High Commissioner for Refugees, *The State of the World's Refugees: In Search of Solutions* (New York: Oxford University Press, 1995), p. 57.

[2] GORDON A. CRAIG and ALEXANDER L. GEORGE, *Force and Statecraft: Diplomatic Problems of Our Time,* 3rd ed. (New York: Oxford University Press, 1995), p. ix.

[3] ARNOLD WOLFERS, "Statesmanship and Moral Choice," in *Discord and Collaboration: Essays in International Politics* (Baltimore, MD: Johns Hopkins University Press, 1962), p. 47.

[4] Joseph S. Nye, Jr., *Understanding International Conflicts: An Introduction to Theory and History,* 2nd ed. (New York: Longman, 1997), pp. 19–24.

[5] Stephen Decatur's Toast, *Oxford Dictionary of Quotations* (New York: Oxford University Press, 1980), p. 173.

[6] Joseph S. Nye, Jr, *Nuclear Ethics* (New York: The Free Press, 1986), p. 33.

[7] Michael Walzer, *The Revolution of the Saints: A Study in the Origins of Radical Politics* (New York: Atheneum, 1969).

[8] Jack Donnelly, *International Human Rights,* 2nd ed. (Boulder, CO: Westview Press, 1998), pp. 7–8.

[9] Jimmy Carter, "Commencement Address at University of Notre Dame," *The New York Times,* May 23, 1977.

[10] Statement of Purpose, *Amnesty International Report 1997* (New York: Amnesty International, 1997).

[11] Maurice Cranston, *What Are Human Rights?* (New York: Basic Books, 1964).

[12] Jack Donnelly, "Post-Cold War Reflections on the Study of International Human Rights," *Ethics and International Affairs* 8 (1994), 104.

[13] Henry Shue, *Basic Rights: Subsistence, Affluence, and U. S. Foreign Policy* (Princeton, NJ: Princeton University Press, 1980).

[14] See V. Spike Peterson and Anne Sisson Runyan, *Global Gender Issues* (Boulder, CO: Westview Press, 1993) .

[15] Robert O. Keohane, "International Relations Theory: Contributions of a Feminine Standpoint," *Millennium Journal of International Studies,* vol 18, no. 2 (Summer 1989), 245–253.

[16] Francis Fukuyama, "Women and the Evolution of World Politics," *Foreign Affairs,* vol. 77, no. 5 (September/October 1998), 24–40.

[17] These statistics are calculated from *Freedom Review* (January-February 1997).

[18] Seyom Brown, *New Forces, Old Forces and the Future of World Politics, Post-Cold War Edition* (New York: HarperCollins, 1995), p. 123.

[19] Arthur Schlesinger, Jr., "Has Democracy a Future?" *Foreign Affairs,* vol. 76, no. 5 (September/October 1997), 7.

[20] Immanuel Kant, *Perpetual Peace and Other Essays* (Indianapolis: Hackett, 1983), pp. 107–143.

[21] Bruce Russett, *Grasping the Democratic Peace* (Princeton, NJ: Princeton University Press, 1993), Michael Doyle, "Liberalism and World Politics," *American Political Science Review,* vol. 80, no. 4 (December 1986): 1151–1169; and Michael E. Brown, ed., *Debating the Democratic Peace: An International Security Reader* (Cambridge, MA: MIT Press, 1996).

[22] Edward D. Mansfield and Jack Snyder, "Democratization and the Danger of War," *International Security,* vol. 20, no. 1 (Summer 195): 5–38.

[23] Walter C. Clemens, Jr., *Dynamics of International Relations: Conflict and Mutual Gain in an Era of Global Interdependence* (Lanham, MD: Rowman and Littlefield, 1998), p. 298.

[24] Fareed Zakaria, "The Rise of Iliberal Democracy," *Foreign Affairs,* vol. 76, no. 6 (November/December 1997): 22–43.

[25] Ibid., p. 24.

What Is the Future of World Politics?

PART IV

13

Population, the Environment, and Economic Development

CRITEX:

"Lifeboat Ethics"

SUPPOSE for the moment that a wealthy relative has given you a vacation on a cruise line as a reward for the excellent job that you did in this class! On the first day of the cruise, the ship's crew has a drill in which all of the passengers go to assigned places on the ship in order to prepare for a disaster. The ship is equipped with enough lifeboats for all of the passengers (unlike the *Titanic*).

As luck—of the bad variety—would have it, your ship runs into a submerged iceberg (like the *Titanic*) and begins to sink. Not to worry; you proceed to your preassigned evacuation area. As the ship begins to take on water and begins to sink, the captain orders everyone to abandon ship. A panic ensues; a number of frantic passengers jump into the water, and several of the lifeboats cannot be released from their cleats and cannot be lowered into the water.

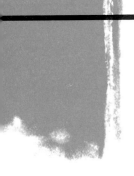

You are fortunate to be on one of the functional lifeboats. Your boat is lowered into the water, and it is immediately surrounded by a number of the passengers who have jumped into the water. The officer on your boat announces that the lifeboat can accommodate an absolute maximum of 60 passengers; anymore will cause the boat to capsize. You and the other passengers are confronted with several excruciating questions:

- There are ten available places in your boat. How should you decide which passengers are allowed into your boat: the first ten to board it? Children, old people, the sick?
- What about the people in the water? Would you allow them to climb over the sides of the boat? Would you prevent, by force if necessary, more than ten coming on board?
- Would your thinking about these questions be different if you were one of those in the water rather than in the lifeboat?
- To what extent is this metaphor applicable to contemporary world politics?

This hypothetical scenario is based on the work of controversial ecologist Garrett Hardin, who has argued that the world is analogous to a lifeboat in that it can support a limited number of people and that its **carrying capacity** is challenged by the number of people in the world.[1] According to Professor Hardin, wealthy, developed states should not intervene to assist poor, developing states; such action is analogous to allowing more passengers on an already overloaded lifeboat. As Professor Hardin has written:

> **Lifeboat ethics** is merely a special application of the logic of the commons. The classic paradigm is that of a pasture held as common property by a community and governed by the following rules: first, each herdsman may pasture as many cattle as he wishes on the commons; and second, the gain from the growth of cattle accrues to the individual owners of the cattle. In an underpopulated world the system of the commons may do no harm and may even be the most economic way to manage things, since management costs are kept to a minimum. In an overpopulated (or overexploited) world a system of the commons leads to ruin, because each herdsman has more to gain individually by increasing the size of his herd than he has to lose as a single member of the community guilty of lowering the **carrying capacity** of the environment. Consequently he (with others) overloads the commons.[2]

INTRODUCTION

This chapter focuses on the "lifeboat" that we call earth and seeks to analyze the interactive effects of the growth in population, environmental degradation, and economic development—topics that are profoundly important in contemporary world politics. In order to accomplish these objectives, various aspects of these topics are reviewed. At the end of the chapter, the steps that have been taken to address these problems are described.

Throughout this chapter, the interaction of population, environmental degradation, and economic development is analyzed. These three factors can be conceptualized as a kind of triangle, as shown in Figure 13.1.

POPULATION GROWTH

In 1997, the population of the United States was approximately 270 million people; this was the total world population in 650 AD. It took a thousand years—until 1650—for the world's population to double to 500 million. It took 200 years (1850) for population to double again to 1 billion people, and then just 80 years (1930) for it to double again to 2 billion. World population reached 4 billion by 1974 and as of 1996 was 5.77 billion (5,770,000,000).[3] The United Nations has estimated that the world's population will continue to increase until the year 2,200, when it will stabilize at 10.73 billion.

Will the world be able to sustain this many people? For at least 200 years, people have debated this question. In 1798, the Reverend **Thomas Malthus** published an essay in which he argued that while food production increased arithmetically, population increased geometrically. According to Malthus, the greatest problem facing the world was "that the power of population is indefinitely greater than the power in the earth to produce subsistence for man."[4] If this is true, then population will at some point outpace the capacity to feed all of the people. For two centuries, Malthus has been wrong; various agricultural and technological advances

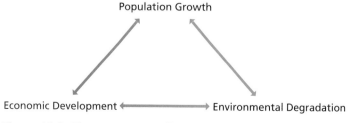

Figure 13.1. The Interactive Effects of Global Variables

have enabled world food production to feed the world's people; however, some argue that Malthus will eventually be proved correct; the only question is how long that will take.

As we think about the growth in the world's population, consider the following striking facts:[5]

- In the second half of the twentieth century, world population has increased more rapidly than ever before.
- In 1994, world population grew by more than 100 million, a number equal to the entire population of Mexico or about 40 percent of the U.S. population.
- Currently, the world's most populous state is the People's Republic of China with 1.2 billion people, about one-fifth of the world's total.
- Early in the twenty-first century, the population of India will overtake that of China.
- In 1950, 33 percent of the world's population lived in developed states; that decreased to 23 percent by 1995 and is projected to decrease to 16 percent by 2025.
- As of 1996, the percent of the population in Africa under the age of 15 years old was 45 percent; in South America 35 percent; in Asia 32 percent; in the United States 21 percent; and in Europe 19 percent.

The world's population has not only grown dramatically, as all of the above statistics indicate; its distribution has also changed significantly. In the mid 1700s, about 3 percent of the world's people lived in cities. That increased to 29 percent by the 1950s; to 40 percent by 1995; and is projected to increase to 60 percent by 2025. One result of this redistribution of people from the countryside to cities has been the growth of large, "megacities." In 1985, the population of Mexico City was 17 million. It is projected to increase to 24 million by 2000. During the same time span, the population of São Paulo, Brazil, is projected to increase from 15 to 24 million.

ENVIRONMENTAL DEGRADATION

Ecology may be defined as "the branch of biology that deals with the relations between living organisms and their environment."[6] There are several principles of ecology that are important to keep in mind. First, "we can never do one thing."[7] The great environmentalist and Sierra Club founder John Muir perhaps stated this principle the best: "When we try to pick anything out by itself, we find it hitched to everything else in the universe." Second, in ecology (as in social and political affairs), actions often have unintended consequences.

An example will help to clarify both of these principles. Early in this century, scientists developed a poison to kill pests that had previously infested and even wiped out crops. This new insecticide, DDT, contributed to both increased agricultural output and improved public health. Ornithologists found that a number of species of birds were decreasing to the verge of extinction and found out that the cause was DDT. Largely due to scientists' criticism of its deleterious effects, DDT was pulled off the market in 1972, and a number of birds, including pelicans and peregrine falcons, made dramatic recoveries. This example illustrates the two principles of ecology mentioned above: DDT did not just kill pests; it had the additional, unintended consequence of killing birds.

The threat of **environmental degradation** can be summarized in nine major categories: (1) greenhouse-induced global warming, (2) ozone depletion, (3) atmospheric pollution, (4) loss of agricultural land, (5) deforestation, (6) depletion of fresh water supplies, (7) depletion of fisheries, (8) acid deposition, and (9) the loss of biodiversity. We will review the potential effects of each of these developments on world politics ... and possibly on you.

Greenhouse-Induced Global Warming

Over one hundred years ago, a Swedish chemist by the name of Svante Arrhenius described the warming effects of increased carbon dioxide in the earth's atmosphere.[8] The great majority of scientists who have studied the problem of **global warming** believe that human activities, particularly those involved with the burning of fossil fuels, are altering the world's climate.[9] In fact, some scientists believe that the term "global warming" is "a misnomer for a phenomenon that should be referred to as anthropogenically induced climate change."[10] Whatever it is called, the basic dynamics of this phenomenon are rather simple: the atmosphere is transparent to the sun; energy enters the earth's atmosphere and some of it is reflected off the earth's surface back toward space; **greenhouse gases,** such as carbon dioxide and other substances that result from burning fossil fuels, trap some of the reflected energy and warm up the earth. Recent studies have noted the increased temperatures of the earth. Although temperature records based on thermometer readings only go back about 150 years, scientists are able to measure past temperatures using indirect means such as examining the annual growth rings in trees and evidence contained in fossils. Based on these studies, scientists have reconstructed temperature variations in the northern hemisphere back to the year 1400. They have concluded that the twentieth century has been the warmest century in the past 600 years and that the warmest years of that entire period were 1990, 1995, and 1997.[11]

Estimates of the extent of global warming vary, but a five-year study by the Intergovernmental Panel of Climate Change, a United Nations-sponsored group of 2,500 of the world's leading atmospheric scientists from twenty-five different countries predicted that the world's temperatures would increase by 1 to 3.5 degrees Celsius by the year 2100.[12] A 1991 study by the U.S. National Academy of Sciences concluded that "greenhouse warming poses a potential threat sufficient to merit prompt responses."[13] There could be at least three major effects from such global warming: climate change (some areas would get warmer, others would get colder), some organisms would be affected, and sea levels would rise.

The UN panel concluded global warming could increase sea levels from six inches to three feet. Such a rise in the world's oceans could be devastating to many of the world's countries; particularly hard hit would be island states. For example, 80 percent of the Maldives, a collection of almost 1,200 islands in the Indian Ocean, are only three feet above sea level. Thirty-five countries have joined together to form the **Alliance of Small Island States** to call attention to the devastating consequences of global warming and its effect on increasing the world's sea levels. Island states would not be the only affected areas. Bangladesh could lose 18 percent of its land mass, and the Netherlands could lose 6 percent. The United States would also be affected. Researchers at the University of Southern California (USC) studied the likely effects of global warming on Ventura County, the area north of Los Angeles. Based on projections made by the United Nations task force on global warming and their own calculations, the USC group predicted that the sea level in Ventura County would rise by two feet by 2040. If this were to occur, houses of more than 9,000 people could be damaged and flooding could occur within a block of the shoreline.[14]

The cost of global warming is significant. In 1997—the hottest year on record—more than $60 billion of economic damages were caused from weather-related disasters. As of the end of 1997, such losses caused more than $200 billion in damage, an amount equal to more than four times the total losses for the decade of the 1980s.[15]

Ozone Depletion

Next to the earth's stratosphere is a layer of ozone, which acts as a filter for harmful ultraviolet radiation from the sun. A second layer of ozone has been created by the industrial revolution. More recently, chemicals call **chlorofluorocarbons (CFCs),** used in manufacturing furniture stuffing, refrigerators, and air conditioners, and in cleaning electronics, are entering the atmosphere and will remain there for decades. In fact, even if the world were to agree to stop using CFCs today, they would continue to have harmful effects for the next 100 years. These harmful effects include blindness from cataracts, skin cancer, reduced immunity, and the destruction of crops and marine life.

Since the 1970s, scientists have noted increased ultraviolet (UV) radiation levels in the southern hemisphere. In 1985, scientists discovered a hole the size of Australia in the ozone layer over Antarctica. This discovery has had very real impact on people in Australia and New Zealand; following the discovery of the hole in the ozone, people became concerned about the dangers of increased UV radiation. One saying is "Today's skin cancer victims are yesterday's sun worshippers."

The international community became concerned about ozone depletion and, in 1987, 154 states signed the **Montreal Protocol** calling for the eventual elimination of the production of CFCs. The protocol was strengthened in 1990 and 1992. By the mid 1990s, the agreement had made a difference; according to the respected British magazine, *The Economist:* "Good news for sunbathers: the concentrations of ozone-gobbling chemicals in the earth's atmosphere fell last year [1995] by 1.5 percent, the first recorded decline since the invention of CFCs." [16]

Atmospheric Pollution

Anyone who has ever lived in or even visited a large urban city has undoubtedly noticed the difference between the air quality of the city and the countryside. Unfortunately, this difference is not just cosmetic; the poor quality of the air of many of the world's cities affects people's health. A tragic episode of pollution affecting people occurred in London in 1952 when a deadly combination of fog mixed with soot caused by the burning of coal caused 4,000 deaths. Today, in some cities and areas of the world the problems are also tragically obvious. The World Health Organization and World Bank estimate that 2.7 million people die each year from illnesses caused by air pollution; of these 1.56 million are Asians. [17]

The Pollutions Standards Index is used to measure carbon dioxide, sulfur dioxide, and other pollutants in the air. In U.S. cities, the index rarely goes above 100; a reading of 300 results in warnings advising people to remain indoors with doors and windows shut, and a level of 400 indicates emergency conditions that could lead to premature death of elderly and sick people. In the early 1990s, these were some Pollutions Standards Index readings: Calcutta (390), Beijing (370), Jakarta (280), Hong Kong (120),

TABLE 13.1					
Air Pollution Takes Its Toll					
		Indoor Pollution Caused primarily by smoke from cooking and heating fines		**Outdoor Pollution** Largely attributed to industrial and automobile emissions	
Region	Deaths:	Rural	Urban	Urban	Total Deaths
India		496,000	93,000	84,000	**673,000**
Sub-Saharan Africa		490,000	32,000	*	**522,000**
China		320,000	53,000	70,000	**443,000**
Other Asian and Pacific countries		363,000	40,000	40,000	**443,000**
Latin America and Caribbean		180,000	113,000	113,000	**406,000**
Former socialist economies of Europe		*	*	100,000	**100,000**
Established market economies		0	32,000	47,000	**79,000**
Middle East		*	*	57,000	**57,000**
Total Deaths		1,849,000	363,000	511,000	**2,723,000**

*Not available.
According to the World Health Organization, at least 2.7 million people die each year from illnesses caused by air pollution.
Source: The New York Times, November 29, 1997, page A 6. Copyright © 1997 by *The New York Times*. Reprinted by permission.

Manila (90), New York (60) and Tokyo (40). Clearly, the residents of the first three cities listed live in a dangerous environment.

In the autumn of 1997, Indonesian and Malaysian farmers burned forest in order to clear land for farming. This burn-off had serious consequences in terms of deforestation (discussed below), but it also caused serious air pollution throughout Southeast Asia. The smoke spread as far as Singapore, Malaysia, Thailand, and the Philippines, encompassing an area inhabited by 200 million people. In September 1997, the pollution index hit 700 in Kuching, Malaysia, and 839 in Sarawak.

Loss of Agricultural Land, Desertification, and Erosion

A motorcyclist and his family wear masks to protect themselves from the smog as they wait in line at a Kuala Lampur gas station.
Source: Associated Press; published in *The New York Times,* September 25, 1997, p. 1; *Los Angeles Times,* April 5, 1998, p. A 13.

If the amount of good agricultural land were unlimited, then there would be no problem with increased population growth because the world's supply of food could meet the demand of the world's population. In the lexicon of ecology, the **carrying capacity** of the earth could be increased to feed the world's people. Unfortunately, agricultural land is finite; at present total worldwide cropland equals approximately 1.5 billion hectares. Optimistic estimates of the total arable land on earth, including both current and potential arable land, fall between 3.2 and 3.4 billion hectares. Experts believe that the best agricultural land has already been cultivated and that there is increasing pressure in areas surrounding cities to convert flat agricultural land into housing and factories because building costs are low. Thus the land that is left is "less fertile, not sufficiently rainfed or easily irrigable, infested with pests, or harder to clear and work."[18]

Due to both natural and human-made causes, the earth's agricultural land is decreasing. When humans build on agricultural land, it is no longer available for farming. Because of the loss of topsoil due to erosion, deforestation, and insufficient fallow periods, many areas of the world suffer from **desertification.** Currently experts estimate that 15.6 million acres (6 million hectares) are lost to desertification every year. The respected demographer Vaclav Smil has estimated that "two to three million hectares of cropland are lost annually to erosion; perhaps twice as much land goes to urbanization, and at least one million hectares are abandoned because of excessive salinity."[19]

Deforestation

Forests, particularly the rain forests of the earth, are disappearing at an alarming rate. Many scientists are concerned about the worldwide destruction of forests because they perform a similar function for the earth that the lungs perform for the human body: they cycle out waste and pollution from the world's air supply and add valuable oxygen to it. Throughout the world, the short-term perspective is taking precedence over the long-term perspective. Local owners of forest resources want to capitalize on their holdings, sometimes ignoring the effects of such actions on the future. For example, in the Philippines logging concessions are granted for a period of 10 years; yet, it takes 30 to 35 years for secondary growth to mature. Unfortunately, up to 40 percent of the harvestable lumber is wasted. The end result of the attempt to capitalize on this resource is clear: early in the twentieth century there were 17 million hectares of forests in the Philippines; today only 1.2 million hectares remain.

In many areas of the world, the interactive effects on the environment of population and the drive for economic development are dramatically evident. Indonesia's population is growing at the rate of 2 million per year, and the government plans to clear 40 million acres of rain forest by 2020, in order to accommodate the growth in population.[20] In the autumn of 1997, farmers in Southeast Asia and Brazil adopted the same environmentally destructive technique to clear more land for agriculture: they started fires to burn forested areas. The World Wildlife Fund estimates that 12 to 15 percent of the Brazilian rain forest has disappeared. Satellite images indicate that 5,800 square miles are deforested each year. In addition, the Woods Hole Research Institute estimates that another 4,200 square miles are thinned by logging beneath the canopy of the rain forest.[21]

Not all **deforestation** is due to the drive for economic development; some results from other human activities. Prior to the long war fought within its boundaries, Vietnam was one of the most forested regions of the world. However, since 1945, its forest cover has been reduced from 43 percent of the country to 28 percent, as a result of both peacetime economic exploitation and the spraying of defoliants, such as "agent orange," by U.S. planes.[22] Overall, it is estimated that Asia has lost 50 percent of its forest cover during the past 30 years.[23] A disturbing fact is that, according to satellite data, deforestation figures indicate a 34 percent increase from 1991 to 1997.

Depletion of Fresh Water Supplies

Three decades ago, when I was in Boy Scouts and hiked in the Sierra Nevada Mountains of California, I never carried water and often did not boil or purify it. That would be a big mistake today because much of the fresh water supplies in the streams and lakes of the United States are infected with a nasty parasite, giardia. The pollution of American streams and lakes, however, pales by comparison with some other countries. For example, Asia's rivers contain on average 20 times more lead than those in western, developed states.[24] In addition, the average river in Asia contains 50 times as much bacteria from human feces than guidelines from the World Health Organization allow.[25]

A particularly difficult problem exists in Russia, where the Soviet government for many years paid inadequate or no attention to the contamination of fresh water supplies from nuclear waste. Norwegian and Russian scientists found that one site, the Mayak reprocessing plant in the southern Ural mountains, consistently leaked five times more radiation than that leaked at Chernobyl.[26] The potential effects of this pollution could extend far from Russia because toxic waste in the form of plutonium (one of the most toxic known substances) and strontium-90 has seeped into Lake Karachay which feeds into the Arctic Ocean. Scientists also discovered a number of large containers of spent nuclear fuel sitting in the open air at a waste site on the Kola Peninsula in northern Russia.[27] Nuclear pollution is particularly problematic because of its long-lasting effects; radon and radium have a half-life of 80 thousand years, while plutonium's half-life is 500 thousand years.[28]

At present, access to potable water is a problem for 40 percent of the world's population. According to China scholar John Bryan Starr, "In 1995 factories and cities in China discharged 37.3 billion tons of sewage and industrial wastes into waterways and coastal waters. More than a quarter of the nation's freshwater supply is polluted, and 90 percent of the water flowing through its cities is impotable."[29] Between 1980 and 2000, worldwide water usage is expected to double. A number of experts believe that access to and control of water supplies will constitute a *casus belli* (cause of war) in the future.

Depletion of Fisheries

Since 1989, the world's marine catch has stopped increasing. Throughout the 1980s, catches of the most valuable species, such as cod and halibut, were lower than in the 1970s, even though the capacity of the world's fishing fleets had increased.

Many Asians, particularly those in southern China and Hong Kong, prefer the freshest fish possible, and many restaurants buy live fish and place them in tanks until they are cooked. With the economic upturn in southern China, there has been a corresponding increased demand for live fish. The easiest way for fishermen to catch live fish is to distribute sodium cyanide into the water around coral reefs. This chemical kills smaller fish, but only stuns the larger ones, which are then netted and sold to restaurants. Recall Professor Garrett Hardin's principle of ecology: "We can never do one thing." That is certainly the case with cyanide fishing, which winds up killing the coral reefs from which many fish and other marine organisms derive their sustenance. Throughout the Pacific, coral reefs have been significantly damaged by cyanide fishing.

Acid Deposition

Sulfur dioxide and nitrogen emitted by industrial factories and automobiles turn into diluted sulfuric and nitric acid when they come into contract with moisture. When these chemicals go into the atmosphere, they mix with water molecules and then reenter the earth's atmosphere as **acid rain.** This stunts the growth or kills fish in lakes and streams, pollutes ground water, and causes respiratory problems. It is estimated that acid rain has destroyed 28 thousand square miles of forest in 15 Eastern European states, and at present Sweden has no fresh water lakes that are not polluted by acid rain. In Chongqing, China, the rain is so acidic that its pH level is equal to three, about the same as Chinese vinegar. And this issue is a significant one in the relationship between the United States and Canada.

Loss of Biodiversity

The eminent Harvard entomologist, Professor Edward O. Wilson, has estimated that 27 thousand species are disappearing each year, 74 each day and 3 each hour.[30] The World Conservation Union maintains a "Red List" of endangered species. In April 1998, this organization concluded that one in eight plant species in the world and one in three in the United States was threatened by extinction.[31]

So what? What difference does the loss of biodiversity make? Several examples may help to answer this question. Prescription drugs are often developed from esoteric plants and animals, such as the rosy periwinkly plant found in Madagascar. The drug developed from this plant is used to treat childhood leukemia, and thanks to this drug, survival rates for this disease have increased from 20 percent to 80 percent. It is estimated that only 2 percent of known plant species have been tested for their possible medicinal uses.[32] Or consider a fungus that wiped out one-fifth of the U.S. corn crop in the 1970s. A wild strain of corn, teosinte, was found in Mexico and was used to develop a strain of blight-resistant corn. Had it been available earlier, it is estimated that U.S. farmers would have avoided losses of $1 billion. At the time that it was discovered in Mexico, only ten hectares of teosinte remained.

WHAT HAS BEEN AND CAN BE DONE?

The problems described in this chapter are significant, and the international community has noted and addressed a number of the direct and indirect issues related to population growth, environmental degradation, and economic development. The United Nations, for example, has sponsored a number of conferences concerning these issues (see Box 13.1). At a minimum, these conferences have served a "consciousness raising" function, alerting the world's population to significant, international issues. In some cases, these conferences have resulted in specific programs of action.

ECONOMIC DEVELOPMENT

Often the international debate concerning environmental degradation and protection turns into a predictable, fruitless debate between those from developed countries who argue that the developing states should do more

---

BOX 13.1   United Nations Conferences on Global Issues

On population:
   1974: Bucharest, Romania
   1984: Mexico City
   1994: Cairo, Egypt

On women:
   1975: Mexico City
   1980: Copenhagen
   1985: Nairobi
   1995: Beijing, China

On the environment:
   1972: Stockholm, Sweden
   1992: Rio de Janeiro, Brazil
   1997: Kyoto, Japan
   1998: Argentina

---

to address the problems described in this chapter and those from advanced-industrial states who point their fingers at developing countries, scolding them for not doing more to limit population growth, save rain forests, curb air pollution, and improve the quality of fresh water. Those from developing states argue that they are concerned, in some cases literally, with the survival of their citizens and that concern about the environment is a luxury of rich countries.

There are many ways of thinking about the levels of development of the world's states. Several decades ago, journalists, politicians, and professors wrote and spoke of two kinds of states: rich developed states and poor developing states. (An explanation about terminology is needed here. Poor countries have been referred to as "underdeveloped states," "less-developed countries" [LDCs], and "third world" states. Throughout this text, I have used the term "develop*ing*" for two reasons: it is less pejorative than the other terms, and it is the term generally preferred by people from these countries.) Going beyond the dichotomous rich/poor, developing/developed categorization, the World Bank has classified states according to a threefold distinction: low income, middle income, and high income. Table 13.2 classifies the world's states according to income and region for the year 1997.

This table graphically shows that most of the world's low-income states are located in Africa, followed by East Asia and the Pacific, Eastern

TABLE 13.2

Classification of Economies by Income and Region, 1997

Income group	Subgroup	Sub-Saharan Africa		Asia		Europe and Central Asia		Middle East and North Africa		Americas
		East and Southern Africa	*West Africa*	*East Asia and Pacific*	*South Asia*	*Eastern Europe and Central Asia*	*Rest of Europe*	*Middle East*	*North Africa*	
Low income $765 or less		Angola, Burundi, Comoros, Eritrea, Ethiopia, Kenya, Madagascar, Malawi, Mozambique, Rwanda, Somalia, Sudan, Tanzania, Uganda, Zaire, Zambia, Zimbabwe	Benin, Burkina Faso, Cameroon, Central African Republic, Chad, Congo, Côte d'Ivoire, Equatorial Guinea, Gambia, The, Ghana, Guinea, Guinea-Bissau, Liberia, Mali, Mauritania, Niger, Nigeria, São Tomé and Principe, Senegal, Sierra Leone, Togo	Cambodia, China, Lao PDR, Mongolia, Myanmar, Vietnam	Afghanistan, Bangladesh, Bhutan, India, Nepal, Pakistan, Sri Lanka	Albania, Armenia, Azerbaijan, Bosnia and Herzegovina, Georgia, Kyrgyz Republic, Tajikistan		Yemen, Rep.		Guyana, Haiti, Honduras, Nicaragua
		Botswana, Djibouti, Lesotho	Cape Verde	Fiji, Indonesia, Kiribati	Maldives	Belarus, Bulgaria, Estonia	Turkey	Iran, Islamic Rep., Iraq	Algeria, Egypt, Arab Rep.	Belize, Bolivia, Colombia

Middle-income	Subtotal: 158								
Lower $766–$3035	Namibia Swaziland		Korea, Dem. Rep. Marshall Islands Micronesia Fed. Sts. Papua New Guinea Philippines Solomon Islands Thailand Tonga Vanuatu Western Samoa		Kazakhstan Latvia Lithuania Macedonia FYR[a] Moldova Poland Romania Russian Federation Slovak Republic Turkmenistan Ukraine Uzbekistan Yugoslavia Fed. Rep.[b]		Jordan Lebanon Syrian Arab Republic West Bank and Gaza	Marocco Tunisia	Costa Rica Cuba Dominica Dominican Republic Ecuador El Salvador Grenada Guatemala Jamaica Panama Paraguay Peru St. Vincent and the Grenadines Suriname Venezuela
Upper $3036–$9,385	Mauritius Mayotte Seychelles South Africa	Gabon	American Samoa Malaysia		Croatia Czech Republic Hungary Slovenia	Greece Isle of Man Malta	Bahrain Oman Saudi Arabia	Libya	Antigua and Barbuda Argentina Barbados Brazil Chile Guadeloupe Mexico Puerto Rico St. Kitts and Nevis St. Lucia Trinidad and Tobago Uruguay
Subtotal:	26	23	21	8	27	4	10	5	34

TABLE 13.2 (continued)

Classification of Economies by Income and Region, 1997

Income group	Subgroup	Sub-Saharan Africa		Asia		Europe and Central Asia		Middle East and North Africa		Americas
		East and Southern Africa	West Africa	East Asia and Pacific	South Asia	Eastern Europe and Central Asia	Rest of Europe	Middle East	North Africa	
High income ($9386 or more)	OECD[d] countries			Australia Japan New Zeland Korea, Rep.			Austria Belgium Denmark Finland France Germany Iceland Ireland Italy Luxembourg Netherlands Norway Portugal Spain Sweden Switzerland United Kingdom			Canada United States

Non-OECD countries	Reunion	Brunei
		French
		  Polynesia
		Guam
		Hong Kong
		Macao
		New
		  Caledonia
		N. Mariana
		  Islands
		Singapore
		OAE[c]
						Andorra
						Channel
						  Islands
						Cyprus
						Faeroe
						  Islands
						Greenland
						Liechtenstein
						Monaco
							Israel
							Kuwait
							Qatar
							United Arab
							  Emirates
									Aruba
									Bahamas, The
									Bermuda
									Cayman
									  Islands
									French
									  Guiana
									Martinique
									Netherlands
									  Antilles
									Virgin Islands
									  (U.S.)

Total:	210	27	23	34	8	27	28	14	5	44

[a] Former Yugoslav Republic of Macedonia.

[b] Federal Republic of Yugoslavia (Serbia/Montenegro).

[c] Other Asian economies—Taiwan, China.

[d] Organization for Economic Cooperation and Development.

Income group: Economies are divided according to 1995 GNP per capita, calculated using the *World Bank Atlas* method. The groups are: low-income, $765 or less; lower-middle-income, $766–$3,035; upper-middle-income, $3,036–$9,385; and high-income, $9,386 or more.

Source: World Bank, *World Development Report 1997: The State in a Changing World.* New York: Oxford University Press, 1997, pages 264–265.

YOU IN WORLD POLITICS

So you're interested in joining the Peace Corps? The Peace Corps provides an excellent opportunity for recent college graduates to live and work abroad. It is an agency of the U.S. government which sends Americans overseas, usually for two years, to developing countries, to assist with economic and social development.

Volunteers often work on their own in rigorous physical conditions. Aside from living abroad, Peace Corps volunteers get independent management experience at a very young age. As a result, Peace Corps experience is highly valued by employers hiring for international jobs. For further information, call 800/832–0681.

Alternatives to the Peace Corps

There are a number of nongovernmental organizations that sponsor Peace Corps-like programs. An excellent description of such programs is *Alternatives to the Peace Corps: A Directory of Third World and U.S. Volunteer Opportunities* edited by Becky Buell, Victoria Clarke, and Susan Leone and published by Food First Books, Institute for Food and Development Policy (145 Ninth Street, San Francisco, CA 94103, telephone: 415/864–8555).

Europe and Central Asia, and the Americas. At the other end of the spectrum, most of the world's high-income states are located in Europe, East Asia and the Pacific, and North America, and are members of the Organization for Economic Cooperation and Development (OECD). There are many middle-income states, particularly in Latin America.

Cathal J. Nolan, the author of *The Longman Guide to World Affairs*, has written:

> There is no consensus about the general meaning of this term [development], or even what indicators should be used to assess it. Yet it is often used in North and South alike to mean the building of institutions and economic infrastructure to steer the modernization of traditional societies. It is closely associated with industrialization and urbanization.[33]

The measurement of development that is most often used is gross national product (GNP) or gross domestic product (GDP) per capita; that is, the value of the total goods and services produced by the citizens and corporations of a country divided by its population. An interesting exercise is to calculate the world's per capita GNP, which can be done using the following figures:

> World GNP is $27,000,000,000,000 (that's $27 trillion for any non-mathematicians!)
>
> divided by total world population, which is 5,700,000,000
>
> *World per capita GNP* = $4,737

Consulting Table 13.2, one can see that this means that the world's average per capita GNP lies in the upper-middle-income category ($3,036–$9,385).

While many in the past have thought of development as a good process, there are some very real threats posed by development and its effects on the environment. One of the greatest concerns the increased use of fossil fuels, which contributes to global warming. At present, there are 144 million automobiles in the United States which has a population of 270 million. Thus, there are almost two people for every car in the United States. In China at present, there are approximately 7 million automobiles. As China develops and prospers, its citizens will undoubtedly want cars, but if the same ratio of people to cars is achieved in China as in the United States, the consequences for the global environment in both developed and developing countries—rich and poor alike—will be disastrous.

A number of economists and social scientists have called for development that can be sustained by the international community. If one accepts the principle that the earth has a limit to its "carrying capacity" (the quantity and quality of organisms it can sustain), then there must be some limit to development. The idea of **sustainable development** therefore emphasizes moderate consumption patterns, technologies that are appropriate to the societies in which they are employed, and the use of resources balanced with their renewal. In 1987, the United Nations published a comprehensive report on this subject, and in 1996 the U.S. President's Commission on Sustainable Development issued a report which concluded that "efficiency in the use of all resources would have to increase by more than 50 percent over the next four or five decades just to keep pace with population growth."[34]

Population growth, environmental degradation, and economic development: these three aspects of contemporary world politics constitute a kind of iron triangle; each one affects the others and these interactive effects cannot be escaped.

DISCUSSION QUESTIONS

1. Was Thomas Malthus correct or incorrect in his predictions concerning population and resources?

2. Some skeptics dismiss environmentalists as alarmist "tree-huggers." To what extent do you think that environmentalists' claims concerning environmental degradation and its consequences are alarmist?

3. What are the attributes of "sustainable development" as opposed to other types of development?

KEY TERMS

acid rain
Alliance of Small Island States
carrying capacity
chlorofluorocarbons
desertification
ecology
environmental degradation

global warming
greenhouse gases
lifeboat ethics
Malthus, Thomas
Montreal Protocol
sustainable development

RECOMMENDED PRINT, MULTIMEDIA, AND INTERNET SOURCES

Print

CAIRNCROSS, FRANCES. "Environmental Pragmatism." *Foreign Policy* 95 (Summer 1994): 35–52.

Commission on Global Governance. *Our Global Neighborhood.* New York: Oxford University Press, 1995.

EHRLICH, PAUL, ANNE EHRLICH, and JOHN HOLDREN. *Ecoscience: Population, Resources, Environment.* Stanford, CA: Stanford University Press, 1979.

GELBSPAN, ROSS. *The Heat Is On: The High Stakes Battle Over Earth's Threatened Climate.* San Francisco: Addision-Wesley, 1997.

"Global Warming." Special Section. *The New York Times,* December 1, 1997.

GORE, ALBERT. *Earth in the Balance: Ecology and the Human Spirit.* New York: Plume, 1993.

HOMER-DIXON, THOMAS F. "On the Threshold: Environmental Changes as Causes of Acute Conflict." *International Security,* vol. 16, no. 2 (Fall 1991): 76–116.

———. Environmental Scarcities and Violent Conflict: Evidence from Cases." *International Security,* vol. 19, no. 1 (Summer 1994): 5–40.

LEVY, MARC A. "Is the Environment a National Security Issue?" *International Security,* vol. 20, no. 2 (Fall 1995): 35–62.

MAHLMAN, J. D. "Uncertainties in Projections of Human-Caused Climate Warming." *Science,* vol. 278 (21 November 1997): 1416–1417.

MATHEWS, JESSICA TUCHMAN. "Redefining Security." *Foreign Affairs,* vol. 68, no. 2 (Spring 1989): 162–177.

MCKIBBEN, BILL. *The End of Nature.* New York: Random House, 1989.

MYERS, NORMAN. "Environment and Security." *Foreign Policy,* no. 74 (Spring 1994): 23–41.

PORTER, GARETH and JANET WELSH BROWN. *Global Environmental Politics.* Boulder, CO: Westview Press, 1991.

SCHNEIDER, STEPHEN H. *Laboratory Earth: The Planetary Gamble We Can't Afford to Lose.* New York: HarperCollins, 1997.

WILSON, EDWARD O. *The Diversity of Life.* Cambridge, MA: The Belknap Press of Harvard University Press, 1992.

WIRTH, DAVID A. "Climate Chaos." *Foreign Policy,* no. 74 (Spring 1994): 3–22.

Video

Chernobyl: The Taste of Wormwood. Princeton, NJ: Films for the Humanities and Sciences. Provides on-site images and interviews with the survivors.

The Greenhouse Effect and Global Climate: Jessica Tuchman Mathews. Princeton, NJ: Films for the Humanities and Sciences (30 minutes).

Hole in the Sky: The Ozone Layer. Princeton, NJ: Films for the Humanities and Sciences (52 minutes).

Paul Ehrlich and the Population Bomb. Princeton, NJ: Films for the Humanities and Sciences, 60 minutes. Contains footage from around the world as well as interviews with Ehrlich and his critics.

CD-ROM

Chernobyl: The Dead Zone. Princeton, NJ: Films for the Humanities and Sciences. Contains video, photographs and documents of the world's worst nuclear accident.

Internet

Amazing Environmental Organization Web Directory (provides capability to search various environmental organizations): http://www.webdirectory.com

Earth Times: a daily electronic news source focusing on environmental, development and population issues: http://www.earthtimes.org

Environment link (one of the largest information sources concerning the environment): www.environlink.org

Environmental News Network (provides news from a number of sources and links to other environmental sites): http://www.enn.com

Environmental Protection Agency's information on global warming: http://www.epa.gov/

Greenpeace: www.greenpeace.org

International Food Policy Research Institute: http://www.cgiar.org/ifpri

International Institute for Sustainable Development: http://iisd.ca/

University of Oregon, "The Challenge of Global Warming":
        http://gladstone.uoregon.edu/~eaglej/

Rainforest Action Network: http://www.ran/org

Science: http://www.sciencemag.org

Sierra Club: www.sierraclub.org

UN Conference on Environment and Development: www.ciesin.org/

UN Development Program (UNDP): http://www.undp.org

UN Environment Program: www.unep.org

UNESCO: http://www.unesco.org/

UNICEF: http://www.unicef.org

US Agency for International Development: http://www.info.usaid.gov

US Environmental Proection Agency (global warming information):
        www.epa.gov/globalwarming/index.html

US Nuclear Regulatory Commission: www.nrc.gov

World population "clock": http://www.webstreet.com/

World Resources Institute: www.wri.org/

Worldwatch Institute: http://www.worldwatch.org/

ENDNOTES

[1] See GARRETT HARDIN, "Lifeboat Ethics: The Case Against Helping the Poor," *Psychology Today* (September 1974) and "Living on a Lifeboat," *Bioscience* (October 1974).

[2] GARRETT HARDIN, "Carrying Capacity as an Ethical Concept," in George R. Lucas, Jr., and Thomas W. Ogletree, eds., *Lifeboat Ethics: The Moral Dilemmas of World Hunger* (New York: Harper and Row, 1976), p. 120.

[3] "The Population Explosion Slows Down," *The New York Times,* November 17, 1996, p. 3.

[4] T. R. MALTHUS, *An Essay on the Principle of Population as It Affects the Future Improvement of Society* (London, 1798), quoted by Paul Kennedy, *Preparing for the Twenty-first Century* (New York: Random House, 1993), p. 5.

[5] FRANCES CAIRNCROSS, "Environmental Pragmatism," *Foreign Policy* 95 (Summer 1994).

[6] *Webster's New World Dictionary* (New York: World Publishing Company, 1966).

[7] HARDIN, "Carrying Capacity," p. 124.

[8] SVANTE ARRHENIUS, *The London, Edinburgh and Dublin Philosophical Magazine and Journal of Science,* vol. 41, no. 237 (1896).

[9] See, for example, R. A. HOUGHTON and G. M. WOODWELL, "Global Climate Change," *Scientific American,* vol. 260, no. 4 (April 1989): 36–44.

[10] SARAH DOHERTY, DAVID BATTISTI, ROBERT CHARLSON, RICHARD GAMMON, CONWAY LEOVY, and J. MICHAEL WALLACE, "Climate Flip-flop," *Atlantic Monthly* (May 1998), 13.

[11] RAYMOND S. BRADLEY and MALCOLM K. HUGHES, *Nature;* quoted by William K. Stevens, "New Evidence Finds This Is Warmest Century in 600 Years," *The New York Times,* April 28, 1998, B 13.

[12] L. Brown, M. Renner and C. Flavin, *Vital Signs 1997* (New York: W. W. Norton, 1997), p. 58.

[13] William K. Stevens, "Science Academy Disputes Attack on Global Warming," *The New York Times,* April 22, 1998, A 20.

[14] Daryl Kelley, "Ill Tidings of a Rising Sea," *Los Angeles Times,* March 25, 1997, B 2.

[15] Brown, et al. *Vital Signs 1997*, p. 70.

[16] *The Economist,* June 15, 1996, 18.

[17] Nicholas D. Kristof, "Across Asia, a Pollution Disaster Hovers," *The New York Times,* November 28, 1997, 1.

[18] World Resources Institute, *World Resources 1990–91* (Washington, DC: WRI, 1991), p. 5, cited by Thomas F. Homer-Dixon, "On the Threshold: Environmental Changes as Causes of Acute Conflict," *International Security,* vol. 16, no. 2 (Fall 1991), 93.

[19] Vaclav Smil quoted in Homer-Dixon, "On the Threshold."

[20] David Lamb, "Southeast Asia Paying High Toll for Prosperity," *Los Angeles Times,* April 5, 1998, A 12.

[21] Diana Jean Schemo, "More Fires by Farmers Raise Threat to Amazon," *The New York Times,* November 2, 1998, 8.

[22] Lamb, "Southeast Asia," A 12.

[23] David Lamb, "Indonesian Fires Cloud Future of Southeast Asia," *Los Angeles Times,* September 25, 1997, 1.

[24] Ibid., A 13.

[25] Nicholas D. Kristof, "Across Asia, a Polluted Disaster Hovers," *The New York Times,* November 28, 1997, 1.

[26] See Environment Link website: www.envirolink.org/pubs/rachel/rhwn191.html

[27] Valonda Bruinton, "Arctic and Nuclear Contamination," *Washington Post,* December 7, 1995, 5.

[28] See the U.S. Nuclear Regulatory Commission's website: www.nrc.gov/NRC/radwaste.html

[29] John Bryan Starr, *Understanding China* (New York: Hill and Wang, 1997), p. 171.

[30] Edward O. Wilson, *The Diversity of Life* (Cambridge, MA: Harvard University Press, 1992), p. 280.

[31] William K. Stevens, "One in Every 8 Plant Species Is Imperiled, a Survey Finds," *The New York Times,* April 8, 1998, 1.

[32] World Wildlife Fund and World Wide Fund for Nature, *The Importance of Biological Diversity* (New Haven, CT: Yale University Press, 1992).

[33] Cathal J. Nolan, *The Longman Guide to World Affairs* (White Plains, NY: Longman, 1995), p. 91.

[34] U.S. President's Commission on Sustainable Development, 1996; quoted by Bill McKibben, "A Special Moment in History," *Atlantic Monthly* (May 1998), 77.

Intrastate Violence, Peace Operations, and Preventing Deadly Conflict

CRITEX:
Stopping Genocide

*t*HE problems of the twenty-first century will not be those of traditional power confrontations. They are more likely to arise out of the integration, or disintegration, of states themselves, and affect all actors on the world scene irrespective of ideology.

Sir Michael Howard[1]

Six million Jews were killed in Nazi concentration camps during World War II. **Six million**—the number is beyond comprehension. The filmmaker Steven Spielberg helped people to understand the Holocaust in human terms in the film *Schindler's List.* Historians, too, have helped people who did not live through the Holocaust to understand. Historian Raul Hilberg spent 12 years of his life researching and writing a detailed, comprehensive history of *The Destruction of the European Jews.*[2] In this book, the

285

author describes in great detail the organization and operation of the concentration camps, but the most poignant passage of the book recalls:

> The father was holding the hand of a boy about ten years old and was speaking to him softly; the boy was fighting his tears. The father pointed to the sky, stroked his head, and seemed to explain something to him…. I remember a girl, slim with black hair, who passed close to me, pointed to herself, and said, "Twenty-three"… The people completely naked went down some steps which were cut in the clay wall of the pit and clambered over the heads of people lying there, to the place where the SS-men directed them. Then they lay down in front of the dead and injured people; some caressed those who were still alive and spoke to them in a low voice. Then I heard a series of shots….

The founders of the United Nations hoped to achieve a number of objectives in founding the new international organization. Chief among these was to prevent World War III, but they also hoped to eradicate **genocide**—the purposeful, systematic extermination of a religious, ethnic, or national group.

In retrospect, what could individuals, states, and the international community have done to stop the Holocaust? Could these same actions be implemented in the contemporary world to stop genocide? Why or why not?

THE GROWTH OF INTRASTATE AND ETHNIC VIOLENCE

Since the end of the Thirty Years' War in 1648, the international system has been based on the interaction of states. In previous chapters we have seen how the logic of world politics has been based on the foundation of this interaction. We have also seen that nonstate actors have become increasingly important in recent decades. Nowhere is this tragically clearer than in the area of conflict and war. Consider the following facts of contemporary international life:

- Since the end of World War II, there have been at least 90 conflicts that can be classified as "civil wars";[3]
- "The proportion of states in the world suffering from some form of civil conflict has remained fairly constant, at around 25 percent, in recent decades…."[4]

- A recent study lists 52 internal conflicts in the 1994–1998 period.[5]

- An interagency U.S. task force estimated that the number of people who are affected by internal conflicts is approximately 42 million, and in 1994 the cost of assisting the victims of internal wars was $7.2 billion;[6]

- The increasing incidence of civil war has affected the victims of war. The Carnegie Commission on Preventing Deadly Conflict has noted: "In some wars today, 90 percent of those killed in conflict are noncombatants, compared with less than 15 percent when the century began."[7]

- Since the fall of the Berlin Wall in November 1989, more than 4 million people have been killed in violent conflicts, and there are more than 35 million refugees and internally displaced persons around the world.[8]

Given these facts, it is not surprising that current UN Secretary General Kofi Annan has noted, "In the world today intrastate conflict is the face of conflict."[9] The crises over Bosnia and Kosovo have tragically confirmed the Secretary General's observation.

While the frequency and pervasiveness of **internal conflict** is not in doubt, the causes are. Clearly one of the most important developments that has contributed to the increasing outbreak of internal conflict is the decline of state sovereignty. In recent times, governments have lost control of weaponry, capital, and information, and power has migrated from the public to the private sector. In some states, such as Colombia, state sovereignty has been directly challenged by organized criminal organizations. Beyond the erosion of sovereignty, what are the causes of intrastate conflict?

In his ambitious study of *The International Dimensions of Internal Conflict*, political scientist Michael E. Brown argues that one must distinguish between underlying and proximate causes of intrastate conflict. The former include factors such as weak states, elite politics, widespread economic problems, and problematic group histories. Proximate causes include factors such as "internal, mass-level factors (bad domestic problems), mass-level problems (bad neighborhoods), external, elite-level factors (bad neighbors); or internal, elite-level factors (bad leaders)."[10]

Some journalists and popular writers ascribe the causes of intrastate and **ethnic conflict** to the "ancient hatreds" that various groups have for one another. For example, in his book *Balkan Ghosts,* which reportedly influenced President Clinton's views on Bosnia, writer Robert Kaplan portrayed the root cause of the conflict as the antipathy that the major ethnic groups in Bosnia had for each other.

Academic analysts, however, tend to discount this explanation of the cause of internal conflict for several reasons. First, academic analysts tend to dismiss any monocausal explanation, and even if "ancient hatreds" play a role in causing internal conflicts, they cannot "account for significant variation in the incidence and intensity of such conflict."[11] Second, even if ethnic hostility exists, it may not result in groups killing one another. For example, the three major ethnic groups existed peacefully for decades in Yugoslavia before they began killing one another, so something besides "ancient hatred" was clearly at work. According to political scientists David Lake and Donald Rothchild, "By itself, ethnicity is not a cause of violent conflict. Most ethnic groups, most of the time, pursue their interests peacefully through established political channels. But when linked with acute uncertainty and, indeed, fear of what the future might bring, ethnicity emerges as one of the major fault lines along which societies fracture."[12]

Ethnic "fault lines" are very much in evidence. Members of ethnic groups identify with one another because of their national origin, tribal affiliation, social organization, and/or common language, religion, or race. Demographers estimate that there are somewhere between 3,000 to 5,000 ethnic groups in the world today.[13] A recent study has identified 233 ethnic groups as targets of discrimination or organized for political assertiveness; this constitutes between 5 and 8 percent of the world's total number of ethnic groups.[14] Of the 194 states that exist today, fewer than twenty—about 10 percent of the world's total—are ethnically homogeneous "in the sense that ethnic minorities account for less than 5 percent of the population."[15] In some states since 1989, ethnic fault lines have resulted in the disintegration of states; to wit Czechoslovakia, Yugoslavia, the Soviet Union, and Ethiopia. In a number of other states, a significant potential for ethnic conflict exists, as Table 14.1 demonstrates.

Ethnic groups often have ties to states outside of the country in which they reside. In some cases the foreign state will provide economic, and

TABLE 14.1

Ethnic Groups Pressing for Independence

Ethnic Group	State
Kashmiris	India
Sikhs	India
Tamils	Sri Lanka
Uigur	China
Tibetans	China
Kurds	Iraq, Turkey, Syria, Iran
Shi'a	Saudi Arabia, Bahrain
Palestinians	Israel
Maronites	Lebanon
Chechans	Russia
Kosovars	Yugoslavia

sometimes even military, aid to ethnic groups in other countries. For example, during the Soviet occupation of Afghanistan, the government of Saudi Arabia provided substantial aid to the Muslim *mujahadin* ("soldiers of God") who were battling the Soviets. When ethnic groups receive aid from foreign governments, domestic disputes can turn into international conflict.

If "ancient hatreds" between or among ethnic groups do not fully explain the causes of internal conflict, what factors do? In an ambitious study of the causes and means to prevent deadly conflict, the Carnegie Corporation of New York identified nine causes of conflict.[16] First, irresponsible leaders such as Pol Pot in Cambodia, Idi Amin in Uganda, or Radovan Karadzic in Bosnia Herzegovina have caused unspeakable human suffering. Second, historical intergroup tensions as among the Serbs, Croats, and Muslims in the former Yugoslavia have contributed to the outbreak of conflict in the former Yugoslavia. Third, population growth, as we saw in Chapter 13 taxes the limits of some states and results in competition for scarce resources. Fourth, increasing crowding in cities, a function of both population growth and urbanization, contributes to the outbreak of conflict. Fifth, economic deterioration can worsen intergroup relations, as was the case in Rwanda. Sixth, environmental degradation can increase intergroup tensions. Seventh, repressive or discriminatory policies have worsened the relationships among various groups. Eighth, corrupt or incompetent governance may contribute to internal conflict. Last, technological development that increases the gap between rich and poor can also increase the gap between or among various domestic groups. Taken together, these factors constitute a "recipe for conflict."

PEACE OPERATIONS

Former New Zealand diplomat Denis McLean has noted, "If war, as Clausewitz famously declared, is a continuation of politics by other means, then **peace operations** represent a continuation of diplomacy by other means."[17] Peace operations include a number of different means designed to reduce conflict and human suffering and to reestablish stability in a conflict-prone situation. A number of prominent individuals and organizations have presented typologies and schemas for these operations. For example, in his 1992 report *Agenda for Peace,* former UN Secretary General Boutros Boutros-Ghali described four possible responses to ethnic, religious, social, cultural, or linguistic strife: (1) preventive diplomacy, (2) peacekeeping, (3) peacemaking, and (4) post-conflict peacebuilding.[18] To these functions can be added one more significant one: peace enforcement.

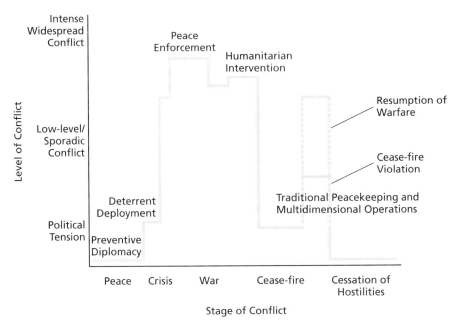

Figure 14.1. Peace Operations and Stages of Conflict
Source: The Henry L. Stimson Center; reprinted from William Durch, ed., *UN Peacekeeping, American Politics, and the Uncivil Wars of the 1990s.* New York: St. Martin's Press, 1996, p. 9. Used by permission.

Both Michael Lund and William Durch have developed typologies of the peace operations and the way in which the various components interact.[19] Figure 14.1 is the typology developed by Durch and shows the various types of peace operations according to the phase and intensity of conflict that forces face when they are deployed to an area of conflict. The horizontal axis shows the normal phases of a conflict from peace to crisis to war and ceasefire and cessation of hostilities. The vertical axis depicts intensity of conflict from political tensions to widespread conflict. Various aspects of peace operations can be identified using this typology.

Sometimes referred to as "an idea in search of a strategy,"[20] **preventive diplomacy** may be defined, following Lund, as "Action taken in vulnerable places and times to avoid the threat or use of armed force and related forms of coercion by states or groups to settle the political disputes that can arise from the destabilizing effects of economic, social, political, and international change."[21] Kofi Annan has underscored the importance of preventive diplomacy by noting that "Prevention is worth a pound of cure."[22] One of the unheralded successes of recent preventive deployment was the deployment of 2,000 UN peacekeepers from nine different countries to Macedonia (approximately 500 of whom were U.S. soldiers) to prevent an expansion of the conflict in the former Yugoslavia into Macedonia.

Peacekeeping refers to what once were called "interposition forces" by third parties, typically the United Nations or a regional international organization. These forces have been dispatched by the UN Security Council with the consent of opposing forces to "help implement peace agreements, monitor cease-fires, patrol de-militarized zones, create buffer zones between opposing forces, and put fighting on hold while negotiators seek peaceful solutions to disputes."[23] These missions are sometimes referred to as "Chapter VI actions" because that section of the UN Charter deals with the peaceful settlement of international conflicts. Since 1945 there have been 48 UN peacekeeping operations; 32 of these operations were established in the decade from 1988–1998. As of July 1998, there were 18 active UN peacekeeping operations, as shown in Table 14.2.

The cost of UN peacekeeping increased significantly during the decade of the 1990s due to the increased number of operations. By 1995, the cost of UN peacekeeping personnel and equipment was $3 billion, more than twice the cost of running regular UN operations. This cost was due primarily to the expense of peacekeeping operations in the former Yugoslavia. These costs fell to $1.4 billion in 1996 and $1.3 billion in 1997. The total estimated peacekeeping costs for the UN in 1998 were under $1 billion. Although all UN member states are obligated under the UN Charter to pay their share of peacekeeping costs, member states owed the UN $1.7 billion in current and back peacekeeping dues at the end of 1998. Of this amount, the United States owed the UN almost $1 billion.

Peacemaking seeks to go beyond peacekeeping's objective of simply keeping opposing sides separated by seeking a brokered solution to conflict. Peacemaking may involve conciliation, mediation, the offering of "good offices," and possibly even the deployment of military forces to establish law and order. In recent years, the UN Secretary General has sent

TABLE 14.2	
UN Peacekeeping Operations as of July 1998	
Africa	Angola, Central African Republic, Sierra Leone, Western Sahara
Americas	Haiti
Asia	India/Pakistan, Tajikistan
Europe	Bosnia and Herzegovina, Croatia, Cyprus, Macedonia, Georgia
Middle East	Golan Heights, Iraq/Kuwait, Lebanon, Middle East Truce Supervision Organization

personal envoys to a number of conflict-prone areas to try to negotiate a peaceful resolution of the problems.

Peace enforcement is a more recent notion that the international community should act through the United Nations and other international organizations to end intrastate and ethnic conflicts, even when the opposing parties do not request assistance. These actions are sometimes referred to as "Chapter VII operations" because that section of the UN Charter refers to actions authorized by the Security Council including blockades, enforcement of sanctions, forceful disarmament, and direct military action. Peace enforcement has been used in relatively few, recent cases, including the Gulf War, Somalia, Rwanda, Haiti, Bosnia and Herzegovina, and Albania. None of these enforcement operations was under UN control; rather, they were directed by a single state or a regional international organization. For example, in Bosnia-Herzogovina, a NATO multinational military force succeeded the UN peacekeeping operation, and in the Kosovo case a NATO military force attacked Serbia in order to halt the "ethnic cleansing" of Kosovo.

CASE STUDIES IN PEACEMAKING: SOMALIA, RWANDA, BOSNIA, AND KOSOVO

Given the increasing frequency of intrastate and ethnic conflict, it is likely that the demand for peacekeeping, peacemaking and peace enforcement will continue into the foreseeable future. A current map of the world with conflicts that resulted in more than 1,000 deaths in any one year shows that conflict was common in the 1990s.

The effects of some of the conflicts depicted in map 14.1 have been ameliorated by the intervention of outside nongovernmental organizations, international organizations, and states. What can we learn from recent peace operations? We will focus here on peace operations in Somalia, Rwanda, Bosnia, and Kosovo.

Somalia

Somalia is a country in the eastern horn of Africa that has had a troubled history since its founding in 1960. In 1969–1970, a Marxist government headed by General Mohammed Siyad Barre took over and opened Somali ports to the Soviet Union. In 1974 a pro-Soviet faction took over in Ethiopia and the USSR shifted its support in the region to this new government. Somalia, in turn, provided support for insurgent forces fighting for independence of the Ogaden region of Ethiopia. The situation worsened, and in 1977 Ethiopia and Somalia went to war. Assisted by Cuban troops,

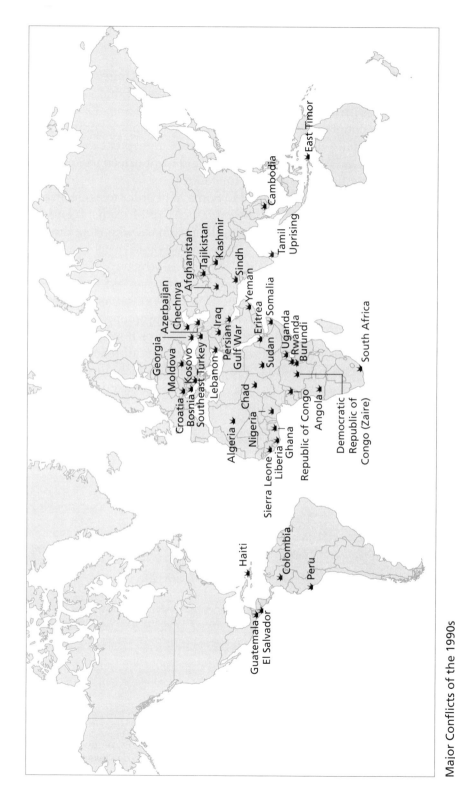

Major Conflicts of the 1990s

Note: Conflicts on this map had at least 1,000 deaths in any one year in the 1990s. There is no authoritative count of the dead in the recent campaign by Laurent Kabila in the Democratic Republic of Congo (Zaire). UN authorities suspect that more than 200,000 Rwandan refugees missing in Central Africa died in the campaign.

Sources: Stockholm International Peace Research Institute, *SIPRI Yearbook: Armaments, Disarmament and International Security,* 1991 to 1997 editions (New York: Oxford University Press: 1991–1997); Ruth Leger Sivard, *World Military and Social Expenditures 1996* (Washington, DC; World Priorities, 1996); "Were 200,000 Slaughtered?" *Foreign Report,* No. 2459, August 7, 1997; Amy Shiratori, "Ogata Urges Japan To Accept Refugees, Spare ODA Budget", Asahi News Service, July 23, 1997. Printed in *Final Report* (Washington, DC: Carnegie Commission on Preventing Deadly Conflict, 1997), p. 12.

Ethiopia defeated Somalia, and Somalia turned to the United States for aid. Throughout the 1980s, intermittent conflict between Ethiopia and Somalia continued with disastrous results for the people of Somalia. Disease and famine were common, and many Somalis left their home country. Exhausted by more than a decade of fighting, a peace agreement was signed in 1988. In 1991, Siyad Barre left the country, and the fourteen major clans of Somalia began to fight one another for control.

In March 1991, the UN intervened in Somalia in order to assist an estimated 200 thousand refugees in the capital city of Mogadishu and to bring good supplies to the more than 4 million Somalis who were threatened with famine. In April 1992, the UN Security Council established the United Nations Operation in Somalia (UNOSOM), which consisted of 50 observers whose mission was to provide humanitarian aid and to promote the end of conflict in Somalia. The UNOSOM observers were not able to achieve their mission due to continued fighting among the fourteen principal Somali clans. UN Secretary General Boutros Boutros-Ghali requested that the United States assist with the delivery of relief supplies. President Bush ordered Operation "Provide Relief" which during a five-month period (August–December 1992) airlifted 28 thousand metric tons of critically needed relief supplies into Somalia.[24]

Emulating armed men, Mogadishu Children Play with Toy Guns
Source: Robert Caputo/Aurora; reprinted in Carnegie Commission on Preventing Deadly Conflict, *Final Report* (Washington, DC: Carnegie Commission on Preventing Deadly Conflict, 1997), p. 160.

The security situation worsened, and in November 1992 a ship fully laden with relief supplies was fired upon and therefore unable to deliver its much needed cargo. Photos of emaciated children accompanied the story about the ship, and public pressure "to do something" mounted. In response, the UN established a multinational coalition, the "United Task Force" (UNITAF), which was to be led by the United States. President George Bush ordered the initiation of Operation "Restore Hope" with the dual mission of providing humanitarian relief and restoring order to Somalia. Significantly, this was the first time in its 47-year history that the UN dispatched troops with rules of engagement that authorized its troops to shoot anyone interfering with the relief effort. Eventually, UNITAF involved more than 38 thousand troops from 21 different countries; of these 28 thousand were Americans.

UNITAF was relatively successful in stabilizing the political situation and distributing food to those who most needed it. Plans called for the termination of UNITAF and the establishment of a permanent peacekeeping force. In March 1993, the UN Security Council established UNOSOM II. Significantly, this was the first-ever UN peacekeeping operation mandated under the Chapter VII peace-enforcement provisions of the UN Charter. The missions of UNOSOM II went well beyond those of UNITAF and called for UN forces to engage in "nation building." The local Somali warlords viewed the new UN mandate as threatening to their power, and on June 5, 1993, Mohammed Aideed's forces attacked and killed 24 Pakistani peacekeepers. The next day, the UN passed a resolution calling for the apprehension of those responsible for the killings. Several elite U.S. Army units—Rangers and the Delta Force—were flown to Mogadishu to apprehend General Aideed. On October 3, the U.S. units received a report that Aideed had been sighted. They attempted to arrest Aideed and were ambushed. Eighteen American soldiers were killed, and 75 were wounded in the bloodiest battle of any UN peacekeeping operation since the 1960 Congo crisis. Pictures of the mutilated bodies of American soldiers were broadcast around the world, and the U.S. public demanded the withdrawal of American forces, which President Clinton ordered.

Somalia is often cited as the first post-cold war peacekeeping failure, but such a criticism is not accurate. First, the attack on U.S. forces came during UNOSOM II, which was essentially a *peace-enforcement* operation and not a peacekeeping operation. Thus, if anything, Somalia was a case of failure to achieve nation building rather than peacekeeping. Second, analysts have estimated that UN and U.S. actions in Somalia from 1992–1995 saved an estimated 250 thousand to 500 thousand lives. It is difficult to consider this a failure. But Somalia affected the way that Americans and the UN viewed peacekeeping operations, as was evident in the Bosnia, Rwanda, and Kosovo cases.

Rwanda

Rwanda is one of the poorest countries in the world. In 1993, annual per capita gross domestic product (GDP) equaled $290. Fifty percent of Rwanda's total GDP was derived from the agricultural sector, and coffee and tea historically made up 80 to 90 percent of total exports.[28] In 1987, the International Coffee Agreement collapsed causing the price of coffee to decline to 50 percent of its 1980 value. This precipitous drop in price had a disastrous effect on the Rwandan economy and served as the backdrop for subsequent events.

For the past four centuries, two tribes—the Tutsi and the Hutu—jointly inhabited the area now known as Rwanda. The Tutsi, primarily cattle herders, were wealthier than the more numerous, poorer Hutu farmers. The area was controlled for a time by Germany and then by Belgium from 1916 to 1962. In 1962, Rwanda and Burundi became separate states when they gained their independence from Belgium. Rwanda was initially governed by President Gregoire Kayibanda, a Hutu, who ruled autocratically until 1973 when Major General Juvenal Habyarimana, a Hutu, staged a coup and took over the government.

Relations between the Tutsi and Hutu periodically flared into open conflict, most notably in 1963, 1966, 1973, and 1990–1993. With each episode of violence, more Tutsi fled Rwanda for surrounding states. By 1992, approximately 8 percent of the Rwanda population of Tutsi was living in exile. Some of these exiles formed armed groups that staged sporadic military raids into Rwanda. In February 1993, the Tutsi militia in exile launched a military offensive that resulted in the displacement of 650 thousand Rwandans. Negotiations were conducted and eventually resulted in a comprehensive peace accord, signed in Arusha, Tanzania, in August 1993. The **Arusha Accords** called for the creation of a coalition government that would incorporate Tutsis in the government and the army and allow for the reintegration of Tutsi refugees into Rwanda. Implementation of the Accords was slow and problematic, and the UN secretary general expressed his concern over the "increasingly violent demonstrations, roadblocks, assassination of political leaders and assaults on and murders of civilians, developments that severely overstretch the resources and capabilities of the national gendarmerie."[29]

Six days after the secretary general issued his report, on April 6, 1994, President Habyarimana of Rwanda and the president of neighboring Burundi were killed when their plane was hit by two missiles as it approached the airfield at Kigali, the capital of Rwanda. The missiles had been fired from a military base controlled by the Rwandan Presidential Guard, elements of which opposed Habyarimana's negotiation with Tutsis. The assassination unleashed acts of genocide not seen since the days of Nazi Germany. In the ensuing three months an estimated 500 thousand to 1 million people were killed and almost 5 million people were forced to flee for their lives.[30] The Carnegie Commission on Preventing Deadly Conflict noted, "this has been one of the most horrifying chapters in human history."[31]

What could have been done to stop this carnage? Following the conclusion of the Arusha Accords, the UN established a peacekeeping force to support implementation of the agreements. This force eventually reached a strength of 2,500 troops and was commanded by Canadian Lieutenant General Romeo Dallaire. The force was stretched to the limit by the daily logistical demands of sustaining the force and by a series of emergencies, such as a coup in Burundi and the resulting refugee crisis.[32] General Dallaire sought authority for an augmented force operating under Chapter VII ("peace enforcement") of the UN Charter rather than Chapter VI ("peacekeeping") in order to: (1) stop the genocide, (2) conduct a peace-enforcement mission, (3) assist in the return of refugees, (4) deliver humanitarian aid, and (4) assist in the cessation of hostilities.

General Dallaire estimated that with 5,000 troops and a mandate under Chapter VII, he could have prevented most of the killing. Why then were his requests not approved? General Dalliare's requests came in the aftermath of the disastrous Somalia intervention, and both the UN and the U.S. government were hesitant to involve themselves in another possible disaster. In addition, the UN, NATO and the U.S. government were trying to figure out what to do about the situation in the former Yugoslavia. As a result, there was little support to send more troops to Rwanda.[33] Therefore, Rwanda became, according to former Assistant Secretary of State for African Affairs Chester Crocker, "the first victim of the post-Somali backlash."[34]

The four cases reviewed in this chapter—Somalia, Rwanda, Bosnia, and Kosovo—are both disturbing and important;

Refugees from Rwanda Stand in Line for Water

disturbing because of the number of people, particularly civilians, who were killed and important because they are likely to be characteristic conflicts in the post-cold war world. How can the international community better deal with such conflicts?

Bosnia

Bosnia-Herzegovina is an area in the Balkans that was part of the former Yugoslavia. For centuries, the Balkan region was the battleground of empire, and at the Battle of the Field of Blackbirds in Kosovo in 1389, the Ottoman Empire defeated the Serbs, and the region fell under control of the Muslim Ottomans. During the eighteenth and nineteenth centuries the Russian and Austro-Hungarian empires made inroads into the Balkans and increased their influence in the region. By 1806 Serbia had established an independent kingdom, and the Treaty of Berlin in 1878 gave control of Bosnia-Herzogovina to the Austro-Hungarian Empire; however, Serbians, based on ethnic and historical reasons, considered Bosnia-Herzegovina to be theirs. So did the Croatians, the second largest ethnic group in the region. In addition to conflicting claims concerning Bosnia, religion also divided the Serbs and Croatians; the Serbs were Orthodox and the Croatians were Catholic. Complicating the problem was the existence of a third large third ethnic group, the Muslims.

In 1908 Austria-Hungary annexed Bosnia, which catalyzed the Balkan Wars of 1912–1913. The assassination of the heir apparent of the Habsburg Empire, Archduke Franz Ferdinand and his wife, by a Serbian nationalist during their visit to Sarajevo, the capital of Bosnia, in June 1914, lit the fuse that ignited World War I. The result of four years of war was 16 million dead.

At the end of World War I, the "Kingdom of Serbs, Croats and Slovenes" was established and was characterized by competition and hostility among the various ethnic groups of the region. Throughout the interwar period, the dominant ethnic groups engaged in terrorist activities against one another. These activities were reinforced, rather than interrupted by the Axis invasion of Yugoslavia in 1941. The Croats and the Croatian terrorist organization, the Ustasha, allied themselves with the Nazis and killed an estimated 500 thousand to 700 thousand Serbs. In turn, the Serbian terrorist organization, the Cetniks, sought to kill as many Nazis and Croats as possible. The Yugoslav partisans were led by Josep Broz Tito, a Croatian communist, who sought to create an effective resistance to the occupying Nazis. At the end of the war, Tito and his partisans proclaimed the establishment of the Federal People's Republic of Yugoslavia and sought to dampen the nationalistic feelings of the major ethnic groups. But these feelings were deepseated and long lasting.

Tito ruled Yugoslavia for 35 years. He was able to maintain the unity of the state by employing a combination of effective leadership and brute force. When Tito died in 1980, many predicted the death of Yugoslavia, a prediction that took a little more than a decade to fulfill. Ethnic Muslims constituted 90 percent of the population of a southern "autonomous region" of Serbia—**Kosovo**—and were in effective control of the province. In April 1987, the Yugoslavian president, Ivan Stambolic, sent his subordinate, **Slobodan Milosevic**, to Kosovo to quell ethnic disturbances between the Albanian Kosovars and the Serbs living in Kosovo. After meeting with representatives of the conflicting parties, Milosevic, a Serb, concluded, "The situation in Kosovo was intolerable … They [Albanian Kosovars] murdered Serbs; they defiled our [Serbian] graves … They will not be allowed to beat you again."[25]

Following his visit to Kosovo, Milosevic embarked on a campaign to depose President Stambolic and an effort to create a "Greater Serbia." After taking control of the Yugoslavian government, in March 1989 Milosevic introduced a new constitution that effectively ended Kosovo's autonomy. Milosevic then extended his campaign for a "Greater Serbia" to Bosnia where he formed an alliance with the Bosnian Serb leaders, **Radovan Karadzic,** and his military chief of staff, General Ratco Mladic.

Yugoslavia's first multiparty election in 1989 led to the victory of nationalists in every republic, and in June 1991, Croatia and Slovenia (Yugoslavia's richest and most western republics) declared their independence. The United Nations imposed an arms embargo on the former Yugoslavian republics. In retrospect, this gave a major advantage to Serbia which controlled the former Yugoslav Army; the militaries of Croatia and Bosnia were at a significant disadvantage. In December 1991, Germany extended formal diplomatic recognition to Croatia and Slovenia.

The first UN peacekeepers were sent to the former Yugoslavia in March 1992. By then conflict had spread throughout the country, and a new, horrific phrase was introduced into the lexicon of politics: **"ethnic cleansing."** This referred to the tactics designed to "expel or frighten people from one ethnic group into abandoning territory coveted by another. It can include the use of terror tactics, mass rape and summary execution."[26] The number of UN troops in the former Yugoslavia was not sufficient to prevent the mass killing of innocent, noncombatants. What had been inconceivable—a repetition of the horrors of the Holocaust—had happened again. When UN forces proved to be incapable of stopping the killing, NATO imposed "no fly zones" and attacked Serb positions on several occasions. But these actions, too, proved ineffective in stopping the killing.

Map of the Former Yugoslavia

On the afternoon of July 10, 1995, Bosnian Serb soldiers attacked Srebrenica, a city that the UN had declared a sanctuary for some 40 thousand
people who sought refuge from the war. The UN peacekeepers in the city
were hopelessly outnumbered and had to watch as some 6,000 people
were rounded up and killed. One account of the carnage reported:

UN Peacekeepers on Patrol in Bosnia
Source: Chris Morris/Black Starr; reprinted in Carnegie Commission on Preventing
Deadly Conflict, *Final Report* (Washington, DC: Carnegie Commission on Preventing
Deadly Conflict, 1997), p. 51.

The Muslim men were herded by the thousands into trucks, delivered to killing sites near the Drina River, lined up four by four, and shot. One survivor, 17-year-old Nezad Avdic, recalled … as he lay wounded among the dead Muslims, a Serbian soldier surveyed the stony, moonlit field piled with bodies and merrily declared: 'That was a good hunt. There were a lot of rabbits here.'[27]

Following the attack on Srebrenica, Serb forces threatened other safe areas. In addition, the Serbs shelled the main marketplace in Sarajevo killing more than 50 innocent civilians. In August three American diplomats died tragically when their armored personnel carrier went off the treacherous road into Sarajevo. These events catalyzed the American and European response: NATO bombed Bosnian Serb military positions and deployed 60 thousand soldiers to Bosnia to implement a new peace agreement negotiated in Dayton, Ohio, by Serbian President Milosevic, Croatian President Franjo Tudjman, and Bosnia Muslim leader Alia Izetbegovic. The provisions of the agreement were implemented in November 1995.

During the four years of the war in Bosnia an estimated 200 thousand people were killed and 2 to 3 million were displaced from their homes. Since the signing of the **Dayton Accord,** there have been no significant instances of genocide in Bosnia.

Kosovo

Kosovo was established as an autonomous province in 1974 by the late ruler of Yugoslavia, Tito, who wanted to decrease the power of Serbia. Kosovo is about the size of the state of Connecticut and at the beginning of 1999 had approximately 2 million residents, 90 percent of whom were Albanian Kosovars and 10 percent were Serbs.

For their part, Serbs have long considered Kosovo to be sacred territory because of an important battle fought (and lost) against Ottoman Turkish forces in 1389. In addition, there are some monasteries in Kosovo that the Serbs, who are Orthodox Christians, highly value.

As noted earlier in this chapter, Slobodan Milosevic came to Kosovo in April 1987 and began his campaign for a "Greater Serbia" here. In 1989, he revoked Kosovo's autonomous status and imposed repressive Serbian rule. This situation was similar to the system of apartheid that existed in South Africa, except in the case of Kosovo, an ethnic-religious minority controlled the other 90 percent of the population.

Bordering on Kosovo is the poorest country of Europe, Albania, whose population is ethnically very similar to Kosovo's. The Albanian economy collapsed in 1990–1991. It rebounded modestly in 1993–1995 and then collapsed again in 1997 due to financial pyramid schemes that had swept the country. The resulting social unrest led to more than 1,500 deaths, widespread destruction of property, and the looting of Albanian army and police weapons storage depots. Military weapons, including powerful combat assault rifles such as the Kalashnikov (AK) 47, were easily available.

Many of these weapons made their way across the Albanian-Kosovar border into the hands of Kosovars who wanted independence from Serbia. For the first time, members of the Kosovo Liberation Army (KLA) had the means to challenge their Serbian oppressors, and they increasingly and more blatantly attacked the Yugoslavian Army and Kosovo police, both staffed almost exclusively by Serbs.

Faced with an increasingly militant and effective resistance and having staked out Kosovo as sacred territory to the Serbs, Milosevic ordered his forces to crack down on the KLA and restive Kosovars at the start of 1998. Milosevic ordered the army into Kosovo during the summer of 1998 and by September, these forces had destroyed an estimated 500 villages and rendered 270 thousand Albanian Kosovars homeless.

Members of the North Atlantic Treaty Organization (NATO) observed Serbia's actions with concern and increasing alarm. In Bosnia, 200,000 people had died and 2 to 3 million had been made homeless, and most informed observers believed that the Serbs were the principal cause of these losses. Leaders of both NATO and the United Nations were concerned that the Serbs might very well attempt to "ethnically cleanse" Kosovo as they had attempted to do in Bosnia.

In June, NATO threatened airstrikes and then did not follow through. In September the United Nations passed a resolution calling for a cease-fire and the re-settlement of the estimated 270,000 refugees. At the end of September, a group of eighteen ethnic Albanian children, women, and elderly people were found massacred; the specter of a repetition of the horrors of Bosnia was very real.

In October, U.S. diplomat, Richard Holbrooke, who had earlier brokered the Dayton Accord concerning Bosnia, arrived in the area to meet with Serbian and Kosovar leaders. As a result of these meetings, Milosevic agreed to a ceasefire, withdrawal of Serbian forces from Kosovo, and the deployment of 2,000 unarmed observers from the Organization for Security and Cooperation in Europe.

A new round of talks was convened in February 1999 at Rambouillet, France, and the Kosovar representative to these talks agreed to accept the terms of the plan which called for: (1) increased autonomy for Kosovo which would remain a part of Serbia, and (2) the deployment of 28,000

**BOX 14.1   The More Things Change,
the More They Stay the Same**

In 1914, the Carnegie Endowment for International Peace released a report on the first Balkan wars of 1912 and 1913. The report prophetically noted: "Reference has already been made to the reflex psychological effect of these crimes against humanity. The matter becomes serious when we think of it as something which the nations have absorbed into their very life—a sort of virus which, through the ordinary channels of circulation, has infected the entire body politic. Here we focus the whole matter—the fearful economic waste, the untimely death of no small part of the population, a volume of terror and pain which can be only partially, at least, conceived and estimated, and the collective national consciousness of greater crimes than history has recorded. This is a fearful legacy to be left to future generations."

Source: Carnegie Endowment for International Peace, *The Other Balkan Wars* (Washington, DC: Carnegie Endowment for International Peace, 1993), p. 269.

Children Play in Front of a Large Target Sign and the U.S. Cultural Center in Belgrade during the NATO Bombing.
Source: Agence France-Presse, printed in *The New York Times,* March 29, 1999, p. A 16.

NATO troops to Kosovo to police the agreement. Milosevic refused to sign the agreement and NATO delivered an ultimatum: sign the Rambouillet agreement or face airstrikes. When Milosevic continued to refuse to sign, NATO began bombing targets in Serbia, Kosovo, and Montenegro on March 24, 1999. The NATO attacks against Serbia were the largest use of military force by the allies since the end of World War II.

As the nineteen members of NATO attacked, Serbian forces increased their attacks on the Albanian Kosovars, who fled the Serbian onslaught in desperation. Within two weeks of the beginning of the bombing campaign, an estimated 800,000 Kosovars had fled the country. The allied bombing, as did the use of bombing during World War II, seemed to stiffen Serbian resistance initially, but Milosevic agreed to peace terms in June 1999 after 78 days of bombing.

PREVENTING DEADLY CONFLICT IN THE WORLD

UN Secretary General Kofi Annan, who previously served as Under-Secretary of the Department of Peacekeeping Operations, has argued that conflict prevention and disease prevention can be thought of in similar terms. A number of other leaders, academics and researchers agree.[35] The members of the Carnegie Commission on Preventing Deadly Conflict noted: "Just as in the practice of good medicine, preventing the outbreak, spread, and recurrence of the disease of deadly conflict requires timely interventions with the right mix of political, economic, military, and social instruments." [36]

In 1994, the Carnegie Corporation of New York funded a major review of the causes and potential prevention of deadly conflict in the world. This project was overseen by a commission of 16 eminent leaders and scholars with long practical and academic experience in dealing with conflict resolution and prevention. In addition, the commission was assisted by an international advisory council of more than 40 distinguished practitioners and scholars. Finally, the commission sponsored research that it felt was needed in understudied areas of conflict prevention. The annual reports, *Final Report* and specialized studies of the commission are all available to the public at the Commission's web site: http://www.ccpdc.org. Given the importance of the Commission's study and findings, this section will summarize those findings.

Three fundamental conclusions constituted the foundation of the Commission's findings. First, "mass violence is not inevitable"; violence does not emerge inexorably and inevitably from "ancient hatreds" or human interaction. Intra- and interstate conflict result from deliberate, political decisions, and these decisions can be affected. Second, "the need to prevent deadly conflict is increasingly urgent." The growth in population, increasing economic interdependence and advance of technology combined with modern communications and weapons technology are an often deadly mix of factors that underscore the need to prevent conflicts from turning massively violent. Third, successful preventive action is possible. "The problem is not that we do not know about incipient and large-scale violence; it is that we often do not act." What is needed is the early, skillful, and integrated application of political, diplomatic, economic, and military measures.

Similar to Michael Brown's characterization of the "underlying" and "proximate" causes of ethnic conflict, the Carnegie Commission has described the strategies for preventing violence as falling into two categories: "operational prevention" and "structural prevention." The former include those measures which are applicable in the face of an immediate crisis, and the latter include those measures "to assure that a crisis will not occur in the first place." [37]

There are four key elements that contribute to operational prevention success. First, there should be a lead actor—an international or regional organization, a country, or even a prominent individual—around which preventive efforts can be organized. Second, there should be a coherent political-military-economic approach designed to stop the violence, provide needed humanitarian, assistance, and integrate all relevant aspects of the solution to the problem at hand. Third, adequate resources are need-ed to support effective preventive engagement. Fourth, and particularly relevant to intrastate conflict, a plan to restore the host state's authority and responsibility is needed.

Structural prevention, also called peace building—requires the devel-opment by states of international regimes, which are implicit or explicit agreements, procedures and or organizations to manage the interaction of states in various issue areas. In addition, states must work for the se-curity, economic well-being, and justice of their citizens. Fairness is a char-acteristic of stable political systems, and the achievement of fairness should be the goal of governments, regardless of their form.

Some Specific Recommendations of the Carnegie Commission on Preventing Deadly Conflict

Preventive Diplomacy:

- States should maintain communication with leaders and groups in crisis.

Economic Measures:

- When necessary, sanctions should be imposed swiftly, comprehen-sively, supported where necessary with forceful measures.
- Governments should explore ways to use targeted measures such as financial sanctions.

The Use of Force:

- Greater accountability and improved safeguards for the control of nu-clear weapons are urgent.
- The development, production, and sale of land mines should be banned immediately.
- Governments should seek a more effective prohibition against the de-velopment and use of chemical weapons.
- The UN needs a rapid-reaction capability to separate adversarial armed groups before mass violence erupts.

Civil Society:

- Nongovernmental organizations should share information, reduce unnecessary redundancies, and promote shared norms of engage-ment in crises.
- Religious leaders should take a more active and constructive role in preventing mass violence.
- The media should develop standards in crisis coverage to assure that adequate attention is given to efforts to diffuse and resolve conflicts.

CONCLUSION

Many people (including the author of this book) assumed that the tragic episode recounted in the introductory critical thinking exercise at the beginning of this chapter was something that was consigned to the archives; that the genocide perpetrated by the Nazis would not be repeated. After all, the Allied states had expended millions of lives and material resources to defeat the Nazi obscenity. Sadly, this proved to be a mistaken view, for genocide has reappeared in a number of cases: in Pol Pot's Cambodia, Idi Amin's Uganda, and more recently in Rwanda, Bosnia, and Kosovo.

Since the end of World War II, there have been a number of successes as well as failures in international peace operations. Despite the presence of peacekeeping forces, conflict in some areas has broken out. In other cases, peacekeeping forces are able to establish the stability necessary for peace. In other cases of successful conflict termination such as Cyprus and Bosnia following the Dayton agreement, it seems that peacekeeping forces are necessary for an indefinite time to deter a resumption of conflict.

With the demise of the cold war, intrastate conflicts have become more common. There is much that individuals, states and the international community can do to stem intra- and interstate violence and conflict. *If only they will.*

DISCUSSION QUESTIONS

1. To what extent is ethnic conflict becoming more common in the world?
2. What lessons do the four cases examined in this chapter—Somalia, Rwanda, Bosnia and Kosovo—provide for the future for peace operations?
3. What are the major stumbling blocks standing in the way of preventing deadly conflict in the future? How can they be overcome?

KEY TERMS

Arusha Accords	Kosovo
Dayton Accords	Milosevic, Slobodan
ethnic cleansing	peace enforcement
ethnic conflict	peacekeeping
genocide	peacemaking
internal conflict	peace operations
Karadzic, Radovan	preventive diplomacy

RECOMMENDED PRINT, MULTIMEDIA, AND INTERNET SOURCES

Print

ALLARD, KENNETH. *Somalia Operations: Lessons Learned.* Washington, DC: National Defense University Press, 1995.

BERDAL, MATS R. *Whither UN Peacekeeping?* Adelphi Paper 281. London: International Institute for Strategic Studies, October 1993.

———. *Disarmament and Demobilisation after Civil Wars.* Adelphi Paper 303. London: International Institute for Strategic Studies, August 1996.

BOUTROS-GHALI, BOUTROS. *Agenda for Peace: Preventive Diplomacy, Peacemaking, and Peace-Keeping.* New York: United Nations, June 1996.

BROWN, MICHAEL E., ed. *Ethnic Conflict and International Security.* Princeton, NJ: Princeton University Press, 1993.

———. *The International Dimensions of Internal Conflict.* Cambridge, MA: MIT Press, 1996.

Carnegie Commission on Preventing Deadly Conflict. *Preventing Deadly Conflict: Final Report.* Washington, DC: Carnegie Commission on Preventing Deadly Conflict, 1997.

Carnegie Endowment for International Peace. *The Other Balkan Wars.* Washington, DC: Carnegie Endowment for International Peace, 1993.

CROCKER, CHESTER A. "The Lessons of Somalia." *Foreign Affairs,* vol. 74, no. 3 (May/June 1995): 2–8.

DANIEL, DONALD C. F. and BRADD C. HAYES, eds. *Beyond Traditional Peacekeeping.* New York: St. Martin's Press, 1995.

DIEHL, PAUL F. *International Peacekeeping.* Baltimore: Johns Hopkins University Press, 1993.

DURCH, WILLIAM J., ed. *UN Peacekeeping, American Politics, and the Uncivil Wars of the 1990s.* New York: St. Martin's Press, 1996.

FEIL, SCOTT R. *Preventing Genocide: How the Early Use of Force Might Have Succeeded in Rwanda.* Washington, DC: Carnegie Commission on Preventing Deadly Conflict, April 1998.

GURR, TED ROBERT and BARBARA HARFF. *Ethnic Conflict in World Politics.* Boulder, CO: Westview Press, 1994.

KEEN, DAVID. *The Economic Functions of Violence in Civil Wars.* Adelphi Paper 320. London: International Institute for Strategic Studies, June 1998.

LAURANCE, EDWARD J. *Light Weapons and Intrastate Conflict: Early Warning Factors and Preventive Action.* Washington, DC: Carnegie Commission on Preventing Deadly Conflict, July 1998.

LUND, MICHAEL S. *Preventing Violent Conflicts: A Strategy for Preventive Diplomacy.* Washington, DC: United States Institute of Peace Press, 1996.

———. "Underrating 'Preventive Diplomacy.'" *Foreign Affairs,* vol. 74, no. 4 (July/August 1995): 160–163.

RENNER, MICHAEL. *Small Arms, Big Impact: The Next Challenge of Disarmament.* Worldwatch Paper 137. Washington, DC: Worldwatch Institute, October 1997.

STEDMAN, STEPHEN JOHN. "Alchemy for a New World Order." *Foreign Affairs,* vol. 74, no. 3 (May/June 1995): 14–20.

United Nations. Department of Peacekeeping Operations. *The Comprehensive Report on Lessons Learned from United Nations Assistance Mission to Rwanda (UNAMIR), October 1993–April 1996.* http://www.un.org/Depts/dpko.

———. *The Comprehensive Report on Lessons Learned from United Nations Operations in Somalia (UNOSOM), April 1992–March 1995.* http://www.un.org/Depts/dpko.

WILLIAMS, MICHAEL C. *Civil-Military Relations and Peacekeeping.* Adelphi Paper 321. London: International Institute for Strategic Studies, August 1998.

Video

Ambush in Mogadishu. Frontline. PBS. Originally broadcast September 29, 1998.

Milosevic. Sixty Minutes II. CBS News. Originally Broadcast April 7, 1999.

No Place to Hide: UN Peacekeeping. A 55-minute video narrated by former long-time UN official Sir Brian Urquhart focusing on the peacekeeping operations of the United Nations.

Yugoslavia: Death of a Nation, 3 vols. Produced by the BBC; distributed by the Discovery Channel, 1996. Traces the disintegration of Yugoslavia and contains video footage of the beginning of the conflict in Kosovo in April 1987 and interviews with all of the principal leaders.

Internet

African Centre for the Constructive Resolution of Disputes:
 http://www.udw.ac.za/UDW/mission/outlook/sstap.html

Carnegie Commission for Preventing Deadly Conflict: http://www.ccpdc.org

Conflict Prevention Resources, Winston Foundation: www.crosslink.net/~wfwp

Institute for Conflict Analysis and Resolution:
 http://www-gmu.edu/departments/ICAR/

Institute on Global Conflict and Cooperation:
 http://www.igcc.ucsd.edu/igcc/igccmenu.html

International Peace Academy: http://www.ipacademy.inter.net/

UN Department of Peacekeeping Operations: www.un.org/Depts/dpko

U.S. Department of State: http://www.state.gov/   Provides information on the department of the U.S. government principally responsible for foreign policy.

U.S. Institute of Peace: http://www.usip.org/

ENDNOTES

[1] MICHAEL HOWARD, *The Lessons of History* (New Haven, CT: Yale University Press, 1991), p. 4.

[2] RAUL HILBERG, *The Destruction of the European Jews* (Chicago: Quadrangle Books, 1961).

[3] CHARLES KING, *Ending Civil Wars,* Adelphi Paper 308 (London: International Institute for Strategic Studies, March 1997), p. 15.

[4] JOHN CHIPMAN, "The Changing Shape of International Relations and Wars of the Future," Pages delivered to the IISS 40th Annual Conference, 1998, p. 7.

[5] DAVID KEEN, "Appendix,"*The Economic Functions of Violence in Civil Wars*, Adelphi Paper 320 (London: International Institute for Strategic Studies, June 1998), pp. 75–79.

[6] JOHN M. GOSHKO, "Regional Conflicts Threaten 42 Million Around World, U.S. Study Finds," *Washington Post* (April 5, 1996), pp. 13–14.

[7] Carnegie Commission on Preventing Deadly Conflict, *Preventing Deadly Conflict: Final Report* (Washington, DC: Carnegie Commission on Preventing Deadly Conflict, December 1997), p. 11.

[8] Ibid., p. 3.

[9] "Remarks by the Honorable Kofi Annan," Conference on Preventing Deadly Conflict Among Nations in the 21st Century, UCLA, April 22, 1998.

[10] MICHAEL E. BROWN, ed., *The International Dimensions of Internal Conflict* (Cambridge, MA: MIT Press, 1996), p. 575.

[11] Ibid., p. 573.

[12] DAVID A. LAKE and DONALD ROTHCHILD, *Ethnic Fears and Global Engagement: The International Spread and Management of Ethnic Conflict,* Policy Paper 20 (San Diego: Institute on Global Conflict and Cooperation, University of California, January 1996), p. 8.

[13] SEYOM BROWN, *New Forces, Old Forces and the Future of World Politics, Post-Cold War Edition* (New York: HarperCollins, 1995), p. 162.

[14] TED ROBERT GURR, *Minorities at Risk: A Global View of Ethnopolitical Conflict* (Washington, DC: U.S. Institute of Peace Press, 1993).

[15] DAVID WELSH, "Domestic Politics and Ethnic Conflict," *Survival,* vol. 35, no. 1 (Spring 1993), p. 65.

[16] Carnegie Commission on the Prevention of Deadly Conflict, *Preventing Deadly Conflict,* p. 151.

[17] DENIS MCLEAN, *Peace Operations and Common Sense: Replacing Rhetoric with Realism,* Peaceworks Paper 9 (Washington, DC: U.S. Institute of Peace, June 1996), p. 2.

[18] BOUTROS BOUTROS-GHALI, *Agenda for Peace: Preventive Diplomacy, Peacemaking, and Peace-Keeping* (New York: United Nations, June 1996).

[19] See Figure 2.1: Life History of a Conflict, in Michael S. Lund, *Preventing Violent Conflicts: A Strategy for Preventive Diplomacy* (Washington, DC: U.S. Institute of Peace Press, 1996), p. 38; and Figure 1.2: Peace Operations and Stages of Conflict, in William J. Durch, ed., *UN Peacekeeping, American Politics, and the Uncivil Wars of the 1990s* (New York: St. Martin's Press, 1996), p. 9.

[20] Comments of Professor BRUCE JENTLESON at the panel on "Preventive Diplomacy," Annual Meeting of the International Studies Association, March 30, 1994.

[21] LUND, *Preventing Violent Conflicts,* p. 37.

[22] ANNAN, "Remarks."

[23] UN Department of Public Information, "UN Peace-Keeping," http://www.un.org/Depts/dpko.

[24] KENNETH ALLARD, *Somalia Operations: Lessons Learned* (Washington, DC: National Defense University Press, 1995), p. 15.

[25] *Yugoslavia: Death of a Nation,* Part I: "The Cracks Appear," Discovery Channel, video. This excellent series contains video footage of Milosevic's visit to Kosovo in April 1987, a chilling video record of conflict in the making.

[26] CATHAL J. NOLAN, *The Longman Guide to World Affairs* (White Plains, NY: Longman, 1995), p. 110.

[27] "Srebrenica: The Days of Slaughter," *The New York Times,* October 29, 1995, p. 1.

[28] U.S. Central Intelligence Agency, "Rwanda," *World Factbook 1994,* CD-ROM version (Grand Rapids, MI: Wayzata Technology, 1994).

[29] UN Security Council, *Second Progress Report of the Secretary-General of the United Nations Assistance Mission for Rwanda,* S/1994/360, March 30, 1994, paragraph 27.

[30] J. MATTHEW VACCARO, "The Politics of Genocide: Peacekeeping and Disaster Relief in Rwanda," in William J. Durch, ed., *UN Peacekeeping,* p. 367.

[31] Carnegie Commission on Preventing Deadly Conflict, *Preventing Deadly Conflict,* p. 3.

[32] SCOTT R. FEIL, *Preventing Genocide: How the Early Use of Force Might Have Succeeded in Rwanda* (Washington, DC: Carnegie Commission on Preventing Deadly Conflict, April 1998), p. 5.

[33] ANDREW KOHUT and ROBERT C. TOTH, "Arms and the People," *Foreign Affairs,* vol. 73, no. 6 (November/December 1994), pp. 47–61.

[34] CHESTER A. CROCKER, "The Lessons of Somalia," *Foreign Affairs,* vol. 74, no. 3 (May/June 1995), p. 7.

[35] See, for example, KEVIN M. CAHILL, ed., *Preventive Diplomacy: Stopping Wars Before They Start* (New York: Center for International Health and Cooperation/Basic Books, 1995).

[36] Carnegie Commission on Preventing Deadly Conflict, *Preventing Deadly Conflict,* p. 35.

[37] Carnegie Commission on Preventing Deadly Conflict, *Preventing Deadly Conflict,* p. 37.

World Politics, the Future, and You

CRITEX:

Your Preferred World in 2050

*I*N THE conclusion to his book *New Forces, Old Forces and the Future of World Politics,* Professor Seyom Brown asks, "Who are the constituents of the emerging world polity?" And he answers: "The conclusion of this study ... is that all of us—no matter where we may live in the world, whatever our national or religious identification, whatever our gender, color, class, or occupation—are its constituents.... The future of world politics is up to us."[1]

Fifty years from now, this course will be a dim memory (if that) in your mind; however, you will have (hopefully) lived a full and rewarding life, and you will be retired or close to it. Undoubtedly, the world will be a very different place from now.

Write a brief essay describing the sort of world that you *hope* exists in the year 2050. Also describe the role that you hope to have played in creating your preferred world.

INTRODUCTION

We have covered, literally and figuratively, the entire world in the last fourteen chapters, and there are many topics that we could still address, but not within the time frame of one course. There are two additional topics to cover before the "ultimate" critical thinking exercise, the final examination. The topics are: (1) future visions of world politics, and (2) what *you* can do about world politics.

POSSIBLE MODELS OF THE FUTURE

Various historians, political scientists, journalists, and politicians have written about the possible future processes and structures of the world. These visions of the future vary considerably from one another. In this concluding chapter, we will review six of the most prominent visions of the future to assist you in your thinking about the future. At the end of the chapter, we will also consider what you can do about world politics.

A World of Democracies: The End of History?

As communism imploded throughout Eastern Europe, former RAND and State Department analyst, Dr. Francis Fukuyama wrote in 1989: "We may be witnessing ... the end of mankind's ideological evolution and the universalization of Western liberal democracy as the final form of government."[2] Dr. Fukuyama referred to this possibility as "the **end of history,**" meaning that the ideological conflicts that have marked the past century's history would be a thing of the past. He argued that democratic political theory had won the ideological competition of the twentieth century and, therefore, the ideological reason for conflict had come to an end. Dr. Fukuyama's thesis stimulated much debate and discussion, and in the years since he first presented his thesis, Dr. Fukuyama has moderated it given the increasing power of conservative, procommunist forces in Russia. Dr. Fukuyama's central thesis, however, seems to be valid; the ideologically based conflicts of the twentieth century seem to have become a thing of the past and are being replaced by conflicts more characteristic of the nineteenth century, ethnically based conflicts.

A Clash of Civilizations?

In 1993 Professor Samuel Huntington of Harvard University published an article in *Foreign Affairs* that elicited more of a response than any article published in this prestigious journal since the publication of George Kennan's seminal 1947 article in which he presented the idea of containment. In his article, Professor Huntington argued that the end of the cold war will not, as Dr. Francis Fukuyama claims, end major conflict in the world. In fact, Huntington argues that with the end of the ideological alliances of the cold war, religion, bloodlines, and cultural heritage have become more important in establishing individual and group loyalty. Defining a civilization as "the highest cultural grouping of people and the broadest level of cultural identity people have short of that which distinguishes humans from other species,"[3] Huntington claims that there are six or possibly seven civilizations in the world: Sinic, Japanese, Hindu, Islamic, Western, Latin American and possibly African. The cold war ideological conflict between communism and anticommunism will be replaced by "a **clash of civilizations**" among these civilizations. Huntington contends:

> Cultural commonalities and differences shape the interests, antagonisms and associations of states. The most important countries in the world come overwhelmingly from different civilizations. The local conflicts most likely to escalate into broader wars are those between groups and states from different civilizations.[4]

Professor Huntington argued that the conflict between the western states and the Muslim countries was likely to be particularly conflictual.

Evidence of the validity of Huntington's thesis can be seen in recent conflicts. The conflict between Chechnya and Russia may be viewed as a secessionist conflict or, according to Huntington, as a conflict between Islam and Orthodoxy. Similarly, the conflict in Bosnia may be viewed as a civil war or as a civilizational battle among Muslim (Bosnian), Catholic (Croatian) and Orthodox (Serb) factions. And the war over Kosovo may also be viewed as a civil war or as a "clash of civilizations" between Muslim Albanians and Orthodox Serbs.

Huntington's critics noted that there were other conflicts, most notably the Gulf War, that were not characterized by a clash of civilizations. In fact, in 1991 Muslims from Kuwait, Saudi Arabia, and other Gulf states fought shoulder to shoulder with soldiers from the United States and Europe against their Muslim Iraqi brethren. This brought out the fact that important differences exist within the same civilization. The split between Sunni and Shi'a Muslims is another example within the Islamic civilization. In the Kosovo crisis, the NATO western states attacked Orthodox Christian Serbia on behalf of the predominantly Muslim Kosovars.

International Relations Becoming Interracial Relations?

In his path-breaking book, Professor Paul Gordon Lauren has noted the underanalyzed influence of racial factors upon world politics and argues that international relations is increasingly becoming interracial relations.[5] Lauren's analysis echoes that of the great African-American scholar W. E. B. DuBois who posited in 1900: "The problem of the twentieth century is the problem of the color line."[6] In proving his case, Professor Lauren cites the blatantly racist writings of some of the greatest thinkers of western civilization, including Aristotle, Plato, Herodotus, and Augustine. Despite the abolition of slavery in the nineteenth century, the racist ideas that had supported slavery lived on, even among some of the most respected leaders of the time. For example, Woodrow Wilson wrote of Asian immigration, "I stand for the national policy of exclusion. We cannot make a homogeneous population out of a people who do not blend with the Caucasian race."[7] Another great leader of the twentieth century, Winston Churchill, reflected Wilson's racist views when he declared, "Why be apologetic about Anglo-Saxon superiority? We are superior."[8]

Lauren does not, as is often the case, only criticize the white, western European states; he notes that while China, India, and Japan have all criticized both the UN and the United States for failing to enforce international agreements against racial discrimination, these Asian countries have ignored their own ethnic prejudices, caste system (in the case of India), and human rights violations. According to Lauren, "It was not that white Europeans held the only attitudes about racial prejudice in the world, but that they possessed sufficient power for conquest to make others suffer accordingly."[9]

Lauren presents strong evidence that history is replete with examples of racist bigotry and that the color line has divided the oppressors from the oppressed. Whether one considers slavery, colonization, World War I or World War II, the abuse of power in the form of racial prejudice has played a role. In this sense, then, international relations is a function of interracial relations.

Rather than simply engaging in a "wrecking operation," Lauren also presents some hope that the problem of race can be overcome: "... the cause of ending discrimination based upon race has been advanced the most when the realities of power and self-interest were balanced with those values of the human spirit.... success has come when those with some degree of power and interest also possess some degree of compassion, a sense of justice, and a moral conviction that all individuals should be treated with respect regardless of the color of their skin."[10]

The Realist Vision: A State-Centric World of Conflict

Throughout this book, we have noted the evolution and development of the nation-state in world politics. Since the end of the Thirty Years' War until the present, states have dominated international relations. Even today, despite the existence of a multitude of nonstate actors such as multinational corporations, international organizations, nongovernmental organizations and other transnational entities, the state perseveres. Those of the realist school of world politics believe that states will continue to dominate world politics.

One of the most prominent of the contemporary realists, Professor Kenneth Waltz, has argued, "If there is any distinctively political theory of international relations, balance-of-power theory is it."[11] Waltz contends that realist theory is the only theory of international relations that meets the requirements for a theory. Certainly when one views the international system, the prevalence of states stands out. For example, the United Nations cannot act independently; it must act with the consent and support of its member states. Similarly, regional organizations such as NATO cannot act without the approval of states.

The Rise of "Illiberal Democracies"?

In an important article published in the influential quarterly, *Foreign Affairs*, the managing editor of the journal, Fareed Zakaria, noted:

> The American diplomat Richard Holbrooke pondered a problem on the eve of the September 1996 elections in Bosnia, which were meant to restore civic life to that ravaged country. "Suppose the election was declared free and fair," he said, and those elected are "racists, fascists, separatists, who are publicly opposed to [peace and reintegration]. That is the dilemma." Indeed it is, not just in the former Yugoslavia, but increasingly around the world.[12]

Like Francis Fukuyama, Zakaria notes the increasing number of democratic states in the world: "Today, 118 of the world's 193 countries are democratic, encompassing a majority of its people (54.8 percent, to be exact), a vast increase from even a decade ago."[13] This is a positive trend; however, there is a disturbing growth of **"illiberal democracy,"** which are governed by leaders who were elected by reasonably respectable elections, but who rule in a manner that is more characteristic of traditional autocracies without the protections of constitutional democracies. Zakaria notes that the number of **illiberal democracies** is growing; in 1990 22 percent of democratizing states could be categorized as "illiberal"; by 1997, the percentage had grown to 35 percent.

Zakaria's analysis contains prescription for United States and western policies; namely, that the constitutional democracies should show more patience with the semi-democratic states that at least "accord their citizens a widening sphere of economic, civil, religious and limited political rights."[14]

Chaos?

Some contemporary analysts of world politics look toward the horizon of the future and are not reassured by what they see. They see increasing ethnic conflict, transnational terrorism, the possible use of weapons of mass destruction and new forms of conflict such as information warfare. Rather than an ordered, stable international system, these analysts see disorder, chaos, and even potential anarchy. Those who hold this vision of the future are not some wild-eyed science fiction writers; two of the most influential writers who hold this vision have had substantial experience in U.S. government service—one in a Republican administration and the other in a Democratic administration.[15] This then is a bipartisan view of a possible frightening future.

WHAT YOU CAN DO ABOUT WORLD POLITICS

During the past academic term, you have studied about the history and politics of international relations. Now we are at the end of our formal consideration of world politics, but there is one topic left: you. What can you do about world politics? The answer varies from plenty to nothing, depending upon what you choose to do.

We started this book by focusing on a tragic figure whose name is not even known, a man captured in a net about to be sent into slavery. The photograph is haunting, like many of the others in this book. In the first chapter of the book, I posed the question, "Are there issues in today's world that future generations will view the way that we today view slavery?" I hope that you have thought about that question and that you have answered for yourself. If there are such issues, then perhaps you will want to think about what you can do to improve the situation, to—perhaps in just a small way—make the world a better place.

We began our study by noting a fact of contemporary life: international politics is becoming domesticated, and domestic politics is becoming internationalized. Whether people realize it or not, their lives are increasingly going to be affected by decisions and actions made in other countries by individuals who do not share their particular citizenship. We saw, for example, that the citizens of the 35 island states of the world are intensely concerned about the problem of global warming because if nothing is done about this problem, the level of the world's oceans will continue to rise, and some of these island states will lose some or even all of their land. But one need not live on an island to be affected by world politics; even those who live in the United States will be affected. What can you do about world politics?

Become More Informed about World Politics

One of the main things that I hope you have learned from this course is how little we know. The more that we learn, the more we learn how much more we have to learn. The world is a richly varied place with many different types of actors. What you have learned in this course may stimulate you to continue to learn about international aspects of the problems that interest and/or affect you. Reading a good daily newspaper or weekly magazine can provide the basic knowledge about the world in which we live.

If you have been interested in this subject, you may want to take more courses in international relations, comparative politics, foreign policy, or the particular areas of the world in which you are interested. And if you are seriously interested in further study of this subject, you may want to go on to graduate school; the appendix provides information on this option.

Get Involved with a Nongovernmental Organization

As noted in Chapter 13, there are many, many nongovernmental organizations dealing with almost every imaginable issue area. Most of these NGOs do not have large budgets and literally survive because of the free labor of volunteers. If you are concerned about a particular issue, read more about it and find out what NGOs are working to solve the problems in this area. Many church groups are involved in hunger relief and development assistance; Amnesty International works against torture and the death penalty and to obtain freedom for political prisoners; Human Rights Watch works to obtain basic human rights for people in more than

70 countries. There is much to be done, and your help is needed. Some of the more prominent NGOs, include:

- Caritas International (Catholic Organizations for Charitable and Social Action);
- Catholic Relief Services;
- Church World Service;
- Cooperative for Assistance and Relief Everywhere (CARE);
- International Rescue Committee;
- Medecines Sans Frontieres (MSF);
- Oxford Committee for Famine Relief (Oxfam);
- Save the Children Federation;
- World Vision.

Become Politically Involved

In my classes, I argue that a political science major is one of the most valuable that a student can choose because the knowledge gained in it can be used for the rest of one's lifetime. Students who take political science courses wind up doing many different things; however, assuming they live in a democratic country, they can all vote. One of the repeated findings of American political scientists is that most Americans are not interested in world politics most of the time. The qualification to that finding is "unless they perceive their interests as threatened." Now you have more knowledge and understanding of world politics than 95 percent of your fellow citizens. One of the ways to exercise your rights of citizenship to the fullest is to work for a political candidate whose views you support.

Think about Working in This Area As An Intern or Professional

There are many opportunities in the foreign policy and world politics field for internships. A number of organizations, including the American Political Science Association publish guides to internships, and this is a good place to start. Also, re-read the "You in World Politics" sections of this book which are a guide to internships, graduate school, and careers in the international relations field. Not many of you may choose to go into this field professionally, but some will, and will be dealing with the issues we have addressed (and undoubtedly many new ones) for your entire professional lives.

YOU IN WORLD POLITICS

So you're thinking about graduate school in international relations? Some universities have schools or programs centered around a two-year interdisciplinary Masters program in international affairs. Originally these schools were designed to produce candidates for the Foreign Service. However, since so few applicants are accepted and since admission is now by examination, these schools have altered their focus and now try to prepare students to work for other government agencies and for international business as well; Georgetown, for example, renamed its program "International Business Diplomacy."

The curriculum stresses international politics, history, and economics; in addition, area specialization is often available. These schools also take placement seriously—an important point to consider. If you're interested in working for the government in international affairs, one of these schools may be your best bet. The utility of their degrees in business is less clear. There is no question that their graduates get jobs with major corporations. However, it's less clear that the degree will suffice for a business career or whether people who have gotten jobs with this degree may have to go back to business school later on.

There are relatively few of these institutions. Two which do not specialize exclusively in international affairs but include domestic concerns as well are the John F. Kennedy School at Harvard and the Woodrow Wilson School at Princeton. The two oldest schools that specialize in international affairs are Fletcher School of Law and Diplomacy at Tufts University and the Nitze School of Advanced International Studies at Johns Hopkins University, Washington, D.C. Also very prestigious are the School of International Studies, Columbia University and the School of Foreign Service, Georgetown University. Programs are also available at the international affairs schools at George Washington University, the Monterey Institute of International Studies, University of Southern California, University of Maryland, American University, and the University of Denver, as well as the Patterson School at the University of Kentucky.

CONCLUSION

The two final questions for you to ponder are: (1) Are you going to keep up your knowledge of world politics? (2) What are you going to do to make the world a better place? The answers to these questions are up to you and you alone.

DISCUSSION QUESTIONS

1. If you were betting $100, what kind of world do you think will exist 50 years from now? Is that the kind of world you would like to live in?
2. What can you do to make the world closer to the one in which you would like to live?
3. How can you keep informed on world political issues after you leave this class?

KEY TERMS

clash of civilizations   illiberal democracies
end of history

RECOMMENDED PRINT, MULTIMEDIA, AND INTERNET SOURCES

Print

BROWN, SEYOM. *New Forces, Old Forces and the Future of World Politics, Post-Cold War Edition.* New York: HarperCollins, 1995.

FUKUYAMA, FRANCIS. "The End of History." *The National Interest,* 16 (Summer 1989): 719–732.

———. *The End of History and the Last Man.* New York: Free Press, 1992.

HUNTINGTON, SAMUEL P. "The Clash of Civilizations?" *Foreign Affairs* (Summer 1993): 22–49.

———. *The Clash of Civilizations and the Remaking of World Order.* New York: Simon and Schuster, 1996.

LAUREN, PAUL GORDON. *Power and Prejudice: The Politics and Diplomacy of Racial Discrimination,* 2nd ed. Boulder, CO: Westview Press, 1996.

WALTZ, KENNETH. *Theory of International Politics.* Menlo Park, CA: Addison-Wesley, 1979.

ZAKARIA, FAREED. "The Rise of Illiberal Democracy." *Foreign Affairs,* vol. 76, no. 6 (November/December 1997): 22–43.

Video

Edward Said in Lecture: The Myth of 'The Clash of Civilizations.' A 40-minute critique of Samuel Huntington's "clash of civilizations" thesis followed by fifteen minutes of questions and answers. Northampton, MA: The Media Education Foundation, 1998.

 Internet

Foreign Affairs website: www.foreignaffairs.org/envoy
Economist: http://www.postbox.co.uk/economist.htm

ENDNOTES

[1] SEYOM BROWN, *New Forces, Old Forces and the Future of World Politics, Post-Cold War Edition* (New York: HarperCollins, 1995), p. 269.

[2] FRANCIS FUKUYAMA, "The End of History," *The National Interest,* 16 (Summer 1989): 719–732. Dr. Fukuyama expanded the argument contained in this article into a book: *The End of History and the Last Man* (New York: Free Press, 1992).

[3] FUKUYAMA, "The End of History."

[4] SAMUEL P. HUNTINGTON, *The Clash of Civilizations and the Remaking of World Order* (New York: Simon & Schuster, 1996), p. 29.

[5] PAUL GORDON LAUREN, *Power and Prejudice: The Politics and Diplomacy of Racial Discrimination,* 2nd ed. (Boulder, CO: Westview Press, 1996).

[6] Quoted by LAUREN, *Power and Prejudice.*

[7] Ibid., p. 83.

[8] Ibid., p. 139.

[9] Ibid., p. 16.

[10] Ibid., p. 290.

[11] KENNETH N. WALTZ, "Theory of International Relations," in Fred I. Greenstein and Nelson Polsby, eds., *Handbook of Political Science,* vol. 8 (Reading, MA: Addison-Wesley, 1975), p. 36.

[12] FAREED ZAKARIA, "The Rise of Illiberal Democracy," *Foreign Affairs,* vol. 76, no. 6 (November/December 1997), p. 22.

[13] Ibid., p. 23.

[14] Ibid.

[15] CHESTER CROCKER, ed. *Chaos* (Washington, DC: U.S. Institute of Peace) and Zbigniew Brzezinski, "Beyond Chaos," *National Interest,* vol. 19 (Spring 1990): 3–12.

Graduate Schools of International Studies in the United States

School of International Service
American University
Washington, DC 20016
202/885–6000

Graduate School of International
  Relations and Pacific Studies
University of California,
  San Diego
La Jolla, CA 92093–0519
619/534–5914
http://irpsbbs.ucsd/irps/
  irpsmenu.html

Edmund A. Walsh School of
  Foreign Service
Georgetown University
Washington, DC 20057–1028
202/687–5763

Elliott School of International Affairs
George Washington University
Washington, DC 20052
202/994–7050

The Graduate School of
  International Studies
University of Denver
2201 S. Gaylord St.
Denver, CO 80208
303/871–2544
gsisadm@du.edu

School of International and
  Public Affairs
1417 International Affairs
  Building
Columbia University
420 West 118th St.
New York, NY 10027
212/854–2167, 854–4841

Graduate School of Public
  and International Affairs
University of Pittsburgh
Pittsburgh, PA 15260
412/648–7640

Woodrow Wilson School
Princeton University
Princeton, NJ 08544
609/258–4836

John F. Kennedy School
of Government
Harvard University
Cambridge, MA 02138
617/495–1155

The Paul H. Nitze School of
Advanced International Studies
The Johns Hopkins University
1740 Massachusetts Avenue, NW
Washington, DC 20036
202/663–5702

Monterey Institute of International
Studies
425 Van Buren Street
Monterey, CA 93940
831/647–4199
admit@miis.edu

Henry Jackson School of
International Studies
University of Washington
Seattle, Washington 98195
206/543–4370
jsisinfo@u.washington.edu

School of International Relations
University of Southern California
Los Angeles, CA 90089–0035
213/740–6278

Fletcher School of Law and
Diplomacy
Tufts University
Medford, MA 02155
617/628–5000

Yale Center for International
and Area Studies
Yale University
New Haven, CT 06520
203/432–3418

American Graduate School
of International Management
Thunderbird School
15249 N. 59th Ave.
Glendale, AZ 85306–6000
602/978–7100
tbird@t-bird.edu

Glossary

This glossary is designed to define briefly the various concepts, important persons, and historical events mentioned in this text. Students should consult the text for a fuller explanation of the term. In addition, the following books are excellent sources for gaining a fuller understanding:

EVANS, GRAHAM. *Penguin Dictionary of International Relations*. London: Penguin Books, 1998.

NOLAN, CATHAL J. *The Longman Guide to World Affairs*. White Plains, New York: Longman Publishers, 1995.

PLANO, JACK C. and ROY OLTON. *The International Relations Dictionary*, 4th ed. Santa Barbara, CA: ABC-CLIO, Inc., 1988.

ABM: see anti-ballistic missile.

absolute advantage: A situation in which a state or corporation can supply goods or services less than other actors, due to the resources of that actor.

Acheson-Lilienthal Plan: See Baruch Plan.

acid rain: Precipitation that has been contaminated with industrial pollutants, nitrogen oxide, and sulphur dioxide.

air-launched cruise missile (ALCM): A pilotless airplane, launched from an airplane, that carries either a nuclear or conventional warhead.

alliance: A formal agreement between or among states to cooperate in military affairs.

Alliance of Small Island States: A group of 35 countries that are surrounded by water and whose citizens are particularly concerned about the problem of global warming because the rise in the world's oceans would cause these island states to lose much territory or to disappear altogether.

Allied Powers: The states that opposed the Axis Powers in World War II, which included the United States, Great Britain, the Soviet Union, China, the free French, and more than 40 other smaller states.

American Revolution: When the British government implemented a number of policies that the Americans found objectionable, fighting broke out in 1775. The Americans declared their independence on July 4, 1776, and defeated the British in 1783.

Amnesty International (AI): A humanitarian, nongovernmental organization that works to improve the condition of prisoners of conscience and opposes torture and capital punishment. It was awarded the Nobel Peace Prize in 1977.

Annan, Kofi: A long-time member of the United Nations staff, formerly assistant secretary general for peacekeeping and currently Secretary General, the head of the UN.

Antarctica Treaty: An agreement signed in 1959 that bans all testing and deployment of conventional and nuclear weapons or disposal of radioactive waste from the continent of Antarctica.

anti-ballistic missile (ABM): A missile designed to destroy incoming warheads or missiles before they reach their intended targets. The difficulty of achieving this task has been compared to "hitting a bullet with a bullet."

appeasement: A policy that attempts to use positive incentives to influence another state's compliance. British Prime Minister Neville Chamberlain unsuccessfully attempted to appease Nazi Germany at the Munich Conference of 1938 by ceding control of Czechoslovakia.

arms control: Policies designed to: (1) reduce the risk of war breaking out, (2) reduce damage should war occur, and (3) reduce the economic cost of preparing for war.

Axis Powers: Germany, Italy, and Japan during World War II.

balance of payments: The summary of a state's international economic activity; reveals a state's trade balance (exports minus imports), foreign aid, and the income of citizens working abroad.

balance of payments deficits: When a state's imports exceed its exports.

balance of power: A system for managing power in the international system in which power is distributed among the member states so that no one state dominates; functioned during the 1648–1914 period in Europe.

ballistic missile: A missile that consists of a rocket and a warhead that follow a flight path determined by the burning of the rocket engine and the force of gravity pulling the warhead back to earth.

Baruch Plan: Based on a proposal by Dean Acheson and David Lilienthal, this plan was presented to the United Nations by the U.S. representative to the UN, Bernard Baruch, in 1946. It called for an international agency to oversee all activities related to nuclear development. In addition, it called for a plan for verification that no states were developing nuclear weapons. The USSR rejected this plan and presented its own, called the Gromyko Plan.

Berlin Airlift: In 1948, East Germany and the Soviet Union closed the access route from West Germany to West Berlin, which lay within East Germany. In response, the United States flew essential supplies to West Berlin.

Berlin Wall: In 1961, East Germany and the Soviet Union began erecting barriers between East and West Berlin to prevent East Germans from escaping to the west. Within several days, these barriers were reinforced with concrete, and the Berlin Wall, one of the most evocative symbols of the cold war, came into existence.

"billiard ball" model: See state-centric model.

Biological Weapons Convention: In 1972, an international agreement was concluded prohibiting the production, storage, or deployment of organisms such as the plague or anthrax to be used for hostile purposes.

bipolar system, bipolarity: An international system dominated by two powerful great powers; the cold war system dominated by the United States and USSR was characteristic of this type of system.

Bismarck, Otto von (1815–1898): German statesman who as Chancellor unified Germany in 1871; considered one of the archetypal realists of history.

Blitzkrieg: This German term translates literally as "lightning war." It refers to the military strategy developed by Germany incorporating integrated land and air operations coordinating tanks and airplanes.

Bolshevik Revolution: Led by Lenin, this upheaval in November 1917 resulted in the toppling of the tsarist government and the establishment of the first communist government in the world.

Bretton Woods System: The conference was held at Bretton Woods, New Hampshire, in 1944 resulted in the establishment of the International Bank for Reconstruction and Development (IBRD) and the International Monetary Fund (IMF). This provided the foundation for a liberal international economic order.

carrying capacity: The maximum number of organisms that a particular system can sustain.

Chaumont, Treaty of: An international agreement among Great Britain, Austria-Hungary, Russia, and Prussia to wage war against Napoleon until victory was achieved.

Chemical Weapons Convention: An arms control agreement signed in 1992 after 24 years of negotiation. The agreement supersedes the Geneva Protocol of 1925 and bans the development, production, stockpiling, transfer, and use of chemical agents designed to be used as weapons.

chlorofluorocarbons (CFCs): A chemical compound found in refrigerators and air conditioners that depletes the ozone.

clash of civilizations: A hypothesis presented by Harvard political scientist Samuel Huntington in 1993 that future international conflict would be based primarily on conflicts between and among the six or seven major cultures: Sinic, Japanese, Hindu, Islamic, Western, Latin American, and possibly African.

classical liberal economists: Economists writing in the 17th century who advocated free trade and free markets; included David Ricardo, John Stuart Mill, and Adam Smith.

Clausewitz, Karl von (1780–1831): A German military strategist who is considered one of the greatest theorists concerning war and strategy. His most frequently quoted observation is that "war is the continuation of politics by other means."

coercive diplomacy: Also called compellence, this is a policy that integrates political and military moves in order to have an opponent stop short of a goal, undo an action, or change the government.

collective security: A system for managing power in international relations that calls for all of the states in the system to identify and universally oppose any aggression in the system. Supported by Woodrow Wilson at the end of World War I, this system was embodied first in the League of Nations and after World War II in the United Nations.

communism: An ideology based on the writings of Karl Marx, Friedrich Engels, and Vladimir Lenin, which calls for the ownership of the means of production by the members of the working classes. The Communist Party ruled the Soviet Union from 1917 though 1991.

comparative advantage: The theoretical foundation of free trade which calls on states to specialize in the goods and services that they are best suited to produce.

compellence: See coercive diplomacy.

compensations: territorial or other inducements used to balance power among states.

Congress of Vienna: The international conference held from 1814–1815, led by the four powers that defeated Napoleon Bonaparte: Austria-Hungary, Great Britain, Prussia, and Russia.

consul, consul-general: A government's official representative to another state who typically deals with nonpolitical issues such as trade and immigration. The consul-general is a senior consular official.

containment doctrine: Also called the Truman Doctrine because this policy was announced by President Truman in 1947; called for the United States and its allies to halt the expansion of communist states. This doctrine was the foundation of American foreign policy from 1947 to the disintegration of the USSR at the end of 1991.

cosmopolitan: One who views world politics not simply as a collection of states, but as a collection of individuals.

crisis management: Attempting to deal with situations that threaten important national goals, have a short time horizon, and surprise decision makers.

Crusades: A series of military attacks launched from Europe with the intention of taking control of Jerusalem and Christian holy sites in the Middle East; these attacks took place from 1095 to 1270.

Cuban missile crisis: The situation that developed in October 1962 when the USSR sought to secretly send and make operational nuclear armed missiles on the island of Cuba. This was the tensest crisis of the entire cold war period and was resolved when the USSR agreed to remove its missiles from Cuba in exchange for a promise from the United States not to invade Cuba and a secret pledge to remove its missiles from Turkey.

custom: One of the sources of international law, custom is regularized behavior among states which can develop into formal laws.

debt crisis: The strain in the international economic system in the 1970s and 1980s caused by excessive borrowing by developing states.

democratic peace: The theory that states which have popularly elected and ruled governments will not go to war against one another. Adherents of this theory favor the spread of democracy throughout the world as a means of making the international system more peaceful.

desertification: The process of arable or grazing land becoming arid desert due to drought or other factors.

détente: A term from the classical lexicon of diplomacy, it originally referred to lessening the tension on the trigger of a crossbow. It now refers to the lessening of tensions between or among states.

deterrence: A concept as old as humanity, deterrence refers to the possession of sufficient power to be able to inflict unacceptable damage on a potential aggressor, in order to convince him thereby not to commit an aggressive act. Deterrence applies both to conventional and nuclear politics.

diplomacy: The system developed to manage orderly relations, particularly negotiation, among states.

diplomatic flexibility: The freedom of states to ally, oppose, or remain neutral toward other states or alliances.

diplomatic immunity: The legal principle that exempts diplomats from being subject to the laws and penalties of the state in which they are posted.

disarmament: Entirely eliminating one type of weapon or all weapons.

divine right of kings: The theory prevalent prior to the French Revolution that rulers are ordained by God and therefore not subject to the review and control of ordinary citizens.

domestic political system: A system of government for controlling a particular territory.

ecology: The study of the relationship of organisms to their environment.

Economic and Social Council (ECOSOC): The United Nations organization responsible for coordinating the specialized agencies of the UN such as the World Health Organization (WHO), the Food and Agricultural Agency (FAO), and the International Children's Emergency Fund (UNICEF).

"end of history": A controversial hypothesis presented by Dr. Francis Fukuyama in 1989 that the fall of communism in Eastern Europe marked the "end of mankind's ideological evolution and the universalization of Western liberal democracy as the final form of government."

environmental degradation: The decline of the ecosystem.

Environmental Modification Convention: In 1977 an international agreement prohibiting the deliberate manipulation of natural processes, such as changing weather or climate patterns, ocean currents, or the ozone layer was signed by 34 states. Since that time many more have signed the agreement.

essential actors: See great powers.

ethnic conflict: Fighting between or among ethnically based groups such as tribes.

European Economic Community (EEC): Founded by the Treaty of Rome of March 1958, this group of originally six states established a customs union among themselves; by 1995, nine more European states had become members. The EEC was the precursor to the European Union.

European Union (EU): The successor to the European Economic Community (EEC). Created by the Maastricht Treaty of 1993. The EU currently consists of

16 member states and has as its overriding goal the greater political and economic integration of Europe.

extended deterrence: The belief that nonnuclear aggression can be deterred by threatening to use nuclear weapons.

feudalism: A social, political, and economic system based on ownership of land and hereditary titles. Feudalism was a hierarchical system in which every member of society had a set place. This system flourished in Europe from the eighth through the twelfth centuries and in Japan from the tenth to the late nineteenth centuries.

flexible exchange rate: An international monetary system in which currency rates are determined by supply and demand.

free enterprise: An economic system in which prices are determined by the market and in which government intervention is minimal.

French Revolution: Because of the extravagant expenditures of King Louis XIV on the palace of Versailles and foreign conflicts, France was close to bankruptcy by the late eighteenth century. In 1789, revolutionaries promising "liberty, equality, freedom," toppled the old regime and ushered in a violent, unstable period until the emergence of Napoleon Bonaparte.

General Agreement on Tariffs and Trade (GATT): An international forum that in 1947 called for international trade to be conducted according to principles of free trade; replaced by the World Trade Organization (WTO) in 1995.

General Assembly: The largest body of the United Nations; each member of the UN has one representative in the General Assembly and voting is according to the principle "one state, one vote." There are currently 185 representatives in this body.

Geneva Protocol: An agreement signed in 1925 which bans the use of chemical or bacteriological weapons. This was not ratified by the United States until 1975.

genocide: The deliberate extermination of an ethnic, religious, or national group; banned by the 1948 Convention Against Genocide.

global warming: The gradual rise in the earth's temperatures due to the increasing concentration of greenhouse gases in the atmosphere.

gold standard: An international exchange-rate system in which the value of each state's currency was fixed to the price of gold. First introduced by Great Britain in 1821, the gold standard was observed periodically, most recently from 1945 to 1971.

Gorbachev, Mikhail (1931–): Selected by the most powerful political body in the USSR, the Politburo, to be the head of the Communist Party of the Soviet Union (CPSU) in March 1985, Gorbachev introduced reforms, including *glasnost* (openness), *perestroika* (re-structuring), democratization of politics, and "new thinking" in foreign policy. These reforms unleashed forces that Gorbachev and the Communist Party could not control and both the CPSU and the USSR came to an end in December 1991.

Grand Alliance: The three largest members of the World War II Allied states: the United States, Great Britain, and the Soviet Union.

grand design and grand strategy: The broad, overarching goals and means of achieving those objectives in a state's foreign policy.

Great Depression: The worldwide decline in economic productivity and investment from 1929 to 1939, which had disastrous consequences for most of the world's states.

great powers: The most powerful states in the international system; during the late nineteenth century these included Great Britain, France, Austria-Hungary, Russia, and Prussia (Germany).

greenhouse gases: Methane, carbon dioxide, nitrous oxide, and chlorofluorocarbons that trap heat in the earth's atmosphere, similar to the way in which a greenhouse traps heat, resulting in global warming.

Green Revolution: The dramatic increase in crop yields in developing countries in the 1950s and 1960s due to the use of fertilizers and genetically engineered varieties of grains and other plants.

Gromyko Plan: The Soviet counterproposal to the United States' Baruch Plan; called for an inspection system to verify that no states had nuclear weapons only after such weapons had been turned over to an international authority. This was unacceptable to the United States.

gross domestic product (GDP): The total value of goods and services produced by a state in one year minus the value of goods and services produced by a state's citizens overseas.

gross national product (GNP): The total value of goods and services produced by a state in one year.

Grotius, Hugo (1583–1645): A Dutch jurist regarded as the father of international law due to the publication of his book, *On the Law of War and Peace.*

Gulf War: In August 1990, Iraq attacked and occupied Kuwait. The United Nations passed eleven resolutions condemning Iraq's action and calling for its withdrawal from Kuwait. When Iraq did not comply, a coalition of the 32 states, led by the United States, Great Britain, France, and Saudi Arabia, attacked Iraqi forces in January 1991 and compelled them to withdraw, and the Kuwaiti government was restored to its prewar position.

hegemon, hegemonic power: A single, dominant power in the international system that is able to influence the operation of the system to conform to its wishes.

Hiroshima and Nagasaki: The two Japanese cities that the United States attacked with atomic bombs in August 1945. These attacks compelled the Japanese leaders to surrender, ending the most costly war in human history.

Hitler, Adolf (1889–1945): Born in Austria, Hitler served in the German army in World War I, became a member of the National Socialist (Nazi) Party in 1919, and was appointed German Chancellor in January 1933. The author of the virulently anti-Semitic book, *Mein Kampf (My Struggle),* Hitler and his Nazi supporters implemented genocidal policies against Jews, Slavs, gypsies, and Catholics. His attack on Poland in September 1939 led to the outbreak of World War II. Hitler committed suicide with his mistress in April 1945.

Hot-Line (Agreement): The direct communications link between Washington and Moscow that is secret, reliable, and fast. Communications between the two superpowers during the cold war, particularly during the Cuban missile crisis, was cumbersome, and the two superpowers agreed in 1963 to install a cable between their two capitals. The cable was later replaced with satellite links.

Hussein, Saddam (1937–   ): The dictatorial leader of Iraq who became president of Iraq in 1979 and who led Iraq into the Iran–Iraq War and the Gulf War (1990–1991).

illiberal democracy: Governments that are elected by reasonably respectable elections, but without the protections of constitutional democracies.

imperialism: The imposition of one state's control over another.

information warfare: The widespread use of information systems, such as computer networks, for hostile purposes.

interdependence: A situation in which the actions and decisions of one international actor affect other actors.

inter-continental ballistic missile (ICBM): Missiles that have ranges of 3,000 miles or more. They are propelled out of the earth's atmosphere and fall back to earth following a trajectory determined by gravity. The USSR tested the first ICBM in August 1957 and this weapon became the principal strategic weapon of both the United States and the Soviet Union throughout the cold war.

intergovernmental organizations (IGO) also referred to as international organizations: Institutions established by governments to deal with a wide range of issues in the international system; examples include the United Nations, the Organization of American States and the Organization of African Unity.

intermediate-range ballistic missile (IRBM), medium-range ballistic missile (MRBM): Missile with ranges of 600 to 2,000 miles (MRBMs) and 2,000 to 3,000 miles (IRBMs).

Intermediate Nuclear Forces (INF) Treaty: An agreement concluded by the United States and the Soviet Union to eliminate from Europe all nuclear forces with a range of 1,000 to 4,000 miles.

internal conflict: Unrest that occurs within a state; intra-state or domestic conflict.

International Bank for Reconstruction and Development (IBRD) also called the World Bank: This intergovernmental organization was founded in 1947 as part of the Bretton Woods international economic system in order to provide assistance to states recovering from World War II. The IBRD attempts to promote free trade, free enterprise, high rates of growth, and economic stability, In recent decades it has provided most of its loans on a long-term, low interest basis to developing states.

International Bill of Rights: The name given to three agreements: (1) the Universal Declaration of Human Rights, (2) the Covenant on Civil and Political Rights, and (3) the Covenant on Economic, Social and Cultural Rights.

International Court of Justice (ICJ): More commonly known as the "World Court," the ICJ is headquartered in The Hague, the Netherlands, and hears cases that are submitted to it with the agreement of the states involved. There are 15 judges who are elected by the Security Council and the General Assembly.

International Covenant on Civil and Political Rights: An agreement signed in 1966, strongly supported by the United States and other western states, calling for the protection of individuals' political rights.

International Covenant on Economic, Social and Cultural Rights: An agreement signed in 1966, strongly supported by the Soviet Union and other communist states, that called for greater economic equality.

international law: The system of rules, customs, and agreements that aims to organize and regulate the behavior of international actors in a number of different issue areas.

International Monetary Fund (IMF): Founded in 1947 as part of the Bretton Woods international economic system, the IMF seeks to maintain monetary stability by helping states to fund balance-of-payments deficits. It currently has 170 member governments.

international political system: The collection of different actors (states) in the world that interact with one another.

international war tribunals: The Nuremberg War Tribunals conducted at the end of World War II served as a precedent for the modern war crimes courts in The Hague, the Netherlands. Trials focusing on war crimes in Bosnia and Rwanda were conducted in the 1990s.

internet: The international computer network that allows for inexpensive and rapid communication throughout the world.

just-war theory: The criteria that should be met for a conflict to be considered legitimate.

Kennan, George (1904–): An American diplomat and academic who served in the Soviet Union; the author of a very influential article in *Foreign Affairs* quarterly that became the basis of the doctrine of containment. Also the author of a number of highly respected books on Russia, the Soviet Union, and U.S. foreign policy.

Kissinger, Henry A. (1923–): Born in Germany, Kissinger's family moved to the U.S. in order to escape Nazi persecution. After service in the U.S. Army, he earned his doctorate at Harvard. He entered government in 1969, when he rose to become secretary of state.

Korean War (1950–1953): In June 1950, North Korea attacked South Korea, which went to the UN Security Council requesting aid to repel the attack. The USSR was boycotting Security Council sessions protesting the UN unwillingness to admit Soviet ally, the People's Republic of China, to membership. Thus, the Security Council was able to approve intervention on behalf of South Korea. Chinese forces intervened on behalf of North Korea. By the end of the war, more than 3 million people had died, mostly Korean civilians.

League of Nations: The brainchild of President Woodrow Wilson, this international organization was established at the end of World War I to implement collective security. Crippled from the start by the United States' failure to join the organization, the League faced a series of challenges in the 1920s and 1930s that it could not meet.

Lenin, Vladimir Ilich (1870–1924): Born Vladimir Ulyanov, Lenin was the leader of the Bolshevik (or Communist) Party at the time of the Russian Revolution in November 1917. Not only an effective and ruthless political leader, Lenin was also a brilliant theoretician, and his collected works fill 55 volumes.

lesser developed countries (LDC): See developing countries.

levels of analysis: Just as natural scientists such as biologists study parts of organisms, particular organisms, species or the interaction of species, social scientists study individuals, states, and the international system.

liberalism: The political philosophy that calls for limited government, the application of reason to the solution of problems of public policy, and the protection of individual freedom. Applied to economics, liberalism supports free enterprise and free trade.

lifeboat ethics: The application of a metaphor comparing the world to a lifeboat that has a capacity to support only a limited number of people.

Limited Nuclear Test Ban Treaty (LTBT): An agreement negotiated by the United States, the Soviet Union, and Great Britain in 1963 to curtail the testing of nuclear weapons in the atmosphere.

Maastricht Treaty: Formally known as the Treaty on European Union, this agreement entered into force in 1993 and called for a common European currency and foreign policy.

Machiavelli, Niccolo (1469–1527): A political philosopher from Florence, Italy, who wrote about how to attain and retain power in a number of works, most notably in *The Prince*. Because he considered power from a secular perspective, some regard him as the founder of modern political science.

Magna Carta: Translates as the "great charter"; in 1215 King John I of England granted certain rights to barons under him. This was significant because it limited the power of the king.

Malthus, Thomas (1766–1834): An English intellectual who argued that population increases faster than the means to provide subsistence for that population.

Manhattan Project: The code name adopted for the project to build the first atomic bomb during World War II. The project developed the two bombs dropped on Hiroshima and Nagasaki in August 1945.

Marshall Plan: Also known by its official name, the European Recovery Program, this U.S. program of financial and economic aid to the victors and vanquished of World War II significantly helped the European countries to recover from the devastation and dislocation of World War II. It was announced in 1947 by then U.S. Secretary of State George Marshall.

Marx, Karl (1818–1883): A German philosopher who co-authored with Friedrich Engels *The Communist Manifesto* in 1853 and *Das Kapital (Capital)*. Marx viewed history as a conflict between two classes: the owners of the means of production and the workers. This conflict inevitably led to conflict. The philosophy is called Marxism.

Melian Dialogue: The appeal by the leaders of the city of Melos to the Athenians during the Peloponnesian Wars (431–404 B.C.) to spare their city. The Athenians destroyed the city, killing the men and making the women and children slaves, causing Thucydides to write that "the strong do what they will, and the weak suffer what they must."

mercantilism: A government economic strategy to increase power by promoting exports and discouraging imports.

Metternich, Klemens von (1773–1859): The foreign minister of Austria-Hungary who convened the Congress of Vienna at the end of the Napoleonic Wars. Also called "the coachman of Europe" because he was able to reestablish the balance-of-power system.

monocausal explanation: A description of why something occurred focusing on only one cause or variable.

Montreal Protocol: In 1987, 154 states signed this international agreement calling for the eventual elimination of the production of chlorofluorocarbons (CFC). The Protocol was strengthened in 1990 and 1992.

most-favored-nation (MFN): Really a misnomer because this means "nondiscriminatory trade." When one state grants another MFN status, it means that the same tariffs and terms of trade are applied to it as to other states.

Munich Agreement: See appeasement.

multinational corporation (MNC): A business enterprise that operates extensively in other states.

multipolar system: An international configuration of states with two or more states.

Nagasaki: See Hiroshima.

Napoleon I, Bonaparte (1769–1821): Emperor of France from 1804 to 1815. He attempted to take over Europe and was almost successful in doing so because of his innovations in drafting people into his army and employing civilians in support of military objectives.

nation: A group of people who feel a common identity because of cultural, historical, and/or linguistic ties.

nationalism: Loyalty and commitment to one's own nation and often the belief that the nation should be independent.

Nazi-Soviet Pact (August 23, 1939): An Agreement concluded by Nazi Germany and the Soviet Union not to attack one another and to divide up areas of Poland.

This protected Germany's eastern front and enabled Hitler to believe that he could successfully attack Poland and western Europe.

neo-mercantilism: The belief that states should seek as large a trade surplus as possible. Japan in the contemporary era is often mentioned as the leading neo-mercantilist state.

Newly Industrializing Countries (NIC): Developing states whose economies are characterized by rapid growth and exports of manufactured goods; included among NICs are South Korea, Singapore, Taiwan, Mexico, and Brazil.

nihilism: The belief that nothing is objectively knowable and that existing social and political institutions must be destroyed in order to achieve improvement for the future.

nongovernmental organization (NGO): Transnational groups of private individuals, including professional associations, philanthropic groups, public-interest organizations, religious groups, and other groups founded upon the common interests of the members.

nonstate actors: Any entity active in world politics that is not a country, including intergovernmental organizations, nongovernmental organizations, and multinational corporations.

North Atlantic Treaty Organization (NATO): A collective self-defense organization founded in 1949 to deter a Soviet attack on Western Europe. NATO redefined its central objectives after the fall of the USSR. The organization currently has 19 members, including newest members, Poland, Hungary, and the Czech Republic. NATO embarked on a controversial policy in 1999 by bombing Serbia.

October War: Also called the Yom Kippur War, this conflict started when Egypt and Syria attacked Israel in October 1973. The USSR provided supplies and military materiel for the Arab states and the United States provided logistical support for Israel. Arab oil-producing states declared an embargo on any states supporting Israel.

Open Door policy: The trade policy followed by the United States toward China from 1849 for the century thereafter. It called for treating all foreign individuals and corporations on a most-favored-nation basis, i.e., on the basis of equality.

Organization for Economic Cooperation and Development (OECD): A group of 25 advanced, industrialized states which exchange information, promote sustainable development, and encourage trade.

Organization of Petroleum Exporting Countries (OPEC): Founded in 1961 by five leading oil-producing states in the developing world, OPEC used its economic power in the October War of 1973 when it declared an embargo on oil shipment to any countries supporting Israel. In recent years, OPEC has not been able to wield as much power as previously, due to flat oil prices.

Outer Space Treaty: An international agreement that entered into force in 1967 that prohibits the deployment of nuclear weapons in space and bans territorial claims.

peace enforcement: An action, typically by an international organization, to end intrastate and ethnic conflict, even when the opposing parties do not request assistance.

peacekeeping: The sending of representatives of third parties, typically an international organization such as the United Nations to help implement peace agreements, monitor ceasefires, patrol demilitarized zones, or to create buffer zones.

peacemaking: Attempts to seek a brokered solution to a conflict.

peace operations: "The continuation of diplomacy by other means"; that is, the process of attempting to encourage peace, including preventive diplomacy, peacekeeping, peacemaking, peacebuilding, and peace enforcement.

Pearl Harbor: The principal U.S. naval base in the Pacific; attacked by Japanese forces on December 7, 1941. Nineteen warships and 120 airplanes were badly damaged or destroyed, and 2,400 Americans were killed. This event created a long-lasting concern among many Americans about surprise attacks.

Peloponnesian War: Fought between Athens and Sparta, two city-states located on the Peloponnese Peninsula of Greece, from 431 to 404 B.C. Modern readers know about this conflict because of the history of it written by an Athenian general turned historian, Thucydides, who is considered by many to be the "father of the discipline of international relations."

Permanent Five (Perm-5): The five members of the United Nations Security Council which remain on the Security Council and do not rotate off: the United States, Great Britain, France, Russia, and the People's Republic of China.

power: One of the most commonly used and least understood concepts in political science and international relations, power has been defined by Professor Robert Dahl of Yale University as "the ability to get others to do what they otherwise would not do." In addition to this definition, there are others that focus on the attributes of power.

preventive diplomacy: Michael Lund has defined this as "Action taken in vulnerable places and times to avoid the threat or use of armed force and related forms of coercion by states or groups to settle the political disputes that can arise from the destabilizing effects of economic, social, political and international change."

primary source: Information obtained from the person who originally released it, including information in newspaper articles, memoirs, interviews, press releases, and speeches.

private international law: The rules and regulations that govern the resolution of conflicts that arise when individuals or corporations have contacts with two or more international actors outside their own state.

protectionism: The use of tariffs and quotas by a state to restrict imports in order to protect domestic industries from foreign competition.

public international law: Rules and regulations concerning government to government relations.

quota: A nontariff barrier to trade which sets a quantitative limit on either the number or value of goods allowed into a country; quotas are economic instruments of protectionism.

realism: A school of thought within the discipline of international relations that assumes that individuals and states are always striving for power and that the best way to manage this struggle is the balance of power. Prominent realists include Niccolo Machiavelli, Thomas Hobbes, Hans Morgenthau, Kenneth Waltz, and Henry Kissinger.

Reciprocal Trade Agreement (1934): The legislation that allowed the president to reduce trade barriers; represented a move toward freer trade.

recognition: A political act formally acknowledging the existence of another state, which carries with it certain legal consequences, rights, and responsibilities.

Reformation: The religious revolution led by Martin Luther and John Calvin in the sixteenth century. Criticizing some of the practices of the Roman Catholic Church, the reformers established a new branch of Christianity, Protestantism.

regional organization: An international organization with member states coming from the same area of the world; examples include NATO, the Organization of American States (OAS), and the Association of South East Asian Nations (ASEAN).

Renaissance: A movement in the fifteenth century that resulted in great artistic and literary accomplishments.

reparations: Damages demanded typically by the victorious states of the vanquished states following a war. After World War I, the Allies demanded that Germany pay rather harsh damages.

Roman Empire: According to tradition, the city of Rome was established in 753 B.C. and the Roman Republic in 509 B.C. The highpoint of Roman rule occurred during the Roman Empire from 27 B.C. to 476 A.D.

SALT: *See* Strategic Arms Limitation Talks.

secondary source: An account of an event based on primary sources such as memoirs, speeches, interviews, and official state documents.

Secretariat: The executive, administrative body of the United Nations which is headed by the Secretary General.

Secretary General: The chief executive officer of the United Nations and the head of the Secretariat. This person is elected by the General Assembly for five-year terms.

Security Council: One of the two main bodies of the United Nations (the other is the General Assembly) which has five permanent members (United States, United Kingdom, France, China, and Russia) and ten members elected among the other members of the UN.

self-determination: The belief that people are entitled to select the type of government under which they live; strongly supported by Woodrow Wilson.

self-help: The belief that a state is responsible for its own security.

Smoot-Hawley Tariff Bill: A trade bill passed by the U.S. Congress in 1930 that significantly increased tariffs and resulted in other states also increasing their tariffs.

sovereignty: The freedom from foreign control in a state; central to the development of the state-centric international system.

sphere of influence: A region controlled by one state.

Sputnik: The translation from Russian means "fellow traveler." This was the name of the first earth-orbiting satellite, launched by the USSR in October 1957.

stability: The equilibrium created in the international system when the great powers accept the existing balance of power and accept the status quo.

Star Wars: See Strategic Defense Initiative (SDI).

state-centric model: The framework of the international system in which countries are the dominant actors.

state moralist: A view of morality that places the interest of the state first and foremost.

Strategic Arms Limitation Talks (SALT): The arms control negotiations conducted by the United States and the Soviet Union that sought to limit the number of long-range nuclear weapons. The first round of negotiations, called "SALT I," were held from 1969 to 1972 and resulted in the Anti-Ballistic Missile (ABM) Treaty and the Interim Agreement on Offensive Forces. The second round of negotiations, called "SALT II," lasted from 1972 to 1979 and resulted in the SALT II Treaty.

Strategic Defense Initiative (SDI): A research program first announced by President Ronald Reagan in March 1983, envisioning the development of a nationwide system to protect the United States from ballistic missile attack.

structural realist theory: The theory in the discipline of international relations that contends that the structure of the balance of power is the best explanation of why states behave the way that they do in world politics.

sustainable development: Economic development that is consistent with the carrying capacity of a particular state or region.

tariff: A fee charged by a state on goods imported into that state.

Thirty Years' War (1618–1648): A series of wars conducted primarily in Germany and fought for religious reasons. This conflict was important historically for two reasons: It resulted in the splintering of Germany into 300 distinct entities, and modern states began to emerge in the aftermath of the conflict.

Thucydides: An Athenian general who wrote *The History of the Peloponnesian War*, one of the classic works of international relations, so respected, in fact, that many consider Thucydides to be the "father of international relations."

trade turnover: A state's exports plus imports.

transnational relations: The activities of nonstate actors across state boundaries.

treaty: A formal agreement concluded between two or more states or international organizations.

tripolar system: A form of the balance of power in which there are three great powers; this was the foundation of the Nixon-Kissinger grand design and grand strategy.

Truman Doctrine: See containment doctrine.

Trusteeship Council: One of the six bodies of the United Nations established by the Charter to administer territories until they were judged to be capable of self-government.

ultimatum: A demand that specifies: (1) what is demanded of the opponent, (2) the punishment that will be inflicted if the demand is not met, and (3) a specific time limit.

unconditional surrender: The termination of a war without prenegotiated stipulation of conditions of ending the war. The most famous case of this occurred in World War II when the Allies agreed that they would accept only the unconditional surrender of the Axis forces.

underdeveloped countries: See developing countries.

Universal Declaration of Human Rights: Adopted by the UN General Assembly in 1948, this proclamation presents political, social, economic, and cultural standards for the world.

Versailles Treaty: The international agreement that resulted from the Paris Peace Conference at the end of World War I. It was signed in June 1919; it placed strict limitations on the German military and called for stringent reparations against Germany.

Vietnam War: The start of conflict in Vietnam can be dated from 1940, when the Vietnamese first began fighting for independence, or it can be dated later when the Vietnamese fought the French, the Japanese, or the Americans. The United States' heavy involvement began in 1964, peaked in 1968 and ended with communist victory in April 1975. The fatalities included 58,800 Americans, 200,000 South Vietnamese soldiers, an estimated 1 million North and South Vietnamese communists and 2 million civilians.

war of attrition: A conflict in which one or both sides attempt to wear out the other side by continuing to prosecute the war even after a stalemate has been reached. The most famous war of attrition occurred during World War I, and the most recent case was the Iran–Iraq war of 1980–1988.

war termination: The process of ending a war via several different means including subjugation, negotiation, and military victory.

Washington Naval treaties: Resulting from a conference held from 1921–1922, these treaties placed limits on what was perceived as the most important single indicator of military power at that time: large warships.

weapons of mass destruction (WMD): These weapons included nuclear, biological, and chemical weapons.

Weimar government: The government of Germany that ruled from 1918 to 1933. This was a progressive, democratic government that was saddled with burdensome reparations payments to the allies. It ended when Hitler became chancellor.

Wilson, Woodrow (1856–1924): The only political scientist to serve as president of the United States, Wilson was a professor, a college president, and governor of New Jersey before serving as President from 1912–1920. The strongest supporter of the concept of collective security and the League of Nations; also supported the concept of self-determination.

World Health Organization (WHO): A specialized agency of the United Nations founded in 1948 that provides advice and direct assistance in preventing, controlling, and even eradicating infectious diseases. It was largely due to the efforts of WHO that smallpox was eradicated by the mid-1970s.

World War I (August 1914–November 1918): Called by some the "Great War" and by Woodrow Wilson "the war to end all wars," this conflict surprised almost everyone by lasting a long time (more than four years) and costing more lives and resources than anyone had anticipated. The war resulted in the significant weakening or disintegration of four empires: Britain, Germany, Austria-Hungary, and Russia.

World War II (September 1939–August 1945): The most costly war of all history, the Second World War began with Germany's attack on Poland and ended with the United States bombing of Hiroshima and Nagasaki. In between those two events, the conflict raged throughout Europe, Asia, and the Pacific, ultimately costing the lives of an estimated 74 million people.

Photo Credits

CHAPTER 1   David Butow/SABA Press Photos, Inc., 2; © Musée de l'Homme, photo R.P. Leray, 4.

CHAPTER 2   Bill Bachmann/PhotoEdit, 18.

CHAPTER 3   Corbis, 36.

CHAPTER 4   Reuters/Gary Hershorn/Archive Photos, 52.

CHAPTER 5   Corbis, 74; Corbis, 79; UPI/Corbis, 80; Hulton Getty/Liaison Agency, Inc., 81; UPI/Corbis, 88

CHAPTER 6   Reuters/Corinne Dufka/Archive Photos, 94.

CHAPTER 7   UPI/Corbis, 116.

CHAPTER 8   Reuters/Goran Tomasevic/Archive Photos, 142; Sygma Photo News, 155.

CHAPTER 9   National Archives, 168; Chu H. Haynie, © 1979 The Courier-Journal, 170; THE FAR SIDE © 1981 FARWORKS, INC./Universal Press Syndicate. All rights reserved. Reprinted with permission, 171; Arme/ICRC, Comité International de la Croix-Rouge, 193; A. de Wildenberg/Handicap International, 194.

CHAPTER 10   Marc A. Auth/New England Stock Photo, 198; AP/Wide World Photos, 209.

CHAPTER 11   Reuters/Peter Andrews/Archive Photos, 216; UPI/Corbis, 225.

CHAPTER 12   Joao Silva/AP/Wide World Photos, 238; Reuters/Arthur Tsang/Corbis, 241; © Tribune Media Services, Inc. All rights reserved. Reprinted with permission, 245; UPI/Corbis, 246.

CHAPTER 13   J. Maier, Jr./The Image Works, 260; Lee Malis/Liaison Agency, Inc., 268.

CHAPTER 14   UPI/Corbis, 284; Robert Caputo/Aurora & Quanta Productions, 294; Chris Romlinson/AP/Wide World Photos, 297; David Brauchli/Sygma Photo News, 301; Boris Subasic/Agence France-Presse, 304.

CHAPTER 15   Linda Mueller/Photographic Resources, 312.

Index